THE JUVENILE JUSTICE SYSTEM

Volume V. Sage Criminal Justice System Annuals

THE JUVENILE JUSTICE SYSTEM

MALCOLM W. KLEIN, *Editor*

 **SAGE Publications**   *Beverly Hills* · *London*

For information address:

SAGE PUBLICATIONS, INC.  SAGE PUBLICATIONS LTD
275 South Beverly Drive   St George's House / 44 Hatton Garden
Beverly Hills, California 90212   London EC1N 8ER

Printed in the United States of America

International Standard Book No. 0-8039-0450-9 (cloth)
International Standard Book No. 0-8039-0451-7 (paper)
Library of Congress Catalog Card No. 75-14632

FIRST PRINTING

HV
9104
·J 87

CONTENTS

PUBLISHER'S PREFACE

The success of past volumes of the SAGE CRIMINAL JUSTICE SYSTEM ANNUALS and the enthusiasm that they have created among scholars and practitioners who wish to contribute to the series (and, in some cases, utilize it in their classes) have prompted us to enlarge the program. Beginning with this volume in 1976 (for at least a two-year trial period) two volumes will appear during each calendar year (one in the spring and one in the autumn). Among the topics selected for future volumes are criminal justice and the victim (to be edited by William F. McDonald), modeling the criminal justice system (under the editorship of Stuart S. Nagel) and corrections and punishment, their structure, function, and process (to be edited by David Greenberg).

We believe that this shift from annual to semiannual publication will enable us to provide more continuous and timely coverage of the criminal justice field—a field that is drawing the interest of ever-growing numbers of social and behavioral scientists, students of law and public administration, policy makers and professionals in the fields of corrections, law enforcement, and the social services. Our expansion of this series is our way of thanking those subscribers, authors, and editors who have encouraged us over the years. We are, of course, eager to learn of our readers' reactions to these plans for expansion—as well as their suggestions for future volumes.

Sara Miller McCune
Publisher

Beverly Hills, California
February, 1976

*for Laurie and Leigh
and for their generation*

PREFACE

It is common in the criminological literature of the 1960s and 1970s to speak of the "nonsystem" of criminal or juvenile justice. We have become so discouraged by the inefficiencies, ineffectiveness, and inequities of our systems of social control that we blame these systems for their intrinsic deficiencies and vituperatively label them nonsystems. It is an unfair label.

What we have, instead, are systems with somewhat ambiguous boundaries and shifting interdependencies. Their mode of functioning is, to an unacceptable degree, unplanned and inadvertent. Thus we have too much of a *re*active and not enough of a *pro*active approach to dealing with criminal justice problems. A *re*active system, no matter how unsatisfactory, is still a system, but one that leaves much room for rational assessment and improvement. This volume is concerned with such assessment and improvement, with specific reference to the juvenile justice system.

Since the late 1960s which saw the publication of the report of the President's Commission on Law Enforcement and Administration of Justice (1967), we have been undergoing a very perceptible period of change and experimentation. It is fashionable—and probably justifiable—to characterize federal commissions as ineffective. Such cannot be said of the Crime Commission, especially in the area of the juvenile system. Programs of diversion and deinstitutionalization, the development of Youth Services Bureaus and community-based treatment programs, and the promulgation of procedures appropriate to the Gault decision have all been greatly accelerated by the Commission's work. Much of this change is reflected in the chapters of this volume.

Perhaps equally important to the current status of the system, although much more difficult to document, is the impact of and reactions to the "war on crime" initiated under the Nixon administration. The most visible impact of this "war" has been the development of the enormous bureaucracy of the Law Enforcement Assistance Administration, the fifty state planning agencies, and numerous regional planning agencies across the nation. The expenditure of billions of dollars through these funnels has had tremendous impact on the component agencies of the juvenile justice system, but seemingly little or none on the volume of delinquency to which they respond. The inequality of impact on system and on delinquency is clearly mirrored in a number of the chapters in this volume.

The opening chapter is the only one not composed originally for this volume. It is an edited summary of a brief conference of scholars which expresses some emerging views on the present and future status of delinquency prevention. The focus is off the delinquent and on the socializing and controlling institutions which seem to produce and treat him. The stance taken is strongly liberal and anti-control, emphasizing decriminalization and normalization while playing down the distinctions between delinquent and nondelinquent youth. The views enunciated in this first chapter are echoed again and again in succeeding chapters.

An interesting example of the echo emerges from Empey's review of the historical context of "adolescence." He suggests that current juvenile justice reforms may merely reinvent some old wheels. It may well be, according to Empey, that current reforms are based on unexamined contemporary values and habits of thought which are therefore self-limiting and unlikely to lead to truly fundamental changes. Clearly, taking account of this historical context leaves us less certain of the moral and legal assumptions underlying our legislation and our preventive and rehabilitative practices for children.

Spergel's chapter reminds us that the juvenile justice system emerges from and operates in a community context, that in fact the justice system is a *subsystem* subsumed under the community. To yield a better grasp of the community/system connections, Spergel undertakes an unusual interorganizational analysis of types of communities, illustrating how variations in community structure are related to variations in delinquency and its control.

The development of system diversion noted by Pink and White and by Spergel involves the community as the absorber of its own delinquents. Prominent issues in this development are highlighted in the paper by Klein and his colleagues. The negative tone in this chapter derives not from failures of diversion programs but from the plethora of unexamined assumptions and unanticipated consequences of these programs which seem to involve system change without the benefit of system measurement.

The chapter by Carter is highly unusual, but in a volume of this sort it may provide a very useful antidote to the scholar's view of someone else's system. Carter lets the cop have his say, in his own words, about his perspective on the system in which he is imbedded. If the policeman does indeed feel so negatively toward the juvenile justice system—and Carter suggests that he must, given the nature of his role in that system—then what hope is there that the system will ever work smoothly?

The Rubin chapter presents one answer to this question: return the system to its status as a criminal court, and let the *court* serve as the fulcrum of the system. Rubin provides a useful overview of the many factors impinging on the juvenile court judge, especially the pressures from community and professional interest groups. Additionally, he portrays the wide variety of court patterns in the United States—so many, in fact, that one might well question whether or not we do have *one* system of juvenile justice.

Like several of the earlier chapters, the piece by Sarri and Vinter on juvenile corrections reminds us of the very *local* (community) stamp on both walled institutions and community-based facilities. This exhaustive review of the current situation is discouraging in its documentation of the lack of change in incarceration rates and in its data-based suggestion that community alternatives do *not* seem to be accompanied by consequently smaller institutional populations. Additionally, Sarri and Vinter provide ample illustration of the many legal and procedural inequities in the correctional terminus of the justice system.

The final chapter, by Gordon, represents somewhat of a departure from the others, being concerned less with the nature of the system and its context than with critical measures of youth behaviors leading to involvement in the system. Gordon provides a brief, concise review of alternative delinquency indices—self-report, victimization, seriousness, prevalence—and indicates something of their complexity and interrelatedness. His own preference for elaboration is prevalence, a relatively undeveloped but important measure. Gordon's analysis of differential racial contributions to prevalence rates may make some readers unhappy. His analysis of the I.Q./delinquency relationships will absolutely enrage many others. Perhaps there is no better way to finish a volume like this than to provoke a genuine controversy.

If the editor may be allowed a personal word: I am very grateful to the contributors of this volume who were so willing to contribute brand new materials to a venture that must at first have seemed highly ambiguous. I invited them to work in areas of their own expertise, but to do so with an emphasis on the *system* aspects, on the inter-component areas so traditionally omitted in criminological texts. *I* knew what I wanted, but the contributors had to interpret my fantasies as best they could. I could not be more delighted with the outcome. The opportunity to put all these materials together has renewed my own hope that conceptual and perhaps practical progress can indeed be made.

Malcolm W. Klein
Los Angeles
November, 1975

Chapter 1

DELINQUENCY PREVENTION:
THE STATE OF THE ART

WILLIAM T. PINK and
MERVIN F. WHITE

INTRODUCTION

Prevention strategies receive little attention in the delinquency field. In 1973 a group of experts gathered in Portland, Oregon, to participate in a two-day invitational seminar convened by the Regional Research Institute at Portland State University. The task was to provide perspectives on new directions in delinquency prevention. The following is a report of their meeting. It shows plainly that they believe we treat delinquent youth badly, sometimes even stupidly.

Contrary to the beliefs of those who administer it, they said, the juvenile justice system does not work. It may feed and clothe the judges, jailers, and

AUTHORS' NOTE: *This paper was edited from* Delinquency Prevention: A Conference Perspective on Issues and Directions, *1974, and is a report of a conference among David Bordua, Lois Defleur, LaMar T. Empey, Peter Garabedian, Donald Garrity, Don C. Gibbons, Malcolm W. Klein, David Matza, Kenneth Polk, Clarence Schrag, and James F. Short, Jr. The conference was sponsored by the Regional Research Institute for Human Services at Portland State University, Portland, Oregon, 1973. Edmund V. Mech was project coordinator.*

agencies dealing out justice; but those being processed through these hands are none the better for it. In fact, they are the worse. Furthermore, the system's hands are clumsy and cannot sort the children who fall into them. All are tossed in the same bag, the rapist with the runaway.

How to make sense in the way we handle juvenile delinquents was the issue of the conference. As conferees saw it, until we begin to treat "institutional" causes and deficiencies we will have no cures. That means finding out just how we can transform the homes, the schools, the neighborhoods, and the churches that these children come from. How can we get them to work together to meet their fundamental responsibility toward youth? It is the rare judge or jailer who can help a child find his way. But the family, with a little help, might be able to. Getting him a job he likes might help. Making school curricula more relevant to his life might help. Finding a way for those who shape him to work together, that indeed might help. Such programs as these might prove far less costly than the current juvenile justice system. We owe it to our youth to rethink the business of how we prepare them for the world they must make their way in. This report is a step in that direction.

CONFERENCE AIMS

Everyone wants to prevent delinquency. Yet views in the field of prevention seem naive, vague, and out of touch with research. Basic concepts in the field lack precision, and few attempts have been made to build programs around consistent theoretical concepts. Accordingly, to explore the state of the art in delinquency prevention, a panel of theorists, researchers, and analysts in the field of delinquency met early in 1973 for an intensive two-day delinquency prevention seminar.

The prevention proposals of conference members were wide-ranging and ambitious. Among other things, they discussed proposed changes in juvenile statutes, keeping juveniles out of the courts, and broadly reforming society. Debate was lively and at times intense, but it did not yield a blueprint for preventing delinquent behavior. Such a blueprint would require data that do not exist. Conferees also observed that in the long run some delinquent behavior will remain, however effective a society's efforts at reform.

The conferees agreed that the following social changes were needed: (a) delinquent youth should be helped to reenter the mainstream of community life, and (b) institutions should work together more efficiently to prevent delinquency. The conferees viewed the conference as a chance to sort the issues and lay out the directions for change.

Almost at the outset, two types of institutions were identified.

The first type are those that maintain bounds or set limits. They include such institutions as the police, courts, prisons, and parole boards. These institutions are controlled by and mainly concerned with illegitimate behavior. They deal with individuals who have violated society's legal norms and who have been processed through the legal justice system: the majority of youth have no contact with such institutions. The thoughts and deeds in such institutions center on social control. They tend to be negative and separatist in nature. Their detached position from the mainstream casts doubt on their ability to resocialize the youth who encounter them.

A second type of institution seeks to help youth establish a legitimate identity. It includes the school, the family, employers, peers, and political groups. The emphasis in such groups is essentially positive. They are concerned with fostering acceptable identities, relationships, and opportunities. They tend to relate to youth very differently from institutions concerned with controlling and rehabilitating the "bad."

Attempts at delinquency prevention have typically been concentrated in negative institutions. Over the years we have failed to appreciate fully the bad effects of removing delinquents from mainstream institutions (especially the home and school) to rehabilitate them. The conferees felt that for most adjudicated youth a segregated and highly punitive rehabilitative process was bound to fail. Changes that would affect the workings of these two types of institutions and their interrelationships were proposed. Conferees emphasized the need for everyone concerned to work together. They argued that juveniles not be branded as delinquent, that they be kept out of court, that the juvenile justice statutes be reformed, and that there be well-integrated reforms in schools, jobs, and communities.

The following sections are an attempt to organize the somewhat disparate views voiced during the conference. This document should not be construed as a surefire blueprint for preventing delinquency. It is primarily intended to clarify issues, point to directions of change, and stimulate research.

DELINQUENCY PREVENTION: SELECTED PRINCIPLES

The current state of the art regarding delinquency prevention and rehabilitation programs can be summed up in a few words. By and large, nothing we have done has seemed to work. Experimental studies have usually failed to produce results any better than those achieved by conventional correction programs. As for the latter, whatever good they do seems unrelated to their programs. Offenders who go straight apparently do so independently of their correction experiences.

The reasons for our failure are varied and complex, but some can be identified. For one thing, most correction activities represent a crude form of intuitive tinkering or trial-and-error tactics directed at offenders. They have not grown from a clear theoretical substructure which has defined the "illness" to be "cured." Many programs have proceeded with no clear notion of what constitutes delinquency or criminal behavior.

Some correction efforts have a theoretical framework which specifies an image of the offender and links this image to certain intervention tactics thought to be appropriate. However, most of these efforts are based on the notion that offenders are psychologically sick. Also, most have been designed to resocialize individuals. But it has become clear that most conventional lawbreakers are not psychologically sick and do not need their psyches altered. Programs that center on the individual may be wide of the mark. Perhaps the delinquent and the criminal are the offspring of social systems rather than aberrations unrelated to the rest of us or our institutions.

This perspective views delinquency as a complex concatenation of behavior and events. We do not agree that if we could only discover what is really wrong with juvenile delinquents, we could try to change their behavior with recreation programs, reality therapy, street work programs, or some other strategem to make them lawabiding. Delinquency has many dimensions. To understand it we must study juvenile behavior, the workings of the police, juvenile courts, and other segments of the social control machinery and how these operations influence delinquents. Then too, rational responses to delinquency must be based on some understanding of the legal dimensions of the problem and the state of public opinion. Legislators and citizens control the resources of delinquency control programs; they specify other restraints on prevention endeavors; and they constitute part of the delinquency problem in other ways as well. A truly adequate explanation of the delinquency problem must include how it relates to such basic features of the American economy as the idleness it forces on the young and the deficiencies of the social order that have alienated the young. In short, in matters of reform, we need to study the criminal influences of modern society rather than tinker with individual delinquents and criminals.

Some might argue that we know too little to spell out a delinquency prevention theory in detail. But we have an abundance of facts about the form and scope of delinquency in contemporary America, police responses to delinquent conduct, and other matters of that sort. Accordingly, the conventions in the pages to follow are not simply uninformed guesses. They represent a set of stock-taking propositions drawn from the research.

A further comment on research is needed. Delinquency prevention work should be a two-pronged affair: various kinds of basic research must be done side-by-side with activities suggested by the theory. Many remarks and suggestions in the pages to follow treat new lines of research which need pursuing.

We present below certain selected generalizations or delinquency principles.

Principle One: Delinquent Infractions versus Delinquency Rates

We need to distinguish between juvenile delinquency, defined as infractions committed, and official rates of delinquency such as police statistics, court cases, and the like. Although the rates reflect the infractions, they sometimes only slightly correlate with the total incidence of infraction. A high delinquency rate in a neighborhood may not necessarily reflect a high incidence of delinquent infraction. It may, instead, reflect police behavior, community concern, or some other phenomenon.

Delinquency programs usually seek to lower the incidence of infractions among youth. Most people regard delinquency prevention as getting youngsters to cease certain annoying behaviors. However, another approach might be to try to reduce delinquency rates. For example, a sizable portion of the problem could be disposed of entirely by removing omnibus clauses from juvenile court laws. Although youths might remain incorrigible, wayward, and the like, their activities would no longer concern the court, and these cases would not appear in delinquency rates.

Principle Two: Degree of Delinquency Involvement

The delinquent-nondelinquent dichotomy is incorrect and misleading. Evidence from self-report and victimization studies suggests that it is a rare person who never violates the law. Most persons break the law often and with no bad effects. A few do so in a predatory or violent way. Still fewer break laws regularly. Finally, a very few derive their livelihood from criminal behavior and are committed to crime as a way of life. The first type ordinarily receives little official attention, while the last is judged to be criminal. Although some confirmed criminals began as delinquents, not all started that way. Moreover, most delinquents do not graduate into a life of crime.

Principle Three: Specialization of Delinquent Behavior

Delinquent behavior varies in frequency, duration, and seriousness. It may also become specialized as in the careers of drug users, sex offenders, strong-arm robbers, and assaultists. Some specialized offenses are of little social significance, while others like violence may be of great concern. However, many control agencies seem to be oriented toward individual acts or single instances of conduct rather than to degree of specialization, involvement, or seriousness.

Principle Four: Delinquency Rates

The rate of delinquency in a community is influenced by both the number of infractions committed by youth and by the degree of police surveillance in the area; therefore, a high volume or increasing rate of delinquency does not necessarily mean that the community is experiencing a crime wave.

Principle Five: Delinquency Rates and Public Opinion

The public's perception of the delinquency problem is also a reflection of the degree of political emphasis on "crime in the streets." When legislators and other influential citizens define delinquency and crime as a social problem, the citizens in the community generally perceive it as such. The mass media also structures the delinquency problem for the public.

Principle Six: Identifying Predelinquent Youths

Programs attempting to identify predelinquent children should be planned and carried out with great care, if indeed they are to be used at all. To date, there are no reliable methods by which children can be classified into this category, or any other category for that matter. Until such procedures are established, programs attempting to identify predelinquents and give them special treatment should be discouraged. Delinquency is often a transitory rather than developmental process. Situations are important in producing infractions. Programs aimed at identifying predelinquents risk locking youths into the delinquent role by the processes of labeling and self-fulfillment.

Principle Seven: The Police and Discretionary Behavior

There is little or no evidence to indicate that proactive police work in the area of juvenile activities is desirable. The police agency which disposes of most petty juvenile cases on the street with admonitions and tongue lashings is probably following the soundest policy.

Principle Eight: Research on Official Discretion

The ambiguity of legislative language makes it necessary for the police, the prosecution and defense, the courts, and correctional workers to exercise discretion. (Their heavy workloads require those engaged in criminal justice to enforce the law differentially. Full enforcement is impossible, even if it were desirable.) Therefore it is not enough for researchers merely to point out that discretion occurs or that it benefits certain law violators. We need research aimed at testing discretionary decisions and at managing those decisions more effectively.

Principle Nine: An Expanded Role for the Juvenile Court is Unwarranted

Evidence does not indicate that court intervention in cases of petty or casual infraction is generally useful. It may often be harmful. In short, the fewer the juveniles in court, the better. Juveniles should not be judged delinquent quasi-officially through such devices as informal probation. Such practices have not proven to have a useful effect. Moreover, policies of that sort raise ethical and legal questions.

Principle Ten: Diverting Youth from Juvenile Courts

Youth Service Bureaus and other agencies designed to divert juvenile offenders from the official juvenile court machinery appear to be desirable, since most infractions are minor in character and not reliable predictors of adult maladjustment. However, some evidence from Youth Service Bureaus indicates that these agencies receive mostly new cases rather than youngsters who have been diverted from the court. Diversion processes tend to increase the number of children in official and semi-official hands, rather than shrink it.

Principle Eleven: Deficiencies of Current Programs

Delinquency programs are often poorly planned, uncoordinated, and work at cross-purposes. We must learn to plan, coordinate, and judge better if we are to control delinquency. Delinquency programs are often impeded by community agencies whose policies "hoard" or "lock-out" certain youth.

Delinquency programs are often carried out not for their proven value, but for political reasons. Funds for planning grants, demonstration projects, and so forth, are allocated largely on the basis of political expediency. But political considerations should not override other considerations in determining which agency or group of officials is to be responsible for a given domain or program. Nor should they be the basis for awarding grants.

Delinquency control agencies and officials have a stake in keeping delinquency alive and in perpetuating current programs, whether they work or not. The juvenile justice system, including the schools, police, juvenile courts, probation departments and juvenile institutions, represents a substantial investment of the community's resources. Hence, we cannot solve the delinquency problem until working alternatives are found. These include redefining the problem, changing official functions and roles, retraining personnel, and allocating and using redirected resources.

Juvenile delinquency is largely an economic problem, and functions positively for the country's economy. Many citizens earn their living "changing people" one way or another: Delinquents are the bread and butter of correction workers, academic theorists, and research-consultants. Perhaps if the problem were reduced, we would have to find a substitute for them to work on.

Principle Twelve: Community Corrections:
Reintegrating the Offender

The notion that we ought to put delinquents in parole programs in the community rather than in institutions has caught the imagination of correction officials, state legislators, and the general public. Yet it is not clear what community corrections means. Numerous programs, many of them contradictory and with no rationale, are being carried out around the country. No doubt behavior can be modified, but reintegrating the offender will require changing social institutions and attitudes and activities of the citizenry. So long as there are legitimate rewards for illegitimate conduct, our social institutions will tend to encourage violations of the law.

THE LEGAL SYSTEM

Throughout the conference heavy attention was devoted to juvenile status offenses, that is, criminal offenses for which an adult could not be charged. Truancy, incorrigibility, and running away are recurring examples of status offense behavior.

Conferees were nearly unanimous that juvenile status offenses be made noncriminal. They recommended in effect that omnibus clauses be removed from juvenile court statutes.

A persistent concern of recent years has been the need to clean up legal definitions of delinquency. Status offenses were first included in statutes on the assumption that committing minor offenses suggests either a difficulty in adjustment or the beginning of a criminal career. Clearly, these statutes are a blank check for discretionary intervention in handling youth.

The evidence, however, calls into question whether committing minor offenses leads to either emotional disorders or a career in crime. Studies of children labeled as delinquent, particularly those based on self-report data, show that a high proportion of youth commit status offenses while growing up. Yet, only a small proportion become criminals. Moreover, to assume that status offenses are symptomatic of an underlying pathology far outdistances the evidence. Indeed, such activities are probably characteristic of adolescence generally. To view these behaviors as delinquent and to involve youth in legal institutions may create unwarranted identity problems. Conferees emphasized that research on the influence of such official involvement in the lives of adolescents remains speculative.

At the same time, to offer treatment to youths who have committed status offenses is also questionable. The sparse research on treatment programs suggests that intervention in status or non-status offenses does not rehabilitate. Often it may create hard-to-reverse illegitimate identities and disrupt existing socialization patterns. Doing nothing officially may be a good way to treat certain status offenses.

Obviously, ceasing to brand our wayward youth will not remove all nuisance behaviors; we should expect these to occur as part of the price of growing up. Conferees proposed that such offenses be handled by the community rather than by the courts.

Removing status offenses from juvenile court statutes will almost certainly call in question the legality of much child service programming. Because the police and other social control agents often refer cases to child care agencies rather than the juvenile court, this practice is likely to receive careful scrutiny from legal rights sources.

What do we do then with the adolescent who feels that he can now behave badly and get away with it? Conferees agreed that such behavior must be controlled—not by the law but by the family, school, neighborhood, and church. Members agreed that a juvenile court judge cannot be a substitute father, and a detention program cannot replace a family. They were similarly skeptical of helping agencies used by courts to treat the problem.

THE JUVENILE JUSTICE SYSTEM

Conferees suggested that two aspects of the juvenile justice system be reformed: (a) the philosophy of the court and (b) the structure of the court.

The juvenile court's philosophy guides and influences the system's actions. This philosophy (parens patriae) asserts that delinquent children should not be imprisoned but protected by benevolent authority and helped by trained professionals to overcome the cause of their delinquency. As noted by the Supreme Court, the parens patriae philosophy, while humanitarian in intent, has not been realized within the justice system, and it seems unlikely that it ever will be. Too often, in the name of benevolence, our youth are branded and confined to what seem to them to be junior jails and prisons.

Four suggestions for restructuring the court and its philosophy were made by conferees:

1. Purpose of the Court

They proposed that the court function only to set limits or maintain bounds. This principle has several implications:

(a) The court should not engage in social reform. Its function should be to administer juvenile justice.

(b) Status offenses should be removed from juvenile codes. Whenever feasible, such behavior should be treated as noncriminal. The present overdose of intervention creates a negative attitude in youth toward the legal process.

(c) As for other punishable offenses, ideally every delinquent act should be dealt with quickly and efficiently to make such actions costly. The police should concentrate on the predatory acts of juveniles (i.e., crimes with victims) and on providing prompt due process in the courts. (See also item 3 below.)

(d) The courts should properly respond to the past and present acts of a youth but not anticipate his future acts. It should cease to punish youth for potential future misconduct. We cannot prognosticate from an individual's misdeeds. The practice is comparable to punishing car manufacturers who have deceived us for abuses we suspect they might commit.

2. Correctional Reform

Effective prevention policy requires that the courts give convicted juveniles a real chance to reenter the community. We need radically different correctional programs than now exist. The court must have a working relationship with the school, the family, and peers so that delinquents can pass easily from one to the other. Such a relationship is critical to correction and reform.

3. Understanding Status Offenses

We must treat juvenile misconduct as unacceptable and calling for amends but not be mystified by it or unforgiving. We must confront those misbehaving immediately and, if needed, contact the family, neighbors, teachers, friends, or others who can see the youngster gets the word. We need not call on officials or experts.

It is common practice to refer a young offender to a specialist rather than send him to court. The burden for carrying this out rests heavily on the police and court. In complex cases, it calls for special youth guidance and defense. If the community took youth in hand, parents, teachers, and the youths themselves could call on specialists for help, and the courts or police would not be needed.

Panel members generally favored greater tolerance of juvenile misbehavior, especially when crime is not involved.

As for youths more deeply involved in lawbreaking, even they were seen as likely to be handled better by communities than by the courts. Such an approach would free the court and correction agency to deal with serious and persistent young offenders.

4. Integrating the Juvenile Justice System

New programs not well understood and accepted in the courts will either not be used or will be co-opted and made ineffective. Well integrated relationships must be built between new programs and the present system, particularly with the police. Otherwise, such programs will have no impact, or will be shaped to fit existing patterns.

THE COMMUNITY SYSTEM

Conferees were attracted by the prospect of community reform, of getting the family, the school, the employer to take much of the responsibility now falling on the court. Delinquency, they thought, could best be prevented by helping youth to find a place in the community. The conferees offered many ways communities could change.

Increased urbanization and industrialization have increased professionalism in agencies responsible for solving social problems like delinquency. These agencies have failed to solve the problems. Furthermore, they tend to become disengaged from the community or at best are peripheral to community life. Efforts should be made to strengthen their effectiveness.

Proposals were made to bring together these community and neighborhood institutions. The proposals made focus on present institutions and how they function, and how they are related to each other and to the larger community.

1. The School

School experiences need to be changed in the following ways:

(a) Tracking and grading practices should be examined. The present system has deleterious effects on adolescents in the lower tracks who are in effect bound to a working-class future at an early age. This tends to kill motivation and breeds poor school work and adjustment and a final dropping out. Such students often do not respect themselves and see no payoff in conforming to society.

A youngster should be free to choose his future status. To stratify youth before they know what is happening is both unfair and prejudicial. Negative labeling was cited as the cause of such problems. Both advocates and skeptics of labeling theory emphasized that research is needed into how school practices and the world of work relate.

(b) The curriculum should be continuously revised to make it relevant for all youth passing through the system. Students constantly complain about courses like math, English, and history which they see as having little or no value for them as adults. We do not suggest that adolescents always know what is best for them, nor do we mean that they should not have math, English, and history. But these courses should be restructured to address particular interests and uses. The present system is geared to produce college students at the expense of those not viewed as college material. Youth put on nonacademic tracks are often given courses poor in value, and judged to be so by society. In short, they find themselves stigmatized by society. No wonder they often become delinquent.

(c) Resources within school systems should be equitably distributed to ensure that all schools receive their fair share. Resources were interpreted broadly to include monies, teachers, teaching equipment, and facilities. For too long schools located in the central city have been given second and third choice. Often they select after everyone else has done so. Given our present ghettos, such schools should be given priority in resource allocation. Qualified teachers are badly needed by the inner city schools. School administrators and school boards must address this problem.

2. World of Work Orientation

There is a vital need to link school and work experiences better. The school should take the initiative for this, inasmuch as this link should be a part of the normal socialization experience of youth. This proposal has several implications. Academic training, while important, is not enough in itself to prepare adolescents for productive roles in society. Other types of experiences need to become an intrinsic part of the education of all students. Not only should schools provide classroom and work experience for all who wish it, but this experience should go beyond that traditionally associated with vocational education.

Work experience was interpreted broadly to include exposure to work settings over the full range of occupations in our society. Adolescents should be exposed to and involved in a variety of occupational activities outside the classroom for the experience that would give academic instruction and career guidance more meaning. Such experiences in the work world should carry both academic credit and pay. A major problem with the present system is that the student is insulated from the reality of the adult's world for most of his formative years. The conferees would open to him a full variety of work experiences, from carpentry and mechanics to medicine and law. Work experiences would provide not only a positive setting for the development of a legitimate identity and a stake in conformity, but also rich and stimulating opportunities for teaching.

Clearly such a view requires that we rethink what is meant by education and work, particularly for the adolescent. These interrelated institutions must be reorganized to help all youth, not just those who perform successfully. Clearly, much more is at stake here than just making their academic education relevant to the world of work. By working, adolescents can acquire work attitudes, habits, and orientations otherwise not available to them. Paying adolescents to do such work gives them a stake in conforming.

3. Expanding Work Opportunities

Child labor laws should be changed to permit adolescents to participate fully in the work force. Such participation need not be full-time; it could be part-time and coordinated with the education experience. Conferees reasoned that such changes in the laws would permit hiring adolescents into a wide variety of jobs at present closed to them. They emphasized jobs that are meaningful, require skill, and for which they could be paid on a level commensurate with their level of participation. Since many new social services are needed, creating jobs in this area would both give adolescents a chance to work and provide a desirable service.

Changes in the child labor laws should provide for such protections as work disability insurance and other benefits of adult workers.

Concerted efforts should be made to create employment opportunities for adolescents in agencies which work closely with them. Attention should be given, for example, to school, recreation activities, juvenile justice system programs, and delinquency prevention programs as possible job sources. Adolescents should be involved in meaningful ways in such programs. In a unique way, they have the insights and skills needed for working with others who require social help because of academic failure, misconduct, lack of recreational skills, and so on. Adolescents have credibility with others their age, and can often achieve rapport more easily than adults. This practice would help offset the limitations of professionals from sociocultural backgrounds different from adolescents who need help. Professionals are often seen as agents of a hostile authority system.

4. A Community Perspective

Communities should build programs around activities meaningful to the entire community in which all youth, not just the good or bad, can take part. Community programs designed to involve all youth avoid the stigma attached to spoiled image programs (programs in which only those with a "bad record" are allowed to participate). Several points should be noted concerning this departure from customary prevention programming.

(a) The programs outlined here should cover the full range of community life, interrelating school, recreation, work, religion, political life, policy-community relations, and the juvenile justice system.

(b) These programs should be coordinated with each other and with the other institutions of social life so they are complementary rather than competitive.

(c) As far as possible, these programs should be directed by persons and organizations outside the juvenile justice system. That is, they should be funded, directed, and supported by the legitimating institutions of the community.

(d) The programs should involve youth of *all* backgrounds in their planning, organization, and execution.

(e) The primary objective of such programs should be to involve as many youth as possible in community life. They should not work solely to benefit delinquent youth.

DECRIMINALIZING JUVENILE OFFENSES

Conferees sought to develop a productive definition of delinquency. Three definitions were discussed:

(a) delinquency as *juvenile acts which result in arrest or referral to juvenile authorities;*

(b) delinquency as *any juvenile act which violates the law;*

(c) delinquency as the *incidence of deviant youthful careers,* whether or not the specific delinquent acts are responded to officially.

The first definition, which is associated with officially recorded rates, was quickly rejected as overly narrow and conceptually deficient. Delinquency prevention was seen to include not only more effective rehabilitation but also a cutback in first offenses. To support this expanded view, the distinction was made between the logic and structure of the juvenile justice system and primary socializing institutions. To propose reform only in the justice system was to ignore that most youth derive legitimacy outside this system. Prevention, to be effective, must change both types of institutions and integrate those changes so the two can work together. Over the two days of the conference the conferees addressed several key reforms in both types of institutions.

Support was unanimous for decriminalizing juvenile status offenses by repealing the omnibus clauses of the juvenile court statutes. This action was proposed for compelling reasons:

(a) the desire to strengthen support for the criminal codes in general;

(b) concern about the interpersonal relationships in an increasingly bureaucratic society;

(c) concern about the negative labeling of youth caught in the juvenile justice system; and

(d) a desire to reduce officially recorded delinquency rates.

Substantive reform of the criminal codes is the foundation for both effective procedural reform and for aspects of the law. Any criminal code must have legitimacy; that is, it must have the respect of the population. The normative structure of any social system constantly changes; what was once unacceptable may later become respectable. Recent changes in the homosexual laws in Britain is a good example. Juvenile status offenses are now prime candidates for removal from the criminal codes, for at least five reasons.

First, self-report data from a number of studies indicate that many youth commit status offenses; however, only a small minority are apprehended. The volume of such acts is overwhelming. Officials can only respond selectively to them. Such selective enforcement, particularly when it discriminates against some sociocultural groups, decreases respect both for legal codes and the whole legal process.

Second, removing these activities from the statutes would free the police to work on more serious crimes. At present, the volume of status offenses is a burden on police and reduces the time they can devote to serious crime.

Third, by definition the status offenses are victimless in character. That is, they generally involve no official complaint of injury or loss of property. In fact, parents and school officials tend to be the major sources of referrals. They tend to turn to the legal system to intervene in problems not essentially illegal in nature. Such widespread legal intervention has tended to free the family and school in particular from taking a more active role. Legal intervention permits both parents and school officials to ignore their role in these problems and place the blame on the supposed pathology of the offending child.

Fourth, since a very large proportion of delinquency involves status offenses, removing them from the statutes would reduce official rates significantly. It would not, of course, necessarily reduce the incidence of such acts in the community; but it would open the way for a variety of nonlegal social responses and interventions now either nonexistent or weakly implemented. Several conferees argued that it would be dishonest and dangerous to encourage a community to change its statutes without offering substitute controls. None suggested that status offenses be ignored. They simply suggested that juvenile justice agencies are not adequate to the task of rehabilitating masses of youth. By permitting professional central agencies to proliferate, we have neglected to generate new institutions in neighborhoods and communities to do the tasks so freely given to the juvenile justice system.

Finally, there was concern that responding legally to status and some non-status offenses may, in fact, harm youth socially. Such negative labeling tends to hamper the careers of youth. Thus, the legal response may not only be needless but destructive.

A lone, forceful dissenter among the conferees expressed misgivings that such action might tie the hands of an agency by removing its legal right to intervene:

If we do away with the so-called omnibus clause, then the law ceases to provide any kind of guidance for intervention. I think most of the reason for having all of these non-criminal offenses was that people guessed that these were the things which if allowed to continue would result in criminal conduct. . . . Once you take those out of the delinquency statutes . . . there's no legal or statutory guidance for intervention at all.

While this plea of caution was acknowledged, the other conferees felt that nonlegal community-backed intervention would have a far better effect on youth than intervention now in use.

DIVERTING YOUTH FROM THE COURTS AND
DOING NOTHING OFFICIALLY

The panel's discussion of alternative intervention models was hampered by a lack of empirical evidence to support one over another. As one conferee suggested:

. . . it seems to me that most of the guys working in the field of delinquency and crime are agreed that we know really very little about definitions, causes, or control. . . . I've been concerned about reasons for such ignorance after many years of research . . . all kinds of prevention programs [have been] instituted, mostly without any real good evidence of achievement or accomplishment. I'm coming to the view that there are several reasons for our ignorance. . . . it's not only the scholars and researchers who share responsibility . . . but I think public officials, administrators, legislators, and others share responsibility for our ignorance in the sense that the programs of delinquency prevention . . . just have never been implemented, so far as I can tell. I don't know of any clear case in which a planned or proposed program was truly implemented . . . the way it was planned.

While conferees agreed that clearer research concepts were desirable, they generally conceded that current rehabilitation efforts have proven ineffectual and costly. One of them observed:

The level of rehabilitation currently achieved with institutional programs can be matched by a variety of alternative non-incarcerating programs at great savings of time, money, and personnel. . . . The data suggest that we can do the same things without the institutions much more cheaply and easily, and we can do it right now.

Another added:

> The Silver Lake experiment . . . found very little difference after one year
> between experimental and control groups. Yet, the cost for the experi-
> mental program in the community was one-third of the one in the
> institution, which meant for every thousand kids treated that way, you'd
> save three million dollars.

To divert youth engaging in status offenses from the juvenile justice system
was judged theoretically sound for several reasons.

First, since such behaviors are not good indicators of future delinquency,
intervention would be more effective if undertaken by organizations based in the
primary socializing institutions.

Second, such organizations would intervene in a mainstream community
setting rather than in an insulated and segregated system. Thus, the adolescent
would experience the least possible disruption to his life at home, school, or
work.

Third, a variety of social action organizations would develop which could
stimulate communities to address their own problems.

Fourth, it would reduce the possibility of adjudicated individuals becoming
involved in what Lemert defines as secondary deviance. This assumes that the
least contact with the stigmatizing institutions the better: youth in nonlegal
community-based programs are more likely to avoid being identified in negative
and humiliating ways.

Fifth, diverting youth would take the justice system out of the business of
enforcing morality in areas better left to other social institutions and permit it to
concentrate on predatory behaviors.

Another response to status offenses—referred to as normalization—is to treat
them as being characteristic of adolescents in general, rather than as indicating
either individual pathology or the prelude to a criminal career. Youth should
neither be routinely thrust into the justice system nor referred to community
agencies for treatment. Many, in fact, would be far better off if nothing were
done to them at all. (There was much discussion concerning whether to treat
first-time offenders in this way.)

An official policy of doing nothing represents one end of the continuum;
community-based, nonprofessionalized organizations represent the other. No
conceptual model for these structures was presented since conferees felt such
organizations should be community specific, but several examples were cited:
citizen concern groups, housing project block groups, school based groups, and
Youth Service Bureaus.

Several dangers in restructuring community organization were noted. First,
for such organizations to be effective, they must be fully legitimated by the

community in which they function. Failure to gain such a mandate will make them just as irrelevant to community life as present treatment programs. Second, any intervention must be coordinated with the present system of justice. Without such a link, the new program will probably be co-opted by the old, and prove ineffective. Third, unless such programs are carefully planned, they will identify and label youth just as efficiently as do justice programs; then the change will have been for nothing. One of the conferees asserted:

> There's a concern I have with saying exactly what we mean by strengthening the community . . . because it seems to me, from knocking around the communities I've worked in, that some young people get identified pretty quickly as rotten kids—whatever that means—and then the institutions that they relate to, including the family, but also other institutions, begin to pick them up on their various kinds of institutional radar. Now one of the kinds of consequences of strengthening the community, if we're not careful, is that we intensify these radar processes so that the youngster . . . loses his ability to negotiate some kind of freedom and flexibility . . . which means that we have to take on the questions . . . how can we provide the institutions resources to take kids who are seen as rotten and make them something else?

An effective prevention policy, then, would reform the juvenile codes and the juvenile justice process to give youth engaging in status offenses and criminal acts a real chance to reenter the community. Clearly, this perspective calls for radically different correction programs than have existed. At minimum, it requires that we develop social control groups capable of working with the primary socializing institutions so that delinquents can pass easily from one to the other. This reintegration process was seen as critical to reform.

REACTIVATING BASIC COMMUNITY SYSTEMS

In their several theoretical perspectives on delinquency, conferees identified a number of critical issues: (a) the need to distinguish between the working logic of social control institutions and primary socializing institutions; (b) the need to identify sources of discontinuity in the socialization process that make it difficult for youth to adjust; (c) the need to revitalize the primary institutions (especially school, work, and family) so they can function better; and (d) the need to link the diverse programs better.

Conferees then considered a series of program reforms in social control and primary institutions and their impact on young people. Two points were emphasized in the discussion:

(a) Delinquency can best be understood as a function of the pattern and structure of the total adolescent experience, an outcome of the way young people are processed by their institutions. Certain practices were seen to deny socially acceptable and personally gratifying roles to many adolescents.

(b) Effecting reform only in institutions of social control has not and probably will not prevent delinquency.

Young people are most likely to acquire a legitimate identity if they have a stake in conformity, that is, if they develop a sense of competence, usefulness, belongingness, and personal power. The majority of our youth form a legitimate identity outside the institutions of social control. Attention should be turned to how the primary socializing institutions function to produce youth with legitimate identities and a stake in conformity.

In any social system a few will have emotional, physical, and intellectual difficulty in growing up. Such difficulties are unrelated to the structure of the institutions through which they pass. Some individuals will have difficulty as a direct result of the socialization process. Such people are casualties of the system: their failure is a direct outcome of institutional logic. While casualties of the first type may best be treated individually, casualties of the second type call for institutional change.

Several sources of malfunction in the socialization process were detailed.

First, the institution may be inadequate to socialize all youth. Families, for example, may not be able to provide a stable and supportive environment. Homes may be broken, parents inadequate, resources insufficient. Similarly, the school may be unable to provide the experiences needed for all students to succeed as adults. That is, the logic of the school may bar young people from experiences that would give them a stake in conformity. Inadequacies of this nature can cause major maladjustments in the larger social system.

Second, the relationship between these primary institutions may endanger adjustment either because it is too loose (i.e., parents are unconcerned with or intimidated by the school) or because peer groups, parents, and the school hold different values. Institutions may compete openly for the attention and loyalty of young people, and this in turn creates disharmony.

Third, these institutions are not equipped to prepare young people for adult roles. The training they offer ill prepares most adolescents to enter the job market. For example, by upgrading college preparatory courses, the school limits the futures of students assigned vocational courses. A growing body of research suggests that this is just what is happening. Research also indicates that failing in school and/or being assigned to non-college courses is strongly related to delinquent behavior.

Fourth, institutions may come to adopt the norms, values, and goals of sociocultural groupings in the larger society and promote these to the exclusion of other groups. Such basic institutions as the schools and the church tend to promote uniformity in norms, values, and goals. Conflicts of interest tend to be resolved most often in favor of the subcultural groups who control the power structure in the society.

Many critics of education have focused on the extent to which predominantly middle-class values are fostered in schools to the exclusion of other life-styles. For many adolescents the school becomes an alien environment. Failure in it is not only a daily reality, but escape is difficult, if not impossible.

Fifth, research on tracking practices in schools suggests that while this practice may benefit students with high grades in college prep courses, it is very often harmful for students with low grades in other tracks. The latter tend to develop illegitimate identities, drop out of school, and engage in delinquent behavior. Once a young person has acquired a negative identity in school, it is almost impossible for him to shake it; and there is nowhere else he can go to get a new identity.

Status, then, in the school and the community, is largely a function of the adolescent's success in school. As youngsters mature, the school increasingly becomes the focus of their lives. Almost everything they do is located in or concerned with the school. Their friends tend to be schoolmates; their major activities are school-related, even afterhours activities. Their family lives are organized around school. Problems experienced in school become, by definition, problems that relate to and have repercussions in all other areas of their experience.

Given the dominance of adults over youth, in the school (which requires that youths be largely passive) keeping out of trouble is difficult even for students who are succeeding. For those who are not, the difficulty is compounded. To the extent, then, that young people fail in school, they will be more prone to delinquent behavior. Those factors which contribute to failure and low status must be changed so that the school can give all students the chance to succeed.

Presently, the logic of our schools requires that a proportion of students fail. There is mounting evidence that the tracking system in the schools may be biased in favor of the middle-class student. Inasmuch as movement is restricted between tracks, existing status differences are solidified. Students placed in lower tracks are subjected to increased social pressures and negative social definitions of themselves and their abilities, a practice that in effect locks them into low status futures (i.e., working-class occupations).

Such stratification often characterizes whole school systems. This seems to be true of schools located in the central city or ghetto neighborhoods. These schools serve primarily minority group members and other students of predominantly lower class background (who traditionally do poorly in school).

Teachers and administrators in these schools allocate status according to the racial and cultural stereotypes they hold. The power of the school to promise future success (i.e., to award high status, a diploma, and a career choice) is a critical feature of an institutional analysis of delinquent behavior.

Evidence suggests that misbehavior, if detected, is likely to compromise the high status of students headed toward successful careers (students doing well in college-bound courses); therefore, their delinquent involvements are low. Failing students, however, are not likely to feel so restrained: misbehavior will not greatly affect the working-class future toward which they are headed.

Reforms in the school, then, were seen as critical to effective prevention. Not only must the schools learn how to reintegrate adjudicated delinquents, but they must also learn how to keep delinquency from beginning.

Contact between the school and other social institutions was also seen as important to prevention. Adolescence has been reduced to a passive period in life, a period of waiting. Education isolates young people physically from other areas of life in the community and prohibits them from taking part in them. Young people are neither encouraged nor permitted to work in many areas in society, areas in which adults develop much of their identity. It is illegal for adolescents to leave school until they have reached a certain grade or age. Thus, they are denied entry to, and firsthand knowledge of, many jobs. Child labor laws severely restrict youngsters from many work experiences even if they have dropped out of school. The laws presently require young people seeking work to do so on a part-time basis. Such work is often menial and irrelevant to their skills and interests. Furthermore, adolescents are discouraged, if not prohibited, from participating in other adult activities, such as getting married and establishing an independent residence.

Conferees urged that we attempt to connect all types of education to the world of work. We might, for instance, give all students some type of on-the-job experience. Firsthand experience on a job would enable him to relate classroom activities to the world and hence better enable him to choose between careers. Such an integration would offer rich opportunities for teaching.

Education should do more than prepare a student for life academically. It is a period in which adolescents acquire work attitudes, habits, and orientations by joining the work force. Paying them for their work gives them a stake in conforming. Schools, recreational activities, justice system programs, prevention programs, and the wider community are prime sources of jobs for young people.

Finally, apropos of integrating the reforms, conferees urged that:

First, for such reforms to be effective they must be backed by both the community and the young.

Second, community prevention efforts must not become collection agencies of rotten kids. Programs must include all types of youth in activities conducive to success in life.

Third, all primary and control institutions should be involved in the revitalization process. Planning and action groups should reflect the pluralistic nature of the community. Ongoing programs should be continually revised to remove elements that are not functioning.

Fourth, both adults and youth should be involved in all planning and programming.

Fifth, a professional agency approach to community problems should be avoided at all costs.

Chapter 2

THE SOCIAL CONSTRUCTION OF CHILDHOOD, DELINQUENCY AND SOCIAL REFORM

L a M A R   T.   E M P E Y

The juvenile justice system is now undergoing changes that are every bit as revolutionary in character as those that led to the construction of the first prisons and houses of refuge following the War of Independence or, later, to the creation of the juvenile court itself. These changes can be encapsulated into a now familiar list of catchwords, all starting with D:

(1) *Decriminalization.* Reduce the number of legal rules by which juveniles can be defined as delinquent, particularly those covering so-called status offenses. Juveniles should not be prosecuted and receive penal sanctions for behavior which, if exhibited by adults, would not be prosecuted.

(2) *Diversion.* Divert more first-time and nonserious offenders from legal processing. The goal of any official action should be to normalize behavior. This is best accomplished by nonlegal rather than legal institutions.

(3) *Due Process.* Extend the constitutional protections of due process to juveniles, not only in cases involving charges of criminal conduct but in cases involving issues of dependency, neglect, or moral turpitude.

(4) *Deinstitutionalization.* Remove correctional programs from places of confinement and locate them in open community settings. Their purpose should be to integrate the offender into the nondelinquent activities of the community, not into the routine of a reformatory.

Efforts to implement these catchwords are not without opposition and certainly not without ambiguity. But the changes they symbolize, and the ideology upon which they are constructed, have become the property of the establishment. They represent an official perspective that has widespread support, not only among legal scholars, influential commissions, social scientists and governmental bureaucracies, but among many practicing police, judges, and correctional people. We have reached one of those points in history where growing dissatisfactions with the past generate widespread and often fervent support for significant change. The four D's indicate a pervasive disillusionment with the juvenile justice system as a parent surrogate for children and portend new ways of organizing that endeavor.

A fascinating, but often ignored, fact is that we have been through all of this before. The words of our new play are contemporary, the plot is changed somewhat, and the list of characters is different, but the ideological fervor is much the same. Consider just a few events from what really is only our recent past.

Enthused by their successful War of Independence and by the philosophy of the Enlightenment, American colonists at the turn of the century rewrote their criminal codes, reduced the severity of their punishments and, as gestures of humanity, constructed houses of refuge and prisons for juvenile and adult offenders, and orphan asylums for destitute children (cf. Rothman, 1971; Barnes, 1972; McKelvey, 1968). By 1870, when people were no longer satisfied with these panaceas, the famous Cincinnati Prison Congress was convened. In its classic Declaration of Principles, the Congress fervently rejected the assumptions upon which existing practices had been built and outlined new ones, but, paradoxically, they did not advocate doing away with the places of confinement they so heartily condemned. Rather, they stressed the importance of dressing them up with several new innovations: the indeterminate sentence, classification of inmates, the "marking" system, and parole. Those were the catchwords of the last quarter of the nineteenth century. Incorporated into a reformatory for young offenders, they would furnish the new solution for juvenile misconduct (cf. Henderson, 1910; Hart, 1910).

Finally, in 1899, after it was clear that the reformatory was not a panacea either, the juvenile court was created. We all know what followed. For much of the twentieth century, the invention of a special court for children has been hailed as a significant human achievement (Mead, 1918; Aichorn, 1964). Said

Charles Chute (1949: 7), "No single event has contributed more to the welfare of children and their families. It revolutionized the treatment of delinquent and neglected children and led to the passage of similar laws throughout the world."

It has only been in recent years that disillusionment has mounted to a high pitch. But now, criticisms range all the way from those that say the juvenile justice system has simply failed to live up to the ideals originally set for it (President's Commission on Law Enforcement and Administration of Justice, 1967; Supreme Court of the United States, 1966) to those that describe it as a blatant attempt to "achieve order, stability and control while preserving the existing class system and distribution of wealth" (Platt, 1974: 367). It would be difficult to find someone whose dissatisfactions do not fit somewhere between these two extremes. More important, it would be difficult to find many people who do not believe that the changes now being advocated will somehow help to reform the system. For quite different reasons, both conservatives and liberals believe that current reforms will meet their expectations.

It is this very fact that should give us pause. As David Rothman (1971: 14-15) has so cogently pointed out, there is a prevailing tendency to regard major societal innovations as "reforms," as improvements over those that existed before. The prison, for example, was regarded as a humane improvement over prior methods of punishment, or the juvenile court as an improvement over older methods of dealing with the problems of childhood. Yet, it would be difficult to maintain, in light of subsequent events, that either innovation was a pure and unmistakeable step in the progress of humanity. To do so, Rothman suggests, would not only be bad logic but bad history.

If such is the case, how should today's innovations—the four D's—be regarded? Are they progressive steps in the treatment of the young? Do they merit the support of wise and well-meaning citizens. Let me paraphrase Rothman's answer (1971: 15): If we are to describe any or all of the four D's as "reforms," we will be taking for granted precisely what ought to be the focus of investigation. We should be asking not only whether the proposed reforms will represent improvements over existing conditions but whether they are superior to *other possible alternatives.*

This is a large order to fill. Not only does it suggest that, as a societal collectivity, we share a common set of values and that we know what those values are, but that we have appropriate methods for determining whether changes in policy and practice will result in a successful implementation of those values. Rothman (1971) used historical analysis as his method for evaluating prisons and other places of confinement as innovative reforms. But after-the-fact analysis, as valuable as it is, is quite a different thing from attempting to assess contemporary innovations while enthusiasm for them is high and while they are still being implemented. It is much easier to use the accumulated events of history as a basis for making judgments about the congruence of value and practice than it is to predict whether, for instance, the decriminalization of status offenses will somehow improve the lives of children. The obvious point is that most social innovations are not the result of rational and systematic investigations but simply products of an ongoing social process for which social scientists have limited understanding and over which they have even less influence. Does this mean, then, that social science, indeed society itself, must be primarily reactive rather than proactive in evaluating social innovations? One would hope that the answer is "no," but it depends upon the viability of two kinds of analysis.

TRADITIONAL EVALUATION

The first kind of analysis involves the traditional kinds of monitoring and evaluation with which we are most familiar. As a method of evaluating the consequences of decriminalization, Morris and Hawkins (1970) suggest that every legislature should have a standing law revision committee charged with the task of reviewing constantly the adequacy of existing laws and the impact of any changes that are made. Rubin (1970) goes even further. He recommends that any alteration, either in basic legal rules, or in the administration of them, be tried on an experimental basis. Any time that new rules call for radical alterations in the services rendered by the justice/correctional system, an experimental design should be set up to see if the new social alternatives that are used are any better. Research would be conducted regularly to determine what the effects of legal changes actually are.

The concept of *diversion* has received a great deal of attention, and a variety of programs have been suggested for implementing it—changes in police, welfare, and school practices (cf. Lemert, 1971; Cressey and McDermott, 1974). Although there are times when this concept is simply another euphemism for delinquency prevention, it does include a variety of newer ideas (Polk and Kobrin, 1972; Ohlin, 1970; Empey and Lubeck, 1970; Caplan and Nelson, 1973; Klapmuts, 1974). Some disciplined efforts to evaluate diversionary programs are also under way or have been completed. Some examples are Reckless and Dinitz's (1972) evaluation of a school-based intervention program; Klein's (1973; 1975) experimental study of diversionary programs conducted by law enforcement agencies; or the study of a comprehensive program of youth development and delinquency prevention conducted by the California Youth Authority (cf. Knight et al., 1974). These and other studies will help to indicate whether, in fact, diversion in lieu of legal processing actually decreases subsequent law violation and the incidence of a variety of other youth problems.

The idea that the constitutional protections of *due process* should be extended to juveniles is being monitored in large part by courts themselves. Beginning with the landmark decisions of Kent (1966) and Gault (1967), there has been a comparative flood of new decisions extending the procedural rights of children, not only in cases involving criminal conduct, but in those in which issues of dependency and neglect, the right to treatment, the right to free speech and expression, or the rights of children as distinct from those of parents are involved (Browne, 1973; Weinstein, 1973, 1974; Morales v. Turman, 1974). Although this kind of monitoring is not the same as evaluation research, its social impact is probably much greater because it both symbolizes important changes in the societal concept of childhood and represents official efforts to see that the concept is implemented. It is the quality control element in the arena of legal social engineering.

Finally, because of a growing disenchantment with the notion that captivity can successfully correct lawbreakers, or compensate for cases of parental and social neglect, the movement to *deinstitutionalize* correctional programs has a rather long history. There have been some nonexperimental studies of probation (England, 1957; Smith, 1971) and several experimental studies of both nonresidential programs (Empey and Erickson, 1972; Palmer, 1971; Lerman, 1968) and residential group homes (McCorkle et al., 1958; Empey and Lubeck, 1971). Also under way is an important study of Massachusetts's recent efforts to close entirely all of its state training schools and to substitute community programs for them (cf. Ohlin et al., 1974). While none of these studies indicate that deinstitutionalized programs are a panacea, they do suggest that community programs are at least as effective as institutions in decreasing lawbreaking, that they usually operate with less cost, that they are not of great danger to the community, and that they reduce the negative effects of incarceration on young people (cf. Adams, 1974, for a summary).

Added to evaluational studies of the type just described, traditional kinds of research on police, court, and correctional practices contribute important kinds of information to the overall understanding of the juvenile justice system (Black and Reiss, 1970; Bouma, 1969; Goldman, 1963; Piliavin and Briar, 1964; Cicourel, 1968; Emerson, 1969; Street et al., 1966). How well do existing practices conform to the ideals expressed in traditional conceptions of childhood and juvenile justice? How are official decisions made and implemented? How efficient is the system in achieving its announced goals for both society and the child? How does the system actually operate, both formally and informally? Such research has often been of great value if for no other reason that that it has often highlighted great discrepancies between the ideal and the real and, if not suggesting solutions, has implied the need for recasting current practices or finding alternative approaches.

Limitations of Traditional Research

With all that it has contributed, traditional forms of research have had serious limitations in terms of their ability to provide a proactive assessment of such social innovations as decriminalization, diversion, due process, and deinstitutionalization, especially when it is recognized that, in total, these imply a vast realtering of the way juvenile justice, childhood, and social order in our society are conceived. The implications are profound and require a broader perspective than most of our criminological research thus far has taken.

We are indebted to two relatively recent developments for calling our attention to these matters: the revival of interest in conflict theory and the recent publication of a number of new works on the history of childhood. Adherents to the conflict perspective argue that most social scientists have failed to heed Roscoe Pound's (1922) dictum that if we are to understand both law and legal systems, we must pay greater attention to their interlocking relationships with the social and cultural orders (Turk, 1969; Quinney, 1970, 1974; Chambliss, 1974). These theorists are probably correct in suggesting that most social scientists have failed to pay much attention to the history and derivation of legal rules, particularly where delinquency is concerned. Except for Platt's (1969) valuable study, little information is available on the extent to which such basic constructs as society, childhood, and delinquency are socially conceived and reinforced by those people in society who have the power to translate their conceptions into law. One does not have to accept the Marxian or counter cultural interpretations that some conflict theorists adduce from their analyses to recognize the importance of further attention to these matters (cf. Edwards et al., 1972; Quinney, 1974; Horton, 1966; Roszak, 1969; Teodori, 1969).

If evaluational or systems research is conducted without attention to the value constructs that set the context within which both that research and justice practices and programs operate, then the findings from such research will have limited implications for proactive conclusions. Today, for example, we have obviously grown disenchanted with the nineteenth-century image of childhood and with the way the reformers of that period attempted to use legal machinery as a method of reinforcing it. But what new image or images are being projected? What forces are tending to produce them? What are their consequences likely to be?

If one looks only at innovative efforts and programs themselves, it is extremely difficult to get any answers to these kinds of questions. The reason is that such programs are locked into a deviance perspective. They focus upon illegitimacy rather than legitimacy, upon departure from rules rather than conformity to them. Thus, when new programs are organized, the usual tendency is to search out those factors that are presumed to cause deviant behavior and then to define some mode of intervention that will address those causes (cf. Polk and Kobrin, 1972). The rules themselves are taken for granted. Hence, the ideal image of what is being sought remains implicit rather than explicit. Even worse, research only compounds this lack of explicitness when it measures program success in terms of its ability to prevent or decrease illegal behavior. Not only are we left without any clear picture of what the program is supposed to be doing for children that is different, but how, if it does, both children and society will be benefitted.

Heavy reliance upon a deviance perspective is understandable if the child population in question is a criminal population. Programs should be concerned with reducing predatory behavior, and measuring whether they are able to do so. But even in this instance, program goals, and related research, are presumably concerned with helping children to live up to some ideal standard of conduct. What is that standard? In what terms is it a desirable standard, both for society and the child? The more one moves away from a criminal population, moreover, the more it becomes important to have some answers for these questions. If we are to make more informed guesses as to whether innovations are improvements over existing conditions, or whether other alternatives might be preferable, attention by research and program people to these issues is required.

CONCEPTUALIZING PROACTIVE RESEARCH

The foregoing suggests, in short, that a proactive stance toward any social innovation requires that we do more to place it, and research upon it, in an appropriate social context. In the case of children and juvenile justice, it seems to me that questions like the following would be important: What is the history of such social constructs as childhood, deviance, and juvenile justice in our society? How has that history set the stage for our contemporary social order as it relates to children? What is, or might be, the role of children in that order? In the face of cultural pluralism, what segment(s) of society tend to set the standard against which conformity and deviance among children are defined and enforced? What new concepts of childhood seem to be emerging and what are their implications for the way innovative programs for children in trouble are run?

While questions of this type have been asked about society in general, they have not been asked about children and they have been given almost no attention by criminologists. They would not only demand greater heed to the way we formulate our research questions, and to the topics on which we conduct research, but would probably require a different ontological stance as well. Using both historical and contemporary trends, we might hope to do a more defensible job of assessing the implications of contemporary innovations with respect to the ways childhood and juvenile justice are organized.

THE INSIGHTS OF CHILD HISTORY

Historians, like social scientists, admit to an almost total neglect of the history of childhood. But, as mentioned above, a number of recent works are beginning to fill the void. Of particular interest is the tendency of those works to cast new light on the nineteenth-century invention of juvenile delinquency and the creation of a juvenile court. When placed in the total context of Western changes in the concept of childhood, and society's organization of it, these inventions take on different meaning. The remainder of this paper is devoted to the pre-twentieth-century derivations of that meaning.

Indifference to Children

The modern system of juvenile justice exists because of widespread beliefs that children are different from adults, more innocent, less capable of criminal intent and, therefore, in greater need of both protection and disciplined guidance. Hence, it may come as some surprise to find that children, in Western civilization at least, have not always been viewed in this way. If historians are correct, our concept of childhood, like delinquency, is a relatively new invention. Childhood has not always been a time in the life cycle to which much importance was attached (Ariès, 1962; Laslett, 1972; Bremner, 1970; Hunt, 1970; de Mause, 1974; Stone, 1974). Indeed, the opposite was often true. De Mause (1974: 1), for example, says that "The history of childhood [in western civilization] is a nightmare from which we only recently began to awaken." And while Stone (1974: 29) is somewhat more cautious, he still concludes that the historical treatment of children is a "catalogue of atrocities."

Infanticide or abandonment of newborn infants were regular practices in ancient civilizations and were not uncommon in Europe as late as the seventeenth and eighteenth centuries. Newborn infants were thrown into rivers, flung into dung heaps, left to be eaten by animals of prey, or sacrificed to gods in religious rites. The bones of child sacrifices are still being discovered in the walls of buildings constructed all the way from 7000 B.C. to 1843 A.D. (de Mause, 1974: 25). Apparently the killing of legitimate children was only slowly reduced during the middle ages, and the practice of killing *il*legitimate ones persisted even into the nineteenth century. In seventeenth-century England, for example, midwives had to take the following oath because of the apparent persistence of infanticide (Illick, 1974: 306):

I will not destroy the child born of any woman, nor cut, nor pull off the head thereof, or otherwise dismember or hurt the same, or suffer it to be so hurt or dismembered.

Cultural beliefs tended to define which children should and should not survive. Any child who was not perfect or seemed to cry too much was generally killed; boys were considered to be of much greater value than girls; and infanticide, rather than contraception or abortion, were methods of controlling family size. Two sons might be raised, possibly three, but seldom more than one girl (cf. de Mause, 1974: 26; Marvick, 1974: 283-286).

Even for those infants allowed to live at birth, survival was tenuous. Up to about the eighteenth century, most children of well-to-do or even average parents spent their earliest years in the care of a wet nurse. The police chief of Paris estimated in 1780 that of approximately 21,000 *recorded* births, 17,000 were sent to the country to be wet nursed; only 700 by their own mothers (de Mause, 1974: 35). The practice of wet nursing was apparently denounced by moralists from the time of the ancient Greeks onward because of its apparent harm to infants. Many did not survive because commercial wet nurses were often cruel and malnourished themselves, and even killed their own infants in order to extend their money-making milk supply (Stone, 1974: 29).

Other infant raising practices such as swaddling, burning babies with a hot iron to prevent "falling sickness," dipping them in ice water or rolling them in the snow to harden or to baptize them, as well as disease and filth, took a high toll (Robertson, 1974: 410-412; Tucker, 1974: 242; de Mause, 1974: 31-37). Indeed, a high death rate among babies and young children may have been a major reason that childhood, as a place in the life cycle, received so little attention. As late as the seventeenth century, approximately two-thirds of all children died before the age of four (Bremner, 1970, I: 3-4). "Before they are old enough to bother you," said one Frenchman, "you will have lost half of them, or perhaps all of them" (Ariès, 1962: 38).

Under such conditions, says Stone (1974: 30),

No parent could retain his or her sanity if he or she became too emotionally involved with such ephemeral creatures as young children. Aloofness, or the acceptance of God's will, or sending one's children away from home were three natural solutions to this problem of how to deal with their deaths.

Thus, Ariès (1962: 28-29) maintains that various languages of the middle ages and later did not possess words to distinguish babies from bigger children, and people had no conception of adolescence. And Skolnick (1973: 333) says that people believed that infants existed " . . . in a sort of limbo, hanging between life and death, more as a kind of animal than a human being, without mental activities or recognizable bodily shape."

Child-raising practices beyond the years of infancy revealed the continuance of relative indifference, at least in our terms. Upon reaching the age of seven, children of the poor and aristocracy alike became apprentices in the homes of others (Ariès, 1962: 35). This was the way they were prepared for adulthood. The social life in which they participated was highly communal. The equivalent of our middle class lived in large households holding as many as twenty-five people—parents, apprentices, relatives, servants, and visitors—while the large floating lower class population, whose life, if not less communal, was spent in smaller dwellings, on the streets, and in the fields.

Prevailing conditions meant that the behavioral rules of the time were vastly different from our own. Measured by contemporary standards, says Ariès (1962: 394),

> It is easy to imagine the promiscuity which reigned in those rooms [of the communal household] where nobody could be alone, . . . where several couples and several groups of boys or girls slept together (not to speak of the servants of whom at least some must have slept beside their masters . . .), in which people foregathered to have their meals, to receive friends or clients.

Ariès's comment points to the apparent fact that children were not spared a full and participatory role in all aspects of existence: sex, work, life, and death. He concludes, as a result, that, because children were not segregated by age as they are today, they led a happy and sociable life: they were the natural companions of adults.

Other historians are far less sanguine (de Mause, 1974; Lyman, 1974; Tucker, 1974; Illick, 1974; Bremner, 1970; Stone, 1974). While children were not segregated from adults, historians contend that their status was at the bottom of the social scale. In antiquity, both boys and girls were sometimes placed in brothels, suffered castration and clitoridectomy, and then became the sexual playthings of adults. The literature of the Renaissance is likewise full of moralist complaints about the sexual abuse of children. The apprenticeship system, which persisted well into the nineteenth century, even in this country, led to the exploitation of child labor. Finally, methods of social control were often brutal and countenanced severe beatings with whips, rods, and cudgels. In short, even if one took a temperate view, he might conclude as Stone (1974: 29) did that children in Western civilization, until very recently, have not counted for much. Legal institutions designed to protect them from neglect, as we define it, or to punish them for lewd conduct, drinking, or staying out late, would have been ludicrous and totally anachronistic.

Discovery of Childhood

The forces that eventually led to a more contemporary view of childhood apparently had their origins in the early Renaissance and, for a long time, existed coterminously with the conditions just described. Christian beliefs had long stressed the innocence and frailty of children, although, in practice, people had not paid much attention to them. During the fifteenth and sixteenth centuries, signs of ambivalence and change began to appear. People were warned to do a better job of selecting wet nurses (Ross, 1974: 185); the color white came to symbolize children (Tucker, 1974: 232); children became a source of amusement for adults, like little dogs or puppies (Ariès, 1962: 129); and children in paintings began to look like children rather than mature dwarfs (Ariès, 1962: 33).

By the late sixteenth and seventeenth centuries, criticisms of prior child-raising practices grew pronounced. Although the Renaissance, the Protestant Reformation, the commercial revolution, and the discovery of the New World were undoubtedly influential, most historians suggest that the real innovators, insofar as children are concerned, were a relatively small band of moralists, churchmen, and schoolmen, both Catholic and Protestant (Ariès, 1962: 330, 412; Illick, 1974: 316-317; Marvick, 1974: 261; Bremner, 1970, I). A moralization of society was taking place in which the ethical aspects of religion were gradually taking precedence over the ritualistic. Efforts were being made to reshape the world and to do so, in part, through children.

Children were seen by the moralists as rather odd creatures, fragile, innocent, and sacred, on one hand, but corruptible, trying, and arrogant on the other. What children must need, they felt, is discipline and training. Their premature induction into the adult world not only injures them but affronts adults. The remarks of two Puritan reformers in 1621 capture this moralist theme very well (Illick, 1974: 316-317):

> The young child which lieth in the cradle is both wayward and full of affections; and though his body is small, yet he hath a *reat* [wrong-doing] heart, and is altogether inclined to evil. . . . If this sparkle be suffered to increase, it will rage and burn down the whole house. For we are changed and become good not by birth but by education. . . . Therefore, parents must be wary and circumspect.

What was emerging, of course, was the modern concept of childhood; namely, the idea that, until a child has been given distinctive preparation, he is not ready for life. Until he has been subjected to a sort of moral and educational quarantine, he cannot be allowed to join the adults (Ariès, 1962: 411-412). In support of this idea, the moralists stressed the importance of two societal institutions in addition to the church: the family and the school. During the middle ages, children were a common property and, except for a few years, were not raised by their own parents. The moralists, however, placed direct responsibility on parents, a responsibility that, among other things, probably contributed to the emergence of the nuclear family. With respect to that issue, Peter Laslett (1972: 1-89) has shown rather conclusively that the English family became increasingly nuclear during the seventeenth century.

Not entirely trusting corrupt parents, however, the moralists also sought to use the school as a place for moral as well as intellectual training. Unlike the humanists of the Renaissance, who stressed the idea that learning should be pursued by people of all ages, the moralists were particularly concerned with schooling for the young. Hence, they were responsible for opening many of the first schools whose purpose was general education rather than technical training for the clergy (cf. Ariès, 1962). While space precludes a detailed discussion of the evolution of these schools, a recognition of their importance as a social innovation designed to reorganize the lives of the young is what is most important.

The Ideal Child

By the late seventeenth and eighteenth centuries, a vision of the ideal child had been developed and widely projected. The vision is easily deduced by allusion to the child-raising principles set forth in a multiplicity of tracts, sermons, and pamphlets which were common both in Europe and in the American colonies (Ariès, 1962: 114-119; Rothman, 1971: 15-17; Bremner, 1970, I). Briefly, the principles were these:

(1) Never permit children to be alone, since they are not fit to govern themselves.

(2) Discipline, do not pamper, children. They must learn submission and self-control.

(3) Teach modesty. Children should not undress in the presence of others; should not lie in an immodest position, especially girls; should not sleep together if of the opposite sex; should not hear songs, read books, or observe performances that express dissolute passions.

(4) Train children to work. Teach them diligence in some lawful trade.

(5) Above all, teach respect for, and obedience to, authority. Disobedience leads inevitably to dishonor, disease, and death.

In short, the ideal child should be submissive to authority, hardworking, self-controlled, obedient, modest, and chaste. Parents who do not produce such children, and schools that fail to mold them, are suspect. What these principles meant, in effect, was that, over the space of several centuries, indifference to children had been replaced by an increasing preoccupation with them. The significance of this change is difficult to overstate. Before turning exclusively to its impact on the organization of child raising in American society, a few collary matters should be known.

First, historical analyses generally suggest that both the ideal concept and organization of childhood were possessions largely of the middle class (Ariès, 1962: 414-415; Bremner, 1970, I: 343; Platt, 1969). The nuclear family, for example, seemed to have greater appeal for a growing number of entrepreneurs, merchants, and professionals than it did either for the peasant class or the nobility. Middle-class families were inclined increasingly to shrink from the indiscriminate mixing of the generations and the classes in large households and to stress the benefits of family privacy. Formal schooling was likewise seen as particularly useful by the middle class. For a long time schools were privately run, both in Europe and America; and though they sometimes made provision for poorer children, many of the latter either could not, or did not, attend schools, and those who did rarely went beyond the first few grades. Virtually no effort, moreover, was made to educate black and Indian children in the colonies (Bremner, 1970, I: 72-79).

Second, sexual stratification continued. Nineteenth-century French peasants were known to declare: "I have no children, monsieur. I have only girls" (Robertson, 1974: 409). And in Naples, it was customary to hang out a black flag if a girl was born so neighbors might be spared the embarrassment of coming to congratulate the parents. Parents were still not crazy about daughters. Hence, European schools were off limits for girls and remained so for some time (Ariès, 1962: 269-285). In the American colonies, particularly the northeast, girls were taught to read and write but beyond that were still relegated to domestic roles.

Third, changes in the concept of childhood did not mean that all older child-raising practices were eliminated. Child labor, for example, was highly important. Hence, apprenticeship practices continued, although with some class differentials. The American colonies used large numbers of indentured children who were swept off the streets of London and shipped over in wholesale lots (Bremner, 1970, I: 5-9). Native-born children, meanwhile, began work at about age six, but for their parents, not for another family. Boys were not apprenticed until about age fourteen, and girls might not be apprenticed at all.

Finally, methods of discipline remained harsh. The debate was not whether children should be whipped, but at which age it should begin, how and where it should be administered, and until what age. However, the conflicted character of child-raising principles, stressing parental love, on one hand, but stern, unyielding punishment for disobedience on the other, did seem to foster ambivalence (Robertson, 1974: 414-420; Illick, 1974: 326).

CHILDHOOD IN EIGHTEENTH-CENTURY AMERICA

Throughout the middle ages, and as late as the eighteenth century, children participated in acts which, if committed today, could not only result in their being defined as delinquent but could require that their parents be charged with contributing to their delinquency. As soon as they could talk, most children learned and used (by our standards) obscene language and gestures; many engaged in sex at an early age, willingly or otherwise; they drank freely in taverns, if not at home; few of them went to school and, when they did, they wore sidearms, fomented brawls, and fought duels (cf. Sanders, 1970; Ariès, 1962). In modern society, these same acts occur, but they are legally defined as undesirable and authorities are charged with curbing them. We are interested, of course, in how this came about.

It was during the nineteenth century that most laws applicable to children were actually written and the juvenile court created. But only by clarifying their eighteenth century precendents is it possible to illustrate the remarkable societal changes that led to their development.[1] First, let it be said that the influential Puritan reformers justified coming to this country as a method of carrying the gospel to the New World and of permitting the young to escape the corruption of the Old. The fountains of learning and religion had been destroyed, said John Winthrop, such that "most children, even the best wits and of fairest hopes, are perverted, corrupted and utterly overthrown" (Bremner, 1970, I: 18-19).

Although Puritan child-raising practices were by no means universal throughout the colonies, the principles they espoused obviously had great impact upon subsequent generations of nineteenth-century reformers, the principles stressing obedience, hard work, modesty, and chastity. Furthermore, the small towns in which the colonists lived were admirably suited to an implementation of these principles. Life was dominated by a network of three major institutions: family, church, and community. "Families were to raise their children to respect law and authority; the church was to oversee not only family discipline but adult behavior; and the members of the community were to detect and correct the first signs of deviancy" (Rothman, 1971: 16).

The moralist emphasis upon education was carried to the New World, particularly by the Puritans. So committed were they to schooling, in fact, that the Massachusetts Bay Colony passed the first law of its kind in 1642 designed to broaden and enforce the educational as well as the socialization functions of the family (Bremner, 1970, I: 28-29). The new law required that each family teach its children a trade and how to read. Parents who failed could be brought before the authorities, while children who disobeyed could be dealt with severely. But since parents were often ill-equipped to teach their children, the General Court of Massachusetts took the first step in 1647 toward a public educational system (Bremner, 1970, I: 72-73). Connecticut and New Hampshire followed suit: towns of fifty households were supposed to provide a schoolmaster for elementary training while towns of one hundred were expected to have a grammar (secondary) school. But since school attendance at the grammar school level was not required, and was dependent upon private support, it tended to favor the well-to-do. Such distinctions were even more apparent in southern and middle Atlantic colonies where education, particularly for the poor, depended upon churches and their pastors. And for black and Indian children, formal education was simply unavailable. Slave owners had almost total control over black parents and children. Hence, while some whites sought to convert blacks to Christianity, they shied away from educating them. To do so, they believed, would be politically and socially dangerous (Bremner, 1970, I: 317-318).

Deviant Behavior

The colonists were concerned about deviant behavior and adopted harsh methods for dealing with it. But they did not see it as a critical social problem in the sense that they blamed themselves for it, nor did they expect to eliminate it (Rothman, 1971: 15). The reason lay in their religious explanation of deviance. They equated crime with sin and assumed that the seeds for both are inherent in everyone. By nature, people are forever inclined to the temptations of the flesh. While careful training and submission to authority might help to control evil impulses, such impulses could never be eliminated. Hence, the colonists were not bothered by any strong inclinations to rehabilitate offenders. Rather, sin demanded retribution.

Colonial criminal codes defined a wide range of behaviors as criminal, from parental disobedience to murder, and drew few distinctions between adults and children, or between major and minor offenses. Any offense was a sure sign "that the offender was destined to be a public menace and a damned sinner" (Rothman, 1971: 15-17). If an offender were allowed to escape, everyone would be implicated in his crime and God would be displeased.

Punishments served protective as well as retributive functions. Because police departments, as we know them, did not exist, the wide use of public whipping, placement in the stocks or pillory, branding, or public hangings all helped to reinforce public morality through mechanisms of shame as well as mechanisms of pain and fear. By sending an offender to the gallows, moreover, a community could be rid of his dangerous presence forever. And since the colonists did not believe in reform, they built no prisons. That invention was still to come (Barnes, 1972).

There was at this time no distinct legal category called juvenile delinquency. Americans still relied on the English common law which specified that children under the age of seven could not be held guilty of serious crime. Between the ages of eight and fourteen, their legal status was ambiguous. Juries were expected to pay close attention to the child and if it was felt that he or she could discern right from wrong, he or she could be convicted and even sentenced to death. Anyone over the age of fourteen was presumably judged as an adult, although some colonies made exceptions. The inclination to put children to death, however, or to whip them in public, may have been less common than originally thought (cf. Bremner, 1970, I: 307-308; Platt, 1969: 183 ff).

Poverty

Of crucial significance to our understanding of nineteenth-century views of childhood and delinquency is the colonial conception of poverty. Unlike nineteenth- or twentieth-century Americans, the colonists accepted the long standing Christian belief that the poor would always be with us. But, again, they did not lament the presence of poverty as evidence of a tragic breakdown in social organization. Rather, they "serenely asserted that the presence of the poor was a God given opportunity for men to do good" (Rothman, 1971: 7). Because of the presence of poor widows, orphaned children, or unfortunate families, persons at all levels of society could be benefitted. The poor could be given charity, and industrious stewards could do God's work by providing it. The one exception was the idle ne'er-do-well who might be told to move on to some other town. Otherwise, poor adults did not live in constant dread of the poorhouse, and children, simply because they were destitute, did not face the prospect of placement in an orphan asylum. Indeed, neither type of institution existed.

There is perhaps no better way to sum up the ambivalent feelings that must have been associated with the stern, yet caring, character of dominant eighteenth-century child-raising practices than the following lines penned by Anne Bradstreet, an eighteenth-century, New England poet (Illick, 1974: 326). Lamenting the death of her eight-year-old granddaughter, she wrote:

> Farewell dear babe, my heart's too much content,
> Farewell sweet babe, the pleasure of mine eye,
> Farewell fair flower that for a space was lent,
> Then ta'en away unto Eternity.

But, in writing about the birth of a new grandson, she expressed prevailing sentiments about the inherent depravity of children:

> Here sits our grandame in retired place
> And in her lap, her bloody Cain newborn.

Responsibilities for raising the right kinds of children were not without tensions.

NINETEENTH-CENTURY ENLIGHTENMENT

Colonial social organization did not survive long into the nineteenth century. After the War of Independence, Americans were subjected to a series of changes which were intoxicating but altered irrevocably the tight-knit communities to which they were accustomed.

Changes in Belief

The first of these changes was ideological. Whereas the religious doctrines of the past two centuries had suggested that people are inherently depraved and foreordained to a particular destiny, the American Constitution and the Declaration of Independence were based upon the philosophy of the Enlightenment, a philosophy that was individualistic and stressed universal and unlimited human progress. Through the use of reason, and by applying the principles of democracy, humankind could reach unlimited heights. The consequences of such thinking were often dramatic.

Just as they began to cast off the strictures of some of their theological beliefs, Americans began to feel that their eighteenth-century methods of social control were obsolete (Rothman, 1971: 57-59). Feeling that the legal codes of the mother country had stifled their better inclinations, and seizing upon the Enlightenment writings of people like Cesare Beccaria (1809), they revised both their criminal codes and vastly reduced the severity of their punishments (Barnes, 1972: 106-107). Americans had a grand mission to fulfill, and one way to do it was to uplift a formerly helpless segment of mankind, the criminal class (Rothman, 1971: 60-61).

Ways by which this mission could be accomplished were suggested by new explanations for deviant behavior that began to emerge at the turn of the century. More and more, there was a tendency to reject the assumption that crime and sin were synonymous. In its stead, grew the belief that deviancy could be traced back to family corruption and an absence of discipline. Orphaned children, or the children of drunken and licentious parents, were those most likely to fall prey to temptation and vice. What was lacking in the lives of deviant children and adults was an adequate preparation for life.

Another social evil, community corruption, was soon added to that of family disorganization (Rothman, 1971: 57-59). So familiar are the profound demographic changes of the nineteenth century that there is no need to repeat them here. Suffice it to say that, in 1750, there were only about one and a quarter million people in the country. By 1850, the figure had reached over twenty-three million, only the beginning of an incredible growth (cf. U.S. Bureau of the Census, 1955). Simultaneously, as manufacturing and commerce increased, as the movement westward began in earnest, and as the size and density of major cities grew markedly, the simple social organization of colonial towns was no longer adequate. But, while this was true, the memories of small, tight-knit towns remained fresh in the minds of many influential people. Hence, when they looked about them and saw growth, instability, and change, they concluded that these factors also promoted deviant behavior. Community disorder went hand-in-hand with the disorder of unstable families.

Such thinking demanded a major intellectual turnabout. Rather than preoccupation with the sinner, reformers now had to be concerned with the forces that shaped him, a significant turnabout indeed, and it had paradoxical consequences: If, on one hand, crime and misconduct were endemic to societal life, and not to the human soul, then they could be rooted out or at least greatly reduced! If the offender was no longer innately depraved, he could be redeemed! If there were young children in danger of becoming criminal, their misconduct could be prevented! The grounds for optimism were considerable.

On the other hand, the impact of such thinking could do little to alter the child-raising principles derived from the eighteenth century. Indeed, if families and communities, and not the devil, were at fault, then greater stringency, if anything, was required. Parents were warned of the awful consequences of an absence of discipline and admonished to take stern measures against any loss of family control. Likewise, the attention of community leaders was directed toward the sources of societal corruption: the taverns, the houses of prostitution, the gambling houses, and other sources of vice that abounded in growing and transient cities. So sensitive to these matters were nineteenth-century reformers, says Rothman (1971: 76), that "they stripped away the years from adults and made everyone a child." While societal ills could be eliminated, unyielding measures would be required. But how? If the powers of community cohesion were being stripped away, and if the use of corporal and capital punishment were to be reduced, what new mechanisms of social control and socialization could be found?

The Institution as Panacea

Out of many possible alternatives, leading reformers chose institutional confinement, prisons for adults and houses of refuge and orphan asylums for children. Asylums for abandoned children had been used in Europe for some time, but the idea that places of confinement could be used effectively to reform criminals or to substitute for family and community as the best method to raise children was entirely new (Barnes, 1972: 122; McKelvey, 1968: 6-11; Rothman, 1971: 208-209). It was no accident either that the first houses of refuge and asylums appeared around 1825 in the most populous cities and states. The progressive destruction of colonial social organization led to the belief that child-saving institutions could become society's new super parents.

Houses of refuge were to become family substitutes, not only for the less-serious juvenile criminal, but for runaways, disobedient children, or vagrants. Well-run institutions that incorporated both parental affection and stern discipline could only work to the child's benefit. Orphan asylums would likewise serve the same purposes for abandoned or orphaned children, for the children of women without husbands, or for those children whose parents were unfit. These children should not be penalized merely because they were the offspring of degenerates or paupers (Rothman, 1971: 207). Older colonial practices, of course, continued to operate in many rural areas, but the communities or states that had asylums or refuges were considered to be the progressive ones. The construction of such facilities signified not a disregard for children, but an overwhelming preoccupation with them. The concept of parens patriae was embodied in obvious physical structures.

By 1850, criticisms of the new super parents had begun to mount; by 1870, there were overwhelming demands for change. Rural oriented and paternalistic middle-class reformers, however, were on the horns of a dilemma. On one hand, rather than becoming model super parents, child-saving institutions had become prison-like warehouses for ever larger numbers of children from the margins of society. Rather than turning out ideal children, they were producing young things who marched, thought, and acted like automatons (Bremner, 1970, I: 696-697; Rothman, 1971: 258-260).

On the other hand, the need for child saving seemed to be greater than ever. By the early 1850s, immigrant children constituted almost three-quarters of the New York Refuge, over half of the Cincinnati Refuge, and two-thirds of the Philadelphia Refuge (Rothman, 1971: 261-262). The parents of these children were often penniless when they arrived in the United States and ended up crowding into the ghettos of Eastern cities and swelling the ranks of the unemployed. All the things that reformers feared most were coming to pass. Furthermore, their Janus-like reactions to children and their old fears about lax families and corrupt communities could only have been exacerbated by the development of new social theories and scientific study. In the last half of the nineteenth century, Americans were subjected to the thinking of social

Darwinists (Hofstader, 1959) and to the results of biological studies like those of Cesare Lombroso (Vold, 1958: 50-51). If they were correct, there was need to worry about the impact of physical depravity, as well as bad environment, on the young. These new emphases upon processes of natural selection and biological depravity could only have helped native-born Americans to take the new and strange customs of immigrant groups as evidence of inherent inferiority.

Such ideas certainly appeared in the thinking of leading reformers. Enoch Wines, the most prominent reformer of the 1870s, described the criminal as being the consequence of three great "hindrances": "depravity," "physical degeneracy," and "bad environment" (Henderson, 1910: 12, 19). Peter Caldwell, a reformatory superintendent, said that a typical delinquent is "cradled in infancy, imbibing with its earliest natural nourishment the germs of depraved appetite, and reared in the midst of people whose lives are an atrocious crime against natural and divine law and the rights of society" (cf. Platt, 1969: 52). And the Illinois Board of Public Charities warned that "every child allowed to grow up in ignorance and vice, and so to become a pauper or a criminal, is liable to become the progenitor of criminals" (cf. Platt, 1969: 130). Poverty, and now perhaps depravity, had become the inevitable precursor of the worst nightmare of all, the delinquent child.

It was likely for reasons such as these that, despite the initial failure of the institution as a super parent, a new generation of reformers after the Civil War merely reaffirmed its utility. The task of saving children, if anything, had taken on more monumental proportions. Hence, reformers reasoned that the fault with surrogate places of child raising lay in poor execution, not in concept; the methods, not the goals, had been bad. Furthermore, the literature of the period reveals the persistent ambivalence of people toward potential or actual offenders, young or old. On one hand, the Cincinnati Prison Congress of 1870 stressed the importance of reward rather than punishment, of cultivating self-respect rather than self-denigration (Henderson, 1910: 39-63). Yet, when these principles were translated into action by Z. R. Brockway (1910) at the country's model reformatory, the stress was upon a "monarchical" type of control marked by a stringent regulation of the young person's life.

At any rate, some new names for places of confinement were found: "reformatories" for young criminals and "industrial schools" for children who need "to be kept safe for a year or two" (Hart, 1910: 72). Guidelines stressed the importance of locating both institutions in the country; reaffirmed the idea that they should emulate the character of a well-disciplined family and community; and, for the law violator, added the indeterminate sentence, a "marking" system, and parole supervision (Hart, 1910; Henderson, 1910: 39-63; Brockway, 1910; Platt, 1969: 54). The institution was dressed up in a new ideology and sent out again to rescue children. Reformers were prepared to help children no matter how long it took. There were a few dissenters, of course, and most southern states did not bother with special institutions for juveniles (Bremner, 1970, I: 672; Platt, 1969: 61-62). Otherwise, the new reformatory movement swept the country. By 1900, however, it had come full circle, just like the refuge movement before it. It was not a panacea.

CREATION OF THE JUVENILE COURT

From our privileged vantage point, it does not seem surprising that places of confinement should fail as super parents. Even if reformatories had been built on every street corner, it is unlikely that they could have done much to stabilize the effects of immigration, urban growth, ideological change, industrialization, and social mobility, or to have served as a parent surrogate capable of producing the same kind of person as a nuclear family located in a rural community. The means were totally inappropriate for the goals. Indeed, it was a whole constellation of educational, economic, legal, and social problems which, in addition to the failure of institutions, led to the eventual creation of the juvenile court. By the end of the nineteenth century, that creation seems to have been a part of a larger effort to invest the problems of childhood with an even greater rank and to give them an even more dramatic place in the whole of society.

When the juvenile court was actually created, it strengthened the traditional concept of parens patriae, gave legal sanction to the stratification of society by age and, for the first time, located responsibility for official action in a unique legal body for children. Much broader in concept than the reformatory, it was to become an even more powerful super parent. The law was to be "liberally construed to the end . . . that the care, custody, and discipline of a child shall approximate . . . that which should be given by its parents . . . " (Revised Statutes of Illinois, 1899, Sec. 21). Because the court was empowered to take a child from an unfit home, it need not wait until he is " . . . in jails, bridewells, and reformatories after he has become criminal in habits and tastes, but [can] seize upon the first indications of the propensity as they may be evinced in his conditions of neglect or delinquency . . . " (Report of the Chicago Bar Association Committee, Oct. 28, 1899. Cf. Platt, 1969: 138-139).

Platt (1971: ix) prefers to interpret the enormously broad powers granted to the juvenile court in Marxian terms. The primary goal of nineteenth-century child saving, he says, was not the welfare of children but the maintenance of control by a group of rural and paternalistically oriented child savers who were the captives of major corporations and financial institutions, people who had been co-opted into securing the existing political and economic order. "The child savers were concerned not with championing the rights of the poor against exploitation by the ruling classes but rather integrating the poor into the established social order and protecting 'respectable' citizens from the 'dangerous classes'."

There is much in late nineteenth-century history to support such a view. Prior to the Civil War, several states passed laws requiring that children attend school, that those under twelve be prohibited from employment, and that the workday of a child over twelve be limited to ten hours. Such laws, however, proved unworkable. Employers ignored them; many children worked rather than attending school; and parents, particularly in hard-pressed immigrant groups, joined in circumventing the law. Thus, as the country industrialized, child employment went up, not down. According to the census of 1870, one out of every eight children was employed (to say nothing of children who worked for parents) but, by 1900, the figure had risen to one out of six. Many child laborers, particularly in southern mills, were between the ages of ten and thirteen (Bremner, 1970, I: 559). It was the poorer classes who found the employment of children, to the exclusion of school, an economic necessity. And just as poorer children were the ones most likely to be found in child saving institutions, so they were the ones most commonly found in sweat shops.

Such evidence notwithstanding, a Marxian interpretation probably does not do justice to the events of history. If there is anything to the notion that American behavior toward children was a reflection of cultural changes that had been going on in Western civilization for centuries, then some heed has to be paid to the total context of those changes, not just to the economic and political. Consider the example just cited.

For centuries, children of all classes had been expected to work, and their labor was viewed both as socially productive and personally beneficial. Given the vestiges of the long-standing practice of apprenticing children to others and the undeniable stress that American colonists had placed upon the virtue of hard work, the fact that children were employed should not be too surprising. Nonetheless, values favoring child labor were being increasingly opposed by those who took a developmental view of childhood and who emphasized the importance of education. Hence, the employment of children generated efforts at reform led by social workers, lawyers, women's groups, and even some industrialists. Like the moralist reformers of the sixteenth and seventeenth centuries, they used such terms as "cannabalism," "child slavery," and "slaughter of the innocents" to describe the treatment of working children (Bremner, 1970, II: 601-604). Nor should it be forgotten that in middle-class American homes, like those in Victorian England, children were not exactly indulged (Robertson, 1974). Perhaps it was no coincidence that, by 1899, the year the juvenile court was invented, twenty-eight states had passed more stringent laws to control child labor. Again, enforcement lagged behind concept, but there is no gainsaying the fact that the educational value gradually gained ascendancy.

The key question is whether we are to view the nineteenth-century treatment of children through late twentieth-century spectacles or through the spectacles provided by earlier history. Though we now find ourselves at intellectual odds with, if not morally repulsed by, the beneficent presumptuousness of nine-teenth-century child savers, we must also ask whether that presumptuousness was somehow worse than the practices of infanticide, abandonment, sexual exploitation, and indifference in the Middle Ages. As recently as a century or two before, American colonists had been inclined to blame the innate depravity of the child for sins and to punish him severely. Now, they were tending to externalize blame and to seek "treatment" rather than punishment. Indeed, given the whole history of punishment, one of the most significant elements of the first juvenile court act may be its justification of a special children's court on the grounds that its principal purpose was child care, not retribution. Such changes in perspective were considerable.

It is interesting to speculate what might have happened had the first Illinois court been declared unconstitutional, as some thought it should be (Lathrop, 1925), or had the New York view prevailed that the primary concern of a juvenile court should be with due process and proper adjudication, not placement and care (cf. Hart, 1910, chaps. 11, 19, 20, 21). Although they were few in number, some court decisions began to appear in the late 1800s which anticipated those of the 1960s by attempting to set limits on the power of the state over children. One such case was *People v. Turner* (55 Ill. 280. Cf. Bremner, 1970, II: 485-486) wherein a boy who had been confined as a status offender was discharged from custody: "The disability of minors," the majority opinion noted, "does not make slaves or criminals of them. . . . Even criminals cannot be imprisoned without due process of law. . . . Why should minors be imprisoned for misfortune?"

Would a separate court for juveniles that duplicated adult procedures and constitutional provisions have been preferable, particularly in the context of the nineteenth century? At present there are many who might agree that it would. But to agree without attention to the profoundly significant changes that have occurred in the concept and organization of childhood since the days of the horse carriage would be to overlook a great deal.

On one hand, the preoccupation with childhood has continued to grow throughout much of the twentieth century. The social construction of childhood has become much more elaborate: the age-grading of society has become an accomplished fact, and the length of child dependency has increased; a host of developmental theories have been expounded, elaborated, and reified to explain a biological and social process of growth among the young that would not even have been thought to exist a few centuries ago; parents have often been overwhelmed by injunctions to take that process into account; a whole constellation of professional, as well as moralist, child savers—pediatricians, teachers, social workers, child psychiatrists, judges, and correctional workers— has been institutionalized to assist parents; numerous manufacturers, retailers, and entertainers have been organized to appeal to a lucratively subsidized youth market; new groups of black and brown children, not fully integrated into the institutionalized developmental process, have struggled for entry; and a large collection of social scientists and scholars has been subsidized to make sense of all this. For much of this century, then, the ideological and institutional structures of society have been geared to a developmental view of childhood.

On the other hand, the past decade has been marked by increasing resistance to this way of organizing childhood: during the 1960s, college and some minority youth protested their political and social impotence; the voting age was lowered and younger people began to engage more heavily in the political process; a powerful movement was begun to eliminate sexual discrimination throughout the life cycle; changing mores have not only stressed greater sexual freedoms but may signal important alterations in the institution of marriage, especially as ever larger numbers of young women begin to pursue a career; a series of court decisions support the view that children should be treated as persons in their own right; and the four D's themselves portend important changes in the legal treatment of the young. The ideal image of childhood is changing and implies greater precociousness than earlier child savers might have thought possible.

But these are not the only changes of great significance. A decline in the birthrate, combined with an increase in life expectancy, is creating a societal population that is growing older. For the first time, American society, along with some other Western societies, is witness to a changing population pyramid that will likely grow increasingly heavy at the top, a phenomenon largely unknown to prior civilizations. For example, the growth in population from 1950 to 1970 was lowest for people under forty-five, 30.5%. By contrast, the population of people over sixty-five increased by 63%. Even more striking was the growth in the number of people over seventy-five, 97%, from 3.9 million in 1950 to 7.6 million in 1970 (U.S. Dept. of Commerce, 1971).

Such trends may hasten a decline in our protective stance toward the young. Ever larger numbers of older people will have to be supported by a proportionately smaller and younger segment of the population. Resources and attention formerly directed to the young may be turned to the elderly, a possibility that could significantly affect efforts to assist those segments of the youth population who need it most. A decrease in the privileged status of the young, moreover, may bring increased demands for accountability, particularly where criminal acts are involved. Magnified demands for retribution are not an impossibility. In short, the list of possible implications is great. Hence, it is clear that a proactive and thoughtful approach to current innovations in the organization of childhood and juvenile justice would direct more attention to these matters and attempt to anticipate their eventual impact. This is the one way that contemporary social science might appear to make twentieth-century child saving a somewhat different venture from nineteenth-century child saving.

N O T E

1. The framework for this analysis relies heavily upon David J. Rothman's provocative work, *The Discovery of the Asylum* (1971). Attention is invited to this work for greater detail and extended documentation of many of the points made here.

R E F E R E N C E S

ADAMS, S. (1974) "Measurement of effectiveness and efficiency in corrections," in D. Glaser (ed.) Handbook of Criminology. Chicago: Rand McNally.

AICHORN, A. (1964) "The juvenile court: is it a solution?" pp. 55-79 in Delinquency and Child Guidance: Selected Papers. New York: International Universities Press.

ARIES, P. (1962) Centuries of Childhood (translated from the French by Robert Baldick). New York: Alfred A. Knopf.

BARNES, H. E. (1972) The Story of Punishment (2nd ed. rev.). East Orange, N.J.: Patterson Smith.

BECCARIA, C. (1809) Essay on Crime and Punishment (American ed. trans. by Stephen Gould). New York.

BLACK, D. J. and A. J. REISS, Jr. (1970) "Police control of juveniles." American Sociological Review 35 (February): 63-77.

BOUMA, D. H. (1969) Kids and Cops. Grand Rapids: Wm. B. Erdmans.

BREMNER, R. H. [ed.] (1970) Children and Youth in America: A Documentary History. 2 vols. Cambridge: Harvard University Press.

BROCKWAY, Z. R. (1910) "The American reformatory prison system," pp. 88-107 in Charles R. Henderson (ed.) Prison Reform and Criminal Law. New York: Russell Sage.

BROWNE, E. W. (1973) Child Neglect and Dependency: A Digest of Case Law. Reno: National Council of Juvenile Court Judges.

CAPLAN, N. and S. D. NELSON (1973) "On being useful: the nature and consequences of psychological research on social problems." American Psychologist (March): 199-211.

CHAMBLISS, W. J. (1974) "The state, the law and the definition of behavior as criminal or delinquent," in D. Glaser (ed.) Handbook of Criminology. Chicago: Rand McNally.

CHUTE, C. L. (1949) "The juvenile court in retrospect." Federal Probation 13 (November): 7.

CICOUREL, A. V. (1968) The Social Organization of Juvenile Justice. New York: John Wiley.

CRESSEY, D. R. and R. A. McDERMOTT (1974) Diversion from the Juvenile Justice System. Ann Arbor: National Assessment of Juvenile Corrections.

de MAUSE, L. [ed.] (1974) The History of Childhood. New York: Psychohistory Press.

EDWARDS, R. C., M. REICH, and T. E. WEISSKOPF (1972) The Capitalist System: A Radical Analysis of American Society. Englewood Cliffs, N.J.: Prentice-Hall.

EMERSON, R. M. (1969) Judging Delinquents: Context and Process in Juvenile Court. Chicago: Aldine.

EMPEY, L. T. and S. G. LUBECK (1970) Delinquency Prevention Strategies. Youth Development and Delinquency Prevention Administration. Washington, D.C.: Government Printing Office.

――― (1971) The Silverlake Experiment: Testing Delinquency Theory and Community Intervention. Chicago: Aldine.

EMPEY, L. T. and M. L. ERICKSON (1972) The Provo Experiment: Evaluating Community Control of Delinquency. Lexington: D.C. Heath.

ENGLAND, R. (1957) "What is responsible for satsifactory probation and post-probation outcome?" Journal of Criminal Law, Criminology and Police Science 47 (March-April): 667-677.

GOLDMAN, N. (1963) The Differential Selection of Juvenile Offenders for Court Appearance. New York: National Council on Crime and Delinquency.

HART, H. H. [ed.] (1910) Preventive Treatment of Neglected Children. New York: Russell Sage.

HENDERSON, C. R. [ed.] (1910) Prison Reform and Criminal Law. New York: Russell Sage.

HOFSTADER, R. (1959) Social Darwinism in American Thought (rev. ed.). New York: G. Braziller.

HORTON, J. (1966) "Order and conflict theories of social problems as competing ideologies." American Journal of Sociology 71 (May): 701-713.

HUNT, D. (1970) Parents and Children in History: The Psychology of Family Life in Early Modern History. New York: Basic Books.

ILLICK, J. E. (1974) "Child-rearing in seventeenth-century England and America," in L. de Mause (ed.) The History of Childhood. New York: Psychohistory Press.

KLAPMUTS, N. (1974) "Diversion from the justice system." Crime and Delinquency Literature, NCCD 6 (March).

KLEIN, M. W. (1973) "Issues in police diversion of juvenile offenders," in Gary Adams et al. (eds.) Juvenile Justice Management. Chicago: Charles C Thomas.

――― (1975) "Labelling, deterrence and recidivism: a study of police dispositions of juvenile offenders." Social Problems (in press).

KNIGHT, D., R. GOLDSTEIN, and J. GUTIERREZ (1974) Organizing for Youth Development and Delinquency Prevention. Sacramento: California Youth Authority.

LASLETT, P. (1972) Household and Family in Past Time. Cambridge: Cambridge University Press.

LATHROP, J. C. (1925) "The background of the juvenile court in Illinois," in The Child, the Clinic and the Court. New York: New Republic.

LEMERT, E. M. (1971) Instead of Court: Diversion in Juvenile Justice. Center for the Study of Crime and Delinquency, NIMH. Washington, D.C.: Government Printing Office.

LERMAN, P. (1968) "Evaluating the outcomes of institutions for delinquents." Social Work 13 (July): 55-64.

LYMAN, R. B., Jr. (1974) "Barbarism and religion: late Roman and early medieval childhood," in L. de Mause (ed.) The History of Childhood. New York: Psychohistory Press.

McCORKLE, L. W., F. L. BIXBY, and A. ELIAS (1958) The Highfields Story. New York: Henry Holt.

McKELVEY, B. (1968) American Prisons. East Orange, N.J.: Patterson Smith.

MARVICK, E. W. (1974) "Nature vs. nurture: patterns and trends in seventeenth century French child rearing," in L. de Mause (ed.) The History of Childhood. New York: Psychohistory Press.

MEAD, G. H. (1918) "The psychology of punitive justice." American Journal of Sociology 23 (March): 577-602.

MORRIS, N. and G. HAWKINS (1970) The Honest Politician's Guide to Crime Control. Chicago: University of Chicago Press.

OHLIN, L. E. (1970) A Situational Approach to Delinquency Prevention. Youth Development and Delinquency Prevention Administration. DHEW. Washington, D.C.: Government Printing Office.

――― R. B. COATES, and A. D. MILLER (1974) "Radical correctional reform: a case study of the Massachusetts youth correctional system." Harvard Educational Review 44 (February): 74-111.

PALMER, T. B. (1971) "California's community treatment program for delinquent adolescents." Journal of Research in Crime and Delinquency 8 (January): 74-92.

PILIAVIN, I. and S. BRIAR (1964) "Police encounters with juveniles." American Journal of Sociology 70 (September): 209-211.

PLATT, A. M. (1969) The Child Savers. Chicago: University of Chicago Press.

――― (1971) "Introduction to the reprint edition." History of Child Saving in the United States, National Conference of Charities and Correction. Chicago, 1893. Reprint edition, Montclair, N.J.: Patterson Smith.

――― (1974) "The triumph of benevolence: the origins of the juvenile justice system in the United States," in R. Quinney (ed.) Criminal Justice in America. Boston: Little, Brown.

POLK, K. and S. KOBRIN (1972) Delinquency Prevention Through Youth Development. Youth Development and Delinquency Prevention Administration, HEW. Washington, D.C.: Government Printing Office.

POUND, R. (1922) An Introduction to the Philosophy of Law. New Haven: Yale University Press.

QUINNEY, R. (1970) The Social Reality of Crime. Boston: Little, Brown.

――― [ed.] (1974) Criminal Justice in America. Boston: Little, Brown.

RECKLESS, W. and S. DINITZ (1972) The Prevention of Juvenile Delinquency: An Experiment. Columbus: Ohio State University Press.

ROBERTSON, P. (1974) "Home as a nest: middle-class childhood in nineteenth-century Europe," in L. de Mause (ed.) The History of Childhood. New York: Psychohistory Press.

ROSS, J. B. (1974) "The middle-class child in urban Italy, fourteenth to early sixteenth century," in L. de Mause (ed.) The History of Childhood. New York: Psychohistory Press.

ROSZAK, T. (1969) The Making of a Counter Culture. Garden City, N.Y.: Anchor.

ROTHMAN, D. J. (1971) The Discovery of the Asylum. Boston: Little, Brown.

RUBIN, T. (1970) Law as an Agent of Delinquency Prevention. Youth Development and Delinquency Prevention Administration, DHEW. Washington, D.C.: Government Printing Office.

SANDERS, W. B. [ed.] (1970) Juvenile Offenders for a Thousand Years. Chapel Hill: University of North Carolina Press.

SKOLNICK, A. (1973) The Intimate Environment: Exploring Marriage and the Family. New York: Little, Brown.

SMITH, R. L. (1971) A Quiet Revolution: Probation Subsidy. Youth Development and Delinquency Prevention Administration, DHEW. Washington, D.C.: Government Printing Office.

STONE, L. (1974) "The massacre of the innocents." New York Review of Books (November 14): 25-31.

STREET, D., R. D. VINTER, and C. PERROW (1966) Organization for Treatment. New York: Free Press.

TEODORI, M. (1969) The New Left: A Documentary History. New York: Bobbs-Merrill.

TUCKER, M. J. (1974) "The child as beginning and end: fifteenth and sixteenth century childhood," in L. de Mause (ed.) The History of Childhood. New York: Psychohistory Press.

U.S. Bureau of the Census (1955) "Revised projections of the population of the United States, by age and sex: 1960-1975." Current Population Reports, Series P-25, No. 123 (October), Washington, D.C.: Government Printing Office.

U.S. Department of Commerce (1971) Bureau of Census Reports, 1950-1970. Washington, D.C.: Government Printing Office.

U.S. Supreme Court (1966) Kent v. United States. 383 U.S. 541:555:6.

––– (1967) "In re Gault." Task Force Report: Juvenile Delinquency and Youth Crime. President's Commission on Law Enforcement and Administration of Justice. Washington, D.C.: Government Printing Office.

VOLD, G. B. (1958) Theoretical Criminology. New York: Oxford University Press.

WEINSTEIN, N. (1973) Supreme Court Decisions and Juvenile Justice. Reno: National Council of Juvenile Court Judges.

––– (1974) Legal Rights of Children. Reno: National Council of Juvenile Court Judges.

Chapter 3

INTERACTIONS BETWEEN COMMUNITY STRUCTURE,
DELINQUENCY, AND SOCIAL POLICY
IN THE INNER CITY

I R V I N G   A.   S P E R G E L

Almost no form of antidelinquency effort has escaped evaluation and negative judgment (Martinson, 1974). There is strong doubt as to whether any form of treatment, rehabilitation, or correction works. Recently a variety of "innovative" strategies has arisen: diversion (Cressey and McDermott, 1974; Klapmuts, 1974), radical non-intervention (Schur, 1973), "close-down correctional institutions" (Bakal, 1973), positive peer culture (Vorrath and Brendtro, 1974), behavior therapy (Stumphauzer, 1973), changing juvenile justice systems (President's Commission on Law Enforcement and Administration of Justice, 1967), etc. Many of these approaches are expected to result in lower costs than those of traditional programs. Current policy makers and administrators are

AUTHOR'S NOTE: *Funds for the exploratory research on which this chapter is partly based were obtained from the School of Social Service Administration, University of Chicago, through a grant of the Social Rehabilitation Service, Department of Health, Education, and Welfare (S.R.S. 98 P-0500, 1972-73). Joseph Galaskiewicz and Brenda Strickland aided in data collection and preliminary analysis. Special thanks are due John Schuerman, John Korbelik, Tom Young, Charles Shireman, Malcolm Klein, and Anne Kincaid for ideas, criticisms, and other assistance.*

apparently convinced that there is little to lose—certainly not money, or political friends except some prison guards, a handful of diehard professionals, and a few misguided or confused citizen groups. However, there is also an underlying tendency to hedge one's bets. Regardless of persuasion or discipline, almost everyone seems to be interested in community-based or community-relevant programs. Programs of reform are somehow linked to the notion of community.

But what is the community? How should it be used? What should it become? After all, in many theories of cause, it is the community or social structure which somehow created delinquents to begin with. How is it that the community which "made" delinquents will now cure them? How specifically should the community deal with the delinquency problem?

This chapter addresses some of these questions and is based on the findings of an exploratory community research and the speculations that arose from them. The chapter is divided into four parts. Part I provides background ideas, a preliminary model of community structure, and data on population and delinquency characteristics of four inner city Chicago areas. Part II compares aspects of these community structures and their relation to units of the juvenile justice system. Part III seeks to develop a typology of communities focused on the generation of different patterns of delinquency. Part IV analyzes and criticizes certain current strategies of delinquency prevention in light of the foregoing.

PART I. INTRODUCTION

A fairly extensive literature, particularly in sociology, deals with the relation or effects of certain demographic, social, cultural, and subcultural variables on deviancy (Clark and Wenninger, 1962; Cloward and Ohlin, 1960; Cressey and Ward, 1969; Kobrin, 1951; Shaw and McKay, 1942; Cohen, 1955; Miller, 1958; Levy and Rowitz, 1973). Traditional theory and research have centered on the influence of norms and values, and the role of criminals, police, court officials, politicians, representatives of churches, and social service agencies in the socialization of delinquents (Tannenbaum, 1938; Whyte, 1955; Sutherland and Cressey, 1966; Thrasher, 1963; Cloward and Ohlin, 1960; Shaw and McKay, 1931; Spergel, 1964; Suttles, 1968). While there has been persistent interest in the effects of community on delinquency, the idea of community has apparently been difficult to conceptualize in specific terms. It has been treated as something given, general, amorphous—a backdrop for the development of delinquent subcultures, gangs, and "defective" or alienative interpersonal relations. Thus, there has been little if any systematic study of community—for example, as a complex of organizations—related to delinquency.[1] However, it may now be possible to do so in light of recent community and interorganizational theory and research.[2]

Communities may be defined as interorganizational fields in which the basic interacting units are "centers of power with linking mechanisms" (Aiken and Alford, 1970). Interorganizational forces and not social characteristics of a particular population or social problem may produce social policy (Turk, 1970: 14). The interorganizational approach suggests that communities or sets of organizations need not be conceptualized in global terms or as idealized types, but in terms of product outcomes—total outcomes—of the interactions of specific organizational variables (Aldrich, 1971). One author has demonstrated that interorganizational factors may even be capable of predicting urban social phenomena without reference to individual or interpersonal sources of variation (Turk, 1970: 16). However, interorganizational and community variables, although significant, are probably less than sufficient in accounting for deviant behavior.

Of special importance in the study of community has been the idea of integration. The components of community integration have been described in terms of horizontal and vertical organizational relations. Horizontal integration is said to exist when the relations of the local community's different units are closely connected to each other through various interactions and common orientations. Vertical integration is said to characterize the local community when the relations of its organizations are primarily oriented to units, often at different hierarchic levels of extracommunity systems (Warren, 1972).

The relation of community and interorganizational patterns to deviancy, particularly delinquency, has in the past been examined, mainly metaphorically rather than analytically. The ideas of "social disorganization," lack of institutional controls, and the lack of effective relationships with, and of power among, organizations have been used by social theorists and practitioners to describe communities and explain the presence of high deviancy rates.[3] Whether communities are indeed fragmented or disorganized and the extent to which those conditions, if they exist, contribute to deviancy have been a source of controversy for many years.[4]

Strategies of delinquency control and prevention have made reference to the community as a basic resource for rehabilitation or prevention of delinquency. Delinquency has been viewed as a result of lack of social and economic opportunities for youth in various low income communities. Action programs during the era of the Great Society attempted to apply opportunity theory at the community level (Hunter, 1968; Marris and Rein, 1973; Weissman, 1969a; Clark and Hopkins, 1969), but the idea of community was overgeneralized making it equivalent to social environment or societal structure (Cloward and

Ohlin, 1960; Fleischer, 1966). It did not clearly identify different organizational sectors, their components and interrelationships.

More recently, the relation of community to delinquency control has been expressed in terms of three strategies of intervention: diversion, community-based programming, and coordination. In the diversion strategy the purpose is to avoid labeling youths as delinquents, in particular by diverting them at various points from the juvenile justice system and its stigmatizing processes.[5] A key, albeit controversial, notion is that it is better to leave youths alone who get into trouble—radical non-intervention (Schur, 1973)—than to attempt to punish, rehabilitate, or protect them through the juvenile court, probation, or correctional sectors of the justice system. It is assumed that the community, or at least not its "formal" justice subsystem, is the best setting for control, prevention, and treatment of delinquency.

The community-based strategy is more program or agency specific as to what should happen to the delinquent so that he does not recidivate.[6] It seeks to treat the delinquent usually outside the juvenile justice system in the context of a variety of particular services, assumed to be more humane, less bureaucratic, more informal than services traditionally available. Little attention, however, is directed to the community as a geographic and normative system influencing not only the delinquent but service programs and agencies themselves.

The third strategy seeks to solve the problem of delinquency, or almost any social problem, by improved service delivery. The "socially disorganized" community is the service-fragmented community. The key problem is the lack of coordination of services for delinquents (Kahn, 1953; President's Commission on Law Enforcement and Administration of Justice, 1967). The rational solution is a system of services which targets the delinquent and controls him, and the conditions that affect him, at all critical service points. But it is also possible to argue that we may have too much coordination; indeed, that coordination—at least a certain type—is a characteristic of the "bad" community. Thus much is made of the value of community directly and indirectly in regard to delinquency prevention and control. Community, however, has been a poorly operationalized concept, and better specification of the idea of community, particularly in terms useful for public policy, seems in order.

Research Formulation

An exploratory research was conducted of four Chicago communities during the fall of 1972 and the winter of 1973 to clarify what was meant by community and its relation to the social problems of its inhabitants, including delinquency. Various definitions were proposed. A community was defined as a set of relationships of people to each other and to the organizations they have created or respond to, usually within a particular territory, based on common tradition, interest, or concern. It could also be an administrative subdivision of the city. The inquiry was restricted to the formal organization defined as an arrangement of roles and positions occupied by a collectivity of individuals, including leadership, whose energies were directed in patterned ways toward the attainment of goals over time and within the context of environmental forces. Only a part of the structure or framework of the community was to be examined: the set(s) of local organizations and their relationships concerned with the social development or social welfare of its residents, including for example, churches, schools, social agencies, police, voluntary associations, businessmen's associations, hospitals, mental health centers, social planning groups, and political clubs.

A tentative model of the relationships of the community welfare structure to the larger environment, as well as to the deviant behavior of the community's population, was used as a basis for data collection (see Figure 1). Special interest was in the identification of community characteristics or intervening variables. The rationale for the model was as follows: in a rapidly changing, complex and differentiated society, a variety of forms of community structure, geographic and nongeographic, have evolved to mediate essential relationships of individuals, families, and primary groups with central authorities. While societal factors, such as access to social and economic opportunity, technological and cultural change, political and social problems, directly affect individual behavior, they may also be significantly mediated and influenced by community structure. Community structure, in part, may be indicated, for example, by the objectives, interorganizational exchanges, or strategies of action of local social welfare organizations. These and other factors might be important in explaining the social adaptation of people in the particular community.

The four inner-city Chicago communities selected—Heart of Chicago, Pilsen, Little Village, and Near West Side—were a convenience sample. These four areas were recognized by tradition and for city planning purposes as distinct communities. For analytic purposes the communities will be labeled as follows: Communal (Heart of Chicago); Pluralist (Pilsen); Transitional (Little Village); and Controlled (Near West Side). The four areas located slightly south and west of the central business district of Chicago were contiguous and stretched six miles west to the edge of the city and two miles north and south. Their total population was 125,000.

Independent Variables

The socioeconomic level of their inhabitants was below that of the city, but there were important differences among the areas, especially between the

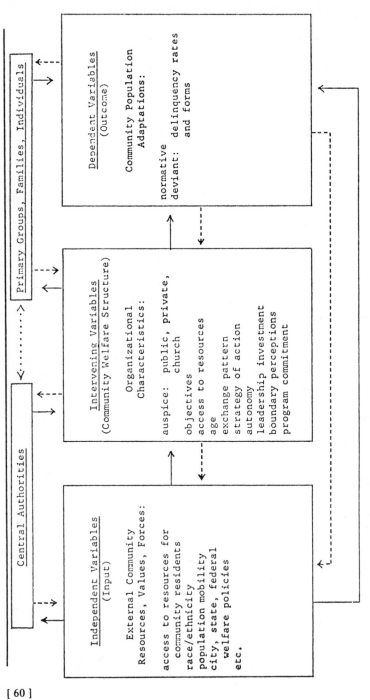

Figure 1. COMMUNITY STRUCTURE MODEL

Central Authorities

Primary Groups, Families, Individuals

Independent Variables
(Input)

External Community
Resources, Values, Forces:

access to resources for
community residents
race/ethnicity
population mobility
city, state, federal
welfare policies
etc.

Intervening Variables
(Community Welfare Structure)

Organizational
Characteristics:

auspice: public, private,
church
objectives
access to resources
age
exchange pattern
strategy of action
autonomy
leadership investment
boundary perceptions
program commitment

Dependent Variables
(Outcome)

Community Population
Adaptations:

normative
deviant: delinquency rates
and forms

———— indicates primary influence.
------ indicates secondary, mainly feedback, influence.
•••••• indicates influence which may be either primary or secondary.

[60]

Controlled community (Near West Side), a very low-income black area, and the other three communities, containing different proportions of middle European, Spanish-speaking, and black populations. The only public housing complex in the four areas was located in the Controlled community. Approximately 10,250 or 53% of its people lived in 2,723 units of low-income public housing. There was a perfect correlation between socioeconomic status and distance from the center of the city. The further the area from the city center, the higher the socioeconomic level of the residents. Mobility rates did not vary in the same way, however. Population turnover was somewhat greater at the periphery than closer to the center of the city.

Socioeconomic status varied, with the Transitional and Communal areas at the higher end, the Controlled community at the lower end, and the Pluralist community in between, but generally closer to the Transitional and Communal areas. Occupational status was mainly blue collar, although the Controlled community had a higher percentage of service and household workers. Average family income was lowest in the Controlled area, about half the city-wide figure, while the other areas were substantially closer to the city average. While Transitional, Communal, and Pluralist communities had a higher percentage of families below the poverty line than the average for the city as a whole, the Controlled community had approximately two-fifths of its population below the poverty line, *four times the city rate*. The male unemployment rate in the Controlled area was almost three times the city rate, but it was only slightly higher than the city rate in the other three areas.

However, there were trend considerations which were altering the socio-economic picture. Between 1960 and 1970, population had increased in the Transitional area, but had fallen in the other three areas, indeed quite drastically in the Controlled area. There had been an important increase in Spanish-speaking and low-income black populations in the Transitional area. Also, there had been a relatively greater improvement in certain economic and housing characteristics in the other three areas. In other words, three of the communities were stabilizing or slightly improving and one, the Transitional area, was slightly deteriorating relative to the city as a whole between 1960 and 1970.

Dependent Variables: Community Problems, Including Delinquency

Community problems were listed and ranked by the representatives, mainly the executives or board chairmen, of 181 organizations in the areas. While crime and delinquency was perceived as the most serious community problems in the Controlled community (29.0%), problems of general education ranked highest in the Pluralist area (26.3%), and problems related to race and ethnicity were most frequently noted by respondents from the other two communities, the

Communal area (23.4%) and the Transitional area (18.6%). Regardless of community, respondents of the public organizations were mainly concerned about crime and delinquency, those from the private agencies most often referred to problems of physical improvement, especially housing; and respondents from the churches were most often concerned with race and ethnic problems. Also, there were differences in the sheer number of major community problems reported by organizations in the four communities. Controlled area respondents reported an average of 2.7 community problems; Pluralist, 2.2; Communal, 1.6; and Transitional, 1.4.

Law enforcement officials perceived a somewhat similar complex and ordering of problems in each of the areas. City police, city corrections workers (Human Resources Department), and county probation officials saw drug use, adult crime, strong-arm robbery, auto theft, youth gangs and poverty as most serious in the Controlled area; drug use, runaways, youth gangs, and poor housing as key problems in the Pluralist community; lack of community solidarity and youth gangs as serious problems in the Transitional community; and insufficient youth activities, runaways, vandalism, and potential racial problems as concerns in the Communal area.

Violent crime for gain appeared to be a dominant pattern in the Controlled community. However, while a tradition of gang fighting was present in the Pluralist community and serious injury and killings occasionally occurred, violence in this community had a different significance than in the Controlled area. Gang fighting emphasized "classic" values of reputation and protection of "turf." Also, gang and delinquency problems were more politicized. For example, the Brown Berets, a major youth organization with a history of street demonstrations for Latino rights but also containing some delinquent youths, was closely integrated into several agency programs. Indeed, the director of the Free Health Clinic regarded himself as a leader of the Brown Berets. Gangs and drug use were lesser problems in the Transitional and Communal area, according to community agency and police reports. However, there was growing concern in the Transitional area with the activity of youth gangs.

Official delinquency rates varied by community. Statistics obtained from the Institute for Juvenile Research based on petitions filed in Cook County Juvenile Court (for youth 12 to 16 years) indicated that delinquency rates for the period 1966-1972 were highest in the Controlled area (206 per thousand) and lowest in the Communal area (81 per thousand) with Pluralist (110 per thousand) and Transitional area (95 per thousand) rates in between. Delinquency rates for the city as a whole were estimated to be slightly below those in the latter two communities (see Table 1). Figures on institutionalization of juvenile offenders obtained from the Illinois Department of Correction suggested proportional and

Table 1. DELINQUENCY RATES (AND COMPARATIVE RANKINGS)
BY COMMUNITY AREAS IN CHICAGO[a]

	1958-61	1962-65	1966-72	Rate Increase (1962-65 to 1966-72)[a]
Near West Side[b]	243 (67)	182 (64)	265 (66)	45.6%
Little Village[c]	88 (44)	66 (38)	138 (51)	110.0%
Pilsen and Heart of Chicago combined[d]	133 (56)	103 (53)	134 (49)	30.1%

a. Rates and rankings were computed from statistics obtained from the Institute for Juvenile Research, Illinois Department of Mental Health. Statistics are based on the ratio of male delinquents (against whom petitions were filed in Cook County Juvenile Court) to 1,000 male population 12-16 years in age. Rates were computed for 75 community areas. The higher the ranking (in parentheses), the higher the relative delinquency rate.
b. The study area is smaller in physical size than that in the larger official Near West Side area. Resident population size and composition are approximately the same, however.
c. Little Village is the same area as South Lawndale. The name of the area was changed several years earlier to improve its image and differentiate it from the area directly to the north, a low income black ghetto.
d. I.J.R. data were not available on these areas separately.

similar patterns in the four areas. Also, delinquency rate trends were different in the four areas. They were increasing at a faster rate in the Transitional than in the other three communities.

Relation of Independent and Dependent Variables

Certain independent variables appeared to be highly statistically related to the dependent variables. Family income was negatively correlated with delinquency rates on an area basis. Mobility patterns and the proportion of blacks in the respective areas were related to the magnitude of delinquency rate change. It is possible, however, that the influence of these and other environmental forces (e.g., federal and city welfare policies) were mediated by community structure. My assumption is that the structure of a community is not only the vehicle for expression of these external forces, but assumes over time a distinctive character of its own and possesses a potential for feedback effect.

Nevertheless, it is important to emphasize the great probable importance of such variables as income and race (or racism) in accounting for delinquency rate. For example, an analysis of 74 Chicago community areas (excluding the downtown Loop area) by characteristics of median family income, proportion of population black, and delinquency rate revealed extremely high correlation coefficients among them (U.S. Department of Commerce, 1972; Chicago Association of Commerce and Industry, 1972; Institute for Juvenile Research, 1973; Kitagawa and Taeuber, 1963). Pearson Product Moment Correlation coefficients between proportion of population black and delinquency rate was −.67, between family income and delinquency rate −.82. A partial regression analysis, controlling for income, revealed that the coefficient of correlation between delinquency rate and proportion of black residents in an area was .56; controlling for race, the coefficient of correlation between delinquency rate and family income of the area was −.64. A multiple regression analysis indicated that the coefficient of correlation of both income level and proportion of population black in a community area to delinquency rate was .88. Finally, both income and race explained 78% of variance in delinquency rate. The variance accounted for by the race factor was 62%; by the income factor, 67%. The addition of race as a second factor provided 11% more explanatory power; the addition of income as a second factor yielded 16% more explanatory power.

In other words, race (but not ethnicity, e.g., Spanish-speaking) and income level seemed independently and, in combination, extremely significant statistically (if we assumed the data were derived from a random sample) in explaining and predicting delinquency rate in a community area (Turner, 1969; Wolfgang et al., 1973; Fleischer, 1966; Friedlander, 1972). The meaning of these findings is subject to a number of interpretations, but they do not indicate that the effects of community structure are entirely negligible. It is the assumption of this chapter that the factors of low income, race, high mobility rate, and inadequate federal or city policies require processing through a series of complex structures or mechanisms, including community structure, delinquent subculture, and defective family arrangements, before the individual youth ends up as a delinquency statistic. Further, it may be argued that the effective organization of community may be a critical means to address changes in these powerful independent factors, only when they are identified and addressed in specific and manageable local impact terms.

PART II. CHARACTERISTICS OF COMMUNITY

Major research interest was in exploration of organizational and interorganizational characteristics, including those of the juvenile justice subsystem, on a community basis. The specific organizational concepts and variables selected were those salient in the literature on community studies[7] and community action programs.[8]

Data were obtained through systematic interviews with 181 directors, executives, or leaders of organizations in the four study areas. This was a 62.8% sample[9] of the 290 formal organizations identified as concerned in some significant way with social welfare or social development. Nine of the organizations were juvenile justice system units. The communities differed in relation to selected structural characteristics: organizational auspice, service boundary, organizational age, resource base, autonomy, leadership investment in community, strategy of intervention, program priorities, objectives, and inter-organizational relations.

Organizational Auspice

Of critical importance was the fact that the communities varied not simply in terms of the numbers but relative distribution of type or auspice of organizations. The Controlled community appeared to have relatively the largest number of public organizations (37.5%) and the smallest number of private organizations (29.2%); the Pluralist area had the largest number of private organizations (56.3%). The Communal and Transitional communities displayed similar patterns in that they both had relatively fewer public organizations than in the Controlled area but more churches than in the Pluralist area.

The Controlled area, the poorest community, did not suffer a lack of formal organization. In fact, just the reverse seemed true: the poorer the residents of the community, the larger the number of organizations, particularly public, relative to population. This made sense, because the poorer the community, the greater the need for public authorities to intervene with a variety of supportive or supplementary institutions and programs. There was no evidence that any of the communities studied lacked organizational life, although there was a different distribution of types of organization. We should note that city police, county probation, and city correction office units were directly located in or physically more accessible to the Controlled community but were outside the other three areas.

Boundaries

The expectation was that, in certain communities, organizations would develop a greater sense of, or identification with, community than would be true in other areas. One indicator of identification was the congruence of program and local community boundaries, particularly in three of the areas (Controlled, Pluralist, Communal) which had similar geographic shape and size. The findings revealed that, while no area had a majority of organizations defining program boundaries coincident (approximately, within a block or two) with community boundaries, the Communal area had the largest number of organizations approaching a majority (44.8%) doing so.

Overall, there seemed to be evidence in each of the areas of distinctive program boundary orientations. Communal area organizations were most community-minded, those in the Controlled area were least community-minded. The Controlled area was most fragmented in the sense that a large proportion of its organizations (43.6%) were oriented to subsectors of the community. Only a small proportion of its organizations (17.9%) were oriented to community boundaries. A substantial number of organizations in the Pluralist community were oriented either to community boundaries (34.3%) or to larger than community boundaries (51.4%). There was little difference as to boundary orientation by type of organization, public, private, or church. In other words, a public organization (e.g., a school) was as likely to serve a small area as a private organization or church. Juvenile justice units uniformly served areas larger than the particular communities.

Organizational Age

The stability of a community's institutions has traditionally been an indicator of the "goodness" of a community, for example, the degree of integration of its value and normative patterns, the effectiveness of its organizational arrangements, its ability to socialize its youth and control deviancy, including delinquency (Thrasher, 1963; Shaw and McKay, 1942; Cloward and Ohlin, 1960). Thus, in those communities where organizations have been established longest, it is thought that the rates of delinquency are lowest. This expectation was partly supported. Communal and Transitional area organizations were generally older, and these communities had the lowest delinquency rates. Controlled community organizations were considerably younger, and the youth population in the area had the highest delinquency rate. However, in the Pluralist community organizations were the youngest of all, but delinquency rates there were much lower than in the Controlled community.

Generally, churches were the oldest and private organizations the youngest in each of the areas. One interesting and significant variation was the age and tenure of the respondents from public organizations in the Transitional area. These respondents were the youngest of all the public officials and held their tenure the shortest period of time compared with public officials in the other areas. In other words, there was evidence of a changing organizational presence and leadership, as well as a changing population, in the Transitional area.

Resource Base

The poorer the community, the more organizational resources generally available. Public agency budgets were larger than those of private organizations or churches. Organizations in the Controlled area had the highest median annual budgets ($123,500), although this was in part due to the large number of public organizations in the sample. Organization budgets in the Transitional area were relatively lowest ($22,000). This may have been due in part to the presence of a relatively large number of small voluntary associations. Church budgets tended to be lowest in each of the areas, except the Transitional community. Also, sources of funding for private organizations and churches in the poorer areas, the Controlled and Pluralist communities, tended to come mainly from outside, but in the Transitional and Communal areas, mainly from inside the areas.

In general, type of staff resources were similar across communities. The proportions of professionals and administrators did not vary much. They were slightly higher in the Controlled and Pluralist than the other two areas. Of special note was the fact that the relative number of paraprofessionals and volunteers was higher in the Pluralist area by factors of 2 and 3 than in the other three areas. There seemed to be significantly more involvement by community people at the program staffing level in this community.

Autonomy

It was expected that the power of a community would be indicated by the structural capacity of its organizations to make autonomous decisions (Yin et al., 1973). The presence of a board or advisory committee indicated capacity to make decisions and exercise influence. A board structure was regarded as evidence of greater organizational capacity to make autonomous decisions than an advisory committee. An organization without a board or advisory committee was viewed as least autonomous.

The data indicated that a majority of organizations in each community had a board or advisory committee. The community with most organizations containing boards and advisory committees was the Controlled area (79.6%). The proportion of organizations possessing a board or advisory group was lowest in the Transitional area (55.8%), with Communal (64.3%) and Pluralist (70.6%) areas in the middle. On the other hand, analysis of only those organizations with a board or advisory committee, eliminating those organizations without either type of structure, revealed that boards were most prevalent in the Transitional (77.4%) and least common in the Controlled areas (43.3%) with the Pluralist community's proportion being 66.6% and that of the Communal area being 55.6%. An unusually large number of private organizations in the Controlled area, more than in the other communities, contained advisory committees rather than boards.

The meaning of the findings based on these and other samples and ways of grouping the data are not entirely clear. What may be indicated is that there probably was a good deal of citizen involvement in decision making in the Controlled area, but the power of the decision making was relatively lower tbere than in the other communities. Overall, the findings suggested that the Pluralist area organizations were probably most autonomous and Transitional area organizations least autonomous.

Leadership Investment in Community

In three of the communities, the majority of respondents lived outside rather than inside the community. The exception was the Communal area, where 52.1% of the respondents resided directly in the community. The percentages for the other areas were: Transitional area, 38.2; Pluralist area, 35.3; and Controlled area, 30.7. Also the data on membership in other organizations revealed that the Heart of Chicago area had the highest percentage of local joiners (72.7%); with the Pluralist area having 60.0%; Transitional area, 58.8%; and Controlled area, 45.2%. Church respondents, generally, were the most likely to live in the area and be members of local organizations; and public agency respondents, least likely. It seemed that Communal area leaders were most invested in their local community and Controlled community leaders, least invested.

Strategic Values

Scales were constructed to indicate the commitment of community leadership to social change (liberal) or social stability (conservative), and to grass-roots (open) or elitist (closed) decision making, orientations (Spergel, 1969). Pluralist area organizational leaders most often scored in the liberal range (33.3%); the leaders in the other communities, much less frequently (13.5%-15.0%). A grass-roots orientation was most common in the Transitional area (40.8%) and least common in the Controlled area (28.9%).

It appeared that Pluralist area leaders were most liberal and quite open. Communal and Transitional area leaders tended to be conservative but open. Leaders from Controlled area organizations appeared somewhat conservative and most elitist or closed in their orientations. The largest proportion of leaders who were both elitist and conservative were located in the Controlled area (21.1%), with Communal area leaders close behind (18.5%). The lowest proportions were in the Transitional (8.5%) and Pluralist (9.1%) areas. (Respondents of juvenile justice organizations tended to be elitist and conservative in their orientations, regardless of type of community.)

While it was to be expected that leaders in relatively better-off communities would be conservative in their goals and somewhat closed in their decision-making patterns, it was not entirely expected that in a very poor community— Controlled area—so large a number of leaders would be conservative and committed to elite decision making. There seemed to be a strong need for stabilization and control of community problems and pressures in the Controlled area.

Program Commitment

There appeared to be limited but expected differences in the pattern of program priorities set by organizations in the various communities. Program commitments were related to the key problems identified. Thus, organizations in the more problem ridden communities set higher priorities for a wider range of general programs and specific types of activities than did organizations in the less problematic, somewhat higher income communities. The rankings on scope and intensity of program commitments in the communities were: Controlled (1st); Pluralist (2nd); Communal (3rd); and Transitional (4th).

Certain activities were of high priority in all areas, for example, individual and group counseling, basic and remedial education. Health, education, day care, and interorganizational meetings—the latter, especially in the Pluralist area—were also of considerable importance. The more interesting differences, perhaps, were in respect to general program commitments. Organizations in the Communal area appeared to be more committed to physical education, recreation, and socialization programs; in the Pluralist and Transitional areas, to school programs. In the Controlled area, the highest priority was given to delinquency control programs. Priorities seemed to be partly related, not only to the reality of problems in the various communities, but also to the way these problems were perceived. For example, the organizations in the Controlled area perceived issues of youth in terms of delinquency prevention and control; organizational leadership in the Pluralist area saw them in terms of youth development, mainly through the schools.

Objectives

Objectives were regarded as important indicators of the fundamental role the organization plays in the community system. The respondent was asked to list his organization's objectives which were placed into approximately 50 categories and then reduced to three major types: services, community planning, and solidarity. *Services* to individuals and families included, for example, education, social, recreation, law enforcement, employment, youth, aging, child care, health care, public aid, welfare services. Service appeared primarily to express the interests and concerns of the larger society for the welfare, education, guidance, care, and protection of (and at times from) the local community population. The function of services was interpreted mainly as the development, support, change, or control of clientele or consumers.

The second major type of organizational objective or purpose was social action or *community planning*. It included mobilization of people around issues or problems, improving agency effectiveness, and the development of community facilities and resources. The function here seemed to be development or change by local organizations of policy and program of other organizations, rather than change or development of the behavior of people as clients directly.

Finally, a third set of objectives was categorized under the rubric of *solidarity*. It included purposes such as: fellowship, cultural identity, biculturalism, good will, community understanding, community pride. Emphasis was on mutual or common identification as well as collective support and interaction by members of the organizations, staff as well as clientele. The function of these objectives appeared to be to bind the individual and organization to each other, as well as to the community and larger society, and vice versa.

It was possible to categorize organizations by statements which indicated an exclusive, predominant, or mixed commitment to one or more of these three types of objectives or goals. This form of analysis revealed differences, mainly by community and to a lesser extent by kind of organization. In general, organizations tended toward specialized objectives, that is, exclusive or predominant purposes: 49.4% of the organizations had a service as their goal, 13.6% concentrated on community planning, 14.2% sought to create solidarity, and 22.7% had a mixed objective or goal orientation. Public organizations seemed to be mainly service oriented (70.8%); private organizations were service (50%) and community planning oriented (26.9%); and churches seemed to be mainly solidarity oriented (45.9%) or mixed (43.2%) in their goal orientations.

However, the differences of goal orientation among the communities were particularly striking (see Table 2). As opposed to 34.5% of the organizations in the Communal area, 69.2% of the organizations in Controlled area were oriented to service objectives; two and a half times as many organizations in the Communal area as compared with the Controlled area were committed to solidarity and mixed type objectives. Organizations in the Pluralist area were most marked in their commitment to community planning objectives. Thus, more organizations, regardless of type, had orientations to service in the Controlled area. A community planning orientation was relatively more characteristic of the Pluralist area; a solidarity orientation was relatively more characteristic of organizations in the Communal area. In other words, there were organizational and community effects present, but community effect appeared stronger. For example, a private organization and a church were more likely to have a major service commitment in the Controlled community; a public organization, a community planning commitment in the Pluralist area; a public organization such as a school, a solidarity commitment in Communal and Transitional communities.

The distinction among juvenile justice system units was best illustrated by the different responses of two of the probation office units, both part of the same county probation organization. In the Pluralist area the objectives were listed as

Table 2. ORGANIZATIONAL GOAL ORIENTATIONS BY COMMUNITY (percentages)

Community	Primary Organizational Orientations to				
	Service	Community Planning	Solidarity	Mixed	Total Orgs.
Communal	10 (34.5)	3 (10.3)	7 (24.1)	9 (31.0)	29
Pluralist	17 (53.1)	6 (18.8)	2 (6.2)	7 (21.9)	32
Transitional	33 (43.4)	11 (14.5)	13 (17.1)	19 (25.0)	76
Controlled	27 (69.2)	4 (10.3)	3 (7.7)	5 (12.8)	39
					176

"helping kids make a proper adjustment and getting them to avoid further contacts with the police; helping the family and community, including the schools, do a better job with kids." In the Controlled area, the objectives were "carry out the mandate of the court; help the kids conform to the law." In both instances, emphasis seemed to be on service to the probationer; however, in one instance, the emphasis was on control, in the other, on rehabilitation. More important, in the Pluralist area, there was also a planning emphasis on use of agency or community resources.

The findings on different patterns of objectives and their functions for organizations seemed indicative of fundamentally different structural arrangements in the communities. In the economically better-off communities, where delinquency rates were also lower, organizations were more focused on solidarity and mixed objectives. In the poorest community, which also had the highest delinquency rate, organizational objectives were highly centered on services. However, in the area where the level of population income was also quite low and the delinquency rate was moderate, organizations were relatively more often committed to community planning objectives.

A key question arises as to whether the establishment of organizations and programs with more and better services is, in and of itself, the best policy for communities and their residents. In the present study, the poorest community already had a relative abundance of services, probably of good quality, but it also had the most serious problems. If there was a cause and effect relationship here, it could mean that the addition of service-oriented programs would make the community situation worse. Or the positive association of service objectives and high community deviance could simply mean that a community with many social problems required much service and indeed received a good deal. The association could also be spurious and suggest that some other factor(s) influenced high rates of deviance. On the face of it, there seemed little support for the notion that extensive service commitment, per se, was associated with, or contributed to, low deviancy in a community.

Interorganizational Relationships

Patterns of relationship with organizations both inside and outside the communities were also viewed as extremely important in providing insight into the determinants of community structure (Mitchell, 1969). The respondents were asked to indicate with which organization there was significant relationship and what was exchanged (i.e., given and/or received) by each organization in a two-way relationship. A great variety of items was exchanged, including clients, staff, funds, facilities, equipment, information, program services, administrative consultation, recognition, good will, moral support. Gross classifications were made based on concepts of focality, amount, direction, distance, and value or "currency" of the things or processes exchanged as well as the character (e.g., conflict) of the organizational relationships.

The communities appeared to differ systematically. For example, different types of organization were central to the exchange networks of each community. The findings indicated there were more relationships or exchanges with public than private organizations or churches in the Controlled community, but relatively more relationships with private organizations in the Communal and Pluralist areas. Index scores or ratios of contact with the different types of organizations are indicated in Table 3.

The amount of activity (i.e., units exchanged with other organizations internal and/or external to the community) varied. The average number of organizational exchanges by community was: Controlled area, 9.1; Pluralist, 5.2; Transitional, 5.0; Communal, 4.8. Activity levels were extremely high in the Controlled area compared to the other communities. However, on the basis of relative volume of items exchanged, the Pluralist area was most oriented to organizations inside and the Controlled area, to organizations outside the community.

Also, while the pattern of internal community relations emphasized the role of private organizations in the Communal and Pluralist areas and the role of public organizations in the Controlled area, the pattern of external community relations was reversed: public organizations played a greater role for Pluralist and partly for Communal areas, and private organizations for the Controlled community. It was as if organizations in one community required public organizations close at hand but in other communities preferred them at a distance.

Furthermore, the level or distance of the outside relationships varied. The Pluralist area appeared to have more relationships with organizations at higher

Table 3. RATIOS OF TYPES OF ORGANIZATIONAL RELATIONSHIPS (CONTACT) WITHIN AND ACROSS COMMUNITIES (Standardized Scores)[a]

Community	Contacts with Other Community Organizations		
(By All Organizations in:)	Public	Private	Church
Heart of Chicago	80.0	108.8	44.4
Pilsen	92.8	106.1	24.6
Little Village	95.3	78.1	40.3
Near West Side	110.5	77.5	28.0

a. The number of organizations by type across communities was controlled. Thus, it is possible to compare relative amounts of contact by type of organization within and across communities, e.g., there was a little less than twice as much contact with public organizations as with churches within Heart of Chicago, and almost twice as much contact with churches in Heart of Chicago compared with Pilsen.

levels of jurisdiction—county, state, and federal levels (46.2%)—than the other communities: Communal, 36.7%; Transitional, 25.8%; and Controlled, 19.2%. On the other hand, the Controlled area had relatively the highest proportion of its relationships with organizations at the municipal and also the district level, that is, the level between the community and the city. In other words, not simply were the levels less distant here, but they were capable of providing more proximate supervision of organizations in the Controlled area.

It was also possible to analyze interorganizational relations by the value of the item or process exchanged. Certain resources were considered more valuable than others. An ordinal scale was constructed in which it was assumed that funds were more valuable or convertible than staff, equipment, or facilities; that these latter were more valuable than program services; that services were more valuable than support or sanction (by most agencies); that support or sanction was more valuable than administrative or consultative services. This kind of classification could also be reduced to a nominal scale in order to establish a more cautious assumption about versimilitude to reality. Regardless of which classification was used, whether organizations received, gave, or exchanged services in relation to inside or outside organizations, the rankings were generally the same. The value of resources exchanged was always highest in the Communal area and always lowest in the Controlled area.

Finally, organizational leaders were asked to identify the organizations both inside and outside the community with which they had had conflict in the previous twelve month period. Striking is the finding that the fewest conflicts,

Table 4. CONFLICTS WITH ORGANIZATIONS INSIDE THE COMMUNITY[a]

Community	Type of Local Organization in Conflict (Inside)			
	Public	Private	Church	Area Wide
Heart of Chicago	.30	.33	.2	.27
Pilsen	.40	.47	3.4	.86
Little Village	.20	.26	.15	.22
Near West Side	.14	.39	0.0	.21

a. Mean Number of Conflicts by Type of Organization and Area with Other Organizations (not specified as to type). The unit of analysis is the organization in conflict with another organization and not the number of conflicts per organization.

whether with organizations located within or outside the community or by type of organization, occurred with one exception (private organizations in relation to organizations inside the community) in the Controlled area. There was even less conflict with organizations outside than inside the Controlled community. Thus, the poorest community with the most severe social problems, the community with most to complain about and with the greatest basis for conflict, had the least interorganizational conflict (Tables 4 and 5).

In general, the poorer the community, the more likely it was to direct more of its conflict to organizations within the community than outside the community. Noteworthy was the extraordinarily high level of conflict by Pluralist area organizations with other organizations in the community and the rather high level of conflict with organizations outside the community in the Communal area. Pluralist area organizations appeared to be in a state of ferment, particularly involving such local organizations as concerned citizen groups, schools, and occasionally social agencies, public and private. Communal area organizations appeared much more antagonistic to external than internal community organizations, particularly public organizations, such as the Housing Authority.

Also, it seemed that private organizations were more conflictual than public organizations in their relations with other organizations inside the community while public organizations were more conflictual in their relations with organizations located outside the community. A tentative explanation might be that private organizations were relatively freer to criticize organizations within the community, which were less likely to control resources or funds. By contrast public organizations were more apt to criticize other organizations, mainly public, which were regarded as competitive and more often located outside the area. We note that, except in the Pluralist area, churches seemed to be the least conflict oriented of the types of organizations.

Table 5. CONFLICTS WITH ORGANIZATIONS OUTSIDE THE COMMUNITY[a]

Community	Type of Local Organization in Conflict (Outside)			
	Public	Private	Church	Area Wide
Heart of Chicago	.70	.56	.30	.52
Pilsen	.53	.13	1.2	.43
Little Village	.25	.26	.25	.25
Near West Side	.18	.08	0.0	.13

a. Mean Number of Conflicts by Type of Organization and Area with Other Organizations (not specified as to type). The unit of analysis is the organization in conflict with another organization and not the number of conflicts per organization.

These patterns of interorganizational relationships suggest the following. The better-off economically and socially the residents of the community, the less active organizations had to be to obtain resources to meet community needs. The poorer the community, the more it had to seek resources outside, but the very poor community could not or was not permitted to go too far. Furthermore, the value of the resources generally available to organizations seemed on a perceived network basis to be greater for the better-off than the worse-off communities. For example, a much higher proportion of informational resources, judged to be of less intrinsic value than some other resources, was exchanged among the Controlled area organizations—probably for surveillance purposes—than in the other communities. Controlled area organizations seemed far more constrained in their development of conflict relationships, particularly with extracommunity organizations compared with the other three communities.[10]

It may be useful to highlight the relation of the juvenile justice system to the particular communities. In general, the juvenile justice units were not central to interorganizational exchange systems in each of the communities, except in the Controlled area, where the city corrections unit, which was intimately related to both juvenile justice and welfare systems, had high status and was one of four organizations at the center of the interorganizational exchange network. The juvenile justice system was relatively most active in the Controlled community, where its units were most often in contact with other public organizations, especially with special programs and personnel established to deal with difficult or troublesome youth. In this area, there was a higher ratio of justice system personnel, particularly police, to population than in the other areas. Juvenile justice units were least active in the Communal area; however, they were relatively more active with private than public organizations. Justice system units were fairly active in the Pluralist and Transitional communities and had about equal contact with public and private organizations.

Justice system units had a different quality of relationship with organizations and population groups in each of the areas. In the Controlled area, the juvenile justice system was not only well integrated with the public sector but with families and various grass-roots groups. Local population groups were highly sensitive to, and sensitized by, special crime control programs (e.g., model cities). They cooperated with and reported a great variety of crimes and delinquencies to the police. This was not true in the other areas. Primary groups and private organizations absorbed aberrant youth in the Communal area. There was a good deal of conflict between population groups and the police in the Pluralist community. Certain private organizations and churches were in a high state of disagreement with the police over their practice of handling juveniles.

We should also note that in the Controlled area there was a great deal of latent or "private" hostility between the police and certain private organizations, particularly those that were militant. But there were no open expressions of disagreement or conflict. Both the police and the private organizations went out of their way to avoid each other.

Finally, the value of the contacts between juvenile justice system units and other organizations differed in each area. It was most substantive—although contacts were less frequent—in the Communal area. Staff exchanges, joint programs, and mutual support were more common. Despite a good many instances of conflict between probation service or the police and community groups in the Pluralist area and to some extent the Transitional community, there were frequent instances of cooperation, and those exchanges were quite substantial and valuable. In the Controlled area exchanges between juvenile justice system and other organizations, private or public, were dominated by requests for information to facilitate surveillance.

In sum, a variety of community structure variables were identified, which possibly reflected underlying conditions conducive to distinctive patterns of delinquency in each community. Formal organizations were viewed as responsible in some manner for and responsive to community problems, including delinquency. However, the complex interaction, the weighting, and the sequencing of these variables were not clearly or firmly established. Thus, what is to be made of these findings? How meaningfully does community structure relate to or influence delinquency patterns? The next section is an attempt at an analytic typology of community and its relation to delinquency.

PART III. TYPOLOGY OF COMMUNITIES

The typology is adapted, in part, from Kornhauser's paradigm of societies based on the accessibility of central elites or authorities and the availability of non-elites or population groups for political mobilization (Kornhauser, 1969: 40). It is also informed by Warren's ideas of vertical and horizontal community integration (Warren, 1972). The Kornhauser formulation is viewed as focusing on the relation of local population groups, including informal groups, to central authorities. The Warren formulation is utilized to specify these various relations through formal organization at local community (horizontal) and at extra community (vertical) levels. It is possible to consider the formal and informal levels of community as related, yet analytically and empirically distinct. Thus, the availability of population groups for social action does not necessarily mean that the community's established organizations are effectively ready for negotiations with central authorities. On the other hand, local organizations may be highly available, although the population may not be mobilized. Also, central or extra-community elites may be differentially accessible or influential in regard to local organizations and local population groups. Table 6, adapted from Kornhauser's paradigm, provides only one set of dimensions for location of four major types of community.

The specific analytic integration of Kornhauser and Warren's ideas is not attempted. The complex interrelationships of these sets of variables would produce a more refined or complex typology than necessary for present purposes. The various forms of organizational and primary group integration, however, will be noted in the discussion. My assumption, furthermore, is that central elites in a democratized mass society (Shils, 1970) are increasingly accessible to both population groups and organizations. Thus, the key issue is the differential character and degree of mobilization of central authorities and of population groups in relation to intermediate formal organizations.

Four general types of community may now be conceptualized: Controlled, Pluralist, Communal, and Mass Movement. Near West Side is an example of a

Table 6. TYPES OF COMMUNITY (Suggested by Kornhauser)

Accessibility or Influence of Central Authorities	Mobilization of Population Groups	
	High	Low
High (Direct)	Mass Movement	Controlled
Low (Indirect)	Pluralist	Communal

Table 7. TYPES OF COMMUNITY BY SPECIFIC VARIABLES

Variables	Types of Community			
	Mass Movement	Controlled	Pluralist	Communal
Independent: Inputs from external environment				
1. Access to economic resources and cultural values	low as to cultural values	low as to economic resources	moderate (but variable)	moderate
2. Race/ethnicity	indeterminate	homogeneous	mixed	homogeneous
3. Population mobility	high	moderate	moderate to high	low
4. City, state, federal policies	(constant)	(constant)	(constant)	(constant)
Intervening: Community Structure				
Organizational:				
1. Auspice	independent (private organization & church)	mainly public	public, private, church	private, church
2. Key objectives	community planning/ solidarity	services	community planning	solidarity
3. Resources	very low	high	moderate	low
4. Age	young	in-between	in-between	old
5. Boundaries	extensive	fragmented	extensive community centered	community centered
6. Autonomy	very high	low	moderate	high
7. Leadership investment (internal community)	very high	low	moderate	high
8. Strategic values	grass roots liberal/radical	elite, conservative	mixed elitist/grass roots, liberal	grass roots/conservative
9. Exchange pattern	fused	imbalanced toward outside organizations	balanced	imbalanced toward internal organizations
10. Program commitment	radical institutional change	deviance control	organizational/ community development	socialization
Dependent: Outcome				
1. Normative adaptation	indeterminate	low	moderate	moderate/high
2. Deviancy (delinquency)	indeterminate	high	moderate	low

Controlled community; Pilsen, a Pluralist community; Heart of Chicago, a Communal community. We do not have a study area to illustrate the Mass Movement community. These general types of communities are summarized by specific variables in Table 7.

Controlled Community

This kind of community is often characterized by an extremely low-income or status-deprived population, located in a ghetto, prison, or total institution. Sources external to the local community exert an overwhelming influence on the social relations of the people through formal organization. Public, in contrast to voluntary or private, organizations and churches abound and are dominant. The pervasive concern of organizations in relation to the gamut of human problems and needs is services—criminal justice, education, health, housing, recreation, financial aid, legal aid, mental health, family counseling, etc. The scope of interest and involvement in the life of the people by public organization, especially units of city or county government directly responsible for the maintenance of law and order, is very wide. Local private organizations or voluntary associations tend to be insufficient in terms of relative numbers or influence. The religious life of the community is often represented by emphemeral storefront or old established churches whose congregations are mainly from outside the area. Voluntary organizations and churches which are present are usually less oriented to solidarity and social action than is true in other types of communities.

While there may be considerable interorganizational activity in the community, it is largely vertically directed, that is, the dominant patterns of communication and resource exchange tend to be controlled by organizations outside the community. A sense of fragmentation of community and programs may be apparent, but the fragmentation and lack of coordination characterizes only horizontal, not vertical organizational relationships. Vertical relationships are highly integrated. Horizontal relationships may be functionally, if not purposefully, fragmented. While there is a high degree of physical decentralization, there is a low degree of political and administrative decentralization by public organizations (Hallman, 1973).

Emphasis in the Controlled community is on the mobilization of clients on an individual, family, or small group basis to become recipients of services. The system needs and seeks clients for services. Emphasis on services tends to personalize problems and direct attention away from larger environmental or organizational problems which affect the residents of the local community. Furthermore, programs in this kind of community emphasize the managerial and supervisory, rather than preventive and curative, aspects of services.

While there is some attention to community planning by organizations, it is mainly for purposes of organizational stability. Citizen groups are mobilized to support and sanction the existing delivery system of services. Effective decision making in regard to policy and planning of programs resides mainly with elites outside the community. The organization of independent local groups which emphasize social change or solidarity is not encouraged and indeed precluded by the service delivery emphasis. What local organizational life is encouraged may be mainly to prevent activities or control tendencies of local people which challenge the basis of social relationship with systems outside the community.

Existing agency or community programs are often carefully monitored and supervised by public coordinative agencies (e.g., local model cities offices) which have extensive resource allocation power. Many local "grass-roots" efforts are quickly co-opted by these coordinative units, if not, then harassed by the police when the programs attempt to innovate services by using deviants themselves as staff, or when the programs are not neatly or closely supervised.

Certain patterns of deviance, however, are permitted and sustained, if not encouraged, through a complex organizational and community feedback system. Organizations sustain themselves only as they can demonstrate the continuing, if not growing, need of the population for more services. Every opportunity is utilized to identify elements in the community, particularly youth, who are deviants or who might become deviants and a threat to authority and management personnel in various local organizations. Deviant youth, especially males, form gangs and are duly recognized for special (stigmatizing) services. Youth groups, especially fighting gangs and strong-arm bands, provide not only status, reputation, and income for their membership, but a highly significant base and focus of community policy and agency services.

Gangs may be a source of identification and stimulate solidarity among sectors of the local population through their threats of and "battles" with non-local residents over "turf." The weakness of formal organization in facilitating solidarity on a territorial basis is partly compensated for at the informal level by the strength of gang or peer relationships. It may also be argued that gang and delinquent activities serve to stabilize the community by stimulating the development of a complex intergroup and interorganizational system. Delinquents, drug users, pushers, the police, and youth workers are known to each other. Each plays an essential role in stabilizing relations of adult groups with organizations within and outside the community. Delinquency is a highly useful problem. Not only does it quickly divert attention from other, more basic and pressing community problems, but it stimulates local support for a service base to control the community. Deviants are thus in constant process of being identified, stigmatized, and controlled to functionally stabilize the community. Public organizations are called upon to help deviants and absorb those who do not have adequate family support, who do not fit into school, work. They supplant the local private system, including the family, and may exercise pervasive influence over wide areas of the lives of people in the community—social, economic, political, cultural. Emphasis on services, especially to individuals and families, becomes a major means to neutralize and channel the energies of the population in a manner which is least threatening to the external society.

Pluralist Community

This type of community may develop in low, middle, and mixed income level, inner-city, suburban, and rural areas. In the liberal tradition, the Pluralist community is assumed to be best adapted to conditions of social change and the interests of the democratic society. A variety of organizations—public, private, or voluntary, and church—is present, with private agencies or voluntary organizations exercising key influence. Organizations on a continuing basis seek to address local problems and improve local conditions.

A premium is placed on the development of local organization to express and meet the corporate interests and needs of people. The presence and influence of external organization, particularly the public agency, is limited, if not challenged. A climate of contest, sometimes conflict, is generated. Public agencies have low prestige and are under continuing pressure to be responsive to local interests; however, community issues may not necessarily polarize the community, since interests are usually partialized. Organizational combatants at one time may be collaborators at another. A good deal of solidarity among organizations, grass roots and primary groups, is created, as autonomous organizations join together periodically to achieve common objectives. Considerable attention is directed to interorganizational relations both within and outside the community to achieve distinctive community objectives. The influence of local private organizations is clearly dominant. Public organization appears to be more decentralized, politically and administratively if not territorially, than in the Controlled community.

While the needs and problems of individuals and families are also stressed, it is done in a manner that emphasizes the positive development of people and institutions rather than the control of deviant behavior. For example, there is probably more concern with improving the educational achievement of individual youth than with preventing and controlling their delinquent behavior. When recognition of a problem of delinquency cannot be avoided, concern may be focused on the efficiency of the police department or the effectiveness of the schools in dealing with "problem" youth. The basis for youth gang behavior may be formulated in larger environmental or community structural terms: the gang is viewed as a response to lack of social, educational, or economic opportunities or lack of means to involve youth in community development or local social reform. Community leadership arises which stimulates the provision of new or additional resources or the change of existing programs so that the developmental needs of people, including youth, are better served.

Efforts may be made to co-opt and even politicize the gang, for purposes of social change. Gang members, especially their leaders, are viewed as resources in a continuing struggle to improve social conditions in the community. By contrast, in the Controlled community the youth gang is viewed by formal organizations as essentially an expression of the defects of individuals and the group. The object of agency services is to rehabilitate individual members and especially to contain the gang so that it constitutes a minimal threat to established authority. In the Pluralist community, the objective is to incorporate deviant youth into local social, cultural, even political structures.

In the Pluralist communities, deviancy rates are moderately high but may be in the process of decline, particularly if private and voluntary organizations are successful in aiding or forcing public organizations, including juvenile justice units, to modify their mode of identifying deviant behavior. Public agencies in due course may change their definitions, procedures, and even programs. Attitudes and behaviors of individuals and families shift simultaneously and interactively in a direction more compatible with the expectations and values of the official representatives of the external community, which themselves have been modified. A primary commitment of local community leadership is changing or developing the policies of public agencies; a secondary interest is changing individual behavior.

No doubt more conflict between the agencies of the juvenile justice system and local organizations occurs in the Pluralist area. On the other hand, there is more interaction, participation, and also considerable cooperation as each seeks to influence the other.

Communal Community

This is a classic, and perhaps idealized, form of community still prevalent in working and lower middle class urban (Gans, 1962) as well as rural (Gorse and Beran, 1973) areas. It is a form viewed as desirable by conservative and utopian thinkers, and derives in part from a conception of the medieval community where the individual and his family were highly integrated into community life, where role and status were functional to the development and survival of the community and its protection from outside threat and attack. Solidarity, common interests, local traditions, and kinship ties are stressed. Social alienation, deviance, including delinquency and mental illness, are low as each individual is accorded a relatively clearly defined role and meaningful status in a stable social and cultural system.

The small communal society, because of its low level of deviance and its satisfaction with local institutions, places limited value on services or social action. It is concerned primarily with the maintenance of its system of social relationships largely through joint participatory experiences, fellowship activities, and traditional ceremonies. It celebrates consistency and continuity in its role succession, leadership, and authority patterns. It depends mainly on family, primary groups, voluntary associations, and churches to deal with a variety of personal and community problems when they arise. These problems tend not to become salient public issues, but are handled informally.

There are relatively few public but many voluntary or private organizations and churches in the community. Ethnic, kinship, primary group ties are pervasive and integrated with formal organizations, sometimes resulting in long standing competitive or conflictual as well as cooperative patterns of inter-organizational relationship. Patterns of conflict, however, are structured and serve to knit the community even more closely together. For example, the aberrant behavior of youth is expected, channeled, and even ritualized. Aggressive or delinquent group behavior may serve to fulfill the requirements of communal rites of passage from one age-grade role to another. It may even be functional for purposes of recruiting youths with certain talents into illegitimate or quasi-legitimate associations. Legitimate and illegitimate sectors of the community are integrated and perform complementary or supplementary functions. The term deviancy seems to lose its meaning in such a framework of integrated values and relationships.

The patterns of social organization extend over decades. So-called outside organizations, including local public organizations such as parks and police precincts, have long histories in the community and have been almost fully co-opted to meet and support the needs of the local culture and system of social relationships. The influence of external authority is minimal, except as it serves to protect local interests. Furthermore, the local units of central authority are used to interpret, mediate, and advocate local wishes and interests. Public agencies, compared to those in other types of communities, are the most politically and administratively, although not necessarily physically, decentralized. The church plays an especially important role in the community. During normal quiescent periods it is a focus for solidarity expression and during crises it is an instrument of social action by various interrelated local interests. The church serves as a center for the coalition of autonomous groups, religious and nonreligious. Churches protect the traditional values of the community and provide leadership in warding off outside threats.

There is a tendency, however, to xenophobia, an intolerance of new programs and considerable suspicion and resistance to social and cultural change. Such communities are not always able to withsatnd the influence of rapid change, particularly the entry of new groups with significantly different values and behavior into the area. The community structure is weakened; it may "fragment" or "disintegrate," that is, become more vertically oriented. This process is now occurring in Little Village which was identified as Transitional, its community structure changing from a communal to some other type.

Mass Movement Community

Although the current research did not identify such a community, theory and social reality suggest the existence of a Mass Movement community. The concept of a Mass Movement community may appear to be a contradiction in terms. A collection of ill-defined associations, primary or family groups in a particular territory, or, indeed, without a territorial base, may or may not meet the requirements of a community structure. Ordinarily, a community indicates the relation of groups or sectors of a population to each other over time. Furthermore, inherent in the notion of modern community is the presence of intermediate organizations or associations to mediate the relationships of individuals, families, and other primary groups with central authorities and agencies often located outside the community.

The Mass Movement community structure is based on a shifting aggregate of individuals, primary or informal groups—large or small—and no stable intermediate organization. The Mass Movement structure is directly available to central authority and its local representatives. In times of crises, or extremely disruptive social change, established organizations in a community or a set of communities may no longer function effectively. Mass movements arise when intermediate organizations are no longer able to bridge relations between local population groups and authorities. These populist or chiliastic movements include such recent social and political phenomena as the civil rights movement, urban uprisings, prison riots, campus disruptions. The Mass Movement community is based on the presence of individuals and small groups who are suddenly and extraordinarily mobilized and committed to influence directly the policies of central authority or its representatives. Immediate, direct action is required, and in the process individual and group attitudinal and behavioral transformations occur, resulting in "deviant" behavior.

These social movements may arise within the context of the other three types of community, although they are probably most likely to occur due to failures of intermediate organizations in the Controlled community, or possibly in the Pluralist community under conditions of extreme conflict among local organizations and extreme politicalization of deviant groups.[11] The breakdown of established structures, furthermore, may stimulate at least a temporary polarization of attitudes and behaviors. Existing intermediate organizations, or their segments, dissolve and become integrated into the protagonist mass movement or the antagonist authority structure, public or private.

Under conditions of Mass Movement, specialization or differentiation of organizational function no longer occurs. Relationships oriented to solidarity, social action, and service are fused in the white heat of revolutionary fervor. The interests and needs of individual, primary group, and tentative intermediate organization are highly interrelated and interdependent.

The mass movement, however, threatens the basic structure not only of the local community but the larger society itself. It may generate revolutionary conditions and precipitate decisions which serve to destroy or restructure basic institutions. However, it would appear physically, psychologically, and organizationally impossible to sustain a Mass Movement community (i.e., keep it mobilized) for any extended period. In time, stable intermediate organizations must be reestablished. The Mass Movement community is then transformed into one of the other forms of community.

It is difficult to establish the extent and nature of deviancy in the course of a mass movement. During the period of mass involvement, old norms and values may be destroyed, new forms of legitimate behavior may arise. Criteria for deviant behavior are not clearly or consensually determined. They depend on the perspective and position of the person judging, particularly as to whether he is identified with movement or anti-movement interests. One man's delinquent activity is another man's heroism. Furthermore, definitions of deviancy (e.g., sit-ins, destruction of property, draft evasion, even assault) and their consequences tend to change over time. Much depends on whether the movement is judged to be successful, after the fact.

Parenthetically, it might be noted that during the height of the civil rights movement or even during the civil disruptions of the 1960s, while certain delinquents and gang leaders, individually, were active participants, there is no evidence of gang sanction in support of these mass movement efforts. If anything, the evidence suggests that gangs were prone to pursue traditional objectives and even to support police efforts in the control and prevention of riots (Spergel et al., 1969; Kalberg and Suttles, 1974). In other words, even delinquent structures are threatened during periods of social or mass movement.

While four ideal types of community have been described above, no real community represents a pure type. Nevertheless, each real community probably has a dominant or characteristic interorganizational structure within certain political constraints.[12] Each community is highly organized but in a different way. The Communal community has a relatively strong horizontal structure, although its various groups are not ordinarily in a state of active mobilization, and relatively weak vertical pattern of organization. The Controlled community has a relatively weak horizontal but a strong vertical interorganizational structure. In the Pluralist community, horizontal and vertical patterns of social organization are moderately well developed and in a state of relative balance. The Mass Movement community probably has the most active and intense form of horizontal and vertical organizational integration, but it is short-lived. It depends least of all on the presence of formal intermediate organization.

Furthermore, each type of community structure seems to produce a characteristic pattern of processing delinquents which affects both delinquency rate and form. Thus, in the Controlled community more violent crime occurs and is probably more often stimulated, reported by citizens, and officially recorded. Also this type of crime may be relatively easy to manage and confine to a given territory. In the Pluralist community, a more diverse pattern of delinquency occurs. Relatively more larceny, runaways, and white-collar crime probably take place and are reported by an active citizenry and a sensitized police force. Delinquency may well be more politicized in this community, and certain types of crime may be overreported or underreported at particular times by certain sectors of the community population. In the Communal area antisocial acts (e.g., vandalism or drug use) are least likely to be defined as delinquent or serious and officially reported. Problems of "delinquency" tend to be handled informally, with least reference to the apparatus of the juvenile justice system. Youth are engaged in those forms and frequencies of "delinquency" least disruptive to ongoing community systems, legitimate and illegitimate.

Finally, it is important to observe that little theoretical or empirical work relating community structure to delinquency patterns has been done in recent years, despite the extensive development of Great Society and criminal justice programs. Community theory may be particularly useful in linking a variety of recent theories of delinquency formation and persistence. If we can construct it, such theory may be useful in connecting macrosociological theory, for example, anomie (Merton, 1968), opportunity (Cloward and Ohlin, 1960), cultural (Miller, 1958), and subcultural (Cohen, 1955) theories, with microsociological theory, for example, drift (Matza, 1964), labeling (Lemert, 1967), and group process (Short and Strodtbeck, 1965) theories.

Community structure theory may provide useful intervening notions for explaining the process by which larger social, cultural, and economic pressures or constraints lead to variable patterns of delinquency among different sectors of the populations. It may now be possible to reconcile certain apparently contradictory findings, for example, that delinquency rates based on self-reports do not show significant variations by class or size of city while official statistics do (see, for example, Bersani, 1970; Institute for Juvenile Research, 1972).

Attempts to correlate delinquency rates and forms with unique factors, such as father's occupation or education (Nye, Short, and Olson, 1958), race, community size (Institute for Juvenile Research, 1972) have been simplistic and unrelated to the complex interaction of social, cultural, economic, and political factors distinctively patterned on a community basis (Clark and Wenninger, 1962). Both self-reported delinquency data and official statistics tend to focus on different dimensions of social phenomena and are almost always aggregated —separately—without reference to community boundaries or differences. Thus, contradictory findings may not be contradictory after all. They are due to atheoretic aggregation of data and lack of understanding of the different functions of community structure.

Also, it is possible that many of the mixed or negative findings of a great deal of evaluative research on the effectiveness of delinquency control programs may be due in some measure to the influence of differential community structures. Thus, delinquency prevention programs which strongly emphasize service type programs may increase rates in certain communities, especially the Controlled community. For example, the use of detached workers (Klein, 1968, 1971) or professional police officers (Wilson, 1968) might in the worst areas, Controlled communities, enhance delinquency creating processes.

A service orientation, supplemented by a community development orientation, might be more effective in a Pluralist community. It is possible thus to account for a significantly lower rate of delinquency after social work intervention among youth gang members in certain white, better-off, areas but no change among youth gangs in certain lower class, black areas as reported by W. B. Miller (1962). Community structure concepts would also be useful in explaining why service approaches have failed in highly solidary communities (Whyte, 1955). Do-gooders are likely to be ignored or driven out of these highly (horizontally) integrated or cohesive communities (Spergel, 1964).

PART IV. COMMUNITY POLICY AND DELINQUENCY CONTROL

A community structure perspective is not sufficient for a complete analysis of, or prescription for, delinquency problems. It represents a partial but important approach. Thus, for each of the types of community, there are distinctive larger environmental or societal determinants which must be recognized as basically, but not necessarily more directly, causative of delinquency, for example, relative level of income, mobility of residents, race, and certain larger policy and cultural constraints. These fundamental determinants operate through, are interactive with, and may be amenable to the influence of local organizations. Certain of these larger environmental determinants may also be at times more significant than others, depending on the community. For example, income differences, lack of basic opportunities, and racism may be relatively more determinative of delinquency in a Controlled community; increasing mobility may account more for deviancy in a Communal area in transition; and certain government policies and programs may be especially influential in the determination of delinquency patterns in a Pluralist community.

A community structure approach provides a set of conceptions of a community as a basis for more effective social policy. It would also appear to be a basis for better analysis of current strategies of delinquency control such as diversion, services, and coordination.

Diversion

The strategy of diversion has much to recommend it, although what is precisely meant by diversion is far from clear. It is presumably based on a theory of labeling concerned with the development of secondary rather than primary deviance. An important consideration is that aberrant children and youth, especially of lower income or minority group origin, be accorded the same treatment as middle and upper class youths, that is, essentially ignored by the juvenile justice system. Somehow, low income and minority group youth will then be in a better position to struggle through and survive the difficulties of growing up. The youth, if left alone or treated "informally" by the police, courts, and "do-good" agencies, will be better off.

The strategy, however, may sidetrack attention from basic community factors generating delinquency.

> The emphasis on diversion, unfortunately, diverts our attention from the etiology of juvenile offenses. It serves to focus on the problem of secondary deviance rather than on the problem of preventing juveniles from engaging in *initial* acts of deviancy. As a consequence, the proactive process of delinquency prevention is downgraded in favor of expanding our reactive capabilities. We suggest that opinion leaders and decision makers within juvenile justice systems must worry not only about reform of juvenile courts and correctional programs, but also about the conditions in homes, schools, and community that launch children in the march toward the door of the juvenile court in the first place. [Cressey and McDermott, 1974: 61-62]

The diversion strategy emphasizes a return of the delinquent to community with insufficient reference to what capacity the particualr community has to rehabilitate the delinquent, and how that capacity may be increased. The community itself, particularly the Controlled community, may constitute a form of incarceration. The slum is a prison of sorts.

Furthermore, the diversion strategy may place the burden for changing a complex and often intransigent community system too much on the delinquent himself. The power of the delinquent in this contest would seem very minimal. The idea of diversion may require the youth to return to community to sink or swim on his own. It may emphasize

> a relationship between the community and the youth, such that the youth assumes greater responsibility for his orientations, exerts more influence in the relationships over those decisions affecting him, and is increasingly rewarded for his achievements and for other behavior considered appropriate. At the same time, the community, noting the increasingly responsible behavior of the youth, allows him greater power to influence decisions affecting him and progressively rewards him for his achievements and appropriate behaviors. [Pappenfort, 1974: 2-3]

A close look at the implementation of a diversion strategy raises questions about the role and amount of help that an agency or community group can supply to delinquents:

> What is being done by the program staff to encourage support of youth in the community? What is actually being done by other community agencies and by residents to support the successful reintegration of youth? Are the youth really being aided or are they being hassled? Are the schools receptive and if not, what is being done about setting up alternative schools? [Coates, Miller, and Ohlin, undated: 41-42]

While these questions begin to focus on the characteristics of community structure which support youth, the diversion strategy is still primarily linked to a particular agency or client approach. Individual agencies are expected to tailor-make programs for particular youth. This strategy is essentially ad hoc and represents a kind of a casework approach to social change. It does not demonstrate an awareness of the complexity and force of a system of organized community relationships.

The critical principle is not simply that vulnerable youth be diverted from the juvenile justice system, but also that the capacity of the private welfare system in certain communities be modified or improved to deal effectively with youth. Diversion out of one system requires increasing the absorptive capacity of another or reciprocal system. The greater the absorptive capacity of the private welfare system, including the churches, families, and grass-roots groups, the less likely that youths will be referred or reported as deviants to the public or official system.

Services

The unquestioned value attributed to social welfare services may signify the most serious failure of current strategies. The general assumption, particularly by social reformers and progressive practitioners, is that so long as programs seek humanitarian purposes—treat, rehabilitate, and serve the individual needs of youth, especially if they are community-based—they are desirable and should be extended. Such services cannot possibly do any harm, and perhaps can do a variable amount of good. But services function essentially to change and develop individuals, mainly to fit them better into a variety of societal roles regarded as desirable. A services approach fundamentally assumes the appropriateness of these roles and the correctness of social or institutional arrangements supporting them. Furthermore, services in certain kinds of communities may emphasize in effect, rather than intent, the supervision and management of people rather than their social development. This approach may be in error when applied in the Controlled community and is of extremely limited impact in the Communal area.

There is very little attention paid by social agencies, public or private, to programs that meet the collective or solidarity needs of both individuals and organizations or institutions. Services have come to be judged by the proficiency with which they adjust or "manipulate" deviant youth socially and psychologically. Fundamentally, the youth or his social situation, sometimes including his family, are treated as atomized entities unrelated to a community whose elements require simultaneous or interactive change and development. A service agency may succeed in getting the youth temporarily to conform to institutional expectations but at the same time increase his alienation. The youth may not be permitted meaningfully to interact with the structure or underlying character of the program of the helping organization. He is not provided adequate opportunity to share in responsibility for its development or change. A basis for initial identification and solidarity is not created.

Services have become differentiated, technicized, professionalized, and thus increasingly disconnected from community development and solidarity functions. While there is some recognition of the need for organizational development, especially through use of paraprofessionals and advocacy to modify services delivery, the rationale for use of paraprofessional or indigenous workers primarily shores up the services approach. The purpose of the indigenous worker or volunteer is to facilitate communication of the client with the professional and the service offered. The rationale serves a technical means for more economic use of manpower and better dispersion of services.

Thus, there has been little emphasis by social agencies on programs which maximize the identification of the individual with the organization, his community, and society, and shared responsibilities in implementing such programs. But this is not to deny that sometimes social agencies in better-off communities, occasionally social movement organizations, and most often youth development agencies in other societies give priority to programs that demonstrate solidarity with community or nation-state. Institutions that promote social solidarity are particularly weak in market economies where the overriding emphasis is provision of the technical means for competition in the race for personal success rather than collective social development.

A strict services approach inherently alienates the individual and his family from community and society. It tends to contribute to deviancy. A social strategy that emphasizes solidarity encourages shared sentiments, values, and consensual behaviors. Services do have positive value for creatively adjusting the individual to his environment, but their effectiveness is maximized only to the degree that they are part of a larger strategy of community solidarity and societal development.

Coordination

Coordination represents a positive, if not universal, value. It is basic to public policy and social planning. In the past decade or more, it has seemed fresh with promise. Some officials would marshall the whole range of social and rehabilitative services at least for the proximate purpose of coordination:

> The "essence" of any social service delivery system, according to the Commissioner of the Social and the Rehabilitation Services Administration for the U.S. Department of Health, Education, and Welfare is to marshall all resources in a coordinated way to bring the client to his best functioning level. [National Advisory Commission on Criminal Justice Standards and Goals, 1973: 51-52]

Coordination and service delivery system are cognate if not identical ideas. Both seek to prevent delinquency by increasing the responsiveness and meaningfulness of services. The client is to be brought to his best functioning so that his delinquency is consequently reduced. Magically, coordination is also expected to cure or prevent a whole range of social and personal disorders and foster the good community:

> An effective service delivery system, in addition to upgrading the quality of life for its clients, can reduce the feelings of alienation many citizens have, increase the confidence of those citizens in public and private institutions, and foster citizen cooperation with these institutions. [National Advisory Commission on Criminal Justice Standards and Goals, 1973: 51]

But are the implications of the presence or absence of coordination clear? Coordination seems to mean bringing organizations or programs closer together. However, do criminal justice organizations need greater coordination? Even the writers of the Commission report cited above have second thoughts about whether service systems and communities are fragmented and whether coordination is really the "true" value:

> The relationships among the parts of the criminal justice system and between the systems and the community's other institutions, governmental and nongovernmental, are so intimate and intricate that a change anywhere may be felt everywhere. . . . A reform like organizing a youth services bureau to which the police and juvenile court, and parents and school officials as well, could refer young people will require an enormous amount of planning. Such a bureau will have to work closely with the community's other youth serving agencies. It will affect the caseloads of juvenile courts, probation services, and detention facilities. It will raise legal . . . [National Advisory Commission on Criminal Justice Standards and Goals, 1973: 56]

There is apparently uncertainty at high levels of government as to what coordination requires and whether it is good or bad. Concern may be expressed that coordination simply extends government control without helping young people or contributing to their rehabilitation and delinquency reduction. The question of the relation between coordination and social control on the one hand and youth development and social justice on the other is not resolved.

> A youth services bureau that places a high priority on interagency coordination would contribute little to the development of opportunities for indigenous adults and youth vulnerable to the justice system to share legitimately community responsibility for reducing crime and delinquency. Maintaining social control primarily through the efforts of professionals and specialists may merely extend governmental control, without encouraging the development of a responsible community of youth and adults concerned with the equitable administration of justice.

> In short, interagency coordination would enhance social stability, while youth development and community involvement would foster social change. [National Advisory Commission on Criminal Justice Standards and Goals, 1973: 68]

A community structural approach is useful because first, it suggests that communities are quite well organized already. Second, it poses the question of direction of interorganizational relations or coordination. The critical issue becomes: Should the community be organized less or more vertically or horizontally? Each type of coordination has different implications for creating and dealing with the delinquency problem. Certain policies as to coordination are therefore appropriate or inappropriate depending on type of community. It could be argued that there is already too much vertical coordination in Controlled communities; that what is needed is relatively more horizontal coordination, for example, interorganizational activity in relation to program sharing and social action. It could be argued that there is too little vertical and too much local integration in Communal areas. Youth development in terms of wider societal considerations or values is being impaired. Of course this might mean a rise in delinquency rates. Finally, it is possible that patterns of coordination are highly variable in Pluralist communities and sometimes stress needs to be given to one type of coordination rather than to another.

Because of the present lack of understanding by policy makers and advisors of the relation of community structure to the development of deviancy, including delinquency, there is much confusion about what coordination is and what it is expected to do. The consequences of ignorance are particularly serious in regard to the Controlled community. Those who advise, administer, or monitor programs in slum or Controlled type communities may contribute more to an increase than to a decline in delinquency.

Conclusion

Both local organizational leaders and public policy makers have a role to play in the development of community structures which contribute to the reduction or control of delinquency. They must begin to think and perceive the problems of people in community related terms. They need to focus on the development and change of specific structural characteristics of community. Government needs to become more aware of its immense power to develop or destroy communities and to lower or raise delinquency rates. Greater vision and creativity by federal policy makers is required to foster the vitality of local community with minimal official or direct management. Also greater federal financial outlay for local development programs will undoubtedly be required, directly or indirectly.

A final caveat is that a community approach should not be construed as a "new" panacea for deviancy problems. An effective community strategy must be part of a larger societal regenerative approach, emphasizing adequate income and employment policies, the elimination of racism, and the highest commitment to the social democratic development of people.

NOTES

1. However, see W. B. Miller et al. (1968). The authors provide an interesting and insightful organizational analysis, but do not set their analysis within a community frame of

reference. Furthermore, they do not relate different kinds of interorganizational relations to different delinquency rates or patterns of delinquency.

2. See, Turk, 1970; Warren, 1972; Mitchell, 1969; Aiken, 1970; Mott, 1970; Aldrich, 1071; Clark, 1973; Cumming, 1968; Levine and White, 1961; Litwak and Meyer, 1966; Litwak and Meyer, 1974.

3. See Bloch, 1972; Clinard, 1966; Dunham, 1965; Faris, 1948; Hunter, 1968; Kahn, 1953; Kahn, 1963; Mowrer, 1942.

4. For example, see Feagin, 1974; Jacobs, 1961; Gans, 1962; Merton, 1968; Whyte, 1955.

5. See Tannenbaum, 1938; Cressey and McDermott, 1974; Lemert, 1967 and 1971; Klapmuts, 1974; Norman, 1972.

6. Duxbury, 1972; Gemignani, 1972; Perlman and Jones, 1967; National Advisory Commission on Criminal Justice Standards and Goals, 1973; Spergel, 1969; Weissman, 1969b.

7. Babchuk, 1970; Bell and Newby, 1971; Emery and Trist, 1965; Fellin and Litwak, 1968; Greer, 1962; Hawley and Wirt, 1968; Hillery, 1968; Janowitz, 1967; Kornhauser, 1969; Liebow, 1966; Rossi and Dentler, 1961; Mitchell, 1969; Sussman, 1969; Stein, 1960; Suttles, 1968; Terreberry, 1968; Tocqueville, 1945.

8. Alinsky, 1946; Altshuler, 1970; Arnstein, 1966; Brager and Purcell, 1967; Cahn and Passett, 1971; Davies, 1966; Fantini, Gittell, and Magat, 1970; Hallman, 1970; Hallman, 1973; Kotler, 1969; Kramer, 1969; Mogulof, 1970; Ross, 1958; Spergel, 1972; Spiegel, 1968; Twentieth Century Fund, 1971; Yin et al., 1973.

9. There were no significant differences in the proportions of the various types of organizations comparing universe and samples in Pilsen, Little Village, and Heart of Chicago. There was a difference ($p = .05$) in New West Side. The difference disappeared if private and church units were combined and compared with public organizations.

10. Classic notions about the prevalence and importance of value conflicts, including those between legitimate and illegitimate groups (Kobrin, 1951; Shaw and McKay, 1942) need reexamination. The findings of the present exploratory research suggest there may indeed by very little expressed conflict among organizations in high delinquency areas. The precise mesh of norms and values of the various groups and organizations should be studied.

11. Some observers believe that modern society is increasingly vulnerable to mass movement because of the weakened condition of intermediate structures, the increased mobilization of primary groups, and the increased accessibility of central leadership. Large sectors of the population are mobilized, and central authorities are overly accessible or responsive to their interests and needs. The rapidity of technical and social change, the alienative consequences of bureaucratic processes, and disaffection with central authorities are key external factors assumed to be responsible for the breakdown of systems of intermediate organizations. It has been suggested that "mass behavior" occurs at a "low rate and in peripheral spheres" in Communal communities; at a "higher rate" in Pluralist communities, but when it occurs in Controlled communities, it is more likely to impinge on its vital centers in its explosive outbursts (Kornhauser, 1969: 51-52).

12. The influence of external environment patterns, particularly at federal and city levels, but increasingly at the state level, with the advent of revenue sharing, should be again emphasized in the development and also the distribution of community welfare structures. Thus, during the 1960s, some cities because of political and cultural traditions, were more likely to encourage and support certain types of community structures than others. For example, a "machine" city such as Chicago may have stimulated the development of

relatively more Controlled and Communal structures than other cities. A "reform" city such as New York may have encouraged the greater development of Pluralistic communities in this period.

REFERENCES

AIKEN, M. (1970) "The distribution of community power: structural bases and social consequences," pp. 487-525 in M. Aiken and P. E. Mott (eds.) The Structure of Community Power. New York: Random House.

——— and R. R. ALFORD (1970) "Community structure and innovation: the case of urban renewal." American Sociological Review (August): 650-665.

ALDRICH, H. (1971) "Organizational boundaries and inter-organizational conflict." Human Relations 24 (August): 279-293.

ALINSKY, S. D. (1946) Reveille for Radicals. Chicago: University of Chicago Press.

ALTSHULER, A. A. (1970) Community Control. New York: Pegasus.

ARNSTEIN, S. (1966) "A ladder of citizen participation." Journal of the American Institute of Planners 35 (July): 216-224.

BABCHUK, N. (1970) The Voluntary Association in the Slum. Lincoln: University of Nebraska Press.

BAKAL, Y. [ed.] (1973) Closing Correctional Institutions: New Strategies for Youth Services. Lexington, Mass.: Lexington Books, D. C. Heath.

BELL, C. and H. NEWBY (1971) Community Studies. London: Allen and Unwin.

BERSANI, C. A. [ed.] (1970) Pp. 107-215 in Crime and Delinquency. London: Macmillan.

BLOCH, H. A. (1972) Disorganization, Personal and Social. New York: Alfred A. Knopf.

BRAGER, G. A. and F. P. PURCELL [eds.] (1967) Community Action Against Poverty. New Haven, Conn.: College and University Press.

CAHN, E. S. and B. A. PASSETT [eds.] (1971) Citizen Participation: Effecting Community Change. New York: Praeger.

Chicago Association of Commerce and Industry. Research and Statistics Division (1972) Community Area Participation for the City of Chicago. 1970 Census data by 75 Community Areas.

CLARK, J. P. and E. P. WENNINGER (1962) "Socio-economic class and areas as correlates of illegal behavior among juveniles." American Sociological Review 27 (December): 826-834.

CLARK, K. and J. HOPKINS (1969) A Relevant War Against Poverty. New York: Harper & Row.

CLARK, T. N. (1973) Community Power and Policy Outputs. Beverly Hills, Calif.: Sage.

CLINARD, M. B. (1966) Slums and Community Development. New York: Free Press.

CLOWARD, R. A. and L. E. OHLIN (1960) Delinquency and Opportunity. New York: Free Press.

COATES, R. B., A. D. MILLER, and L. E. OHLIN (undated) "The labelling perspective and innovation in juvenile correctional systems: an analysis based largely on the Massachu- setts experience." Law School, Harvard University (mimeo).

COHEN, A. K. (1955) Delinquent Boys: The Culture of the Gang. Glencoe, Ill.: Free Press.

CRESSEY, D. R. and R. A. McDERMOTT (1974) Diversion From the Juvenile Justice System. Ann Arbor: University of Michigan Press.

CRESSEY, D. R. and D. A. WARD [eds.] (1969) Pp. 737-912 in Delinquency, Crime, and Social Process. New York: Harper & Row.

CUMMING, E. (1968) Systems of Social Regulation. New York: Atherton.

DAVIES, C. J., III (1966) Neighborhood Groups and Urban Renewal. New York: Columbia University Press.

DUNHAM, H. W. (1965) Community and Schizophrenia. Detroit: Wayne State University Press.

DUXBURY, E. (1972) "Youth Service Bureaus in California." Progress Report No. 3.

EMERY, F. E. and E. L. TRIST (1965) "The causal texture of organizational environments." Human Relations 18 (February): 21-32.

FANTINI, M. D., M. GITTELL, and R. MAGAT (1970) Community Control and the Urban School. New York: Praeger.

FARIS, R.E.L. (1948) Social Disorganization. New York: Ronald.

FEAGIN, J. R. (1974) "Community disorganization: some critical notes," pp. 123-146 in M. P. Effrat (ed.) The Community: Approaches and Applications. New York: Free Press.

FELLIN, P. and E. LITWAK (1968) "The neighborhood in urban American society." Social Work 13 (July): 72-80.

FLEISCHER, B. M. (1966) The Economics of Delinquency. Chicago: Quadrangle.

FRIEDLANDER, S. L. (1972) Unemployment in the Urban Core. New York: Praeger.

GANS, H. J. (1962) Urban Villagers. New York: Free Press.

GEMIGNANI, R. J. (1972) "Youth services systems." Delinquency Prevention Reporter. U.S. Department of Health, Education, and Welfare. Youth Development and Delinquency Prevention Administration (July-August).

GORSE, W. J. and H. J. BERAN (1973) The Criminal Justice System of Lincoln. Columbus: Ohio State University Press.

GREER, S. (1962) The Emerging City: Myth and Reality. New York: Free Press.

HALLMAN, H. W. (1973) Government by Neighborhoods. Washington, D.C.: Center for Governmental Studies.

――― (1970) Community Corporations and Neighborhood Control. Washington, D.C.: Center for Governmental Studies.

HAWLEY, W. D. and F. M. WIRT [eds.] (1968) The Search for Community Power. Englewood Cliffs, N.J.: Prentice-Hall.

HILLERY, G. A., Jr. (1968) Communal Organizations: A Study of Local Societies. Chicago: University of Chicago Press.

HUNTER, D. E. (1968) The Slums: Challenge and Response. New York: Free Press.

Institute for Juvenile Research (1973) Chicago Delinquency Rates, 1928-1972. Department of Mental Health. Chicago: Institute for Juvenile Research.

――― (1972) Juvenile Delinquency in Illinois. Department of Mental Health. Chicago: Institute for Juvenile Research.

JACOBS, J. (1961) The Death and Life of Great American Cities. New York: Alfred A. Knopf.

JANOWITZ, M. (1967) The Community Press in an Urban Setting. 2nd ed. Chicago: University of Chicago Press.

――― (1961) Community Political Systems. New York: Free Press.

KAHN, A. J. (1963) Planning Community Services for Children in Trouble. New York: Columbia University Press.

――― (1953) A Court for Children. New York: Columbia University Press.

KALBERG, S. and G. D. SUTTLES (1974) "Inarticulate protest: gangs, the police, and politicians in Chicago during 1964-1970." Paper presented at Burgess Seminar, Department of Sociology, the University of Chicago, April 13 (mimeo).

KITAGAWA, E. M. and K. E. TAEUBER (1963) Local Community Fact Book: Chicago Metropolitan Area, 1960. Chicago: Chicago Community Inventory.

KLAPMUTS, N. (1974) "Diversion from the justice system." Crime and Delinquency Literature 6 (March): 108-131.

KLEIN, M. W. (1971) Street Gangs and Street Workers. Englewood Cliffs, N.J.: Prentice-Hall.

——— (1968) From Association to Guilt: The Group Guidance Project in Gang Intervention. Los Angeles: Youth Studies Center, University of Southern California.

KOBRIN, S. (1951) "The conflict of values in delinquency areas." American Sociological Review 16 (October): 653-661.

KORNHAUSER, W. (1969) The Politics of Mass Society. Glencoe, Ill.: Free Press.

KOTLER, M. (1969) Neighborhood Government: The Local Foundations of Political Life. Indianapolis: Bobbs-Merrill.

KRAMER, R. (1969) Participation of the Poor: Comparative Community Case Studies in the War on Poverty. Englewood Cliffs, N.J.: Prentice-Hall.

LEMERT, E. M. (1971) Instead of Court: Diversion in Juvenile Justice. National Institute of Mental Health. Washington, D.C.: Government Printing Office.

——— (1967) Human Deviance, Social Problems, and Social Control. Englewood Cliffs, N.J.: Prentice-Hall.

LEVINE, S. and P. E. WHITE (1961) "Exchange as a conceptual framework for the study of interorganizational relations." Administrative Science Quarterly 5 (March): 583-601.

LEVY, L. and L. ROWITZ (1973) The Ecology of Mental Disorder. New York: Behavioral Publications.

LIEBOW, E. (1966) Talley's Corner: A Study of Negro Street Corner Men. Boston: Little, Brown.

LITWAK, E. and H. J. MEYER (1974) School, Family, and Neighborhood: The Theory and Practice of School-Community Relations. New York: Columbia University Press.

——— (1966) "A balance theory of coordination between bureaucratic organization and primary groups." Administrative Science Quarterly 11 (June): 31-58.

MARRIS, P. and M. REIN (1973) Dilemmas of Social Reform. 2nd ed. Chicago: Aldine.

MARTINSON, R. (1974) "What works—questions and answers about prison reform." Public Interest 35 (Spring): 22-54.

MATZA, D. (1964) Delinquency and Drift. New York: John Wiley.

MERTON, R. K. (1968) Social Theory and Social Structure. Enlarged ed. New York: Free Press.

MILLER, W. B. (1962) "The impact of a 'total community' delinquency control project." Social Problems 10 (Fall): 168-191.

——— (1958) "Lower-class culture as a generating milieu of gang delinquency." Journal of Social Issues 15 (Summer): 5-19.

——— C. B. RAINER, and R. McNEIL (1968) "Delinquency prevention and organizational relations," pp. 61-100 in S. Wheeler (ed.) Controlling Delinquents. New York: John Wiley.

MITCHELL, J. C. [ed.] (1969) Social Networks and Urban Situations. Manchester, Eng.: Manchester University Press.

MOGULOF, M. B. (1970) Citizen Participation: The Local Perspective. Washington, D.C.: Urban Institute.

MOTT, P. E. (1970) "Configurations of Power," pp. 85-100 in M. Aiken and P. E. Mott (eds.) The Structure of Community Power. New York: Random House.

MOWRER, E. R. (1942) Disorganization, Personal and Social. Philadelphia: J. B. Lippincott.

National Advisory Commission on Criminal Justice Standards and Goals (1973) Community Crime Prevention. Washington, D.C.: Government Printing Office.

NORMAN, S. (1972) The Youth Service Bureau. Paramus, N.J.: National Council on Crime and Delinquency.

NYE, F. I., J. F. SHORT, and V. J. OLSON (1958) "Socioeconomic status and delinquent behavior." American Journal of Sociology 63 (January): 381-389.

PAPPENFORT, D. M. (1974) "Deinstitutionalization of adjudicated delinquents in Illinois: a concept paper." School of Social Service Administration, University of Chicago, June 15 (mimeo).

PERLMAN, R. and D. JONES (1967) Neighborhood Service Centers. Office of Juvenile Delinquency and Youth Development. Washington, D.C.: Government Printing Office.

President's Commission on Law Enforcement and Administration of Justice (1967) Challenge of Crime in a Free Society. Washington, D.C.: Government Printing Office.

ROSS, M. B. (1958) Case Histories in Community Organization. New York: Harper.

ROSSI, P. H. and R. A. DENTLER (1961) The Politics of Urban Renewal. New York: Free Press.

SCHUR, E. (1973) Radical Non-Intervention. Englewood Cliffs, N.J.: Prentice-Hall.

SHAW, C. R. and H. D. McKAY (1942) Juvenile Delinquency and Urban Areas. Chicago: University of Chicago Press.

——— (1931) Social Factors in Juvenile Delinquency: A Study of the Community, the Family, and the Gang in Relation to Delinquent Behavior. National Commission on Law Observance and Enforcement: Report on the Causes of Crime, Volume II. Washington, D.C.: Government Printing Office.

SHILS, E. A. (1970) Pp. 1-36 in Selected Essays. Chicago: Department of Sociology, University of Chicago.

SHORT, J. F., Jr. and F. L. STRODTBECK (1965) Group Process and Gang Delinquency. Chicago: University of Chicago Press.

SPERGEL, I. A. (1972) Community Organization: Studies in Constraint. Beverly Hills, Calif.: Sage.

——— (1969) Community Problem Solving: The Delinquency Example. Chicago: University of Chicago Press.

——— (1964) Racketville, Slumtown, Haulburg. Chicago: University of Chicago Press.

——— C. TURNER, J. PLEAS, and P. BROWN (1969) Youth Manpower: What Happened in Woodlawn. Chicago: School of Social Service Administration, University of Chicago.

SPIEGEL, H.B.C. [ed.] (1968) Citizen Participation in Urban Development. Volume I: Concepts and Issues. Washington, D.C.: N.T.L. Institute for Applied Behavioral Science.

STEIN, M. R. (1960) The Eclipse of Community: An Interpretation of American Studies. Princeton: Princeton University Press.

STUMPHAUZER, J. S. (1973) Behavior Therapy with Delinquents. Springfield, Ill.: Charles C Thomas.

SUSSMAN, M. B. [ed.] (1969) Community Structure and Analysis. New York: Thomas Y. Crowell.

SUTHERLAND, E. H. and D. R. CRESSEY (1966) Principles of Criminology. 7th ed. Philadelphia: J. P. Lippincott.

SUTTLES, G. D. (1968) The Social Order of the Slum. Chicago: University of Chicago Press.

TANNENBAUM, F. (1938) Crime and Community. Boston: Ginn.

TERREBERRY, S. (1968) "The evolution of organizational environments." Administrative Science Quarterly 12 (March): 590-613.

THRASHER, F. (1963) The Gang: A Study of 1,313 Gangs in Chicago. Abridged and with a new introduction by J. F. Short, Jr. Chicago: University of Chicago Press.

TOCQUEVILLE, de A. (1945) Democracy in America. Vols. I and II. New York: Alfred A. Knopf.

TURK, H. (1970) "Interorganizational networks in urban society: initial perspective and comparative research." American Sociological Review 35 (February): 1-19.

TURNER, S. (1969) "The ecology of delinquency," pp. 27-60 in T. Sellin and M. E. Wolfgang (eds.) Delinquency, Selected Studies. New York: John Wiley.

Twentieth Century Fund (1971) CDC's: New Hope for the Inner City. New York: Twentieth Century Fund.

U.S. Department of Commerce, Bureau of the Census (1972) 1970 Census of Population and Housing, Chicago, Illinois. Parts I and II. Washington, D.C.: Government Printing Office.

VORRATH, H. H. and L. K. BRENDTRO (1974) Positive Peer Culture. Chicago: Aldine.

WARREN, R. L. (1972) The Community in America. 2nd ed. Chicago: Rand McNally.

WEISSMAN, H. M. [ed.] (1969a) Community Development in the Mobilization for Youth Experience. New York: Association Press.

––– (1969b) Individual and Group Services in the Mobilization for Youth Experience. New York: Association Press.

WHYTE, W. F. (1955) Street Corner Society: The Social Structure of an Italian Slum. Enlarged ed. Chicago: University of Chicago Press.

WILSON, J. Q. (1968) "The police and the delinquent in two cities," pp. 9-30 in S. Wheeler (ed.) Controlling Delinquents. New York: John Wiley.

WOLFGANG, M. E., R. M. FIGLIO, and T. SELLIN (1973) Delinquency in a Birth Cohort. Chicago: University of Chicago Press.

YIN, R. K., W. A. LUCAS, P. L. SZANTON, and J. A. SPINDLER (1973) Citizen Organizations: Increasing Client Control Over Services. Santa Monica: Rand Corporation, R-1196-HEW.

Chapter 4

THE EXPLOSION IN POLICE DIVERSION PROGRAMS: EVALUATING THE STRUCTURAL DIMENSIONS OF A SOCIAL FAD

MALCOLM W. KLEIN
KATHIE S. TEILMANN
JOSEPH A. STYLES
SUZANNE BUGAS LINCOLN
SUSAN LABIN-ROSENSWEIG

Evaluation technology has slowly but steadily grown both in sophistication and in acceptance by those involved in public policy (Struening and Guttentag, 1975; Guttentag and Struening, 1975). Concurrently, simplistic reliance on idealized experimental designs has yielded to more comprehensive if less controlled approaches to the "so what" questions about social programs. We pay more attention to the objectives and values or "utilities" (Edwards et al., 1975) of various audiences or publics related to such programs. This paper deals with a type of social program to which such thinking is just beginning to be applied. By pinpointing selected structural dimensions of the program as it has developed in the past few years, we can highlight an assortment of evaluative criteria to which attention must be paid. We believe these are prototypical of dimensions and criteria in many components of the juvenile justice system.

AUTHORS' NOTE: *Materials for this chapter were gathered in part with support from Grant No. MH26147-01 from the National Institute of Mental Health and from Grant No. 74-NI-99-0045 from the National Institute of Law Enforcement and Criminal Justice, Law Enforcement Assistance Administration, U.S. Department of Justice. Points of view or opinions stated in this document are those of the authors and do not necessarily represent the official position or policies of HEW or the Department of Justice.*

The type of program to which we refer is generally called *diversion*. In the present instance we shall concentrate specifically on police diversion programs for juvenile offenders.

The importance of specifying measurable dimensions for evaluating police diversion programs has been underscored by conclusions from a recent, exhaustive review of published and unpublished reports on these programs:

> The central results of the . . . project surround the analysis of the twenty-two police diversion evaluation studies located. These were subject to severe limitations in the Internal Validity area in that they tended not to formulate problems clearly or to frame and test hypotheses carefully. Often the target population of the study was not exactly described and there was little hope of determining whether or not the programs "worked" because objective tests of this question were absent.
>
> In the Methodology area, far too often study populations were inadequate, analytic methods were inexplicit and of questionable utility, appropriate data were lacking, statistical tools utilized were limited, "treatment" influences were only some among many possible explanations for results, supportive evidence from extra-study sources was non-existent, and logical leaps were involved in moving from data analysis to discussions of conclusions.
>
> Studies reviewed tended to be consistently superficial or to major on one or two (often semi-extraneous) aspects of diversion at the expense of several others. Typical differences in analytic rigor involved careful analysis of cavalierly collected data, or vice-versa, and great attention to the possible program implications of findings resting on almost no data collection at all.
>
> The studies inclined toward inconsistency. Changes in analytic approaches repeatedly crept into studies mid-stream. Worse, often one could not tell whether there was any internal consistency or not, save unflawed lack of clarity.
>
> The External Validity question goes to whether or not studies of the same or like phenomena achieved similar results. It is difficult to determine whether structured diversion programs increase the level of diversion—one of their main purposes. Whether or not diversion leads to less penetration of the criminal justice system and less recidivism remains unknown. It can be concluded that sometimes diversion programs "work;" by no means all of them do. What distinguished the successful approaches is not known. There may be no structural components that can guarantee effectiveness. [Neithercutt and Moseley, 1974]

We use the term diversion henceforth to refer only to the process of turning suspects or offenders away from the formal system. *Referral* will mean the process by which the police initiate the connection of the juvenile to a non-justice-system agency, public or private (Klein, 1973). Thus one can have diversion with or without referral, and one can have referral with or without successful contact and treatment at the referral agency. The distinction between diversion and referral is critical to much of the following discussion. With this distinction in mind, we now move to six issues which raise major evaluative questions, each such question providing objectives and values associated with the many audiences of diversion programs.

1. THE DIVERSION EXPLOSION

Easily the most striking single dimension of diversion programming is its enormous recent growth. Significantly stimulated by the President's Commission (1967), nurtured by the "national strategy" for delinquency prevention promulgated in the early 1970s (Gemignani, 1972; Polk and Kobrin, 1972), and given enormous funding by regional and state arms of the Law Enforcement Assistance Administration in the mid-1970s, diversion has national backing and scope and is almost epidemic in proportions.

Some measure of recent changes can be made by reference to descriptions of the diversion and referral situation in Los Angeles County in 1970 and 1971. Research was carried out in those two years to determine the level of referral activity of all the police departments in the county. These included the two behemoths, the Los Angeles Police Department and the Los Angeles County Sheriff's Department, and 45 smaller independent departments serving cities ranging in population size from 1,000 to 400,000 persons. On the basis of interviews with 77 juvenile officers and over 40 police chiefs and on the basis of data available from the departments, Klein (1975) concluded:

> Juvenile officers do not seek out, nor are they urged to seek out, suitable referral agencies. By the same token, few private agencies offer themselves as willing absorbers of delinquency. Thus the modal number of private agencies known to our smaller-city juvenile officer respondents . . . was two! In six cities, the officers in 1970 could not name a single private agency to whom youngsters might be referred.

> Nor is this "accidental" or temporary ignorance of resources. Exactly half of the 1971 respondents reported *belonging to no* community organizations in the communities they served. Half did not live in the community served. Yet the median number of police associations for these same officers was two and a half. The situation was even worse in the LAPD and LASD. In these two agencies, officers in one quarter of the stations could not name *any* community resources.

Lack of information is not the only problem; the nature of the occasional referral process was often less than wholehearted. About half of the 45 independent cities reported making referrals *directly,* that is, by contacting the referral agencies personally. In the LAPD and LASD, only 2 of 31 officers reported using such direct referrals. The others merely told the arrested youth or his parents that they should go to selected agencies. Twenty percent of the officers in the smaller departments and 45% of those in the LAPD and LASD said they *never* made referrals. The modal response in the other departments was that they made "two or three a month." Clearly, then, police referrals of juveniles to community agencies was at best a minor practice and an ill-defined policy area.

Corroboration for this conclusion comes from a survey of 119 private agencies which were selected for a survey on the basis of their reported appropriateness for police referrals in Los Angeles County. A summary statement from that survey concludes (Klein, 1975):

> The first conclusion we can offer is that the diversion process is, at best, minimal. Of 119 private agencies queried for the year 1969, three reported receiving referrals from LAPD, two from LASD, and eight from one or more of the other . . . departments. In all, these connections led to 428 referrals. By way of contrast, there were 6,142 referrals to 84 of the 119 agencies from probation, court, and correctional components of the system. Available private agencies are used for rehabilitation, but not for diversion. . . . These data come from personal interviews and question-naires. Almost none of the police agencies keep a *record* of referrals to community agencies. The recording necessitated by the FBI and the state's Bureau of Criminal Statistics likewise makes no explicit reference to such referrals. That is, the "System" expresses no interest in and therefore receives no information about the workings of its input and diversion module.

There is no reason to think that this situation described for the Los Angeles area would not have applied equally well to any metropolitan area in the early 1970s. That the referral level did not *have* to be so low was amply demonstrated by a pilot project carried out in one police station in 1970 and reported recently by Lincoln (1975). This station had made almost no referrals in the prior year. Yet under the leadership of a police lieutenant who sought out available agencies and proselytized his juvenile officers,[1] a total of 35 juvenile offenders were referred to local agencies during the first 40 days of the pilot project. Thirty-two of these made the agency connection and initiated counseling. The experience with this pilot project became the opening wedge for officials in Los Angeles County to expand referrals in the Sheriff's Department. From a 1968-69 figure of 119, the Department increased its "referrals to social agencies" to 896 in 1971-72, 1,349 in 1972-73, and 1,646 in 1973-74. The 1974-75 figure has been projected to 2,098 by the head of the juvenile diversion unit.

This particular department's obvious enactment of a diversion policy and dramatic increase in referrals is impressive, yet it is typical of what has been taking place generally. A survey of police departments in Los Angeles County in 1973, conducted by a County agency, described active diversion/referral programs in 14 departments, and minor or informal programs in 20 others. Our own detailed survey only a year later, in 1974, identified diversion/referral programs in 37 departments. It was the plan of the Regional Criminal Justice Planning Board, the local dispenser of LEAA funds, to have 60 cities involved in its diversion system by the end of 1975. The board designated over four million dollars to support these programs within the county during that year.

A recent review of diversion programs throughout the state of California provides equally impressive numbers (Bohnstedt, 1975). Seventy-four projects funded by the state planning agency and active in 1974 were identified, to the exclusion of those funded from other sources. Of these 74, 9 were located in Los Angeles County and involved, at most, 15 police departments. Using what we know in detail about the Los Angeles County figures and the percentages of projects funded specifically by the state planning agency, we can extrapolate from these figures to estimate that there were probably between 150 and 200 projects throughout the state. And even more have been funded in 1975. The overall rate of expansion is shown by the data taken from this same state survey: of the 74 projects, 12 were in their third year, 27 were in their second year, and 35 were in their first year. The explosion in diversion projects is continuing.

Finally, it should be noted that the federal government itself, through the Law Enforcement Assistance Administration, is launching its own direct participation. Using funds authorized under the Juvenile Justice and Delinquency Prevention Act of 1974, LEAA has announced the decision to underwrite an eight-and-a-half million dollar program for the development of model juvenile diversion programs across the nation. Fortunately, it is planned to commit a portion of these funds to evaluating these model programs. This diversion program follows directly on the heels of another eight-and-a-half million dollar program to fund model programs for the deinstitutionalization of status offenders, a clear form of juvenile diversion. In reality, then, we are speaking of a seventeen million dollar direct federal investment in juvenile diversion projects.

2. ALTERNATIVE RATIONALES FOR DIVERSION

As clear as it has become that there is a diversion "explosion," it has become equally clear that the rationales for diversion are multiple, are conflicting, and are both manifest and latent. The explosion seems to be serving several ends, with the obvious implication that any comprehensive evaluation of diversion programs must concern itself with the degree to which each of these several ends is attained.

A concise and hard-hitting summary of diversion activities in California (Public Systems Inc., 1974, chap. 4) has noted four major rationales underlying the current explosion. The first of these is that increased diversion overrides "the system's inherent biases" in releasing and detaining suspects by stressing and legitimating explicit criteria which, ipso facto, are more equitable and universalistic. This fits nicely with the growing "professionalism" of police work as the latter is defined in terms of the application of less personal discretion (Wilson, 1968).

The second rationale is that increased diversion will decrease the volume of cases inserted into the juvenile justice system. Since the vast majority of these cases do not consist of serious adult-like offenses, there is indeed considerable opportunity to find alternative means for handling them outside the system. These alternatives range from intensive community treatment programs, to outright release, to what Edwin Schur has designated as "radical non-intervention" (1973). So long as diversion *does* mean movement away from the system of cases otherwise destined for system insertion, and does not mean nonsystem treatment of cases formerly released without treatment (Vorenberg and Vorenberg, 1973), then this rationale seems well served by police diversion programs. The fact is, however, that programs actually launched by police departments are often characterized by the second meaning more than by the first, that is, providing treatment in lieu of outright release.

The third rationale is simply that, ceteris paribus, diversion processing is less expensive than system processing, certainly to the system itself and probably to the overall community as well, even if alternative treatment programs are provided. The volume by Public Systems Inc. (1974) provides savings estimates ranging from thousands of dollars on the local level, to billions of dollars on the national level.

The fourth rationale is the one with the greatest theoretical import, the avoidance of stigmatization as delinquent, "bad," or criminal. In this sense, diversion is the practitioner's operationalization of labeling theory. Although the esoterics of labeling theory are not known to most system officials, the basic implications of self-image changes and differential societal reaction are frequently encountered. So long as these implications are not explicitly juxtaposed against the implications of a deterrence philosophy, many police are sympathetic to actions that will avoid stigmatizing juvenile offenders. This seems particularly true of juvenile officers and higher officials with command responsibilities. It seems least true of experienced or older patrol officers.

In addition to these four rationales, two others are frequently encountered both in the field and in the relevant social science literature. Often voiced by the police, in particular, is the concern that relatively naive young offenders will become contaminated through contact with more sophisticated and recalcitrant offenders during periods of detention or incarceration. To the extent that diversion prevents the exposure of the one to the other, it is seen as an effective preventive measure.

Finally, there is the widely held desire to find procedures, outside the juvenile justice system, to provide help for young offenders whose very status *as* offenders seems to signal the need for help. Diversion *from* the system with referral *to* a helping agency satisfies the various personal and institutionalized propensities to respond to the need to provide service as well as to prevent recurrence of the problem behavior. To most people, help offered within the context of the justice system is suspected of having little effective impact; help offered in an alternative context—one already accepted and established, such as the mental health and/or welfare system—is "known" to be effective. As the Vorenbergs have noted, a diversion program " . . . offers the promise of the best of all worlds: cost savings, rehabilitation, and more humane treatment" (1973: 151).

If the foregoing material does indeed represent more than a summary of the views of various writers and policy makers, if it does indeed represent the acting rationales of the practitioners who carry out juvenile diversion programs, then it should be possible to document this in interviews with such practitioners. Recent interviews with juvenile officers in 35 police departments with diversion programs have been completed by the writers of this chapter. The results do *not* yield the same picture.

The interviews reveal that police motives for diversion are often not what is commonly implied by the term "diversion." The criteria which the police state they use in deciding to refer a juvenile are examples of this subtle change in the meaning of diversion. Asked specifically about criteria for referral, 18 of 35 officers mentioned "offense seriousness" as a factor, but probing indicated that it is *low* seriousness which convinces the officer to refer the juvenile. Similarly, greater willingness to be referred, not resistance, leads to referral; shorter prior arrest records (two priors or less) lead to referral; younger offenders are preferred for referral over older ones; if the officer's estimation is that the youngster is not likely to be rearrested, that youngster is preferred for referral over the one judged more likely to be arrested. Thus the composite picture of the more referable offender seems to be of the young, minor offender with little or no record, who is unlikely to be rearrested in any case. This picture fits the profile of the youngster who heretofore whould have been released outright, for whom referral represents *increased* intervention rather than diversion *from* system intervention.

Thus, it can be suggested from these interviews that, while there is clearly a desire in some police departments to divert juveniles from the system, the more common feeling is that referral should be used as an alternative to simple release. In short, the meaning of diversion has been shifted from "diversion from" to "referral to." Ironically, one of the ramifications of this is that, in contrast to such earlier cited rationales for diversion as reducing costs, caseload, and the purview of the justice system, diversion may in fact be extending the costs, caseload, and system purview even further.

For anecdotal illustration, we cite the case of one rather large department which has attempted to explicate diversion and referral criteria by specifically listing cases for which diversion may *not* be employed. Cases may not be diverted and referred in this department if they involve:

(1) felony offenses resulting in death or serious injury;

(2) known gang members;

(3) more than two prior arrests;

(4) offenders already on probation or parole;

(5) crimes against police officers, school personnel (teachers, administrators, or any other regular employee), or employees of the recreation department;

(6) offenses that disrupt school or recreation department activities or destroy property of school and recreation departments;

(7) use or possession of a deadly weapon;

(8) offenders judged physically dangerous to the public because of a mental or physical deficiency, disorder, or abnormality;

(9) escapees from probation institutions;

(10) selected vehicle code violations, primarily hit and run, auto theft, and driving under the influence of or in possession of drugs, liquor, or weapons;

(11) a prior arrest with a referral to a treatment agency.

Obviously, this is a department that believes very strongly in a deterrent philosophy and is testing the notion of diversion and referral much as a bather tests his bath water—toes only. This department's overall release rate has varied over the years between 10% and 20%, as opposed to the oft-cited national average of about 50%. Obviously, referrals from this 10% to 20% pool, given the restrictions listed, must yield a miniscule referral rate. This represents the bottom line in juvenile referral programs.

The top line may be represented by another department, located right next to this one, in which almost *every* juvenile slated for release is referred to a local agency; or perhaps by another adjoining department which has established its *own* referral agency. In any event, there has developed a paradox not unlike that in other human service areas. There is a need to provide more effective service for those presenting the most serious problem, a concommitant need to show program impact which is unlikely among the most serious problem cases, and finally a concommitant need to prevent others from becoming serious cases but without knowing who these will be. To date, the dominant trend has been to resolve the paradox by "ignoring" the serious cases while diverting and referring those less in need but more likely to yield pleasing results, since the less serious cases seldom recidivate.[2] Rationales have yielded to practicality and administrative/political considerations.

3. ALTERNATIVE ENCAPSULATION

There are several other issues less critical to the diversion movement than its explosive nature and its rationales, which nevertheless are directly pertinent to the evaluation of the movement and its constituent programs. Among these is what was somewhat facetiously labeled "alternative encapsulation" at a recent working conference called by the U.S. Justice Department's Law Enforcement Assistance Administration.

There is a danger that the attempt to remove young offenders from the juvenile justice system may do so merely by inserting them into another system which might be characterized as the mental health, welfare, or social service system. So long as it is felt that diverted offenders, or "deinstitutionalized" offenders, need service or treatment when we turn them away from the justice system, then ipso facto we are inserting them into an *alternative* system which may be equally pervasive or *encapsulating*. For all we know, it may be equally stigmatizing although admittedly less costly.

One agency administrator recently estimated that 75% of her police referral cases in a diversion project were of the type which normally would be released and would not receive agency counseling. This same spokesman indicated that, if other things were equal, the police referral would receive priority in enrollment into the agency program over regular (nondiversion) clients. Similarly, the developer of a multi-million dollar diversion program stated to us that his clients, however minor their problems might be, would have to take precedence in assignment of treatment resources over "regular" agency clients. "Are you concerned about these 'bumped' clients?" we asked. "Well," came the answer, "I guess that's the way the cookie crumbles." Here, then, we see more than alternative encapsulation: we also see a questionably appropriate set of clients supplanting a traditional set of clients. There is a conflict between two legitimate concerns: the well-being of diversion clients and that of traditional clients.

A major police department makes the relationship between referral and minor offenders explicit in a departmental directive: "Referral agencies should be used *whenever possible with the beginning offender.* 'Counseling and releasing' of offenders should be considered *only in very minor cases* and only when the subject is not likely to repeat deviate behavior" (emphasis added). Ordinarily, first offenders are released by the police unless the offense is so serious as to require petitioning into the juvenile court. Yet in an established diversion program in one large police department under our purview, over two-thirds of the *referred* offenders were first offenders. A special project subsequently initiated by this department which stressed diversion of more serious cases could only reduce this rate to 50% first offenders. To create the diversion population, it was necessary, it seems, to draw heavily from the pool of offenders normally released. Now these offenders are referred to community agencies; they are inserted into a new social service system. Are we merely trading new service for old?

A hint comes from data recently collected on three cohorts of offenders referred to agencies by the department last mentioned. These cohorts of 41, 52, and 27 referred offenders received means of seven, eight and a half, and almost twelve hours of counseling. In a comparable cohort of 82 youths for whom petitions were filed, 20 were subsequently released at intake without treatment, 30 were assigned to "informal probation" with minimal treatment, and all but 6 of the remainder were sent home on probation. Such figures do *not* make it clear that referral is less encapsulating than petitioning. In fact, it becomes clear that referral is equally or even more encapsulating.

4. EXPANSION OF THE SERVICE SYSTEM

If thousands of new clients are being diverted from one system and referred to a second, we might expect the second system to undergo some modification and, most specifically, to expand in sheer size. Clearly such modifications and expansion are now taking place.

Of tweleve programs funded by "Probation Subsidy" funds in Los Angeles County in 1973, ten were juvenile diversion programs. Among these, the funds were used to expand police staffing in six instances and referral agencies in four instances. The largest known diversion agency in Los Angeles County was, by its own account, saved from closing its doors by an influx of funds from police diversion activities which purchased agency services. Another had to open a second office as its budget suddenly increased by a third and its counseling load doubled.

In an as yet unpublished report, Dennison and associates (1975) have described one setting in which a small agency with a $50,000 budget quickly expanded into a central mental health facility with a budget of $600,000. They describe another setting in which an agency opened three branches and became a training center for a prominent school of psychology. The authors note, "If there is some chagrin manifested by agencies that feel they have not received their portion of referrals, a number of others have been rescued from extinction."

No head count of new "diversion" agencies or personnel has been undertaken, yet within Los Angeles County alone the authors have seen a number of new agencies and dozens of new staff members. Things have moved far enough for there to have been, in 1975, a *third annual conference* of a new organization called the California Association of Diversion and Youth Service Counselors.[3]

Site visits undertaken by the authors to numerous cities throughout the United States confirm that a similar expansion among service agencies is taking place and accelerating in many localities. We are amused, on occasion, to find the associated jargon to be less than uniform (diversion becomes "divergence," "diversionary," or "deferrment"), but we find this linguistic confusion to be overshadowed by the conceptual and definitional confusions in the rapidly increasing professional literature on diversion. We may only be describing some typical growing pains of a new social welfare movement, but there is a legitimate concern over whether such a service expansion is a healthy and useful development or not.

If the services provided do in fact reap benefits for the referred delinquent clients, reduce the load on the justice system, and accomplish these ends without harm to other client groups, then the concern disappears. But many agencies, programs, and funders have failed to evidence genuine concern with demonstrating and *testing* such benefits. If on the other hand, the services provided amount primarily to a new form of overreach, a larger net within which to encapsulate the diversion client, then the concern must be taken seriously and a moratorium declared until the impact of such alternative encapsulation can be assessed.

If, finally, the service expansion takes on a semblance of permanence, of a new, full-blown system, then its very existence may pose a danger. New systems and new bureaucracies often become self-perpetuating phenomena; they may become resistant to change; they may become attuned to their own needs often at the expense of (or even in ignorance of) client needs. Much of the current activity in diversion, deinstitutionalization, and decriminalization can be interpreted as recognitions of this pattern and attempts to counteract it. But we may be counteracting by creating counterparts, by putting our wolves in sheep's clothing.

5. POLICE CONTROL

There are two control dimensions of immediate concern. The first describes the degree to which diversion programs maintain control over their clients, determining their activities, their options, and the likelihood that additional antisocial behaviors will reinsert them into the justice system. The second control dimension describes the degree to which diversion programs are under the control of, or accountable to, the juvenile justice system—in our case, to the police.

The first issue, program control over clients, has several facets; but we will allude briefly to only two, overreach (i.e., who is controlled) and extensiveness (i.e., how much one is controlled). Interviews with referring officers in 35 police departments, as well as preliminary analyses of data on samples of arrested juveniles in these and other departments, have convinced us that "over-reach" is the predominant pattern. To a very considerable extent, diversion practices are being applied to juveniles who formerly have been released by the police without further action. Thus control is being extended to a larger and less seriously involved sector of the juvenile population. Other writers have recently reported similar findings with unbroken consistency (Vorenberg and Vorenberg, 1973; Kutchins and Kutchins, 1973; Blomberg, 1975; Mattingly and Katkin, 1975).

Extensiveness of control over client lives is illustrated by the range of restrictiveness of treatment programs for referred offenders. At the high control extreme are residential treatment centers in which offenders eat, sleep, often work, may receive educational instruction and other "betterment" lessons (from grooming to encounter therapies), and so on. Control mechanisms may include curfew and grounds restrictions, daily schedules, and behavior modification procedures with specific rewards for approved behaviors and negative sanctions for disapproved behaviors.

More typically, referral agencies vary their control over clients living at home by contracting for expectations, by requiring certain numbers of treatment hours or visits at the agency, by maintaining contact with adults significant to the client (parents, school personnel, peers), and by retaining varying levels of contact with police and court officers concerned with the case. Thus control over clients can be achieved by mutual "contract," by suggestion and expectation, and by threat of reinvolvement with the police, probation, or court.

The other dimension, system control over programs, has emerged with some clarity from the plethora of diversion programs recently instituted. In many—perhaps most—instances, the level of control is determined by the philosophy of the referring agency. For example, one recent paper describes a court volunteer program in which the volunteers may have become merely another arm of the law (Berger, 1975). A report from Cook County describes how juvenile officers, antagonistic to a diversion program, used a legal loophole to subvert the program and actually brought about a 53% increase in incarceration (NCCD, 1975). Thus, to evaluate the impact of control, we need to recognize the means by which the police exercise varying levels of control over program. We list six of these for illustration:

a. *In-house counselors.* Some police departments hire or arrange for the transfer of counselors to work in the department and treat referred offenders. Some of the counselors are probation officers, others are agency counselors on loan, others are private counselors on the police payroll, and occasionally they are, themselves, police officers. In each instance, they are housed in the department, a part of the police milieu, and they are often formally and informally accountable to police officials. The clients, of course, may interpret their counselor's role and their relationship to it as a function of this departmental context.

b. *Police-based agency.* Occasionally, one finds a referral setting established by or in very close collaboration with the police and staffed by a mixture of police and counseling personnel. It may be located on departmental premises or in another, often public, building (school, probation office, welfare office). It may be called a Youth Services Bureau, even though these bureaus were originally designed to be independent of the justice system. The singular feature of this type of program is the sheer visibility of police involvement in the diversion/referral process. To the client, it must be clear that diversion has not meant his "escape" from the justice system. For the nonpolice staff, it must be equally clear that they are intrinsically involved in police business.

c. *Selected referral resources.* Perhaps the most common and understandable means by which control is exerted by the police is through the selection (and occasional modification) of referral agencies. We have found rather consistently a police preference for professionally (psychologically) staffed agencies, agencies without the "flavor" of minority militancy, agencies that do not condone or excuse minor transgressions, such as the use of marijuana, but counsel specifically against each of these, and agencies willing to keep the police informed about client progress or continuation of a delinquent pattern. This latter can be either informal or formal via feedback reports on client progress or renewed misbehavior. This is not to say that the police commonly reject agencies that refuse to provide feedback to them, but such agencies do seem less preferable to those who will join in a more collaborative (and thus controlling) operation.

As a tangential note to this pattern, we can report the increasingly common pattern of police referrals to firemen who serve offenders in some variation of a Big Brother role. For the police, firemen are good bets as referral resources. They are often "cleared" through police files prior to acceptance in the fire department, they have official authority, and they are seen as brothers-in-arms by the police. The young boy looking up at the fireman with adulation and respect is an image peculiarly suited to the police-endorsed, Norman Rockwell mythology of a "straight" America.

d. *Purchase of service.* An increasingly common procedure is for the police to purchase the service of community agencies for treatment of referred offenders. The fee usually is paid contingent upon a minimum number of clients, or a minimum number of treatment hours or visits per client. Obviously, agencies that do not provide what the police want may be cut off from further payments; control may be achieved financially. The epitome of this is an arrangement whereby an agency receives a minimum fee for accepting a client and provides a specified level of treatment, for instance $50 for six client visits. Then, if the client stays "clean"—that is, does not recidivate—for a given period of time such as six months, the agency receives an additional stipend several times as large as the original. Thus it is worth the agency's while to provide effective intervention specifically pinpointed if possible to the reduction of delinquent behaviors. From the police viewpoint, what is being purchased is maximum and time-extended attention to the production of legal conformity. In one such program observed by the authors, this arrangement did indeed yield significantly greater levels of treatment in accordance with the desire of the police agency involved.

e. *Program organization.* On a number of occasions, diversion programs have been initiated by police departments out of frustration with the ineffectiveness of existing procedures. This initiation—an unusual stance for a public agency which is more typically *re*active than *pro*active—includes seeking out, coordinating, and motivating community agencies, seeking public funds and writing grant proposals, seeking facilities and political support, and convincing normally hesitant factions within the police department itself. Once such an effort is expended, there is little inclination to loose the reins and turn control over to others. The stamp of the initiator remains visible, and the program is likely to thrive or die in proportion to the continued concern and involvement of the police. As a result, the character of the program is highly responsive to the philosophy and concerns of the police department.

f. *The directorate.* Many diversion programs, especially those involving more than one municipal jurisdiction, are governed, directed, advised, and supported by boards of directors and advisory boards. Often, one finds police representation on these boards to be disproportionately heavy. Experience also suggests that their voice on such boards is a strong one; one "nay" vote from the police can effectively block a diversion program. McAleenan (1975) has recently described a project with two boards, one of which is comprised solely of community agency personnel while the other is half police and half school personnel. Dennison and associates (1975) portray two projects with advisory boards. In one, 4 of 18 members are police officials; in the other, 5 of 12 including the chairman represent the police.

Other forms of control are obviously possible; our purpose in presenting these, each of which we have observed, has been to highlight the variety of control procedures possible and to make it clear that this control dimension is indeed a prominent one. Diversion programs are far from independent of the juvenile justice system, even though diversion is supposed to mean diversion *from* that system. It seems clear, as well, that programs high on the police control dimension are more likely to be higher on the client control dimension.

However, it is important to emphasize that we have observed a number of police-diversion programs in which the police connection with referral agencies is truly minimal. Diversion here is not so much a project as a habit.

6. COMMITMENT TO DIVERSION

In the preceding sections we have characterized diversion as a fad serving multiple and conflicting goals. Now we turn to the final concern of this chapter, police commitment to diversion. If commitment is genuinely low, then perhaps the question of appropriate evaluation dimensions is moot. But if commitment is more than low—high commitment is perhaps not a realistic expectation—then the evidence for commitment is worth pursuing. Despite the reservations and cautions expressed throughout this chapter concerning the way in which police diversion programs are being carried out, we are satisfied that police commitment to the diversion philosophy is, in general, too entrenched currently to be considered "low." Of course, this still does not characterize it as "high."

Our own interviews in 47 police departments suggested to us as being involved in diversion yielded 35 which characterized themselves as so involved. In 33 of these 35, we inspected 100 randomly selected case files, finding referrals to community agencies in 26 of 33; 7 stations who think of themselves as having referral programs yield *no* referrals in 100 cases.

Still, that leaves 26 who are referring juveniles for treatment of some kind. The range of referral rates is from 1 in 100 to 28 in 100, with most of the stations having fewer than 10. Taking the 33 departments that characterized themselves as having diversion programs, we find a mean referral rate of 8%: 8 in 100 arrestees are referred. Commitment to referral is certainly not high, but the low of a decade ago has been raised considerably.

As important as level of commitment, if we are to understand the relevant issues, are the variables associated with police commitment to diversion. Two sets of variables have been suggested by current research. In their comparison of two multi-city diversion programs, Dennison and associates (1975) have related commitment implicity to (a) levels of political involvement and (b) degree of success sensed by police personnel. Political involvement emerges as paramount in this analysis, especially as exhibited in interorganizational relationships and in threats to organizational "turfs." The authors note, "The lesson is that funding agencies should be thoroughly familiar with the regions to be served before attempting to impose organizational guidelines, and that the regions should be small and well-defined" (1975: 16).

The second set of variables relates directly to the control issue explicated earlier. Specifically, the present authors found from interview data in 34 departments that commitment to diversion was related to whether the counseling was all done within the police department or was placed in community-based agencies. An interesting and rather clear pattern of differences emerges.

First, as might be expected, inhouse programs are positively associated with the structural additions of new divisions or details and new staff. Not so obviously, inhouse programs are positively associated with initiation of the program from inside the department. Conversely, departments using outside referrals were more likely to have remained structurally unchanged and their programs were more likely to have been initiated from the outside, usually by a state or regional planning agency.

Second, inside initiation and inside development of the program are associated with structural changes and with having a period of civic funding, or no funding at all, at some point in the program's history.

The composite picture so far then is one set of programs that were self-initiated and developed, were operating without funds or with civic funding for a period of time, have added staff, and have an inhouse counseling arrangement. Another set of programs, initiated and developed with the help of outside agencies (usually the state planning agency) have always operated on outside government funding, have yielded no structural changes in the department, and refer offenders to outside counseling agencies.

Perhaps more interesting, these historical and structural variables were found to be closely associated with certain attitudinal variables. These represent a dimension of optimism versus pessimism about the program and its effects, including prospects for changing the crime rate, confidence in counselors, and possible effects on public relations. Clearly, optimism was associated with the inhouse programs and pessimism with the outside referral programs. It should be noted that 17 of the 34 programs were strictly outside referral ones.

Thus, although there are a number of departments having self-initiated, self-developed, self-funded programs that have resulted in structural changes in the department—in short, a group of "committed" practitioners of diversion and referral—there are many others that cannot be so described. This latter group, making up a substantial proportion of the recent diversion "explosion," has been induced from the outside to begin programs about which they are not especially optimistic. From our informal contacts and from data inferences, it is clear that the inducement is government money. The question immediately arises: what happens when federal money is withdrawn, as it inevitably will be? Does referral become a thing of the past? Probably not for the self-initiated programs which are clearly operated by juvenile officers committed to diversion. However, it is just as clear, at this point, that the government-initiated programs will probably die unless something happens which changes the attitudes of those officers.

In line with this last remark, it is appropriate to note that, in general, the government-funded projects started more recently than the self-initiated ones. It is possible that there has not been time for the officers in these programs to see positive results and therefore become convinced of the merits of diversion. The opposite possibility is, of course, equally probable. It might be advisable for the state planners to turn their attention to this problem. Succinctly put, funders must face the fact that rationales and commitment behind funding and planning at an administrative level do not necessarily filter down to the operating level of the juvenile officer.

CONCLUSION: EVALUATION DIMENSIONS

The reader may have noted by now that this chapter has paid almost no attention to whether or not diversion "works," especially in the sense of reducing recidivism rates. This omission does not reflect a view that the recidivism criterion is of little consequence; quite to the contrary, we consider it of paramount importance. However, we have been concerned here with a different matter, trying to elucidate a number of additional evaluative criteria which emerge from a structural analysis of diversion programs. These other criteria are often given great emphasis by policy makers. Further, they deal more directly with the connections between the police, as one component of the juvenile justice system, and the system, community, and political contexts within which police programs must operate.

To attend to all criteria may ask too much of any single evaluation group or project. To ignore most criteria has been the history of most groups and projects. But with a reasonable amount of planning, and given the large number and varying forms and settings of diversion programs, a comprehensive evaluation methodology is conceivable. The existence of scores of state and local criminal justice planning agencies should make such comprehensive evaluation possible, or even mandatory. To date, it has not.

NOTES

1. A printed sign on the wall admonished, "Think Referral."

2. McAleenan (1975) has recently noted the case of the diverted juvenile offender aged four and a half years, as well as several others aged five, seven, and nine.

3. Recruitment was facilitated by an announcement from the U.S. Department of Health, Education, and Welfare (OYD, 1975).

REFERENCES

BERGER, R. J. (1975) "An evaluation of a juvenile court volunteer program." Ann Arbor: Institute for Social Research, University of Michigan, mimeo.

BLOMBERG, T. G. (1975) "Diversion: a strategy of family control in the juvenile court process." Tallahassee: School of Criminology, Florida State University, mimeo.

BOHNSTEDT, M. (1975) The Evaluation of Juvenile Diversion Programs. Sacramento: California Youth Authority.

DENNISON, L., L. HUMPHREYS, and D. WILSON (1975) "A comparison: organization and impact in two juvenile diversion projects." Claremont: Claremont Graduate Schools, mimeo.

EDWARDS, W., M. GUTTENTAG, and K. SNAPPER (1975) "A decision-theoretic approach to evaluation research," in E. L. Struening and M. Guttentag (eds.) Handbook of Evaluation Research, Vol. I. Beverly Hills: Sage Publications.

GEMIGNANI, R. J. (1972) "Youth service systems." Delinquency Prevention Reporter. Washington, D.C.: Government Printing Office.

GUTTENTAG, M. and E. L. STRUENING (1975) Handbook of Evaluation Research, vol. 2. Beverly Hills: Sage Publications.

KLEIN, M. (1973) "Issues in police diversion of juvenile offenders: a guide for discussion," pp. 375-422 in G. Adams, R. M. Carter, J. D. Gerletti, D. G. Pursuit, and P. G. Rogers (eds.) Juvenile Justice Management. Springfield, Ill.: Charles C Thomas.

――― (1975) "On the front end of the juvenile justice system," in R. M. Carter and M. W. Klein, Back on the Street: The Diversion of Juvenile Offenders. Englewood Cliffs, N.J.: Prentice-Hall.

KUTCHINS, H. and S. KUTCHINS (1973) "Pretrial diversionary programs: new expansion of law enforcement activity camouflaged as rehabilitation." Presented at the Pacific Sociological Association Meetings, Hawaii, mimeo.

LINCOLN, S. B. (1975) "Juvenile referral and recidivism," in R. M. Carter and M. W. Klein (eds.) Back on the Street: The Diversion of Juvenile Offenders. Englewood Cliffs, N.J.: Prentice-Hall.

MATTINGLY, J. and D. KATKIN (1975) "The Youth Service Bureau: a re-invented wheel?" Presented at the Society for the Study of Social Problems Meeting, San Francisco, mimeo.

McALEENAN, M. M. (1975) "The politics of evaluation in a juvenile diversion project." Los Angeles, Occidental College, mimeo.

NCCD (1975) note in Criminal Justice Newsletter 6 (April 14), p. 2, Hackensack, N.J., mimeo.

NEITHERCUTT, M. G. and W. H. MOSELEY (1974) Arrest Decisions as Preludes to ?: An Evaluation of Policy Related Research, Vol. II. Davis, Calif.: National Council on Crime and Delinquency.

Office of Youth Development (1975) note in Youth Reporter, 75-26030. Washington, D.C.: Government Printing Office.

POLK, K. and S. KOBRIN (1972) Delinquency Prevention Through Youth Development. (SRS) 72-26013, Washington, D.C.: Government Printing Office.

President's Commission on Law Enforcement and Administration of Justice (1967) The Challenge of Crime in a Free Society and Task Force Report: Juvenile Delinquency. Washington, D.C.: Government Printing Office.

Public Systems Inc. (1974) California Correctional System Intake Study. Sunnyvale, Calif.

SCHUR, E. M. (1973) Radical Non-Intervention: Rethinking the Delinquency Problem. Englewood Cliffs, N.J.: Prentice-Hall.

STRUENING, E. L. and M. GUTTENTAG (1975) Handbook of Evaluation Research, vol. 1. Beverly Hills: Sage Publications.

VORENBERG, E. W. and J. VORENBERG (1973) "Early diversion from the criminal justice system: practice in search of a theory," pp. 151-183 in L. E. Ohlin (ed.) Prisoners in America. Englewood Cliffs, N.J.: Prentice-Hall.

WILSON, J. (1968) "The police and the delinquent in two cities," pp. 9-30 in S. Wheeler (ed.) Controlling Delinquents. New York: John Wiley.

Chapter 5

THE POLICE VIEW OF THE JUSTICE SYSTEM

ROBERT M. CARTER

The role of the police is best understood as a mechanism for the distribution of non-negotiably coercive force employed in accordance with the dictates of an intuitive grasp of situational exigencies.

> —Egon Bittner in *The Functions of the Police in Modern Society,* 1970

What the fuck does that mean?

> —Sergeant, Los Angeles Police Department, 1975

USC CAMPUS MEMO

To: Mac Klein
From: Bob Carter
Date: April 4, 1975
Subject: The Police View

Mac,

I'm not at all sure of the "police view" of the justice system. There undoubtedly are as many views as there are police officers. Perhaps these many and sometimes diverse views can be collapsed into one generalized perspective, but there would be a wash-out of individual distinctions and differences.

In any event, the proposed chapter will present a number of dialogues —perhaps a half-dozen—with police officers and sheriff's deputies from the

Los Angeles Basin. I will attempt to elicit comment on a range of subjects from the criminal and juvenile justice systems through police, courts, and corrections. My proposed target population will be officers/deputies with several years of experience who are working on the street—where the proverbial "rubber hits the road"—rather than R&D personnel, planners, captains, etc. I suspect it will be possible to generalize from these various inputs and to summarize the general themes which emerge. The final product may or may not be profound; it will most likely be profane.

ON THE POLICE ROLE

"That would have been an easy question to answer twenty years ago. I remember when I was a kid, I always wanted to grow up and be a cop. . . . I guess all little kids want to grow up to be cops. I really wanted to arrest criminals, lock them up, you know, prove that 'crime doesn't pay.' It's funny, all the kids who wanted to be cops. Hardly any of them give a damn about police now, unless they have a problem. I wonder what causes people to change. Anyway, in theory, the answer is right here on the door, 'To Protect and To Serve.' That's what the police role is supposed to be. But to protect and serve just isn't so. The only people protected and served are criminals. They get the breaks, not the victims, not the witnesses, not the good people. Sit in a courtroom sometime and see who gets fucked around—cases continued, witnesses harassed and insulted, victims made out to be criminals, and plea bargaining. That's the worst! We could catch some dude coming out of a liquor store with a smoking gun in one hand and a bag of money in the other, and he'd walk out of court with ten days suspended for trespassing. Let me ask you, Who gets protected? Who gets served? The whole thing pisses me off.

"The police role isn't just busting people; in fact, there is damn little of that. We spend more time writing reports and waiting in court than making streets safe. People don't like cops. Now, maybe some cops did some stupid things, but most of us are trying to do good. I can live with the fact that people don't like cops, but it bothers me that they don't like me because I'm a cop. And that's true on the street and off duty too. You wonder why we stick together; you almost have to. A bunch of us even went to Dodger Stadium together last night. Nobody understands; non-cops can't understand it. Maybe we don't understand it ourselves. Next time you're in a bar, tell the dude next to you that you're a cop. Watch him come apart. Or try to make it with some broad and tell her you're a cop. Shit. Nothing. People want you around and they don't want you around. They love you, they hate you. They need you, they don't need you.

God, if the role is fuzzy, it's probably because no one really knows what they want from police."

ON THE CRIMINAL JUSTICE SYSTEM

"I think I understand the criminal justice system; at least I understand it academically and intellectually. I have my degree from Cal State. But the system doesn't make too much sense to a street cop. Imagine that you're in a black and white in South Central at 2:30 a.m. And this would be true for 77th, Newton, Southwest, shit, even Lennox and Antelope Valley. When you turn a corner, drive into an alley, or respond to a 211 IP or 459 silent, you don't know what's going to happen. It might be a psycho, a street junkie, some kid on speed, or even some dude who wants to waste a cop. Might not be anything. You don't know. But let me tell you what the justice system is then. It is me and my partner. We have a car, a radio, a backup unit, two 38s, one shotgun in the rack. That is the justice system on the street. To make it complete, you add one criminal.

"There isn't any DA or public defender in that system, no probation officers, no judges. Just me and my partner . . . and some assholes. The rest of the system is sleeping. The only people awake are the cops and the assholes. That's the justice system at night—me and my partner. The rest of the system goes home at 5 o'clock and goes to bed at midnight. We're just getting up. It's kind of funny: our part of the system stays awake all night so that the rest of the system can sleep. We have an 8-to-5 criminal justice system—except for us. A lot of people aren't carrying their weight."

ON ACADEMIA

"Nothing personal, but most professors don't know what they are talking about. They sit on the campus putting out all this good shit about rehabilitation and causes of crime. Most of them haven't ever been on the street; and if you want to know what's happening, you have to be on the street. They haven't seen these assholes after the sun goes down, laughing and scratching, shucking and jiving. Instead of them telling us about crime, we ought to be telling them. If they would spend a couple of days with us, they might find out what's happening. No, they don't want to do that, it might upset all their theories. I've heard some of those theories in school. Bullshit! What has toilet training got to do with anything? Nothing. They ought to be teaching stuff we can use, not all that sociology and social work. Like they say in the army: they don't know shit from shinola. It's a shuck.

"All this liberal bullshit. Some of the teachers are okay, but they are the ones with some street time; they know what it's like. Like that Professor in Florida. The others sit on their ass, smoking a pipe and pulling on their beard. They worry about the fucking criminals. You know, the death penalty stuff. They get in a big sweat if something happens to one of the assholes; you don't see any sweat when a cop takes a round in the chest. Let some nigger get a bloody nose or a head cold in the county jail, and the liberals come apart. It's a lot of shit.

"I've heard all the theories of crime. Let me tell you, crime is caused by assholes. That's the asshole theory. If you want to check that, come on out on the street. See it like it is."

ON THE JUVENILE JUSTICE SYSTEM

"I don't want to sound like a hardass, but we have some really bad young hoodlums on the streets in LA. These aren't the nickel and dime kid shoplifters; they are hardcore. Some of them have dozens of arrests, but they're still out there ripping off people. Some of them have killed people, but they are still out there. The juvenile justice system doesn't take care of the dangerous kids—they are on probation, on parole, on bail, on the street. They are in gangs, with a hardcore leader and a few other psychopaths. They pull pretty good kids into their web—peer pressure or whatever it's called. These good kids start imitating the hardcore, and pretty soon there is a bigger gang. And then the gangs start in on each other—you've seen the paper—someone is always getting cut up or killed in a gang war. And then there is a need for revenge and another killing and so on. We don't have witnesses; nobody sees or knows anything. But even if they did, the system probably wouldn't do much. These pukes are into juvenile hall and out twenty minutes later; seriously, some of these hoodlums are back on the street before I finish the paperwork. If you are going to correct kids, they have to get their hands whacked the first time they put them in the cookie jar, not six months later. Juvenile justice is slow. Jesus, the rights these kids have got. They have more rights than I have: lawyers, witnesses, the whole bag. I'm not talking about the mickey mouse cases; I mean the hoodlums.

"The best example—I mean the worst example—was the narcotics bust last month at the schools. We worked those cases for a long time—undercover and all that—and what happened? The POs and the courts turned them loose, while we still had people working the schools making arrests. It's a wonder no one got killed. Why did they turn them loose? Isn't selling narcotics a crime? Is the school some kind of sacred place where you can commit crime? I tell you, it isn't the cops who are messed up; it's the people. They want us to stop trafficking at the schools, but they don't want us to work the schools. Well, sometimes we can work the schools, but that is 'Officer-Friendly' stuff in the grammar schools.

"You can't get juveniles into the system. The probation officers want to handle the cases and get the subsidy money. Hardly any of them even spend one night in the juvenile hall. It would be good if they got to see the inside. They are put on informal probation, or diversion, or probation, or something. How can you make the streets safe if you can't get the hoodlums off the streets? I don't know what the public wants: they jump us if we make good cases like in the schools, and they raise hell if we don't make the cases and get the hoodlums off the street. Anyway, we are doing our part. We try to clean the streets, but the rest of the people in the justice system seem more concerned about getting those hoodlums rehabilitated by turning them loose. And little crime turns into big crime—don't forget that. If you don't stop these kids the first time, they get worse.

"The system isn't working together: we try to clean up the city; the other people in the system don't seem to have the same goal. You know, leniency breeds contempt. The system has been lenient; maybe that's why gang violence is increasing. You know, we have had about 100 kids killed already this year—and it will spread. Somebody else has to do something. We are doing our part."

ON THE DISTRICT ATTORNEY AND PUBLIC DEFENDER

"I've got about six years in the Department, and things have changed even while I've been a cop. There was a time when the DA was on our side: his job was to prosecute. Nowadays, that doesn't seem to be true. The DA is more concerned with getting the cases closed, and there is a lot of dealing with the PD. That plea bargaining really ended the adversary system, the 'people against somebody.' Now it's all a matter of making the best deal. I may be writing my thesis on plea bargaining. I can understand that the backlog in the courts can be expedited and that bargaining means that neither the DA nor the Public Defender loses a case: they both win. But the public may be losing. Deterrence is kind of lost in a system where you bargain for justice; it seems to me that you are either guilty or not guilty of, say, robbery-one. I find it hard to accept that robbery-one can be reduced to a misdemeanor with a deal for a year in the county [jail] on a weapon possession charge. If you are guilty of robbery, you ought to be convicted and sentenced for it. It might be better to make the case stick if you can.

"I think the DA is overcharging so that he can negotiate down, and that isn't right either. And maybe we don't give as much attention to investigation anymore—after all, the exact charge and sentence is going to be negotiated. There was something majestic about the courts in the old days—whenever they were—guilty or not guilty. The sentences imposed were deserved, not worked out. I imagine that the people convicted are doing a lot less time with the new system; maybe time didn't rehabilitate anyone, but at least the punishment sort of fit the crime. Now the punishment is fitted to meet the needs of the system like crowded courts and prisons. And good cases are thrown out as part of the deal. We see the defendant plead guilty to one count when we really had him cold on a dozen. If they think they beat the system—and I think they are beating the system—the deterrence is gone. It's a sellout to meet system needs."

ON PROBATION AND PAROLE

"I don't know too many POs. Three of them were in a class I took last semester. They seem like pretty good people, but I don't know if they have their heads screwed on right. They have a good education, but they aren't street-wise. They have a job to do, but I don't think that they are getting it done. Our job is to catch these people and get them off the street; their job is, well, I'm not sure. They talk about rehabilitation. But a lot of people on the street haven't even been habilitated. How can they talk about *re*habilitation? And some of those people are real losers.

"I don't think they do much good. Hell, you can't get any of their people off the street on a violation. You have to make a new case. So what good is probation and parole if you have to make a new case every time? Maybe they can't get the judge or the parole board to take these people back, but it's damn sure that you can't get them locked up without a new crime. Matter of fact, a lot of these people shouldn't be on the street in the first place. I know the PO doesn't turn them loose, but they ought to have more clout with the judge or the parole board with all of their reports. I mean, what's the sense of it all? We bust some asshole, and he is back on the street before we get the report written; he's back before we are, especially kids. Jesus, I don't know why we even bother with some of this shit.

"They work pretty good hours—9 to 5—and good pay, too. If one of their cases has trouble, he's got to wait until the office opens. I don't know what happens if the office is closed, but I'd bet nothing happens. Wait until the next day. And they bitch about all the cases they have. They must get conned all the time. We see these fuckers on the street. They are into all kinds of stuff, but the PO doesn't do anything about it. Maybe he can't; maybe he doesn't know; maybe he doesn't give a damn. Anyway, they aren't going to talk these clowns into good behavior. It probably doesn't make any difference how many cases they have. The whole thing is unreal. A lot of crimes in this city are committed by their cases. We keep busting the same people; but, like I say, it doesn't do much good. They keep getting turned loose, and the PO doesn't do much. If some of the people around here with priors would get locked up, crime would really go down."

ON JAILS

"I worked the jail for two years after the Academy. It was a good experience, but I wonder why we have to run the jail. We ought to be on patrol, not in the jail running a correctional institution. And talk about a sorryass group of people; that place is full of losers in there. It's no wonder they got caught; some of those turkeys couldn't walk and chew gum at the same time. Anyway, it might be better if we didn't run the jail. A lot of time and manpower goes into it, and we could be better used somewhere else. I don't know how many people we have on any day, but it must be thousands, like nine or ten thousand. Some of them are convicted, some aren't. We have to keep the women separate and the juveniles separate and the psychos someplace else, and with all that movement back and forth, it would be better for someone else to run the jail. It is a kind of madhouse: people coming, people going, visitors in and out, court appearances, counts of the inmates.

"We don't keep inmates long: maybe the average guy is just there for a couple of days, and chances are he was drunk or something like that. Looking back, it was a good experience working the jail. I mean, seeing the kind of people locked up was an experience, but I wouldn't want to work there for twenty years, no sir.

"It is a well-run place; I mean, it is clean and the food is good and we don't have any escapes, but we don't do too much for the inmates except to keep them locked up. I mean we don't have many programs, but we do keep people locked up for a while."

ON PRISONS

"I don't know too much about prisons—just what I hear and see on the street. But I'll tell you one thing: the fucking inmates are running the zoo. Look at all the trouble they are having: there must have been a hundred stabbings just at 'Q' this year. These people, they were sent to prison to be punished, weren't they? I don't see any punishment. Now, I don't mean we ought to beat them with sticks, but they shouldn't have all the things they got—you know, visits from their girlfriends. We didn't send these people to the joint to get laid, did we?

And the other stuff. I heard that they have a golf course at 'TI,' and these guys get to play tennis. Shit, I don't even get to play tennis.

"Let me tell you something else. Some of these ex-cons on the street are bad news. I don't know what they teach them in prison, but they aren't doing too good on the street. Maybe it's just the parolees we run into; maybe some others are making it. If I were running a prison, I'd have a set of rules. As long as you live with the rules, okay. 'Fuck up, lock up'—that'd be the way I'd do it. But, like I said, I don't know much about prisons, but I see the graduates running through this city. They commit a lot of the crime. Prisons don't seem to help much, but they do keep the animals off the street for a while. A little protection is better than none, isn't it? They shouldn't turn these people loose until they are sure they are going to make it. A lot of them don't make it; they even go back for the same thing. Prisons aren't doing too good a job. They ought to teach the inmates a trade, maybe that would help. But they shouldn't let them out so quick, at least not until there's a good chance they are going to make it out here. This rehabilitating prisoners—I don't think it works. I don't think it can be done. It is like a monkey trying to fuck a football: it can't be done."

ON THE COURTS

"I don't get into court very much, but if there is a messup in the system, that's where it's at. Talk about the high and mighty—that's the judge. I work a good ten-hour day, five days a week. The average judge does half for twice the salary, too. Judges, especially the nine wise men in Washington, have turned the whole thing upside down: I mean the assholes get all the breaks. The criminal has more going for him than we do. And the judges, they get days to think about cases that we have to decide in two seconds what to do. The ones I know about run the courts for their convenience: just the hours they keep shows that. No wonder we wait for months to get a case closed. And Jesus, the courtrooms are a shambles—crowded, noisy, everybody talking. If you talk about justice and visit a muni court with the junkies and winos, and other assorted assholes, you would be depressed. It's a circus, with everybody wheeling and dealing and trading.

"The judge sets himself apart from us; he really isn't any better than us. As a matter of fact, he doesn't know as much about crime as I do. I see it every day. I see the shit on the street, like the victims and puke and blood and shit, tears and everything else. Do you think that judge ever talked to a girl who just got gang-banged by four niggers? He sees them niggers saying 'yes sir' and 'no sir' in court, not 'motherfucker' and 'honky pig.' I'll tell you, if the judges don't get with it, we are going to have tough times on the street. I'm sick of all these fucking rights and I'm sick of all the dealing in court. Now, I don't want you to get me wrong; there are some judges who will put some of these animals away, but there aren't many of them. I am really tired of all this bullshit—the people on welfare, the probation department, the whole scene. I'd give it up, but I've got too much time in—nine years. And it gets worse every year. You don't see the judge worrying about the witnesses—especially police—or the victims, or nobody but the criminal. And look at the sentences they pass out: county jail for rape and robbery; probation, that's automatic for burglaries; and you got to shoot a nun at high noon to get sent to the joint. No kidding, sometimes I wonder if it's worth the hassle. I really didn't mean I'd quit. I like the job, and what else can I do? It's exciting—an eight-hour orgasm."

ON LEAA

"I personally have gotten a lot out of LEAA (Law Enforcement Assistance Administration, U.S. Department of Justice) from the LEEP Program. I've been back in school for the last two years. Should finish at Long Beach next June. It paid for my tuition. I might not have gone back without it, but there was a lot of pressure to go back to school anyway. LEEP made it easier. I probably will have an edge on the sergeant's exam because of it.

"As far as the Department goes, we have a lot of LEAA dollars or CCCJ (California Council on Criminal Justice, the state planning agency that disburses LEAA funds) dollars, I don't know which. We got some equipment, radios, I think, and I know we are going to be tied into a better communication net.

"Except for LEEP and the equipment we received, I don't know if all that money has done a lot of good. I mean, crime is still going up. Maybe it would have gone up faster without LEAA. There are a lot of people employed because of those dollars. The County has a board and the State has CCCJ and the Feds must have a board too; a lot of money goes through their hands. I don't think it's done much good. I mean, it seems like the money is rationed out with a little bit here and some there so that everybody gets something. That's probably good politics, but it may not be the best way to spend it. There doesn't seem to be any plan for spending the money, except to make sure all the departments get something. And nobody is really checking to see if the money made any difference. I know somebody is making sure it isn't stolen or ripped off, but I mean whether the money made any difference. Did all that money—I guess does all that money—make the streets safer? That's the name of the federal law, isn't it? Safe streets?"

ON PREVENTION

"That's kind of difficult. The role for law enforcement is changing. More and more, we are becoming involved in prevention programs. Police have always had crime prevention programs. Police have always had a crime prevention role; that's been accomplished by patrol, shaking doors, stopping suspicious people. But now we are into a different kind of thing: programs with the schools, the neighborhood, different organizations. We even are organizing differently; the basic car plan in LA is a good example of that. All that means is that we are trying to prevent crime directly—like we always did—and also to participate in community programs which will keep youngsters from getting into trouble.

"Don't get me wrong: the old-timers aren't all turned on by this sort of thing. The juvenile bureau is not always in step with them. A lot of the guys with a lot of time in the Department don't believe in all this prevention activity, except what is directly crime-related. You know those people. They'll tell you they didn't join the Department to become a social worker. They want to work patrol or detective bureau, out on the streets. And that is a majority of the people on the Department.

"We get a lot of money for prevention programs. CCCJ gave us a large grant, and we get a lot of mileage from the newspapers for it. But most of the Department doesn't care; they think the money is going into a rathole. You ought to talk to Sergeant ———; he's a classic. He'll tell you straight out that prevention isn't our job: parents ought to be doing more, the schools ought to get rid of the fuckups, and people ought to go to church. He's loud, but he has a lot of silent support."

USC CAMPUS MEMO

To: Mac Klein
From: Bob Carter
Date: October 28, 1975
Subject: The Police View

Mac,

I have discussed the interviews on the preceding pages with a number of police middle managers, sergeants and lieutenants, and there is considerable consensus that the interviews reflect the views of a large segment of the law enforcement community.

There are several techniques for summarizing the content of these dialogues so that a "Police View of the Criminal Justice System" emerges.

The more traditional method would be for me to prepare several pages of prose which tell you in my words what police officers told me in their words. That seems unnecessary, for there is little uncertainty about the police view of things from their commentary. Let me try a different approach. There are five words which come to mind to describe their view: frustration, anger, anxiety, alienation and hostility. Using a standard dictionary definition, the police view of the justice system is one of:

frustration: frustrate (v.) 1. to cause to have no effect; bring to nothing; counteract; nullify; to have no effect . . . ; 2. to prevent from achieving an objective; foil; baffle; defeat.

anger: (n.) 1. a feeling that may result from injury, mistreatment, opposition, etc.: it usually shows itself in a desire to hit out at something or someone else; wrath; indignation; rage; ire.

anxiety: (n.) 1. a state of being uneasy, apprehensive, or worried about what may happen; misgiving.

alienation: alienate (v.) 1. to estrange; make unfriendly; 2. to cause a transference of (affection).

hostility: (n.) 1. a feeling of enmity, ill will, unfriendliness, etc.: antagonism.

To the extent these five words or their synonyms reflect the police view of the justice system, one might ask: why? What do they see as their role? Three words come to mind: pragmatic, moral and guardian.

pragmatic: (adj.) 1. a) busy; active; b) practical.

moral: (adj.) 1. relating to, dealing with, or capable of making the distinction between, right and wrong in conduct; 2. relating to, serving to teach, or in accordance with, the principles of right and wrong.

guardian: (n.) 1. a person who guards; person who watches over, protects, cares for, or defends another person, property, etc.

To summarize all of this, the police see themselves as the pragmatic guardians of the morals of the community. They are the "thin blue line" against the forces of evil. This role is not shared by all segments of the justice system or the community, either philosophically or operationally, and the responses of frustration, anger, anxiety, alienation, and hostility are not unreasonable when the role increasingly is challenged. Perhaps it was always like that; but there seems to be little to suggest the pattern will change in the future.

Chapter 6

THE EYE OF THE JUVENILE COURT JUDGE:
A ONE-STEP-UP VIEW OF
THE JUVENILE JUSTICE SYSTEM

H. TED RUBIN

The eye of the juvenile court judge is a view of the juvenile justice system from the juvenile court bench. The eye is also an "I"; this judge, particularly, views his role from his own subjective values and experiences. He functions as the key person in a system of justice in which many agencies and agents interact, upon which social and political factors and forces impinge.

Juvenile court judges like to point out that their courtrooms are often designed differently from those of other courts. The benches on which they sit and face their clients are not as high off the floor. They are frequently one step up, rather than three. This approach to design seeks to improve the judge's approach to communication with children and their parents, to reduce austerity and formality.

In every county in this country, there is a court that has jurisdiction over juvenile offenses. This court's structure takes various forms. It is sometimes a separate juvenile court organized as a special entity to devote its full-time efforts to the legal problems of children who reside in a limited geographical area. Examples of such a court are the Denver Juvenile Court, the Boston Juvenile Court, and the Juvenile Court for Orleans Parish, Louisiana.

In several states this separate juvenile court is a statewide juvenile court, and juvenile offenses are considered exclusively by juvenile court judges in the various districts of that state. Utah and Connecticut exemplify this structure.

There are other states where juvenile offenses are considered exclusively by family court judges in separately organized family courts throughout that state. The family court includes juvenile jurisdiction and certain family-related matters as well. New York, Delaware, and Rhode Island are examples of statewide family courts, although New York does not include any statewide administration of this court.

More typically, juvenile offenses are considered within the jurisdictional range of a broad-based trial court, either the highest court of general trial jurisdiction, as in California and Florida, or in the lower trial court where lesser criminal and limited-claim civil matters are also heard, as in Maine, New Hampshire, and Arkansas.

There are other variations: juvenile offenses are considered by a juvenile division of the probate court, as in Michigan and much of Kansas; juveniles in certain counties of a state are considered in a separate juvenile or family court, while in other counties their judge is a member of a trial court bench, who also hears a variety of criminal, civil, or probate matters. Alabama, Louisiana, and Colorado illustrate this hybrid structure.

A 1973 survey, which brought responses from 1,314 judges of juvenile jurisdiction, revealed 12.4% of this group were full-time judges who spent their full time on juvenile matters. Further, 86.4% of these judges devoted half-time or less to juvenile matters, and 66.7% spent one-fourth time or less on juvenile matters (Smith, 1974: 33).

These judges had served an average 7.7 years in juvenile jurisdiction; 22.2% of the judges had presided in juvenile jurisdiction less than two years, while 27.8% had served this area more than 10 years (Smith, 1974: 32).

The type of court that incorporates juvenile jurisdiction and the amount of time a judge devotes to juvenile matters influence the judicial view of the juvenile justice system.

The judge of the separate juvenile or family court not infrequently receives less pay than a judge of the court of highest general trial jurisdiction, and is accorded lesser status. Somewhat outside the mainstream of judicial developments, he may become isolated from legal regimen, and preoccupied with rehabilitation and concerns for court clientele. He may ignore the law in his zeal to seek to help persons. He is, however, an effective community advocate for improved probation and social services.

When this jurisdiction is vested in a lower, "inferior" court, there are the same lower pay and status problems, but the judge, who hears a variety of other matters, may place greater stress on law and punishment and be uncomfortable in a part-time juvenile division assignment that requires a broad orientation to social services and social sciences.

When the juvenile jurisdiction is part of the highest general trial court, that court assigns one or more judges to serve in its juvenile division. While the judge assigned to juvenile division is a full-fledged member of the superior, circuit, or district court, or however it is named in the various states, this division still has difficulty achieving equal status with other divisions of the court. Assignment to the juvenile division is sometimes seen as a journey to Siberia, to be completed as soon as possible. On the other hand, some judges have preferred this assignment and retained this responsibility for many years.

For the balance of this presentation, the terms *juvenile court* and *juvenile court judge* shall be used generically to describe the judicial figure and the court setting that is the focus of this article, except where the context requires specification to undergird a particular statement or meaning.

TRANSITION TO A COURT OF LAW

It should stand as a "given" that any court is a court of law, where legal matters are processed according to regularized procedures and rules, where lawyers are central to the presentation of cases, and where there is a developed body of case law upon which judicial decision-making is based. Yet, such a legal environment had not characterized juvenile courts until recent years, and still, today, juvenile court adherence to legal regularity remains erratic.

Until perhaps seven or eight years ago, a minority of juvenile court acts had undergone comprehensive revision since their initial promulgation in the first several decades of this century. Original juvenile court acts had emphasized judicial powers and prerogatives, and had underallocated attention to the countervailing rights of juvenile clients. The breadth of proscribed juvenile behavior brought a vast amount of very normal adolescent experimentation and interpersonal struggles into the juvenile court lair (South Dakota, 1919). Further, the constitution was irrelevant when the purpose was rehabilitation and not punishment (In re Holmes, 1954a). The court was peopled with probation officers, social workers, mental health professionals, school principals, and parents. Few lawyers came out of the woodwork into the juvenile courtroom. The "best interest of the child" was the rhetoric banner and banter. The judge and his helpers, described in historical perspective as white-coated surrogates (DeBacker v. Brainard, 1969), undoubtedly helped many children and families; yet many were more injured than aided (In re Holmes, 1954b).

Too many youngsters suffered long-term detriments from the court's short-term patience. Limited probation services failed to arrest the commonplace violations of probation rules. State industrial and training schools frequently became sterile junior prisons, way stations along the road to more serious adult criminality.

Not until 1966 did the United States Supreme Court issue a formal opinion in review of a juvenile delinquency hearing (Kent v. United States, 1966). The following year, in its second case review, the Court shook the foundations of juvenile court philosophy, enunciating the juvenile court must become a court, its judge must become a judge, good intentions were a poor substitute for regularized legal procedures, and "neither the Fourteenth Amendment nor the Bill of Rights is for adults alone" (In re Gault, 1967).

Less than two months later, the National Council of Juvenile Court Judges, meeting in annual conference, by coincidence, at the Galt Hotel in Fort Lauderdale, Florida, stated, by resolution and somewhat critically that these two decisions "have left unresolved more questions than they have resolved" (Juvenile Court Judges Journal, 1967).

Three months after the Gault decision, the Blue Ridge Institute for Southern Juvenile Court Judges affirmed the traditional juvenile court judge preference for good intentions rather than law.

Its resolution was prefaced by: "Whereas, there are those who would seek to destroy the basic principles of the juvenile court and convert that court into a criminal court for children." Its resolve urged the National Council of Juvenile Court Judges:

A. To be alert as to the magnitude and potential potency of any attack on the Juvenile Courts of our land;

B. To establish the necessary facilities to the end that the National Council be informed of every instance where any Juvenile Court is attacked on constitutional grounds. [Juvenile Court Judges Journal, 1968]

The National Council, dominated by judges fearful that the constitution and lawyers were incompatible with its philosophic priority of rehabilitation, had, in 1966, appointed a Committee on Appellate Litigation, with a charter to file amicus curiae (friend of the court) briefs on appeals of juvenile court cases, in order to present the council's statement on juvenile court philosophy. Since that committee disagreed "upon the principles of juvenile court law to be expounded, or the philosophy to be presented," the council decided against requesting to join in the Gault appeal (Juvenile Court Judges Journal, 1967).

Supreme Court decisions are not self-executing. The implementation of Gault is not dissimilar to the implementation of the Court's school integration decision (Brown v. Board of Education of Topeka, 1954). The requirements of these decisions remain somewhat ignored in many communities some years later. The spirit and letter of Gault are adhered to only in those courts where there is strong judicial respect for law, strong judicial leadership in demanding that court procedures adhere to law, and where organized defense counsel services along with prosecutor offices have assigned effective counsel to this court.

The traditional juvenile court judge had for years discouraged lawyer representation in his court: "the child needs a judge, not a lawyer." But if a lawyer had nonetheless appeared for a child, he was too often deferential to the judge's greater familiarity in this forum. Hired by the parents, he frequently preferred to strengthen the parents' image with the judge at the expense of the status of the child.

Justice Fortas, writing for the Gault majority, set forth the requirement that the juvenile court judge must advise each child before him of his right to a lawyer, and to a free lawyer if his family cannot afford an attorney. This mandate has been (a) rigorously followed, (b) "waffled" on, and (c) largely ignored. Some juvenile court judges will not consider a case in the absence of counsel, public or private. In other juvenile courts, less than 10% of children are represented by attorneys.

There are ways to discourage representation: "Johnny, you can have a lawyer, but I believe you're the kind of kid who would like to speak for yourself"; "Mrs. Jones, Johnny can have a lawyer, but then you would have to take off work and come back here again"; "Johnny, while you can have a lawyer, I have a lot of respect for your probation officer, and I am sure he and I can give you the kind of help you need."

Several state legislatures, notably in California, New York, Illinois, and Colorado, had overhauled their juvenile codes prior to Gault, to provide more checks on the judge and substantially more rights for juveniles. In the aftermath of Gault, countless states revised their legislation, strengthening their legal protections for children, updating their language, tightening their procedures.

Juvenile law reform is both an incomplete achievement and an ongoing process. The acts of a number of states still harken back to the "good old days," while reform-minded states have annual or biennial battlegrounds on Capitol Hill where the more progressive and the more regressive forces of different professional and citizens' groups skirmish between soft-line and hard-line extremes, contesting the need for further legal checks and balances, dividing on who should be eligible for court sanctions, the extent of sanctions, the duration of sanction.

To their credit, and regardless of one's respect for the substantive views of a particular state's group of juvenile court judges, these judges, more than the judges of any other court, participate actively in the legislative sawmill.

The future is clear: law and due process are here to stay in the juvenile court;

prosecution and defense counsel have become permanent members of the court's cast of characters; rehabilitation efforts will be pursued within a legal context.

VARIABLES INFLUENCING JUVENILE COURT JUDGES' VIEWS
OF THE JUVENILE JUSTICE SYSTEM

There is no one type of juvenile court judge. Like members of the U.S. Congress, they represent a wide range of backgrounds, constituencies, personalities, and interests. Most, but not all of them, are lawyers. (In states where the juvenile court is part of the lower court, lawyer judges are not always required.) That the 1973 survey (Smith, 1974) revealed that 69% of the judges had previously held local or state office prior to their judgeship, and in recognition that in most states today, these positions are elective rather than appointive, the observation can be made that these judges are quite close to the body politic, and somewhat adept at fitting their viewpoints and their careers into the parameters of local political acceptability.

A juvenile court judge does not have the cloistered, ivory tower environment which characterizes certain other judgeships. He or she, on virtually any court day, has the "community" and numerous representatives of community agencies participating in the judge's workshop. One or more parents virtually always attend the hearing with their child. Grandparents, aunts and uncles, neighbors, and clergymen help bring the child's world into the judge's perceptual range. A probation officer is present at all hearings, except certain trials, struggling with the difficult role of control agent and helper, a daily reminder to the judge of both judicial power and judicial limitations: this official is subservient to judicial order, but judicial orders are often subservient to probation execution.

Prosecutors and defense counsel, increasingly structured into juvenile court systems, are helpful reminders to the judge that his is a court of law. Yet, counsel do not always function as independently as we might prefer. Certain reciprocities develop between opposing counsel, or between counsel and judge. Certain concessions are made by and between these three agents, and these may be more often felt than verbalized.

A judge's interest in strengthening the legal component of his court depends on certain variables: the state juvenile code; the cultural environment of his court and community, which encourages formalization or discourages legal representation; his county commissioners and whether he wishes to risk this relationship by saddling the county fathers with a higher tax bill for legal representation of juveniles; his own convictions, orientation, and background; his tolerance of legal challenges to his procedures and decisions.

There are other regular visitors to this court: psychiatrists and psychologists from court clinics or public mental health services whose language and style of thought may be received with awe or with skepticism. Some judges are subservient to the professional in this field where they are an intrigued amateur, while other judges are turned off by views they regard as impractical.

And there are the social workers. The protective service workers from the public child welfare agency, constantly in court on battered child, neglect, and other cases, the lady working with mildly delinquent youngsters in foster homes, the person who, in rural areas in some states, functions as a probation officer.

There are also psychiatric social workers from the mental health centers, family social workers from United Way family service agencies, medical social workers from hospital settings, and others.

The judge must understand still others who participate at hearings: the representative of a militant organization working with minority youth; the junior league volunteer spending one or two hours a week with a court child; the neighborhood community center worker, sometimes the key person keeping a child out of further trouble, for which the judge may erringly congratulate the probation officer.

There are school officials, some asking the judge to do something with this child, others saying what they might do for the child.

Victims may be present, many interested in the redress of their injuries, some also interested in justice for the child.

Judges are also aware of police presence in their courts, whether or not a law enforcement official is actually physically present. Judges gauge the political consequences of slapping down an unreasonable search or illegal arrest; they weigh police acceptance of case dispositions, the kinds of decisions following which police may pass critical comments through the community.

The process by which a judge decides whether or not to deprive a child of his freedom is an intricate one. It is a complex of his expectations for himself, his expectations for others, and others' expectations of him. His decision-making is also related to the community rehabilitation alternatives available to his disposition, and to his rating of state institutional resources. It is also a product of the seriousness of the juvenile's offense, the chronicity of his record, the youth's attitude toward his conduct and toward the court, and the extent to which his parents appear able to provide effective controls over his behavior.

There is a certain predictability about judicial dispositions. Minor offenses receive minor sanctions unless this is the fifth or perhaps the tenth such offense. Serious offenses more likely receive serious sanction, particularly if there was injury to a person or substantial injury to property.

The in-between offenses and the moderately chronic records are less predictable. Here, some judges' psychology and philosophy continue to emphasize community corrections; others move toward placement away from home.

A judge's first six months on this bench are less predictable than his dispositions made after a tenure of a year or two. A perceptive judge is constantly striving to make conscious his emotions which are responsive to the interaction in which he is a participant. His attempts to weigh objectively the overt circumstances should be accompanied by self-analysis of his reactions to the presenting circumstances and personages. A judge should also review how he presents himself to the child and his family: too distant, too friendly, too stern, not stern enough, too solicitious of the probation officer, too identified with the parents against the child?

THE MAN-SIZED JOB OF THE JUVENILE COURT JUDGE

The general public considers that the primary job of a juvenile court judge is to make decisions on the array of delinquency and neglect cases which daily enter his courtroom or chambers. This is primary, although some judges slough off as many hearings as they can to referees who assist them, "ditching" the court for the spotlight of a PTA speech, participation on a community agency board of directors, or taking part in one of the many functions of their national organization.

The community role, also known as quasi-judicial activities, is particularly critical in this court, and should be seen as an important part of this judge's job description.

American Bar Association *Code of Judicial Conduct,* adopted in many states, applies to the juvenile court judge and all judges, and upholds judicial activities to improve the law, the legal system, and the administration of justice "subject to the proper performance of his judicial duties," and so long as the broader community participation "does not cast doubt on his capacity to decide impartially any issue that may come before him" (American Bar Association, 1972).

There is little question but that juvenile court judges are far more interested in this broader role than many judges of other courts. Yet, at times, they fail to subject these broader activities to the priority of the proper performance of their in-court judicial duties.

Many juvenile court judges accept the further responsibility to influence the quality and quantity of referred cases which exit the system short of formal court consideration. It is well known that the juvenile justice system contains certain important processing points where "go, no-go" decisions are made. These decisions, executed by nonjudicial personnel—law enforcement officials, school officials, probation officials, prosecutors—may be, and probably should be, significantly influenced by judicial policy and preference.

Preferably, the presiding juvenile court judge would sit down in conference with key representatives of these groups, together with a public defender, a citizens' advisory committee to the juvenile court, and certain representatives of other community agencies, and hammer out this court's role in this community in relationship to justice system goals. This is a pro-active stance, aimed at guidelining those situations police officials should bring to detention, the types of youngsters who should be admitted to detention, those youngsters to be diverted and to where, and the cases requiring formal consideration. The judge is the center of these policy considerations. The other representatives provide the interest and concerns of their respective functions. The end product can be a more effective and more appropriate utilization of existing court and community resources.

For example, one judge may fundamentally prefer to limit formal court processing to more serious and repeated delinquent offenders. Another judge may see the court role more preventively, with its door wide open to parents, schools, and community agencies seeking to buttress their weakened authority over children through the court's powers.

In many communities, police officials refer only 30% to 50% of apprehended youngsters to the court. Urban truancy rates may total 10% or 15%, yet school systems substantially vary as to the extent to which school truancy is referred to the court. Parental reliance upon the court also shows variance.

The judge holds the key to the door, and while entry is better narrowed with the concurrence of key justice officials and citizen representatives, the judge is the most powerful determinant of the passage way.

Juvenile court judges have a further role: that of ultimate accountability for the administration of the court. They should be viewed as responsible for the court's administrative functions: the management of the court calendars and the flow of cases through the court; the maintenance of the court record system and its provisions for security and confidentiality; budget preparation and fiscal controls; space utilization and management for the court and its related program needs; the preparation, promulgation, and monitoring of procedural rules; the administration of the court's personnel system.

It follows, then, that in jurisdictions where probation, and/or detention, and/or a variety of rehabilitation-oriented programs are court administered, the judge, particularly the presiding judge, should exercise overall responsibility for program administration.

The debate is a warm one as to whether courts should administer such services. The patterns vary widely between states and even within states. In

Michigan, juvenile courts administer juvenile probation, juvenile detention, and often a wide range of counseling, educational, and guided work programs. The Florida legislature, in recent years, has transferred these functions to the exclusive hegemony of a state executive agency, the Division of Youth Services. Such programs are operated in California at the county, rather than the state, level as an executive branch department in certain counties, though in other counties the chief probation officer is appointed by the juvenile court judge. Colorado transferred juvenile detention to a state executive agency in 1973, but retained probation as a court function. In certain Southern states, probation is an arm of the court in more metropolitan communities, but is the responsibility of either county or state welfare departments in the remainder of the state.

When they are court administered, these employees are paid by the judicial branch budget and subject to judicial system rules and administration. Here, clearly, the presiding juvenile court judge should have an appointive role with chief program personnel, and concur with their basic procedures and practices. The twin problems are that some judges so dominate and control probation administration that an uncomfortable subservience constrains effective probation delivery. The other extreme is the judge who is cowed by probation, provides them with a blanket approval of whatever they might do, and prefers to assign his time to areas where he is more comfortable.

But a judge, when probation and program services are administered by an executive agency, does have an interfacing responsibility for certain of their practices and procedures, even though they are not under his direct control. This is controversial, and will be resisted by probation officials, and many judges who would prefer to avoid it. Some judicial involvement may take several forms:

1. Where executive branch probation has the power to decide whether youngsters should be admitted to detention, and whether a juvenile referral should be dismissed, handled informally, or result in a formal petition, a presiding judge of the juvenile court should approve the written policies and criteria that guide these decisional processes. It is not the decision of the individual case that should require judicial approval, for this is judicial overreaching and raises significant constitutional questions. Rather, it is a policy approval that is necessary to assert the court's responsibility for the types of cases that enter its jurisdiction. The executive agency should be the major draftsman of such guidelines.

2. A judge requires continuing information on executive probation practices, workload characteristics, supervision practices, and employment practices. A judge who places a youngster on probation should know what is expected to happen in the way of service delivery. He should also know whether the probation department is an equal opportunity employer. He needs information

as to whether juvenile detention centers comply with licensing code requirements and promulgated standards for care. This same principle applies to the
standards of care provided court clientele by both public and private welfare
services, particularly, as to residential care. When a judge entrusts custody to a
given agency, he should have assurance that at least minimum standards of care
and supervision will be furnished.

HOW DOES A JUVENILE COURT JUDGE VIEW HIS ROLE?

The historic rhetoric of the juvenile court, "to help the child," presents severe
problems to the committed juvenile court judge.

The juvenile court grew up as a spin-off from the adult criminal processing
system, and from the centuries old equity courts where rigidities of the law
could be brushed aside in favor of more flexible social needs. The doctrine of
parens patriae was its dominant philosophy: that the juvenile court judge, much
like the King of England around whom this doctrine was initiated, should be the
guardian of all children who needed care or supervision.

A prevention role was authorized with the expectation that, through court
intervention, neglected children would not develop into delinquent children;
that parent-child conflicts could be dealt with so that a runaway daughter would
not become an unwed mother; that truants would be placed in a special school
so they would not later become burglars.

Some of this intervention was effective; much was not. The promise of this
court has not really been actualized, partly because the court's resources and the
community's rehabilitation services have never been adequate or sufficiently
effective. Also, adolescent behavior often fails to respond to seemingly rational
adult measures.

The renaissance of law in the juvenile court in the late 1960s applied some
brakes to these good, although often misguided, intentions. Still, in the
mid-1970s, the child-saving zeal of many judges preempts their legal training.

For example, an Ohio judge, on concluding a delinquency trial, refused to
throw out a case on the technicality that the state had failed to prove the age of
the child. The court of appeals was forced to reverse (State v. Mendenhall,
1969). This problem also occurred with a New York judge who ignored the same
evidentiary failure in his determination to take jurisdiction over a child found
to have in his possession a live round of ammunition (In re Don R. B., 1971).

The preference to sidestep legal and constitutional requirements in favor of a
judge's perception of a child's "constitutional needs," was mirrored in the 1967
resolution of the National Council of Juvenile Court Judges. In rebuttal to our
highest court's declaration that "even a boy is entitled to more than a kangaroo

court" (In re Gault, 1967), the council resolved: "The pressures of urbanization and the upsurge of interest in civil liberty and its constitutional safeguards should not be allowed to confuse the issues in juvenile court cases to the extent that any child before the juvenile court is deprived of the best opportunity the court can possibly provide for him, or that legal precedents which are based on sound common sense and understanding of biological realities, are ignored or overruled" (Juvenile Court Judges Journal, 1967).

The reluctance to grant basic constitutional rights to juveniles continues, despite Supreme Court mandates. Children are still committed to state delinquency institutions, and transferred from juvenile court to criminal court for processing as an adult, without the benefit of legal counsel (Rubin, 1972).

The temptation to intervene without a legal base is not limited to judges. Police officers apprehend youngsters on evidence that does not justify arrest under a state's constitution or statutes, as in one Cleveland case where a juvenile court judge exonerated a policeman's arrest of a juvenile on the hearsay complaint of obscene language and interference with other children's use of the playground. The judge's specious rationale was that the playground surroundings endangered the arrested minor's welfare (In re James L. Jr., 1963).

Other judges, however, have held the law in the highest regard. A New York judge suppressed, as evidence, jewelry valued at $2,000 which was found by law enforcement officials following a "consent to search" given at 2 a.m. by a 15 year old boy who had been questioned for several hours without the presence of parents or counsel: " . . . a Family Court ought to be no less zealous than a criminal court in requiring reality of consent, freely and intelligently given without fear or coercion before permitting contraband discovery as a result of a search without a warrant to be used against them in juvenile delinquency proceedings. Indeed, because of the child's tender years and lack of understanding of his constitutional rights even more rigorous standards than those applied to adults should prevail when it is claimed that a child has knowingly waived a constitutional right" (In re Williams, 1966).

The Gault decision set forth that a juvenile must be advised of his right to silence; of his right to counsel and to free counsel if indigent; that he is entitled to receive a petition which specifies the offense, and the place and date of the charge; and that hearsay evidence is inadmissible at trial. Three years later, the Court held that the standard of proof required for a delinquency conviction must be the criminal court standard, beyond a reasonable doubt (In re Winship, 1970).

A year later it decided the federal constitution did not compel states to provide a right to jury trial for a delinquency offense (McKeiver v. Pennsylvania, 1971a). Adult offenders have a right to a jury trial if the statutory punishment may exceed six months. Juveniles have no such right except where, in about one-fourth of our states, this right is granted by statute or by appellate court decision. Even in those states the jury trial right is infrequently utilized (McKeiver v. Pennsylvania, 1971b).

Most recently, the U.S. Supreme Court applied the constitutional protection against double jeopardy to a juvenile, initially adjudicated for a delinquent offense in a juvenile court, to prohibit his retrial for the same offense in criminal court (Breed v. Jones, 1975).

Other distinctions between criminal and juvenile jurisdiction are that juveniles have not been held to have the right to bail pending court disposition, although certain states authorize bail for juveniles by statute or decision. Further, juveniles have no right to a public trial, and in those states where criminal felonies proceed by way of grand jury indictment, no such procedure is provided for juveniles charged with felony offenses.

Though juveniles have fewer rights than adults, the incarceration of juveniles in correctional institutions has probably occurred at a lesser ratio than with adult defendants. The advocacy by juvenile court judges for improved probation, and community health and welfare services, augmented by citizen interest in facilitating their provision, however inadequate they may be, have brought resources superior to the programs available to the criminal court judge.

What has been happening these past five years or so has been a "criss cross": juvenile procedures have largely absorbed or adapted the legal procedures and constitutional safeguards from the criminal courts; the latter forums have borrowed from the juvenile strength, and increasingly interface with adult pretrial release and diversion projects, and an increased range of community rehabilitation alternatives.

The juvenile court judge's greatest frustration is the absence of readily available resources to meet the educational, counseling, supervision, treatment, and residence needs of his juvenile clients. Inadequate or insufficient detention and shelter care, foster home placements, institutional care, and probation or social service staff were cited as the four most pressing problems facing juvenile court judges from among a list of 14 need areas (Smith, 1974: 36). One judge has stated:

> The lack of appropriate services and facilities for delinquent children and to a much greater extent for neglected children has contributed more than any other single factor to negating the purpose of the court.

> The value of diagnostic studies and recommendations is too often reduced to a paper recommendation. In shopping for placement, probation officers are forced to lower their sights from what they know a child needs to what they can secure. Their sense of professional responsibility is steadily

eroded. The judge, in turn, becomes the ceremonial official who in many cases approves a disposition which he knows is only a dead end for the child. [Polier, 1964: 30]

The judge also views his role in terms both of what the community expects of him and of what justice system agencies expect of him. This, too, brings out the best and the worst in judges. The best, as with the Midwestern juvenile court judge who refused to transfer a juvenile homicide case to the criminal court because he believed the juvenile justice system had a greater capacity to rehabilitate this youngster. He suffered electoral defeat several years later on the political contention of permissiveness. Or the worst, as with the Southern judge who is held in high esteem in his community, in part because he believes that several nights in detention is good medicine for any child apprehended by the police, even though many of these youngsters are later dismissed without formal court processing.

A judge's relationship with law enforcement agencies is an important one. Some police leaders are subservient to the courts; others are highly vocal critics. The judge, appointed or elected to a four- or six-year term in a juvenile court, must achieve a workable balance in this relationship. For the judge assigned to this court for three or six months, or one year, this balance is less critical.

Some judges are deathly afraid of "crossing" the police, and scramble to compromise a legal ruling or a dispositional decision. They would prefer that the police remain unaware that they may be more interested in youth development than community protection.

The judge has a somewhat different problem in relationship to a probation department. To frequently reject probation officer recommendations results in a disgruntled staff. To largely rubberstamp probation recommendations causes problems with public defenders and prosecutors, depending on whether the recommendations lean more toward institutional commitments or toward community rehabilitation alternatives.

A judge's relationship with school officials becomes tenuous when he suggests the court has more important business than to order truants back to school, or when he retains in the community and returns to the classroom a more chronic or more serious offender whom the school had written off, and had hoped not to see again for another year or two.

The judge also views his role by the expectations of the welfare department. In child neglect cases, welfare agency evidence may be socially strong but legally inadmissible; the judicial duty would be to dismiss the case for insufficient proof. But in the absence of adversarially oriented defense counsel, judges not infrequently dismiss their professional concerns as to insufficient evidence, and sustain a finding. They have been seduced into the protective parent role; also, criticism by a welfare agency, charging judicial insensitivity, has been avoided.

Victims and irate neighbors may demand the judge draw blood from a juvenile offender. Juvenile courts, consciously or unconsciously desirous of minimizing unsatisfying confrontations, tend to ignore the victim and fail to notify him of what is happening in the court. Victim presence is not usually required since relatively few juvenile cases go to full trial. But victims are rarely invited to the dispositional hearing, where the judge determines what action he should take concerning the child's misdeeds.

The way newspaper editors view the juvenile court may have substantial impact upon how this judge views his role and responsibility. The managing editor, the city editor, the courthouse reporter may be critical or supportive, dependent upon a variety of factors, both tangible and intangible.

Judges prefer "good press." They may read the daily newspaper more assiduously than they read appellate court decisions. Some judges strenuously court the press. Some editors strenuously press the court. Judges like stories dealing with their frustrations over the shortage of resources available to court children. They get such copy, but now and then they get an exposure of what they do not like: a juvenile on probation who reoffends, holding up a storekeeper with a gun; or, by contrast, and through a subversive leak, a story on a child institutionalized for a very minor offense.

The juvenile court, a social institution, is more vulnerable and more visible than other trial courts. Despite the general privacy of proceedings in this forum, it receives considerable public attention. Judges like to see their names in print, but only in positive reference. They are political animals, and most judges prefer to continue in office. This concern as to their public rating appears quite prominent, without regard to how judges are selected or elected.

Today, in many states, judges still run for election and reelection on the banner of a political party. Elsewhere, their election is on a nonpartisan electoral basis. The reformist model, known generally as the "Missouri Plan," has the governor appointing the judge from among two or three names recommended by a lay-lawyer judicial nominating commission. After a specified period of time, this appointed judge seeks retention, the ballot question reading simply: "Shall Judge X be retained as juvenile court judge? Yes, No." There is no overt campaign for retention unless, as in some states, following organized attack, a judge may obtain approval from his supreme court to campaign formally.

Governors in some states appoint judges with the advice and consent of one or both legislative bodies. Appointment is usually for a defined term of four or six years. Utah juvenile court judges are appointed by the governor from a list of at least two candidates nominated by the Juvenile Court Commission. Their term is six years, following which the same selection process occurs: the juvenile court judge is eligible for renomination by the Juvenile Court Commission; if nominated, he is eligible for reappointment by the governor. Several Utah judges have not been reappointed though they sought to continue in their office. Juvenile court judges have been defeated in reelection or retention efforts when voters decided an incumbent was "too soft," "too harsh," or "too insensitive."

The point is that, whether the system is an elective or appointive one, large "P" or small "p" politics are very much involved with continuation in this position. Continuation appears more assured when judges make no large waves, when they hold to a basic middle ground philosophy, maintain an equilibrium with power groups, and take fewer risks with their decisions.

EMERGING TRENDS IN JUVENILE JUSTICE:
THE JUDGE IN A CHANGING SYSTEM

1. Law and Lawyers

In 1965 a New York City judge wrote out her opinion on the constitutionality of a police stop and frisk procedure, and then went on to point out a shortcoming in the way the court operated, calling for corrective legislation.

Ahead of other states, New York had developed a Law Guardian system which provided extensive legal defense to juvenile defendants in the Family Court. This judge had previously issued numerous opinions that extended due process protections for juveniles. Here, she soundly criticized the absence of a suitable system to provide prosecution counsel:

> As a result of this situation, the Court is all too often required to question the complaining witnesses on the basis of the petition and then have the Law Guardians exercise the right and duty of cross-examination. Such a procedure does not provide for adequate preparation or presentation of the testimony against the child. It also places the Court in the untenable position of having to seek the facts on which a petition of delinquency is based, hear the defense, and then undertake to evaluate and pass on the evidence as a Judge.

> Unless legislation is enacted to correct the present imbalance in legal services and to provide for adequate legal assistance and judicial manpower, there is grave danger that cases will be dismissed for lack of proper presentation, that citizens will be discouraged from seeking redress in the court, and that legal questions will not be given adequate consideration. The present situation inevitably results in injury to citizens, to delinquent children and to the entire community. [In re Lang, 1965]

A strong judge wants a balanced legal system, and this requires effective representation by both prosecution and defense counsel, from beginning to end of a juvenile case. We are in the process of overcoming district attorney reluctance to assign sufficient lawyers to the juvenile court, though, too often, those assigned are the newest members of the staff, and frequently remain in this court only a few months. The mandated right to defense counsel, the acceleration of defense legal challenges, and the relentless rise in delinquent and serious delinquent offenses is forcing the assignment of more prosecutors to this forum. Too many judges remain ambivalent about trials and adversary proceedings and do little to insist upon a more pervasive prosecution presence. In more informal systems, this judge may pass the word to the prosecutor, that, conviction having been secured, he need not appear at the dispositional hearing when the probation report is received.

Judges divide on several other roles for the prosecutor: whether court staff should decide the charge and prepare the official petition, or whether this should be done by prosecution staff.

In the juvenile system, in most states, police refer not to the prosecutor, but to intake probation officers. Probation intake screening has largely been a social one: weighing whether a child's overall adjustment—family, school, peers—and the apparent strengths of the child and the family, matched with the present offense and prior record, merit informal handling, dismissal, or formal petition. Generally, the screening pays only limited attention to the legal sufficiency of the case against the child. The intake officer is not a lawyer. This probation officer tends to presume the child guilty, as does the child himself. From time to time, on charges that would be dismissed for insufficiency if contested, juveniles accept informal probation programs providing supervision and restraints for up to a year, or, if formally filed, admit to offenses and are subject to the whole range of court dispositional alternatives.

More enlightened courts have built a prosecutor screen into their system, the prosecutor refusing to send on to the court perhaps 5% to 10% of police referrals, due to legal weakness, serving as a political buffer for the court and the probation department, vis-à-vis law enforcement.

Most judges give most youngsters a second chance. Most juvenile court acts stress, as policy, the strong preference that juveniles grow up in their own homes. The defense view coincides with that policy. The wise judge also wants defense counsel to operate as a check and a balance on probation overreaching. He may be unhappy that there are now more trials, and the trials take longer, but he has now lived with the Gault decision for a long time, and sees that it was not the death knell of the juvenile court. Or if he is one of the many judges who have assumed this bench since 1967, he is more oriented to the primacy of law in this setting.

This court, still largely a court of the poor, finds a minority of families engaging private counsel for their child. Some judges prefer appointing private lawyers, paying for their services from court funds, in contrast to the public defender model. With the former, there is frequently less challenge to the court's procedures, the lawyer's limited fee discourages serious challenge. These attorneys read the judge, that his honor prefers co-optation to litigation.

Public defenders typically prefer to advocate vigorously, challenge inefficiencies in the system, and lay the groundwork for a judicial decision, in the trial or appellate court, which may benefit a class of youngsters, not only the individual represented.

2. The Movement Toward Unification of Trial Courts

Nationally, there is movement to reorganize substantially a wide variety of courts. State after state is taking a healthy look at the present organization of its courts, eyeing more efficient organization. What is "in" is the direction toward a single trial court, encompassing all courts where initial trials take place. A rather global example of court reorganization occurred in Cook County, Illinois, where some 208 courts (police, magistrate courts; city, village, town, and municipal courts; justice of the peace courts; circuit court; probate court; criminal court; and others) became the Circuit Court for Cook County (Underwood, 1971). The juvenile court in Chicago had long been part of the circuit court, Illinois's highest court of general trial jurisdiction. Its structure was not changed by reorganization.

Florida's reorganization in 1973 was another major model of reform. All trial courts were consolidated into two courts, a county court, which is a "lower" criminal and civil court, and a circuit court, which is the highest court of general trial jurisdiction. In that state, the juvenile court, which had earlier been at the lower level, was replaced in the circuit court. Yet in many other states, the juvenile court remains part of the lower trial court.

Some states have opted for separation, not unification. New York and Delaware created separate statewide family courts. Massachusetts, in 1973, created its fourth separate juvenile court in Bristol. A new juvenile court was created in January 1975 in Topeka, Kansas.

Conversely and typifying the stronger trend, the Juvenile Court for the District of Columbia was absorbed into the new single trial court for the District.

To give up a separate juvenile court is threatening to many judges who have liked their jobs, their power, their recognition. A 1973 resolution of the National Council of Juvenile Court Judges supported placement of the juvenile court in the highest court of general trial jurisdiction, as a specialized division, but resolved that the judges of the juvenile division should serve in that division for their full term, without rotation among other divisions of the court.

This has been the bone of contention: rotation versus specialization. There are strengths and weakness in both approaches. In a number of general trial courts, judges are assigned, frequently for annual terms, to the criminal division, the civil division, the probate division, the domestic relations division, the juvenile division. A year later, these judges are subject to reassignment by the presiding judge; individual judicial preference, seniority, competency of service in a particular division, and overall court needs figure into the next year's assignments.

The assignment of a judge, from another division to the juvenile division, requires a specialized learning period for this judge, and substantial adaptation by probation, prosecutor and defense counsel, and social agency staff members to the new approaches of the new judge. The judge must quickly become acquainted with juvenile law and procedure, and with the rather complex network of rehabilitation services which require familiarity and differential application. A new judge impacts upon a system. A swing, from one judicial philosophy and style to another, tilts and changes a juvenile court, requires many adjustments, and poses certain problems for court and related agency personnel and for court clientele.

The opposite, judicial specialization in a separate juvenile or family court, appears attractive, but is fraught with other problems. Too many cities have had long-term juvenile court judges who have become the personification of the court. These judges dominated court practices, forced probation officer thinking to conform to judicial prejudices, had special ways of winking at the law and avoiding trials, and developed what some have called an illness, where, in time, the judge needed the court more than the court needed him. This was the judge who resisted lawyers and legal challenges. He continues to dominate a number of juvenile courts today, nearly a decade after the emergence of law in this setting. This judge resists court reorganization, but when it occurs, seeks indefinite assignment to the juvenile division.

There are positives to each approach, as well. Rotation shares the ownership, permits a larger number of judges to maintain an interest in the welfare of the juvenile division, and increases their interest in helping out with that division's problems and needs. The juvenile division judge, when reassigned to the criminal division, carries along a more sensitized approach to individualized justice. Criminal division judges, reassigned to juvenile division, bring a strong orientation to law, which is critically needed in juvenile courts. All judges, then, are more a part of the judicial mainstream.

Conversely, with specialization, the central prominence of the judge can be extremely useful in his efforts to improve community services, secure more probation staff, and exploit his knowledge of the juvenile justice system to spur related agencies to more effective services.

In the wake of the movement to reform court structures is the awakening of an old idea, that of a family court, which, in rebirth, would become the family court division of the general trial court (National Advisory Commission, Criminal Justice Standards and Goals, Courts, 1973). For years juvenile court judges have romanticized about their interest in a family court, although few have been implemented in any full sense. To take the juvenile court and the divorce court and form a family court is the simplest model. Yet most existent family courts either lack divorce jurisdiction, or have achieved essentially no integration of these two sections which function, vis-à-vis judges and probation officers, largely without integration. It is likely that we will see a substantial formation of family court divisions in the future, with broad jurisdictions: delinquency and status offenses, neglected and abused children, paternity cases and support of children, the full range of divorce and divorce-related matters, commitment procedures concerning adult and juvenile mentally ill or mentally retarded, and intra-family misdemeanor offenses.

3. Organization of Juvenile Probation and Detention Services

This is one of the nitty gritties. Should probation be organized within the judicial branch under the policy direction of the judiciary, the majority practice today? Or should probation be a function of the executive branch of government at either the state or county level? The same two questions apply to juvenile detention centers, where youngsters are retained pending juvenile court disposition. State by state, organizational patterns vary, and they also may vary within a state.

The average juvenile court judge prefers to hold on to judicial control over probation and detention, retaining his broader power over the probation and detention staff he appoints. Stated positively, there are more employees to carry out his necessary orders to enhance child welfare: authority accompanies responsibility. Stated negatively, there are more employees who obeisantly bow and scrape to enhance his judicial ego needs.

There are examples of both excellent and disinterested juvenile court judges who want nothing to do with the court's administering such programs. And there are good and bad juvenile court judges who insist upon retaining this hegemony, regardless of how well the services are delivered.

There are problems with both models. Probation can be flat, bureaucratic, traditional, or uninspired, regardless of administration. Also, due process abbreviation occurs under either administration.

In Florida, where probation and detention are part of a state executive agency, a judge, who committed a youngster to the Division of Youth Services, unsuccessfully sought to dictate his placement in a confined institution rather than a community residence. He was rebuffed by the division, and rebuffed by the court of appeals (In re J.N., 1973).

In Arizona, where probation is judicially administered and its personnel appointed by the judge, the Arizona Supreme Court denied that such a system deprived a child of due process, a fair trial, or equal protection of the laws.

From another direction, legislation transferring probation from the judicial to the executive branch was held constitutional by New York's highest court (In re Bowne v. County of Nassau, 1975).

The National Advisory Commission on Criminal Justice Standards and Goals opted to give intake and pretrial investigation functions to the judiciary; detention and probation supervision services were allocated to the executive (National Advisory Commission on Criminal Justice Standards and Goals, Corrections, 1973). States with effective judicial spokesmen will largely shun such a split. Where judicial probation services are presently weak and the potential for executive sponsorship improvements strong, legislative shifts will take place. Pending, however, will be additional suits where the judiciary will consider the constitutional home for probation.

4. Status Offenses and Diversion

Should the juvenile courts continue to deal with runaways, truancies, incorrigibility? Should these youngsters be the sole prerogative of community social, educational, and mental health agencies? Should the court acquire jurisdiction over such youngsters only following certification by a community agency that its efforts have been unproductive?

All of this has to do with what is the purpose of the juvenile court, and what are its goals? It also has to do with the viewpoint of a juvenile court judge, the extent of alternative community services, the extent of more serious juvenile offenses, and, possibly, the regularity and vigor of the juvenile defense counsel system.

Juvenile court judges warmly debate this issue. The official position of the National Council of Juvenile Court Judges opposes repeal of these jurisdictional grounds (Arthur, 1974). However, urban judges, particularly, consider that conduct illegal only for children is akin to victimless crime, and the court should concern itself with crimes that have victims. With limited probation and social service resources, this approach argues that the court should apply itself more deliberately to doing a better job with those who offend against persons and property. Conversely, suburban and rural judges more frequently have closer ties to school systems, church organizations, and middle class parents who want to use the court's authority to buttress their sagging controls over wayward children.

Some judges insist that these children, when they appear in court, must have legal counsel. Other judges discourage counsel for these children, expecting the lawyers will clutter the docket with more trials, force children and their parents into more severe adversarial postures, or disadvantage the judge's relationship with the county commissioners when larger bills are sent in for legal services.

Probably few judges perceive how costly this jurisdiction is to the justice system effort to curb more serious delinquency. These youngsters and their parents are allocated extensive slices of valuable police time, detention time, prosecutor and defense counsel time, judge time, intake and supervision probation officer time. Many of these cases require recurrent processing and recurrent hearings. Neither truancy, runaways, nor parent-child disputes typically disappear with the wave of a judge's wand.

Lawyer challenges to the constitutionality of this jurisdiction are increasing, and a few preliminary decisions have held that terminology, such as "in danger of leading an idle, dissolute, lewd, or immoral life," or "habitually disobedient," or "ungovernable," denies constitutional standards of notice and due process.

The issue of whether the court should take jurisdiction over lesser offenses is related to the concept and practice of diversion. Diversion generally refers to removing a youngster from the juvenile justice system prior to a formal adjudicatory hearing with a judge. For centuries, police officers have diverted youngsters away from court systems and back to parents. Probably since the birth of the juvenile court, probation officers have shortstopped certain referrals and handled them by warnings, or by referral to a noncoercive community agency. National estimates suggest that 58% of all referrals to juvenile courts are handled nonjudicially (U.S. Department of Health, Education, and Welfare, 1971). Annual court reports of many juvenile courts indicate that anywhere from 50 to 85% of referrals are handled nonjudicially, although certain New England states still utilize the judge to hear personally all police referrals, although many are judicially dismissed at the initial hearing without any further proceedings.

This is an area where systematic collaboration can be extremely useful. Unsubstantiated police referrals can be effectively shortstopped by a juvenile prosecutor screening out legally weak cases. Truancy referrals can be curbed by court support of a school district's implementation of noncoercive educational alternatives. Lesser delinquencies can be diverted off to youth services bureaus and other youth agencies. Court caseloads can be meaningfully reduced, even in the face of increased community delinquency, where referring sources better understand the limitations on a court's role and use other means of dealing with less serious offenders.

Some juvenile court judges boast that only 15 to 20% of referrals are handled judicially. Yet intake officers and others are largely spinning their wheels with the other 80 to 85%, serving as the open door for screening and informal counseling services which should initially become the responsibility of welfare departments, mental health clinics, and other agencies which long ago relinquished this responsibility to juvenile courts.

A JUDICIAL ADDRESS TO THE JUVENILE JUSTICE SYSTEM

Undoubtedly, too much has been asked of the juvenile justice system. Juvenile courts were asked, and juvenile court judges were all too willing, to accept the responsibility for maintaining the nation's children, youth, and families in a homeostatic equilibrium. This large order, we now painfully know, cannot be filled, given the enormous social and economic problems of this nation, the wide breakdown of the American family, and the swift pace of technological and cultural change. The resources of juvenile courts, even in simpler days, were no match for the less extensive problems of an earlier American society.

The comparatively substantial investment of federal LEAA funds in state and local criminal and juvenile justice agencies has thus far failed to dent the crime and delinquency problem. A few effects of this program are noteworthy in the present context: the first two or three years of lopsided favoritism in funding police demands brought critical cries of a wasteful overarming of law enforcement, as well as the complaint that expanded police personnel could now capture more offenders which, if continued, would paralyze even token efforts at rehabilitation. Corrections, subsequently, received a larger slice of the LEAA pie. By 1973-1974, the courts were dropping their reticence about overhauling their systems, and initiated more aggressive grantsmanship efforts to receive Potomac dollars. The concept of systems planning and balance was beginning to progress.

Rudiments of system were precipitated as local, regional, and state criminal justice councils, by a variety of names, were mandated to review the allocation of these monies. This process brought together, often for the first time, the judges, and the criminal and juvenile justice agencies, including law enforcement, into some form of a planning process. Although ubiquitous backscratching occurred, these councils served to increase communication between these forces, within a context of system needs, and the effects on other parts of a system, when one part was augmented or addressed.

Such a collaborative approach, organized around the limited purpose of allocating federal dollars, could well be exploited by sensitive judges through forming interjuvenile justice system councils, structured to smoke out and resolve dysfunctional elements and practices, to hammer out agreements on the processing criteria used by different subsystem components, and to bring the support of the system to remedying subsystem needs.

Such an approach could spike the chronic police cry that kids, taken to juvenile halls, beat the officer back into the neighborhood, by addressing the criteria that guide police determination of whether a youngster should be brought to detention in the first place. It could help satisfy the police concern that it seldom finds out what happens in the court by developing a responsible court disposition feedback to the police. Collectively, this group could persuade a local district attorney to assign experienced prosecutor staff to this court. It might pressure the court administration to come up with caseflow data showing how long it takes for police reports to be received, for intake decisions to be made, to get to trial, and to complete a dispositional hearing process. It could be a forum where a public defender could show that delaying his entry, until after formal arraignment, has caused more youngsters to remain unnecessarily in jail or in detention. It could be an interprofessional review board where probation failures and successes receive a wider critique. This body might agree on needed changes in juvenile court acts, rules of procedure, or agency policies which could be improved. It could unleash its criticism that welfare departments drag their feet in providing shelter care, foster care, and residential group care. The judge could bring this all about.

Short of such a council, juvenile court judges can assert other leadership to improve the system. They might, for example, negotiate an agreement with a public welfare agency to avoid the slow process of probation referral to the welfare agency for subsidized placement of a child in private residential care, and instead have a judge approve the same placement, as arranged by probation staff.

Judicial participation in the development of police guidelines for discretionary decision-making has been recommended (National Advisory Commission on Criminal Justice Standards and Goals, Police, 1973), and could be a useful assist to a better-balanced system. Such an approach also applies to the prosecutor's office in those states where the prosecutor has the final say so on whether a referral becomes a formal petition. An even stronger role would be indicated for the judge where probation is judicially administered and where the intake responsibility rests with an executive branch agency. In such cases, the guidelines and criteria utilized should be court approved, the judge asserting his responsibility to play a major role in determining the nature of the court's workload.

There are other dimensions of these interfaces which a judge could address. Police interrogation procedures with juveniles are within the boundary of judicial surveillance and approval of procedures. Limitations on removing youth from detention centers, for police questioning and investigation, can be judicially promulgated. Judicial activism can curb due process violations when probation officers use detention centers for short-term restraint of noncooperative probationers. The list continues.

Judicial policy can insist that no child be detained without a written police report spelling out both the offense and the reasons the youngster was not returned to his parents. Judicial policies can shorten detention stays, effectuate speedier court processing, impact upon the specificity of proposed probation programs. The judge can convene school officials, in general, or in an individual case; call for earlier intervention and more limited caseloads for public defenders; and secure the insertion of prosecutors in the legal screening role between the police and the court.

With local and state mental health services, state youth service divisions, and any number of health, welfare, and social service agencies, the judge can be the key engineer of smoother working relationships, of services more responsive to his intentions, of improved communication and reports.

Some judges have dusted off the old legal doctrine of the inherent powers of the court where, when all reasonable efforts to obtain funds for necessary court services have been frustrated, the judge has brought suit to compel funding (Carrigan, 1973).

There is another way judges are beginning to get at intersystem effectiveness. This approach is known as judicial accountability, or judicial responsibility for the enforcement of its orders. For example, a Pittsburgh judge found a director of a county child welfare services in contempt, and fined the director for that agency's failure to properly oversee the placement of a child in a shelter facility. "We hope that this will serve as a warning that this Court sees the obligation of any agency dealing with children in custody as providing such children with adequate care and treatment" (Janet D. v. Carros, 1974).

Judges are increasingly saying: When collaborative agencies are ordered to perform certain services for children within the court's jurisdiction, these orders should be enforced. Enforcement may come when a concerned probation officer or defense attorney brings a deficiency back into court for review. Yet more systematic monitoring methods must be found.

The presiding judge of the Denver Juvenile Court, in 1974, advised Community Group Homes, Inc., whose five residences were largely occupied with juvenile court youngsters, that administrative probation staff would visit these homes, monthly, and unannounced. The agency's executive accepted this directive as a suitable check on his own staff and agency standards, but went one step further: He advised the judge that he would monitor the monitors, and would send quarterly reports to the court and to the state court system, welfare department, and youth services division, reporting on the quality of the monitoring of his program.

One result of a New York study of private and public mental health and social services available to court children resulted in the creation of a special office, partly in response to the finding that private agencies discriminated against minority children. Among other duties, this office monitors the intake practices of residential care facilities, and brings information on this and on the quality of care provided to judicial attention (Schack, 1972).

Concomitant with this direction is the rise of the "right to treatment" doctrine, based on both statutory and constitutional interpretation, that any agency receiving youngsters under court order must meet suitable standards of rehabilitative care. The Indiana Boys Training School and the Texas Youth Council were found by federal courts to be so deficient, regressive, and repressive in their institutional programs as to violate their legal obligations to its residents (Nelson v. Heyne, 1973; Morales v. Turman, 1973). The courts are less often taking a hands-off approach when they give a youngster to the care of another justice system agency.

Judges continue to write countless support letters, run up capitol hills, and urge funding bodies and the general public to help other justice system agencies get the necessary funds to do a better job for juvenile justice.

It is now an old adage that justice system reform is no sport for the short-winded. The mounting tensions and concerns over the juvenile justice system can be assuaged and impressively redirected by the judge who sits in the eye of this hurricane. A judge who better understands himself can better comprehend his vital opportunity to impact upon this system: he senses that the answer "is blowin' in the wind," and that he is central to it.

REFERENCES

(a) Articles and Reports

American Bar Association (1972) Code of Judicial Conduct. Canon 4.

ARTHUR, L. G. (1974) "The Youth Service Bureau—a view from the bench." Soundings. National Center for Youth Development of the National Council on Crime and Delinquency 1 (May-June): 7.

CARRIGAN, J. R. (1973) "Inherent powers of the courts." Juvenile Justice 24 (May): 38-61.

Juvenile Court Judges Journal (1968) Vol. 18 (Winter): 143.

Juvenile Court Judges Journal (1967) Vol. 18 (Fall): 106-107.

National Advisory Commission on Criminal Justice Standards and Goals, Corrections, Standards 8.2, 9.4, 10.1, and 16.1 (1973). Washington, D.C.: Government Printing Office.

National Advisory Commission on Criminal Justice Standards and Goals, Courts, Standard
14.1 (1973). Washington, D.C.: Government Printing Office.
National Advisory Commission on Criminal Justice Standards and Goals, Police, Standard
9.5.3 (1973). Washington, D.C.: Government Printing Office.
POLIER, J. W. (1964) A View From the Bench: The Juvenile Court. New York: National
Council on Crime and Delinquency.
RUBIN, T. (1972) Three Juvenile Courts: A Comparative Study. Denver: Institute for Court
Management.
SCHACK, E. (1972) Juvenile Justice Confounded: Pretentions and Realities of Treatment
Services. Hackensack: National Council on Crime and Delinquency.
SMITH, K. C. (1974) "A profile of juvenile court judges in the United States." Juvenile
Justice 25 (August): 27-38.
UNDERWOOD, R. C. (1971) "The Illinois judicial system." Notre Dame Lawyer 47
(December): 247-266.
U.S. Department of Health, Education, and Welfare (1971) Juvenile Court Statistics.

(b) Case and Statute References

Breed v. Jones, 95 S.Ct. 1779 (1975).
Brown v. Board of Education of Topeka, 347 U.S. 483, 74 S.Ct. 686 (1954).
DeBacker v. Brainard, 396 U.S. 28, 90 S.Ct. 163, 167 (1969).
In re Bowne, v. County of Nassau, 371 N.Y.S. 2d 449 (1975).
In re Don R. B., 320 N.Y.S. 2d 813 (1971).
In re Gault, 387 U.S. 1, 87 S.Ct. 1428 (1967).
In re Holmes, 370 Pa. 599, 109 A. 2d 523, majority opinion (1954a).
In re Holmes, 370 Pa. 599, 109 A. 2d 523 dissenting opinion (1954b).
In re James L. Jr., 25 0.0 2d 369, 194 N.E. 2d 797 (1963).
In re J. N., 279 So. 2d 50 (Florida, 1973).
In re Lang, 44 Misc. 2d 900, 255 N.Y.S. 2d 987 (1965).
In re Williams, 49 Misc. 2d 154, 267 N.Y.S. 2d 91 (1966).
In re Winship, 397 U.S. 358, 90 S.Ct. 1068 (1970).
Janet D. v. Carros (1974). Cited Juvenile Court Digest 6 (July): 139-141.
Kent v. United States, 383 U.S. 541, 86 S.Ct. 1045 (1966).
McKeiver v. Pennsylvania, 402 U.S. 528, 91 S.Ct. 1976, majority opinion (1971a).
McKeiver v. Pennsylvania, 402 U.S. 528, 91 S.Ct. 1976, dissenting opinion (1971b).
Morales v. Turman, 364 F. Supp. 166 (1973).
Nelson v. Heyne, 355 F. Supp. 451 (1973).
South Dakota Revised Code (1919), Section 43.0301. Repealed 1968.
State v. Mendenhall, 21 Ohio App. 2d 135, 255 N.E. 2d 307 (1969).

Chapter 7

JUSTICE FOR WHOM?
VARIETIES OF JUVENILE CORRECTIONAL APPROACHES

ROSEMARY C. SARRI and
ROBERT D. VINTER

The beginning and end of the nineteenth century witnessed the establishment of two social institutions of critical importance to an understanding of juvenile justice in the United States today: the child-caring institution and the juvenile court. Moreover, both of these institutions are now being challenged from a variety of perspectives as to their relative ineffectiveness in achieving the expectations established by society. The Houses of Refuge were begun in 1824 as child-caring institutions for juvenile lawbreakers and other children deemed to be in need of institutionalization (Rothman, 1971). They spread rapidly and became the prototype of our present institutions for juvenile offenders, both

AUTHORS' NOTE: *This chapter was completed in conjunction with the National Assessment of Juvenile Corrections, supported by a grant (NI71-079-G) from the National Institute of Law Enforcement and Criminal Justice, the Law Enforcement Assistance Administration, U.S. Department of Justice, under authorizing legislation of the Omnibus Crime Control and Safe Streets Act of 1968. The authors wish to acknowledge the valuable contributions to this paper by NAJC staff members, including especially Rhea Kish, Paul Isenstadt, Wolfgang Grichting, George Downs, Bill Barton, Elaine Selo, John Hall, and Vann Jones. Responsibility for contents of this chapter, however, rests with the authors.*

public and private. In 1899 the Illinois legislature enacted statutes establishing the juvenile court as a separate entity which was to focus on the rehabilitation of the child. By 1928 all but two states had adopted similar legislation, which emphasized ideologies of treatment and parens patriae but did not modify, as Fox (1970) and Platt (1969) point out, that court's relationship with other elements of the criminal justice system. Great reliance was placed on incarceration of youth in jails and detention or in institutions, under conditions that actually violated nearly all the requirements for treatment and rehabilitation (Schultz, 1973).

Today, 150 years since the establishment of the House of Refuge legislation, correctional administrators, judges, and the public all voice alarm at the high rate of offender recidivism despite the utilization of vastly increased resources. Many seek alternative arrangements, some advocating more social control and punishment, and others encouraging restriction of the domain of agencies dealing with normative violations by juveniles. Simultaneously, greater emphasis is being placed by courts on the rights of juvenile offenders and upon the maintenance of conditions of fairness, humaneness, and justice whenever a person is incarcerated.

The next decade will inevitably present many problems in juvenile justice as the society attempts to resolve dilemmas and contradictions between the protection of the public, enforcement of normative behavior, punishment of the lawbreaker, and rehabilitation of the offender.

This chapter examines some of the issues in juvenile corrections that are problematic throughout the nation, presents selected findings from the NAJC survey of state systems of juvenile justice, correctional programs, and juvenile statutes, and concludes with several alternatives for future policies. Findings have been selected to illustrate the levels and varieties of alternative approaches to the handling of juvenile offenders, but this is not a comprehensive report of the research completed by NAJC. The approach of this report is to provide a critical analysis of crucial aspects of the juvenile justice system as it operates in contemporary United States. Policy and program development in juvenile corrections have been fundamentally hampered by pervasive preoccupation with case studies, exemplary programs, service designs, causal theories, individual outcome research, and professional ideologies. And understanding has been obscured by the general lack of basic, reliable information about the major practices, patterns, and trends in this general field. Without a foundation of objective knowledge about the core phenomena and their dimensions, informed conclusions about desirable innovations are impossible, as are critical points for needed reform or promising directions for change in public policies.

THE PRESENT STATE OF JUVENILE JUSTICE

At least five major themes can be delineated in analyzing contemporary juvenile justice in the United States.

1. *Juvenile justice is essentially a local government vehicle for dealing with fundamental shortcomings of our entire society.* Throughout American history the family and community have been responsible for the socialization of youth and the maintenance of public tranquility. Public education has been freed from its parochial context, but it has effectively avoided obligations to compensate for various shortcomings of family and deprivations of community. The depressed employment situation for young adults has aggravated this stressful situation as fewer and fewer legitimate opportunities become available. Thus, as social institutions fail to solve the problems of youth, the police and courts are pressed into handling an increasing volume of contemporary problems.

The state plays a dominant role in the postadjudicatory processing of and services to youth, but it does little to affect the local community in arrest, diversion, and adjudication processes in most states. These latter processes are critical determinants of who is processed and how they are processed. Experiments such as the probation subsidy in California and other states (Smith, 1971; Bakal, 1973) have reduced the volume of youth committed to state-operated residential facilities, but as yet there is no evidence that they have had a pronounced effect on the number and means of local processing.

Inundation of local justice capabilities has been fostered by three developments: (1) the nation's inability to formulate constructive solutions to a multitude of social problems that severely impact youth, the most vulnerable segment of the population; (2) a heightened but selective sensitivity to moral norms in mass society, with an intolerance of deviant behavior, especially by youth; and (3) an increasing expectation of intervention by *government,* at all levels, to cope with problem situations.[1]

Opportunities and services available through basic social institutions and public programs are simply inadequate for contemporary needs and expectations in health, education, welfare, employment, and so on (Schur, 1973). We, the public, as a nation, are thus far failing to remedy these deficiencies. Having no better alternatives, we proceed to process "youth with problems" into the justice system. We adamantly refuse to acknowledge that morality cannot be enforced by negative sanctions, or to face the ominous implications of the disproportionate—and possibly increasing—numbers of poor and minority-group persons who are absorbed into this system (Kadish, 1967). Until recently the state governments provided little more than central institutions for delinquent children and those "in need of care or supervision," and only some are developing service capabilities remotely commensurate with the new demands upon them.

2. *The operations of the juvenile justice system are grossly overloaded, demonstrably ineffective, and indifferent to fundamental rights.* There are some striking paradoxes. First, we channel many youth with problems into the justice system, but provide only *marginal* resources for it. Reports and evidence everywhere attest to overloading in all parts of the system, from police through courts to correctional programs. Components of the system are typically isolated from other community services and opportunities, and encounter major barriers in gaining access or assistance. Second, we provide almost no diversion *from* the system to rechannel the overload into more appropriate service areas, but set up high levels of diversion *within* the system (Morris, 1974; Cressey and McDermott, 1973). The revolving door assures apprehended youth at least a brush with the system, under the most impropitious circumstances. Third, we retain a sizable number of all youths routed into the system for heroic, extremely costly, and protracted handling in programs whose effectiveness cannot be demonstrated (Allen, 1964). Ironically, those receiving the most extended and severe handling are likely to include youths—especially girls— whose behavior has presented neither danger nor harm to others.

This irony is perhaps the touchstone to the tragic irrationality of the juvenile justice system—"tragic" for the participants and for the nation, and "irrational" if we are to believe its professed purposes. That youths who have not engaged in conduct dangerous to others or to public safety are incarcerated in the same ineffective programs with serious offenders poses grave questions about the true posture of the state toward juveniles. Indeed, the actual workings of the "justice" system require us to ask whether the state really *likes* children. At all points in the processing and handling of youth it offers minimal and reluctant recognition of their legal rights and civil liberties (Renn, 1973). It permits or encourages coercive intervention into the life situations of minors who have committed no offense chargeable under adult criminal laws; it casts most of them aside, stigmatized but unaided; and it reserves a select proportion for involuntary confinement in programs of dubious value. Meanwhile, other community services are denied to most of these youths once they have entered the justice system. The expectation that the justice system can offer effective remedial aid to most youth with problems is as valid as an expectation that the highway department can resolve the energy crisis.

3. *Countervailing developments now provide the bases for potential improvements in juvenile justice across the nation—if their positive elements can be brought into combined focus.* Among these has been the strengthening of individual rights and civil liberties through federal court decisions, and a new

willingness by the courts to handle cases involving state activity in corrections and related areas (Wald and Schwartz, 1974). Legislatures have been slow to anchor these rights, obligations, and constraints in statutory law, which have been only limitedly extended to juveniles.

Minority groups continue to press their claims for equality, equity, and fairness. They have met with grudging recognition and some notable successes. Having no broad political base and lacking powerful allies, however, children will probably become the nation's last oppressed minority. But the responsiveness that other minority groups have kindled can be argued as inevitably working in their favor. Children must secure recognition in law as persons with substantive rights, and the gains won for others must be extended to them.

Developments among state governments offer promise, if their negative potentials can be contained. State governments are gradually becoming less aloof from assuming their proper responsibilities for juvenile justice, and are establishing or expanding *state* agencies to perform certain services that previously were entirely relegated to local governments. Some states are more willing to allocate state resources, to establish minimum standards, and to impose constraints on local units by regulation, monitoring, or supervision. But there are no guarantees that states will be more progressive than local units have been, and we face the risk that state governments will merely *expand* juvenile justice systems, thus recruiting even larger numbers of youth who do not need that kind of intervention. State administrators, to a greater degree than local officials, however, have more freedom and more resources to effect positive changes if they choose to.

There also appears to be growing concern about the high costs of justice system operations, especially for correctional facilities. Increasing competition for state allocations can be joined with a now pervasive skepticism about whether conventional correctional programs are effective, even in maintaining security and control. The chorus of those supporting centralized state facilities has dwindled over the years as authoritative opinion leaders, government bodies, and the mass media have exposed the costliness, the futility and ineffectiveness, and the frequent brutality of prisons and training schools.

4. *"Decriminalization," "diversion," and "deinstitutionalization" are perceived as key concepts for action implementation almost simultaneously with "deterrence," "punishment," and "retribution."* Behavior associated with each of these concepts can be observed in local and state governments throughout the country. The pattern is usually haphazard and almost no attention is given to the fundamental contradiction implied by these contrasting paths. Implementation of strategies associated with the former set of concepts should result in contraction of the juvenile justice system. But one also hears discussion of

expansion and punishment. Comparative analyses reveal that the numbers of juveniles being processed into and through the system is increasing substantially in many states, and particularly in some areas of the system where the risk of long-term harm is aggravated, for example, increases in the placement of juveniles in adult jails (U.S. DHEW, 1974). Counties and municipalities can proceed—and many are—to lock up more youths in jails, and they can reproduce correctional programs (under the guise of community services) that rival any state-level program in punitiveness and ineffectiveness (Mattick, 1974). Community frustration because of increasing crime and ineffective past interventions may result in the waiver of more youth to adult courts for processing as adults into adult programs (Keiter, 1973). In contrast to trends in most European countries, the United States appears to be blurring the differentiation between adults and juveniles for purposes of criminal court processing. When no obvious benefits can be shown to accrue for society from such policies, one can only conclude that punishment and control are primary motivations for such action.

5. *Community conditions and juvenile justice.* The character of juvenile justice is critically shaped by the local community, which can also escalate or alleviate the problems of this system. Community opportunities, resources, and services define the basic life conditions of children and generate the main motives for deviant behavior. Community toleration of youth behavior, or pressure to cope more stringently with it, directly affect the rates and volume of cases presented for formal handling (Cumming, 1968). The responsiveness of community institutions and agencies determines whether youth in trouble will be isolated within the justice system, or will be offered helping bridges toward satisfying and conventional social life (Cressey and McDermott, 1973). The substance of state law delineates which youth behavior *may not* be subjected to legal processing, but forces within the community determine how many of which youths *shall be* channeled for such processing. Evidence from across the nation can be read, at worst, as suggesting collusion among influential community elements to send more and more youths into the justice system; at best, the evidence can be read as revealing a slow drift toward more formal handling and processing of youth rather than *serving* them through basic social institutions. Even under optimum community conditions, we seldom find truly comprehensive and concerted efforts to aid children in trouble outside the justice system. Real diversion and effective community-based programming require a revitalizing of local commitment and institutions on behalf of all youth, but especially those with problems, and new strategies for collaboration to serve youths in trouble away from the court and correctional agency (Arthur D. Little, 1974).

There are fundamental connections between the juvenile justice system and community conditions, and particularly its schools and service agencies. These units play a major role in validating the existence and seriousness of youth problems that allegedly can only be served through court intervention, and thus in legitimating the operations of the entire system as it impinges on juveniles. Minors defined as engaging in deviant but not illegal behavior—especially status offenders—could not be nominated or recruited into the justice system without the consent—witting or otherwise—of professionals and agency spokesmen whom the public regards as having expert knowledge of these matters, and who acquiesce in assertions that there are no other suitable means to deal with such needs and problems. These persons and agencies know well why such youths have not and will not be served adequately through conventional agencies, including the schools, and the real nature and origins of their problems. They should also know—although many may not—what is and what is not happening *within* the justice system. Failure to proclaim that it does not and cannot remedy the problems assigned to it has the effect of authenticating both its rationale and its operations (Ferster and Courtless, 1972). The acquiescence of these persons and agencies has been part of a "noble lie," and in our view constitutes negligence if not culpability.

SYSTEMS OF JUVENILE JUSTICE

Although the term *justice system* has come into common use and is accepted as if it referred to something real, nowhere is there a definition of what is meant, a delineation of the components and boundaries, or a statement of how it works. Observation provides ample support for generalizations about interdependencies among differentiated units and actors having frequent interactions with each other, but whether these approach the criteria of social systems remains doubtful for most of the nation.

The dual aims of NAJC have been to obtain reliable data about the characteristics and operations of several key components of juvenile justice and corrections (e.g., the courts, state corrections agencies, juvenile codes, correctional programs) *and* to examine the interconnections among these components. The understanding generated by each of these directions of research has relevance for the other and for comprehension of whether and how events in one area or at one level are affected by those in another. Thus, for example, we are interested in how substantive differences in state juvenile codes affect the ways that youth are handled through the courts, and in how the policies of state correctional bureaucracies affect the nature and operations of particular correctional programs.

The notion that there are or should be justice systems was promoted in the

report of the President's Commission on Law Enforcement and the Administration of Justice in 1967. It was further embodied in the Omnibus Crime
Control Act of 1968 which led to the establishment of state planning agencies
and critical roles for state government in establishing standards, priorities, and
new programs.

Juvenile statutes and judicial decisions provide the primary normative content
of contemporary justice systems, and courts are acknowledged to be the pivotal
units within the state and federal systems. Judicial codes and related enactments
not only contain provisions that define policies and procedures of courts and
their personnel but also define roles of many governmental agencies. Of critical
importance to the juvenile justice system are the correctional agencies that
render direct services to youth, but also included are planning, funding,
coordinating, and monitoring units.

In addition to the public sector, private organizations at the local, state, and
national levels often assume key roles in planning and provision of services. One
has only to note recent litigation by the Children's Defense Fund and other
organizations to see their significance (Edelman, 1974).

Federal statutes and agencies provide other elements of the so-called juvenile
justice system. Until very recently the federal-state articulation has been
haphazard and infrequent, with the federal role largely restricted to the
provision of grant funds for state and local programs, and the stimulus of a few
major Supreme Court decisions. The passage of Public Law 93-415, the Juvenile
Justice and Delinquency Prevention Act of 1974, offers some promise for a
reversal of past practice, but thus far little actual change has been effected.

STATE-LEVEL JUVENILE CORRECTIONS

Given the structure of federal-state relationships and the absence of
operational national policy, juvenile justice programs, policies, and problems are
essentially either the direct resultants of state government activity, or are
local-level events largely constrained or facilitated by state-level policies and
conditions. Everywhere, of course, juvenile courts are entities of state
government, but they are peculiarly responsive to local circumstances because of
vagueness or broad discretionary latitude in state juvenile codes, historical
patterns, and a status somewhat detached from other judicial structures in many
states. State control over juvenile correctional programs is probably much
greater and certainly much more extensive than has been recognized in the
literature or among professionals in the field. In almost all states the
overwhelming proportions of young offenders are committed to the state and
are handled in diverse correctional programs directly operated by the state

corrections agency or funded in whole or large part by it (U.S. LEAA, 1974). Examination of juvenile justice in general and juvenile corrections in particular must, therefore, address the role of state governments.

NAJC field staff conducted reconnaissance trips for observation and interviewing of officials and interest-group leaders in a majority of the states, and collected standardized data through file examination and interviews with juvenile corrections administrators in all fifty states. Analysis of these materials, and of the voluminous reports and publications issued by state agencies over a period of years, has generated comparative knowledge of state government policies and policy outputs across the nation.

Juvenile justice appears to be a relatively *marginal* area of governmental activity everywhere. This both confounds the difficulties of identifying causes of change and clarifies our discovery of little correlation between states' policies in juvenile justice and their other fiscal and policy decisions. Regardless of how large certain justice budget line items may seem, or how salient litigation or code revision may be to some, the issues and dollars involved are almost insignificant compared to the state resources allocated to public education, or the current issues of energy shortages, unemployment—and even adult corrections. The reality of marginality is also demonstrated by the very small proportions of state LEAA funds allocated to juvenile corrections, and is echoed in a state legislator's report of his difficulties in getting juvenile justice on *any*one's agenda, from the general public to the state legislature. Given this essential marginality, we are not surprised to find that juvenile justice has no general constituency among the states, that few interest groups regularly attend to it, that coalitions of interest groups and political and governmental leaders seldom form to push for change, and that important events (other than incidents of crime) are usually relegated to the inside or back pages of the newspapers. In a very real sense, it is much easier to explain why progress does *not* occur in this area than to trace out the reasons for varying directions and rates of change among the states.

The fact of marginality, however, has not offset the growth of state and local bureaucracies, plus numerous private agencies, that deal with young offenders. In many states a marked series of disjunctures is evident between the activities of these various agencies, especially between the state and local levels. State systems thus often appear as disjointed congeries of units operating in partly autonomous ways, with little coordination at any level. Furthermore, policy and program issues of concern in some states are substantially different from those receiving attention elsewhere; in fact, the policy, structure, or program *solutions* chosen by some states represent the *problems* rejected by other states.

The dominant trends across the states are not, as some would like to believe, toward deinstitutionalization or reforming juvenile corrections or contracting state activities in this area while expanding them through other services to juveniles in trouble. The most prevalent developments have been reorganization, extension, and consolidation of state responsibility and activity, turnover among top administrators, and concern about rising costs. In the past five years 17 states have undergone two or more reorganizations that affected juvenile corrections, and 41 states have had at least one. Juvenile corrections is usually simply caught in the backwash of major statewide reorganizations which, in some states, seem to follow on the heels of each gubernatorial election. In a few states these changes have become almost an annual event, and one state managed to reorganize completely twice in the same month, leaving the executive confused about his mailing address as well as his agency's location in state government.

Through these changes state juvenile correctional services are being variously linked or merged with adult corrections (19 states), or unlinked from adult services and combined with other agencies responsible for youth services. Increasingly, juvenile corrections is being relocated in larger superagencies (31 states). In almost none of these structural reorderings is there a necessary or inevitable change in the agency's operational autonomy, status or resources, or functional responsibilities, and these are dependent on still other arrangements or provisions.

The trend toward *centralized* state responsibility for providing an increasing range of services for young offenders is also marked. Fifteen states have now assumed some or all administrative responsibility for institutions, aftercare, *and* probation services. Local units of government are by no means fading out of the picture, nor are private agencies. Extension of state responsibility and activity also can be seen in funding, standard-setting, monitoring and enforcement of standards, or coordinating local-level services.

The *consolidation* of state-level services appears to be another trend, although its forms are even more diverse. Thus, while 15 states have consolidated probation, institution, and aftercare services into a single state agency (often with local-level involvement), 15 other states have apportioned these responsibilities among separate agencies. Many states are concerned about how best to combine or integrate juvenile justice services with social services, mental health and mental retardation, adult corrections, and more lately with public education, manpower or human development programs, etc. Better integration is sometimes sought by outright merger of two or more of these services, and sometimes by retention of agency status combined under larger "umbrella" or superagencies, as we have noted. Everywhere we have found major problems in achieving closely meshed collaboration among services for young offenders and other youth with related problems or characteristics. Furthermore, these problems persist at all levels of government, and of administration or operation.

There is little consensus among the states about *which* services should be more closely linked to juvenile justice, or about the most appropriate forms for these links among state government agencies. Policy makers differ considerably in their views of which combinations are most desirable or feasible. They have limited knowledge of comparable concerns and developments in other states and, more important, almost no valid information for assessing the actual consequences of one rather than another pattern of interservice consolidation or collaboration between levels of government.

Interviews with state executives and examination of state agency files and statistics yielded much quantitative information which, in combination with data from other sources, provides new understanding about current practices across the nation, about policy outputs of states relevant to juvenile justice and corrections, and about directions of development and change. We are now able to provide informed answers to such questions as: How many juveniles are being handled in the nation's total justice system? Where are these youth located within the system, and how many are assigned to what kinds of correctional programs? What are the costs of operating these programs? To what extent have states moved toward deinstitutionalization and the development of community alternatives to training schools? [2]

Numbers of Youth in Juvenile Justice

Because adequate information procedures are lacking at the local, state, and national levels, it is not possible to report accurately even the number of juveniles who are processed through the justice systems each year. In 1972 at least 1,112,500 delinquency cases were processed by the nation's juvenile courts, based on information from voluntary reports to the U.S. Department of Health, Education, and Welfare (1974). Adding the numbers of delinquents held in detention facilities, jails, institutions, on probation, and so forth easily produces a conservative estimate in excess of 2 million cases. There is no way to determine the extent of overlap, and therefore no reliable means of estimating an unduplicated count of individuals. However, given an estimated child population of 52.8 million between the ages of 5 and 18 in 1972, it can be noted that 1 of every 26 youth is potentially processed as a delinquent each year in the United States. Obviously, were it possible to have an unduplicated count of delinquents, we would learn that some youth are processed many times each year, while the overwhelming majority are processed one or no times (Wolfgang et al., 1972).

Approximately 25% of the 1.1 million juvenile court cases deal with females, and 65% involve youth from urban areas. About 85,000 youth are committed to state public residential programs each year, and approximately 20,000 are handled in local and private residential units (U.S. LEAA, 1974; Pappenfort et al., 1970). Thus, the numbers of youth processed as delinquents are staggering and there is little evidence of parsimony in intervention, as we shall note subsequently. Moreover, there is little reason to be optimistic that positive change is now widespread: NAJC's comparisons between 1966, 1971, and 1974 show as many increases as decreases among states in the numbers of youth handled through certain of these channels.

Jailing and Detention: Perhaps the single most disturbing problem in juvenile justice today is the increasing placement of juveniles in adult jails prior to adjudication hearings or trials. It is estimated that at least 500,000 youth are held in *adult jails* each year and slightly under 500,000 in *juvenile detention* facilities.[3] This total of nearly one million youth vastly exceeds the yearly total of 85,000 of all youth held in all public training schools, ranches, camps, and halfway houses. In other words, for every 10 youth incarcerated in all types of correctional programs, 9 of them are in jails or detention units. Were we to include police lockups and other short-term holding facilities, the numbers would be far higher.

Placement in jails and detention varies greatly from one state to another, from a combined rate of 2.28 per 100,000 youth in North Dakota to 114.62 in New York. Although these facilities are largely operated by local courts and county government, increasingly the state is assuming responsibility for planning, standard-setting, and supervision of program implementation. Since experiences in jails are so overwhelmingly negative for youth, and since admissions have increased rapidly in some areas, state control appears essential if increases are not to continue unabated (Sarri, 1974). There were no youth found in jails in Connecticut, Delaware, Hawaii, Massachusetts, New Hampshire, Rhode Island, and Vermont at the time of the 1970 LEAA census, and these were all places where the state government had assumed substantial responsibility for the operation of jails and detention facilities.

Particularly problematic about the placement of juveniles in jail is the disproportionate representation of status offenders, minority group youth, and females. Statutes governing jailing and detention are notoriously ambiguous and provide almost no protection against inappropriate detention (Levin and Sarri, 1974).

State Institutions: Despite much publicized movement toward the handling of adjudicated delinquents within communities where they live, the traditional training school or public institution continues to be the dominant choice for disposition of juvenile offenders. On an average day in 1974, over 28,000 juvenile offenders were incarcerated in state-operated training schools and camps, while only 5,663 were in state-operated or state-funded community-based residential programs. This represents a substantial reduction from the 35,931 children reported in public training schools on June 30, 1971 (U.S. LEAA, 1974), but given the changes in policies governing the incarceration of status offenders (CHINS, PINS, etc.), it may represent a reduction in primarily these types of cases.[4] However, when compared with an earlier census of all children's institutions in 1966, the institutionalization of juvenile offenders in state facilities shows a consistent downward trend for the nation as a whole: 40,825 juvenile delinquents in state public institutions and 5,585 in local residential facilities were reported then (Pappenfort et al., 1970).

The average daily population of youth in state institutions varied from 56 to 2,858 during 1974, with a mean of 560 for all states. When these data are translated into rates controlling for the total population, major differences in degrees of institutionalization among the states become clear. The highest rate (41 per 100,000) is 19 times the lowest (2.1), and no consistent regional differences were noted. Association with other sociodemographic state characteristics indicate modest negative correlations between rate of institutionalization and percent of states' urbanized populations (−.38), their per capita incomes (−.31), and industrialization (−.44). Thus, wealthier, more urbanized and industrialized states appear less likely to rely heavily on the use of institutions.

Expenditures for institutionalization are of rising concern because of the rapid increases in residential costs in recent years and budget crises in most states. Fiscal data were obtained only for annual operating expenditures, not capital or construction costs, so that they permit determination of per-offender costs, relative levels of fiscal effort, and interconnection between cost measures and other data. States reported spending more than 300 million dollars during fiscal 1974 on the operation of their institutions, ranches, and camps. Twenty-seven states spent less than 5 million, and 7 spent more than 10 million, with a mean of 6.2 million. Annual per-offender costs for institutions, camps, and ranches average $11,657, with a low of $3,798 and a high of $39,625.[5] A correlation of .51 was obtained between states' per capita income and per-offender expenditures, suggesting that wealthier states are more able or willing to spend more per offender in institutional programs.[6]

Community-Based Programs: Widespread interest continues to be shown in the development of community-based correctional programs for offenders —especially for juveniles—as alternatives to more conventional institutional facilities. The conclusions of the President's Commission on Law Enforcement and Administration of Justice authoritatively affirmed the views of many that institutions (and especially larger, closed facilities) had "failed" and that there was much rehabilitative promise in turning to community approaches.

The tremendous variety of conceptions and actual types of community correctional programs existing in 1974 required that we impose our own definition in the collection of data from states about these services. For these purposes, then, we define community-based programs as state-operated or state-funded residential agencies located in urban locales that generally handle between 5 and 30 adjudicated offenders. They are distinguished from institutions not only by their community locations and smaller size but also by their encouragement for offenders' attendance at local schools or their involvement in local employment. These kinds of programs are often referred to as halfway houses, and sometimes as group homes or group care homes (Keller and Alper, 1970). This definition excludes nonresidential, or "day treatment," programs, although in some states a few offenders were allowed to live outside the residential agency.

Only in four states (Massachusetts, Minnesota, South Dakota and Utah) did offenders in community-based programs equal or outnumber those in institutional programs; and in only four other states (Oregon, North Dakota, Maryland, and Kansas) did the number of juveniles in community-based programs roughly approximate the number in institutions. Across the 48 reporting states a mean average of only 18% of all youths in state-related corrections were assigned to community-based programs.

Great variability was observed in state use of community-based corrections: the highest rate of 20.5 per 100,000 is 100 times larger than the lowest rate of .2, and six states reported no state-related community-based programs. In contrast to rates of institutionalization, there are relatively few even moderately strong associations. The correlation with percentages of urbanized population is $-.12$, and .02 with level of income, but a fairly strong negative association $(-.45)$ was found with the percentage of the population having less than five years education, suggesting that community corrections may be more favorably viewed by a better-educated citizenry.

The states spent a total of less than $30 million on the operation of community-based programs in fiscal 1974, and more than half the states spent less than $300,000, only a small percentage of what was spent for institutional care. Average per-offender costs were $5,501, less than half the average institutional cost of $11,657. Use of state funds to develop community-based programs through purchase-of-service arrangements with other agencies (non-profit or commercial enterprises, or agencies of local governments) is more extensive and less costly than direct operation of those programs under state government. The use of outside resources seems to provide greater capacity and more flexibility, and probably greater rapidity of program development, than when the state seeks to expand its own facilities and operative personnel.

Because institutions frequently provide a wider range of services than community-based programs, any direct comparison is extremely complex. A Wisconsin policy paper supported the emphases on community programming because of the "unfavorable cost-effectiveness of incarceration when compared to the cost-effectiveness of probation and parole and other alternatives" (Wisconsin Department of Health and Social Services, 1973). The explanation offered was that institutional programs must invest heavily in custodial staff, with three-fourths of the expenditures going for maintenance costs, and over half the staff reporting themselves as security or supportive staff. In addition, institutional programs duplicated schools, vocational training, and health facilities found in the community. It is often true that these extra services in institutions are provided at a greater cost than would prevail for the same or similar programs in the community.

Foster Care: It is very difficult to obtain reliable information about the placement of adjudicated offenders in state-funded foster homes because data may not be systematically recorded and summarized, or because of variable patterns of retaining such information among the states. Nonetheless, on an average day 8,000 adjudicated delinquents were reported as living in state-funded foster homes. It is noteworthy that this figure is *greater* than the number of offenders in community-based group programs. In fiscal 1974 the states spent $10 million on foster care, far less than on institutional or community-based programs. The cost of maintaining a youth in foster care averaged less than $2,500 per year, so this disposition should be attractive to cost-conscious state legislators and administrators. However, the level of foster care appears to have been on a plateau in many states because the payment per child-day has been too low relative to costs for the foster parents. Thus it has become more and more difficult to recruit competent foster parents without increasing fees and hence costs.

The states ranking highest per capita in assignment of juvenile offenders to state-related noninstitutional correctional programs are as follows: *State-Operated Community-Based Programs*—(1) Florida, (2) Oregon, (3) Michigan, (4) Arizona, (5) North Dakota, (6) Washington, (7) Missouri, (8) New York, (9) Maryland, and (10) Utah; *State-Funded Community-Based Programs*—(1) South Dakota, (2) Oregon, (3) Utah, (4) Massachusetts, (5) Wyoming, (6) Minnesota, (7) Idaho, (8) Kansas, (9) Montana, and (10) Maryland; *State-Operated and State-Funded Community-Based Programs (Combined)*—(1) Oregon, (2) South Dakota, (3) Utah, (4) Massachusetts, (5) Wyoming, (6) Minnesota, (7) Idaho, (8)

Maryland, (9) Kansas, and (10) Montana; *State Foster Homes*—(1) Utah, (2) Wyoming, (3) South Dakota, (4) Alaska, (5) West Virginia, (6) Idaho, (7) Kansas, (8) Maine, (9) Iowa, and (10) Nebraska.

Deinstitutionalization: Ever since the endorsement of community-based alternatives to incarceration by the President's Commission in 1967, advocacy of deinstitutionalization has taken on some of the aspects of a social movement. Despite the lack of a firm foundation of factual knowledge, one can easily find highly persuasive arguments about the advantages of community-based programs. These rationales do not necessarily call for the demise of institutions, but most do seek to reduce the proportion of youth hwo are incarcerated in them. Not infrequently the term "diversion" is used inappropriately to refer to the channeling of youth to community-based corrections in lieu of institutionalization, but this is an improper use of the term, for such youth are not diverted from the juvenile justice system. By "deinstitutionalization" we mean the development and use of community-based programs as alternatives to institutions.

Throughout the United States there is a high level of interest in reducing institutional populations, and, as noted earlier, there has been a substantial reduction nationally in the number of youth placed in state institutions for juvenile offenders.

When comparisons are made between the number of youth who are assigned to community-based programs and those in institutions, almost two-thirds of the states had less than 25% of their offender population in community programs. In fact, six states had no community-based services at all for youth. Only a minority of states have reached significant levels in community programming. There is no geographical basis for the patterns in which Delaware, Texas, and Ohio are lowest and Oregon, Massachusetts, and South Dakota highest in levels of deinstitutionalization.

The lack of association (.04) between deinstitutionalization and states' per capita use of institutional and community programs implies that shifting to community programming does not necessarily reduce the number of juvenile offenders handled by the state. Our findings suggest that community programming is being used as often to *supplement* as to *supplant* institutional services. The evidence does not support an interpretation that community programs are mainly or generally used as alternatives to institutional commitments.

How then do the ten most deinstitutionalized states differ from the ten least deinstitutionalized? The findings in Table 1 reveal marked differences in the average daily population in community programs; for the rate of assignment to

Table 1. PERFORMANCE CHARACTERISTICS OF THE TEN MOST AND LEAST
          DEINSTITUTIONALIZED STATES

	The 10 States Deinstitutionalized	
	Most	Least
Average percentage of daily population in community settings	48.2%	5.2%
Mean per capita rate of assignment to institutions and community programs	2.56	2.18
Rate of institutionalization	1.33	2.07
Average percentage of budget on community programming	27.0%	2.9%
Average per capita cost for institutions and community programs	$1.80	$2.03

institutions and community programs combined, however, the differences are
small and in the opposite direction. Although the economies resulting from
community programming are mostly offset by increased use of institutions and
community services, per capita expenditures are still somewhat lower for the
most deinstitutionalized states.

The Expansion Tendency: One of the most provocative questions surrounding the gradual movement toward community corrections is whether the
states that develop community programs use them to *replace* training schools or
use them *in addition to* training schools. Norval Morris has suggested that, unless
proper safeguards are instituted, the development of community-based corrections will result merely in the placement of more and more persons under
surveillance or control by the state:

> We risk substituting more pervasive but less punitive control mechanisms
> over a vastly larger number of citizens for our present discriminatory and
> irrational selection of fewer citizens for more punitive and draconian
> punishments. . . . The juvenile court itself was a diversionary program,
> aiming to reduce the impact of the criminal law on the young offender and
> to divert him to less punitive, rehabilitative controls. It has swept more
> children within the ambit of the criminal law than if the state had not
> gone coercively into the business of child saving by means of statutes ill
> defining delinquency. [Morris, 1974: 10-11]

Our data show that the development of community corrections is not associated with reduced rates of institutional incarceration. States that place more offenders in community-based programs do not place fewer in training schools, although there are several exceptions. In general, as the number of offenders in community-based facilities increases, the total number of youth incarcerated also increases.

When we examine placements in foster care, this expansionist tendency is further evident. States with high rates of institutional and community-based commitments also have high rates of foster care placements. Even more than community-based programming, foster care appears to be used as an extension of commitments rather than an alternative to them.

CORRECTIONAL PROGRAMS

The NAJC study of correctional programs included community-based residential and day treatment agencies, institutions, and aftercare services. Study of probation and detention services was done in relation to the juvenile court, and the latter findings are not reported here. The correctional programs are grouped into three types for this presentation of the data: (a) "closed" institutions, where the youth are removed from their usual social environment and 80% are confined within the agency all the time; (b) community residential facilities (group homes), where youth can interact with the surrounding community; and (c) day treatment programs, where youth live at home but are required to participate in a daily program at a specific location.

Extensive data were gathered from staff and youth in these programs, from parent organizations, and from official records. The data were collected as a basis for developing comprehensive and systematic statements about the functioning of various types of correctional programs. As such, it is distinct from many other evaluation studies which limit their attention to individual-level variables within the program and to postprogram outcomes for those same individuals. We sought to learn as much as possible about how these facilities operate, what their objectives are, and the level of staff effort required to produce first-order consequences.[7] The research was informed by the proposition that juvenile justice in general, and juvenile corrections in particular, have often failed in the primary mandate of processing and rehabilitating young offenders with a minimum of social dislocation of youths, communities, and resources. Obviously, however, not all aspects of this broad proposition could be examined fully. Attention was therefore concentrated on first- and second-order consequences within the boundaries of the correctional programs and in their environing communities at a specific point in time.

The information reported here is from field studies of a probability sample of 42 programs in a universe of 922 juvenile correctional programs. The universe included all major types of programs, jurisdictions, auspices, sizes, and age ranges.

Our summary presentation of findings from the study of correctional programs will include the following:

(a) Youth characteristics

(b) Staff characteristics

(c) Organizational practices regarding control procedures and humaneness

(d) Some consequences of labeling

Youth Characteristics

1. As the findings in Table 2 show, the mean age of youth was 15.8 years, with a range between 8 and 24 years. The youngest mean-age population was

Table 2. ATTRIBUTES OF OFFENDERS BY TYPE OF CORRECTIONAL PROGRAM

	Institution	Community Residential	Day Treatment
Race			
Minority (%)	54	46	66
White (%)	46	54	34
Age			
Mean (years)	15.7	16.7	16.2
Range (years)	8-24	13-24	12-22
Social class			
Unemployed or working-class parent (%)	59	40	60
Sex			
Male (%)	71	62	84
Female (%)	29	38	16
Prior correctional experiences (mean number of times)			
Arrested	8.0	6.3	6.0
Detention	4.5	4.8	3.4
Jail	3.2	2.0	1.5
Court	5.5	5.7	4.3
Probation	2.0	1.2	1.5
Group or foster home	1.2	1.5	0.3
Institution	1.7	1.0	0.5
(Range of n)	*(1269-1341)*	*(145-152)*	*(224-238)*

observed in institutions (15.7), with 16.7 for community residential and 16.2 for day treatment programs. These findings refute the popular assumption that institutions are places of last resort for older offenders.

2. More than half the youth (55%) belong to minority racial groups, with blacks constituting the largest single group (32.2% of the total sample). Day treatment programs are 67% nonwhite, which appears to be due to their location within central cities of major metropolitan areas. These data suggest an increase in nonwhite percentages during the past decade where comparisons can be made with other similar data. Since the minority percentage of the total national population is approximately 15%, these findings clearly indicate that juvenile correctional programs disproportionately represent minority populations. Overall, however, we have no information showing that minority youth are more delinquent than whites, either in terms of self-reported frequency or engagement in a variety of delinquent behaviors or in terms of the offenses for which they were committed. These findings are generally in accord with Williams and Gold (1972), who observed only small differences in seriousness of delinquency between blacks and whites.

3. Seventy-two percent of all program youth are male and 28% female. This is relatively similar to the proportions of males and females in cases processed by juvenile courts (U.S. DHEW, 1974) but evidences a small tendency for increased incarceration of females. As will be noted subsequently, the differences are dramatically greater when commitment-offense patterns are examined.

4. Reports by youth of prior correctional experiences are extensive in all types of programs, particularly in terms of incarceration in detention, jails, and institutions rather than placement on probation or in foster homes. Youth in institutions do report more frequent experience in the justice system, and this is noteworthy when it is recalled that these are the youngest population. Day treatment programs predominantly have urban males with the least prior experience in juvenile justice agencies.

There are marked variations in the patterns of commitment offense for the different types of correctional programs, as Table 3 reveals. First, the proportion of youth in institutions committed there for status and other minor offenses is high, and surprisingly so for females (50%). It would be expected that youth charged with such offenses might well be handled in day treatment programs or perhaps in group homes. However, when the nature of the status offenses was examined further, it was noted that consistently more males than females charged with school- or family-related offenses are in day treatment centers. Similarly, regardless of offense, females were more likely to be institutionalized.

A relatively small proportion of all these juveniles were committed for person crimes (15%), but particularly significant is the observation that substantial

Table 3. COMMITMENT OFFENSE, BY PROGRAM TYPE AND SEX (in percentages)

	Status[a] Offense	Probation or Parole Violation	Mis- demeanor	Drugs or Alcohol	Prop- erty	Person	(n)
Institution							
Male	23	4	2	6	46	18	(832)
Female	50	1	3	18	14	14	(349)
Community Residential							
Male	50	3	1	10	26	10	(70)
Female	67	3	0	14	12	3	(58)
Day Treatment							
Male	45	3	4	6	30	12	(164)
Female	87	0	0	5	3	5	(37)

NOTE: Determination of commitment offense was based on youth response to the question, "Why were you sent here?"

a. Status offenses include incorrigibility, dependent and neglected, truancy, running away, curfew violations, disorderly, etc.

numbers of such youth are found in all types of programs. This finding would indicate that placement in closed institutions is apparently not essential for all offenders charged with serious crimes, such as those against persons. Staff in the more open, community-based programs reported no greater difficulty handling these youth than did staff in institutions. The concept of "minimal penetration" has become popular among juvenile justice practitioners. If this concept were implemented, we would expect to find more minority youth, females, and younger offenders in open community programs. Similarly, we would expect greater use of mild rather than severe sanctions, but just the opposite is true, for all types of programs.

Staff Characteristics

Many students of human service organizations assert that reduction in social distance between staff and clients is a desirable and perhaps necessary precondition for successful intervention (Grosser et al., 1969; Moos, 1974). In the juvenile correctional programs surveyed by NAJC, similarities rather than differences among staff were noteworthy. When comparing staff with youth, however, there were pronounced disproportions with respect to sex and race. As Table 4 shows, staff are generally young, male, white, married personnel who have been engaged in work with youth for many years. Overall educational background characteristics indicate that they are probably better prepared in

Table 4. STAFF CHARACTERISTICS BY OCCUPATIONAL SUBGROUPS

	Median Age	Male (%)	White (%)	Mar-ried (%)	With Degree (%)	% with 5 Years in			(n)
						Pro-gram	Correc-tions	Work with Children	
Executive	34	80	84	61	63	35	53	85	(48)
Treatment	30	68	68	55	72	21	25	44	(213)
Teaching	35	56	70	66	73	25	26	56	(196)
Living unit	34	52	68	59	29	18	22	33	(260)
Clerical & maint.	39	43	76	73	19	26	30	47	(162)
Aggregate	35	60	73	63	51	25	32	53	(879)

terms of formal education than were personnel in adult corrections last surveyed nationally in 1966 (Joint Commission on Correctional Manpower and Training, 1969).

Minority-group representation among staff is relatively low (27%) considering that 50% of the youth served in these programs are nonwhite. Comparisons, however, with Joint Commission findings (1969) indicate that minority-group staff representation has increased considerably in recent years. With respect to executive staff, improvement is far less apparent, for 5 out of 6 executives were found to be white, and 4 out of 5 male. Male administrators predominate even in the female and coed programs.

Only small differences were observed in staff characteristics when comparisons were made by program type. Community residential agencies tend to have slightly higher proportions of females, and institutional staff are slightly older, less educated, and have longer tenure in their current position.

The average unit has staff of whom 50% have five years prior experience in working with children and 25% of whom have five years prior experience in the program in which they are currently employed. These data suggest relatively longer staff tenure than is often reported for comparable human service organizations.

Staff were asked about their perceptions of the relative importance of a range of goals typically pursued by juvenile correctional agencies (Street et al., 1966). These included educational, custodial, treatment, and organizational maintenance goals. Staff were asked their perceptions of "actual" goals (whose high importance was evidenced by actual practice at the program) and of "ideal" goals (what *"you yourself* think . . . *should be"*). A total of 1,175 staff in the 42 programs responded, with the following summarized results.

1. Five categories of staff concern were identified from their responses:

(a) Treatment aspects of the program

(b) Local community interactions

(c) Staff working conditions

(d) Custodial elements of the program

(e) Interorganizational contacts

2. With respect to *actual* goal priorities, the treatment of youth is perceived as most important by all staff groups. Custodial considerations are second in importance for all staff groups except the executive core, who view these next to lowest. Interorganizational contacts are perceived as least important by all staff groups except clerical and maintenance personnel, who view them as of medium importance.

3. Comparison of actual with ideal goal perceptions shows that executives are reluctant to admit any discrepancies between them. Staff working conditions are thought to be the most neglected and in greatest need of improvement. All staff agree that custodial concerns should be de-emphasized and that treatment should receive greater emphasis. Providing youth a background in vocational skills is viewed as the single highest treatment priority. Perhaps surprisingly, some interorganizational exchanges and local community involvement are perceived as requiring less attention.

4. When comparisons are made by program, despite the alleged primary importance of treatment, de-emphasis of custodial concerns receives the highest "ideal" score across all program types. Perhaps staff view this de-emphasis as an essential precondition for increasing treatment priorities. Staff across all program types view the custodial approach to juvenile offenders as misguided. Ideally, they say, understanding and help are needed if rehabilitation is to be achieved.

Organizational Patterns—Control and Humaneness

Control and Discipline: Control and discipline are deemed to be essential elements of correctional programs, but they are seldom examined from the perspective of program effect or impact upon youth in the long run rather than in the immediate situation. For example, much attention today is given to increasing control and discipline in the public school because of violent behavior by some youth. Yet few persons seem to be apprehensive about possible serious negative consequences of being educated in a highly controlled social environment. In juvenile corrections there is a tendency to consider policies, rules, practices, and "hardware" independently, ignoring the inevitable interrelationships among them, or as inevitable accoutrements of correctional facilities. In the analysis of staff perspectives on organizational goals, custody was viewed consistently second in importance among five areas of concern. But it was also observed that control policies and practices differ widely among correctional programs, so it is appropriate to inquire if there are varying effects on youth.

One of the basic dilemmas administrators face in evaluating the balance between control and treatment is whether or not the program environment facilitates the development of healthy and socially desirable behavior and attitudes on the part of youth. More than a decade ago, correctional administrators adopted the following guideline:

> A too restrictive program defeats its own immediate purpose of main-taining close physical control and defeats the training school's basic function of rehabilitation as well. In deciding what should or should not be permitted, the training school should be guided, as far as possible, by what is normal and natural behavior for youngsters. Because it is caring for many children, among whom are a substantial number who, at least temporarily, require close supervision if further delinquencies are to be prevented, it is necessary for the training school to impose many limitations beyond those found in the average home or community. Within these added limitations, however, the aim should be to let youngsters act and be as much like their contemporaries as possible. [National Conference of Superintendents of Training Schools and Reformatories, 1962: 143]

In a variety of ways—generalized surveillance, sanctioning, and punishing—the institutions in this study impose much tighter and harsher controls than do day treatment or community-based residential facilities. We also observed evidence of more internal disorder in institutions in both administrative and youth reports, but cannot determine if this is a result or a cause of the greater restrictiveness. We also do not know to what extent youth's potential misconduct is thwarted by the more restrictive control in institutions, but we do know that the rules and sanctions that are imposed do not lower the misconduct below that of group homes and day treatment centers. The latter programs do not incur greater costs in terms of disruption and disorderly conduct by youth even though they allow more freedom and flexibility of movement to youth.

Differences between institutions and other facilities can be illustrated with the following findings:

1. *Assignment of youth to discipline rooms or units for misconduct.* Only 43% of the institutions have a policy that youth cannot be held in discipline rooms more than a week, whereas all the day treatment and group homes have such a policy. As a result, youth report greatly different experiences. No one in a group home or day treatment facility remained in discipline units more than two days, whereas in institutions 29% stayed up to six days, and another 29%

remained there between one and four weeks. In addition there were many behaviors in institutions that are more often a basis for assignment to discipline than in the other types of facilities (e.g., fighting, running away, hurting oneself, stealing, homosexuality).

2. *Transfer to other facilities.* If a youth misbehaved, he was more likely to be transferred from a group home or day treatment center than from an institution. Nonetheless, 27% of the institutions also report use of transfer to control behavior.

3. *Differential treatment.* There is no evidence of any systematic modification of discipline and punishment for status offenders as contrasted to youth charged with serious crime, nor is there any evidence of less stringent sanctions in female or coed institutions as compared to male institutions. Obviously, however, the forms of misconduct vary by sexual composition of the unit. It must be borne in mind that at least 31% of the institutionalized youth were status offender commitments (and that proportion increases to 50% for females). Females are dealt with more harshly for relatively minor offenses, and they report more extensive rules governing daily behavior. In fact, sex is a more critical variable in explaining the application of severe sanctions overall.

4. *Youth response to rules.* When asked a variety of questions pertaining to clothing and hairstyle, privacy, contact with family and friends, and so forth, both males and females are more positive about the rules and living conditions in community residential and day treatment programs. Females in institutions expressed the most dissatisfaction with the numbers of rules and restrictions. For coeducational programs dissatisfaction dropped substantially in a variety of areas (e.g., informal daily life, residential conditions, and homosexuality).

Fairness, Humaneness, and Justice: National attention to the lack of standards for the care and treatment of incarcerated youth, and the increase in litigation focused on ensuring basic rights and constitutional safeguards for all youth in correctional programs, reinforced NAJC's concern for adequate standards in our study of correctional programs. The statement of the National Advisory Commission on Criminal Justice Standards and Goals (1973) was used, along with other nationally accepted materials, to formulate measures assessing fairness, humaneness, and justice. Preliminary findings show that nearly twice as many staff as youth report no differences in fairness of treatment because of race or ethnicity. Youth report far more racism than staff, but, interestingly, they also report that racism is most problematic in interaction with other youth rather than with staff. With respect to handling rule violations, substantial proportions of both youth and staff maintain that they would not prefer uniform or undifferentiated application of policies or rules.

Humaneness is a recognized issue in all programs, but it is more salient in youth than in staff responses. The majority of youth are concerned about the amount and severity of punishment. Nearly half express dissatisfaction with the availability of medical or dental services. Observations of our research staff indicate a greater normalization of living conditions and adolescent life-styles. The lack of privacy, insufficient contact with family and friends, and various censorship practices continue to be of concern to large proportions of youth in the residential programs.

Responses about *justice* suggest that the correctional law revolution has not been felt in the juvenile area to the same extent as in adult programs. Most juveniles report minimal contact with lawyers or legal services. A large majority reported that staff do not discuss legal rights with them. Staff responses also indicate little concern with legal rights and intervention or advocacy for youth.

Whether the control practices found in the institutions, community-based residential programs, and day treatment centers in our sample is justified in terms of preventing future delinquency and rehabilitating youth for law-abiding behavior cannot be answered here, but one can ponder how much the isolation and restrictiveness found in some of these programs violates basic conditions of humaneness and justice for juveniles. What kinds of "normal and natural" experiences can be assured by institutions in which most of the youth never go off grounds for school or work, never spend time with others their own age in the neighborhood, have never had a home visit since they arrived, are searched and have their mail inspected, and are subject to rules and punishments they feel are illegitimate? Is it justice that permits some youths who have committed only status offenses to be given harsher treatment in more confining and structured settings than some youth who have committed serious delinquent acts? And is it really necessary for more than a few youth to be regimented and confined for 24 hours a day when more open settings are able to handle serious delinquents? The costs of tight control are heavy both in fiscal resources and human development and growth.

Labeling and Some of Its Consequences

Many students of social deviance (Lemert, 1967; Becker, 1964; Quinney, 1970; Matza, 1969) have pointed to the negative consequences of societal reaction to and labeling of much delinquent behavior by adolescents. It is asserted that when the label of delinquent is officially applied, the youth is stigmatized and embarks on ever more serious behavior, which in turn results in the application of still more negative labels. Despite the plausibility of the argument, data to support theoretical formulations have been lacking, as Klein (1972), Mahoney (1974), and others assert. Fortunately, the survey of offenders contained several items that permit some examination of the stigmatization process. Youth were asked why they were sent to the program in which they were placed and if they perceived that "people think of me as a criminal because I'm here." The latter question does not measure labeling per se but, rather, subjective perception of it. Responses were analyzed with reference to several variables, including patterns of official intervention, commitment offense, type of program placement, staff-youth interaction patterns, and ascribed characteristics of youth.

Analysis of youth responses reveals that 50% of the youth committed to correctional programs thought they were considered criminal. Among first offenders, 34% held these opinions, but there were no significant differences between youth *initially* committed for status rather than criminal offenses. The process apparently starts with the youth's first encounter, regardless of offense, with the justice system. Fewer females than males believed they were considered criminal (46% versus 55%), but there was a smaller difference among females when controls for offense were examined. Among females—by offense type —labeling was perceived by 49% of the criminal offenders and 43% of the status offenders, but among males the range widened—to 60% and 43%, respectively. Race and socioeconomic status do not show a clear pattern of association with perceived labeling.

The subjective probability of being labeled criminal increases proportionally to the frequency and types of contact between the youth and the justice system. Positive correlations, although small, were obtained between a respondent's belief that labeling was likely and the number of times she or he had been arrested (.13), been jailed (.13), been detained (.08), appeared in court (.08), been placed on probation (.07), and been sent to a correctional facility (.07).

Comparison between type of program and expectation of being labeled revealed that 56% of the youth in institutions thought people considered them criminal whereas only 36% in community residential or day treatment programs thought so. Furthermore, within institutions, 58% in public versus 50% in private institutions shared this view. It can be recalled (Table 2) that the mean age in institutions was lower than in the other programs; therefore, these findings are particularly noteworthy regarding the effects of processing.

The most critical variable in understanding some of the dynamics of youth-perceived labeling appeared in the analysis of staff-youth interaction. The findings in Table 5 reveal that youth's supposition of being labeled criminal is negatively related to positive staff-youth interaction. The frequency of perception of negative labeling increases as youth perceive that staff members do not care, punish unfairly, and display a punishment orientation toward youth.

Taken together these responses by youth do not conclusively test critical

Table 5. JUVENILE OFFENDERS' PERCEPTIONS OF STAFF AND OF BEING
         LABELED CRIMINAL (in percentages)

Youths' Perception of Staff	Labeled Criminal	
	Yes	No
Most staff here care.	41	59
Most staff don't care.	70	30
(n = 1745)		
Staff don't punish unfairly.	42	58
Staff punish unfairly.	63	37
(n = 1753)		
Staff don't try to punish.	40	60
Staff try to punish.	62	38
(n = 1756)		

aspects of labeling theory, but they do show clearly that ascribed characteristics of the youth are less related to awareness of being labeled criminal than are the number and nature of his/her contacts with the juvenile justice system, regardless of the offense the youth was first charged with. Moreover, the findings highlight the critical role of staff if the potentially harmful effects of processing are not to be aggravated. They also support the notion of parsimony regarding the type and extent of intervention.

LEGISLATION AND LITIGATION

Statutes

Comparative analysis of the statutes pertaining to juvenile delinquency reveals great diversity of legislative approaches to jurisdiction, definitions, processing, disposition, and treatment of juveniles. To evaluate courts and other types of juvenile justice organizations, therefore, one must be informed of the variable statutory provisions that govern the domain and operation of these units. Moreover, the late sixties witnessed several significant decisions by the United States Supreme Court which were expected to affect statutes and the processing of juveniles.[8] Between the years 1968 and 1972 a total of 33 states effected major changes in their juvenile codes; many of these changes pertained to due process, age definitions, and court structures. This pattern of changes appears to be continuing almost without interruption. It represents a distinct shift from earlier decades: few and minor changes had been made in many juvenile codes since their establishment in the first quarter of the twentieth century.

In theory the juvenile court was created to intervene for rehabilitative and protective rather than punitive purposes, to avoid stigmatizing labels, and to treat each child in an individually helpful way. We surveyed the statutes to determine how they actually reflect this societal mandate (Levin and Sarri, 1974). Our examination of statutes of the fifty states and the District of Columbia indicated that the states vary on most of the following major dimensions: jurisdiction of the juvenile court, definitions of delinquency, procedures for processing of juveniles through all phases of legal processing, court structure and staffing, detention, specification of offenders' rights and due process provisions, disposition alternatives, and the limits of discretion. These variations sometimes extend *within* states where provisions vary among different counties.

Decisions of the U.S. Supreme Court have continued to leave it to the states to decide the crucial question of who is a child and who therefore will be accorded full constitutional protection. It is not surprising that federalism has produced certain dramatic differences. For example, which children will be processed by the juvenile court and which will go through the adult criminal system as adults is basically the function of three statutory variables: age, seriousness of offense, and grounds for transfer to the criminal system. In 32 states and the District of Columbia, the maximum legal age of a child is 17; in 12 states it is 16, and in the remaining 6 it is 15 years. But some states also differentiate by sex although the legality of this practice is questionable;[9] some have complex and elaborate stipulations governing transfer procedures; and others exclude certain serious offenses from the juvenile court's jurisdiction. Very few states have clear, unambiguous provisions—which are necessary for effective administration of justice, particularly in courts that are overwhelmed by large numbers of referrals.

Perhaps the juvenile code provisions that cause the greatest miscarriage of justice are those that define the areas of behavior the juvenile court may regulate. All 51 jurisdictions bring into the purview of the court, conduct that if engaged in by an adult would bring legal action. But, in addition, all states permit the court to intervene for behavior that is not illegal for adults, for example, truancy, incorrigibility, running away, immorality, disobedience, promiscuity, or even just "idling." While all states use the category of status offenses, as these behaviors are usually termed, status offenders are treated with considerable variation. Many states have recently adopted special legislation governing the processing of these "children in need of supervision" (CHINS).

In 1972, 26 states had special categories for such juveniles, but by 1975 that number had dropped to 16, and even in the latter group several states were considering new legislation (Dineen, 1974). One impetus for these changes is the provision in Public Law 93-415, the Juvenile Justice and Delinquency Prevention Act of 1974, which requires that within two years after passage, status offenders not be placed in detention or correctional facilities if federal funds are to be received.

It is debatable, however, whether CHINS or other similar provisions are sufficient to direct youth from the system; often they are transformed from status offenders to delinquents after the second or third status violation. For example, in one state with a separate category for status offenders, 80% of the institutionalized females were truants, runaways, or ungovernables. According to the *Children in Custody* census of 1971 (U.S. LEAA, 1974: 6), 23% of the males and 70% of the females in public correctional facilities were status offenders.

In 41 states dependent and neglected children are not required to be separated from delinquent children in a detention facility. After disposition 17 states allow delinquents and dependent and neglected children to be housed together. Given the vague definitions of *delinquent,* it is not surprising that delinquents and dependent or neglected children are found together not only in detention facilities and jails but also in private institutions and training schools. In several states, large numbers of mentally retarded children can be observed in the same institution with delinquent youth, with little or no difference in program experiences. The recent New York decision in *In the Matter of Ellery C.* (32 N.Y. 2d 588, 300 N.E. 2d 424, 347 N.Y.S. 2d 51 [1973]) held that separate facilities must be maintained for status offenders and delinquents in training schools. The decision of the U.S. Supreme Court in *Robinson v. California* (370 U.S. 660 [1962]) has not been extended to cover youth status offenses thus far, but changes are under way in many states. Judge Orlando (1975) argues that status offense provisions be abolished under the legal concept of "void for vagueness."

The most glaring deficiency of the juvenile codes is their ambiguity and deliberate grants of unlimited discretion. This permits grossly inconsistent administration of justice between cases and among jurisdictions in the same state. Although well-drawn statutes cannot ensure appropriate processing of juveniles, it is unlikely that improper practices will be eliminated without explicit statutory requirements.

Overreach of the law and overuse of criminal sanctions continue in many states despite their relative ineffectiveness in achieving desired goals and despite the generally negative secondary and tertiary consequences. Many years ago Roscoe Pound expressed grave reservations about the extent to which the education, health, and morals of youth had come under the authority of the juvenile court. When these problems are written into statutes as bases for state intervention, parents, neighbors, schools, and social agencies are encouraged to avoid or refer their problems rather than try to solve them.

Many students of juvenile justice have also recommended decriminalization not only of status offenses but also of victimless crimes. In few states, however, have we observed any concerted drive in this direction. In fact, there is some evidence that far more is being accomplished in decriminalization for adults than for juveniles, although it seems patently obvious that decriminalization could be more productive and is more urgently needed for juveniles.

Juvenile Litigation

The fundamental philosophy of the juvenile court laws is that a delinquent child is to be considered and treated not as a criminal but as a person requiring care, education and protection. He is not thought of as a bad man who should be punished but as an erring or sick child who needs help. [Thomas v. United States, 121 F. 2d 908 (D.C. Ct. of Appeals 1941)]

This philosophy is the ever-recurring theme of the juvenile justice system. The words "care," "protection," "erring," and "sick" connote nonpunitive concepts. Today, however, this philosophy is being directly challenged as not in the best interest of a child by a fledgling movement for the legal rights of juveniles (Renn, 1973).

Judicial activism in corrections in the fifties and sixties took one of two courses, institutional reform or crisis strategy. For the former, lawyers began using litigation to make institutions and facilities less oppressive and more conducive to the aims of rehabilitation.[10] In contrast, advocates of crisis strategies became convinced that implementing prisoners' rights upsets the balance of power in institutions and makes them inoperable; further, since institutions respond only when required by events, the advocates of change must provoke crises.

Case decisions in juvenile justice as far back as 1899 emphasized the role of the training school as a "provision of treatment" (Wisconsin Industrial School for Girls v. Clark Company, 103 Wisc. 651, 79 N.W. 422 [1899]). Despite the broad interpretation of treatment in our society by statutory law, case law, and lay language, the United States Supreme Court has not as yet ruled on the inherent right to treatment. Although recognizing the relationship between juvenile proceedings and rehabilitative or treatment needs (Kent v. United States),[11] the Supreme Court has only recently ruled that a party committed under a statute that in some way espouses rehabilitation or treatment has thereby a constitutional right to treatment (O'Connor v. Donaldson, 43 U.S.L.W. 1929).

The right to treatment was used during the late sixties to advance and support the exclusion of certain procedural due processes for juveniles. The "Rich Trade-off Doctrine," evolved from *In re Rich* (125 Me. 373, 216 A. 2d 266), denied the right of trial by jury as an inherent constitutional right for juveniles ("the right to trial by jury could only come in exchange for a right to rehabilitative care taking. Thus the validity of the whole juvenile system is dependent upon its jury to protect it rather than its penal aspects"). With the Supreme Court decision in *McKiever v. Pennsylvania* (403 U.S. 528) and the recognition that it is very difficult to remove the "treatment philosophy which seems to pervade the courts' legal roles," attorneys have begun to try to effect actions to challenge current treatment services in public institutional programs.

Historically, litigation has evolved as an effective instrument for planned social change. Although time-consuming and costly, it often produces permanent change. Attorneys' social activism, along with concerned and interested professionals in the juvenile justice system, should be able to make litigation an increasingly effective tool for change (Wald and Schwartz, 1974). Until now litigation has been directed primarily against abuses of public institutions. However, with the advent of *O'Connor v. Donaldson* (43 U.S.L.W. 1929), *Morales v. Turman* (364 F. Supp. 166 [E.D. Texas 1973]), and *Nelson v. Heyne* (335 F. Supp. 451 [N.D. Ind. 1972] aff'd 491 F. 2d 352 [7th Cir. 1974]), litigation is being utilized as a means for effecting widespread change. Private and community-based programs are also likely to come under careful scrutiny by the courts. From this litigation further definitions of treatment, of problematic behavior, and of procedural rights are likely to be refined by the courts. These actions can be expected to have substantial impact on the juvenile justice system, although, as in the Gault case, the consequences are likely to be uneven throughout the states. Nonetheless, the statements of the court in *Morales v. Turman* are likely to influence the practices current in many juvenile correctional programs today:

> An important incident of the right to treatment is the right of each individual to the least restrictive alternative treatment that is consistent with the purpose of his custody. . . . Just as the state cannot mechanically hospitalize every person found to be mentally ill . . . it may not institutionalize every child that the state's courts declare to be a delinquent. Yet the testimony at trial established that the Texas Youth Council seldom, if ever, places a child committed to its care in any situation except a TYC institution. . . . The TYC has explicit statutory authority for using community-based programs to effect the treatment of children committed to its care . . . but has chosen to ignore that grant of authority and pursue institutionalization as its sole alternative. This choice is not permissible under the Constitution. [Morales v. Turman, memorandum and order, at 180-182]

CRITICAL ISSUES FOR POLICY AND PROGRAM DEVELOPMENT

Contemporary approaches, practices, and problems in juvenile justice have been highlighted in this chapter. It is readily apparent that there are no definitive modalities which are operative across all the states. Moreover, it is apparent that there are many organizational or system practices that are contrary to the stated goals of these organizations, for example, the more stringent sanctioning of younger and female status offenders. Our objective was to describe critical features of the extant system in policy-relevant terms. It is our hope that findings of this order will provide a basis for more informed judgments about policy and programmatic issues.

Failures are easily found, but what seems particularly disturbing today is lack of learning from past experience by key decision makers. New problem-solving mechanisms for long-range planning for youth appear to be urgently needed. There is a tendency for each governmental level or unit charged with an aspect of youth socialization or control to address only its own problems or tasks, with little reference to more general developments or to other organizations working in the area. With the implementation of the Juvenile Justice and Delinquency Prevention Act of 1974, a federal mechanism has become available to facilitate more rational planning by states and localities and by public and private sectors of the society. If more effective planning is to be achieved, a far higher priority must be given to interorganizational activity than was seen as existing by staff surveyed in this research.

The NAJC survey of the organization of state services, of correctional programs, and of statutes has raised many provocative issues which point to the need for policy and program change.

1. *Increase in Juvenile Justice Population:* The population being handled through the juvenile justice system is increasing in many states. This is undoubtedly attributable in part to the increase in the total youth population in this decade, but it is also probable that a higher proportion of those who commit offenses are now being apprehended, diverted, adjudicated, and committed to correctional programs. More governmental resources are being allocated; but given the reductions in other key sectors (e.g., public education and child welfare), there may be a tendency to refer youth to those institutions or organizations with the greater resources. Because of their age and status, many juveniles need social supports in growing up, but it is debatable that the services should be provided under conditions of coercion or in ways that label youth as delinquent when that label is likely to have negative consequences in the long as well as short run. Juvenile justice resources have increased as a result of LEAA

and Juvenile Delinquency appropriations at the same time other youth-serving agencies experienced declines in their resources. Based on reports by youth themselves (Gold and Reimer, 1974), the frequency and seriousness of delinquent behavior did not increase between 1966 and 1972. Yet the news media constantly reported that delinquency was rising. Thus, one is inclined to question the advisability of the national policy that led to this resource shift.

2. *Inadequate Protection of Juvenile Rights in Revised Statutes:* The statutory changes now under way in the majority of states are as negative as they are positive with respect to protection of the rights of juveniles and their general well-being. Although delinquency has been frequently redefined, status offenders have thus far not been removed from the system. Moreover, processing status offenders—such as runaways—through the system, however rapidly, appears to aggravate, not resolve, their problems. Placing them in detention or jail is not only inappropriate but in fact detrimental. The concept of "minimal penetration" is typically inoperative for status offenders.

3. *Racism and Sexism:* Racism and sexism are serious problems in juvenile justice but are not addressed as directly as they have been in the public schools. Solutions cannot be long postponed. When a national subsample of correctional programs shows that half of the confined youth come from minority groups where the proportion of minority persons in the total population is less than 15%, then serious problems must be expected. The young are sensitive to this phenomenon and are less likely to think they have anything to lose by challenging a racist system. Sexism is an equally important problem. Females are discriminated against by more stringent forms of intervention and by more negative sanctions. Furthermore, society hypocritically asserts that it is protecting them and their morality by this action.

4. *Fads in Juvenile Justice:* The in words in juvenile justice today are "diversion," "deinstitutionalization," "community-based programming," and "evaluation"—in about that order of importance. But consistent real-world referents for these concepts are practically nonexistent. For example, "community-based programming" is strongly encouraged by various federal agencies, and states adopt widely different interpretations, from small, secure institutions within cities to open treatment units in other places. We have also observed aftercare and parole programs replete with large caseloads and traditional approaches classified under the community service umbrella. Thus, "community-based service" can become semantic trivia for traditional programs whose physical location in an urban community is the sole basis for

identification as community-based. Residential programs are still utilized more extensively, even though they are almost always more expensive than day treatment. Similarly there is very little true diversion *from* the system, although increased processing of youths has necessarily resulted in diversion *within* the system. Pouring old vinegar into new bottles misleads the public, corrupts the system, and confounds accountability and evaluation.

5. *Intervention Overkill:* "Heroic" intervention costs more, but no evidence exists that it is more effective. We therefore assert that intervention by the juvenile justice system should be more parsimonious in all aspects, and focused toward rehabilitation, not custody. Custody absorbs at least 60% of juvenile corrections funding and, as presently structured, only adds to the criminalization of youth. Rehabilitation focused toward more effective education and greater employment opportunities is preferred by youth.

6. *Right to Service:* Emphasis on diversion fundamentally begs the question of how many or even most youth in trouble should be handled. It would not be necessary to "divert" if communities provided more adequate opportunities and services to youth and if the juvenile system were restricted to handling those who engage in what are criminal acts when committed by adults. These issues must be seen in relation to each other, for it is the status offenders, deprived of adequate aid and service, who are overloading the modest capabilities of the justice system and for whom it can provide the least helpful intervention. Moreover, once inside the system, they are not systematically differentiated from youth who have committed very serious crimes. Processing through the justice system cannot compensate for failures of the family, the school, or the community. The right to treatment now being extended in residential programs should be paralleled in the community by a "right to service"—and to education and to employment.

7. *Child Advocacy:* In a bureaucratized mass society, the promotion of services to meet special needs and the protection of rights require an active constituency, which children do not enjoy in most communities. Broad awareness is needed of who is processed and how they are processed to encourage adult representatives to see that their own basic interests are also at stake. Likewise, the establishment of ombudsmen or children's advocates to provide more effective and speedier redress of grievances within and between agencies would stimulate action on behalf of youth.

8. *Roles for the Federal Government:* New opportunities for the federal government are everywhere to be found. The evidence to date is unclear,

however, that the national government will act to reduce the fragmentation of policies and services to youth at the federal level. Interagency coordination and cooperation is perhaps even more critically important at the national level than at the state level. More attention must be given to determining the sectors to be aided if we are to socialize and prepare youth better than we are doing now. Among the federal government's responsibilities are (1) establishing priorities and standards, (2) channeling resources for strategic aims on longer than a yearly basis, and (3) developing a national information infrastructure that will enable us to know what has been done and what needs to be accomplished.

In A.D. 2000—the Child the Father of the Man

Given the depth of dissatisfaction and conflict with the goals and processes of the juvenile justice system, now may be a particularly opportune time for introducing long-overdue changes. In the year 2000 boys and girls who are being processed through juvenile justice agencies today will be adults expected to contribute to the well-being of society. Rather than evaluation, which addresses only short-term social control goals, the question to be asked is: Will today's juvenile justice programs prepare youth for responsible adulthood? It is unlikely that society will have capable and responsible adult citizens in the year 2000 if there are critical failures, gaps, and problems in its socialization of youth in the 1970s.

NOTES

1. Reports from NIMH (1974) cite increased hospitalization of adolescents for mental illness, another indication that contemporary youth are experiencing greater problems in growing up.

2. The research methodology was informed by Freed (1973), Walker (1969), Hofferbert (1972), and Sharkansky (1970). NAJC's survey (Vinter et al., 1975) provides the data base.

3. On a given date 11,748 youth were held in juvenile detention facilities (U.S. LEAA, 1974), and more than 7,800 in adult county jails (U.S. LEAA, 1971).

4. Dean and Reppucci (1974) reported recently on the number of youth in juvenile correctional institutions, but their information is based largely on 1965-1967 data, and it is obvious that substantial change has occurred since that time in the types of institutions for placement of youth.

5. This measure represents the mean offender-year costs for states' institutional services during fiscal 1974. It is calculated by dividing the 1974 total operating expenditures for state institutions by the 1974 average daily population in each state's institutions, camps, and ranches.

6. There is only a weak association (.23) between states' per capita incomes and their per capita *expenditures* for institutions. It will be recalled that we found a negative correlation (−.31) between states' per capita incomes and their *rates* of institutionalization. These findings indicate that wealthier states are less likely to rely heavily on juvenile

institutions but are much more likely to increase their per-offender costs for these facilities, thus producing a very modest increase in their overall level of effort (i.e., per capita allocations) for these programs.

7. This research was informed by the evaluation critiques of Suchman (1967), Campbell and Stanley (1966), Rossi and Williams (1972), Caro (1971), Riecken and Boruch (1974), and Weiss (1972), among others. All of these analysts have stated that greater emphasis in program evaluation should be placed on organizational-level variables, such as process and effort, in order to learn more about how and why a result is or is not being achieved, not merely what the final outcome is.

8. Among the key decisions were Kent v. United States, 383 U.S. 541, 86 S. Ct. 1945, 16 L. Ed. 2d 84 (1966); In re Gault, 387 U.S. 1, 87 S. Ct. 1428, 18 L. Ed. 2d 527 (1967); and In re Winship, 397 U.S. 358, 90 S. Ct. 1068, 25 L. Ed. 2d 308 (1970).

9. Decisions in Connecticut, Oklahoma, and New York hold such laws to be unconstitutional. See Sumrell v. York, 288 F. Supp. 955 (1968); Lamb v. Brown, 456 F. 2d 18 (1972); and In the Matter of Patricia A., 31 N.Y. 2d 83, 335 N.Y.S. 2d 33 (1972). More recently the U.S. Supreme Court, in Stanton v. Stanton, 43 U.S.L.W. 4449 (April 1975), reversed the decision of the Utah Supreme Court which differentiated minority ages for males and females, but the decision was qualified by the following: "We find it unnecessary in this case to decide whether a qualification based on sex is inherently suspect."

10. The recent decisions by Judge Johnson in Wyatt v. Stickney, 344 F. Supp. 378 (M.D. Ala. 1972) set out 74 guidelines, ranging from appropriate ratios of specific staff to patients, to directing the necessary hygienic facilities for patients.

11. Supra, note 8.

REFERENCES

ADAMS, S. N. (1975) Evaluative Research in Corrections: A Practical Guide. U.S. LEAA. Washington, D.C.: Government Printing Office (No. 2700-00270).

ALLEN, F. A. (1964) The Borderland of Criminal Justice: Essays in Law and Criminology. Chicago: University of Chicago Press.

Arthur D. Little, Inc. (1974) Evaluation of Services Offered by Community Mental Health Centers and ADAMHA-Funded Drug and Alcohol Programs to Juvenile Delinquents. Cambridge, Mass.

BAKAL, Y. (1973) Closing Correctional Institutions. Lexington, Mass.: D. C. Heath.

BAUM, M. and S. WHEELER (1966) "Becoming an inmate," pp. 153-185 in S. Wheeler (ed.) Controlling Delinquents. New York: John Wiley.

BAUM, T. (1965) "Wiping out a criminal or juvenile record." California State Bar Journal 46: 816-830.

BECKER, H. [ed.] (1964) The Other Side: Perspectives on Deviance. New York: Free Press.

CAMPBELL, D. T. and J. C. STANLEY (1966) Experimental and Quasi-Experimental Designs for Research. Chicago: Rand McNally.

CARO, F. G. [ed.] (1971) Readings in Evaluation Research. New York: Russell Sage.

CRESSEY, D. R. and R. A. McDERMOTT (1973) Diversion from the Juvenile Justice System. Washington, D.C.: Government Printing Office (No. 2700-00241).

CUMMING, E. (1968) Systems of Social Regulation. New York: Atherton Press.

DEAN, C. W. and N. D. REPPUCCI (1974) "Juvenile correctional institutions," pp. 865-894 in D. Glaser (ed.) Handbook of Criminology. Chicago: Rand McNally.

DINEEN, J. (1974) Juvenile Court Organization and Status Offenses: A Statutory Profile. Pittsburgh: National Center for Juvenile Justice.

EDELMAN, M. W. (1974) Report of Second Year Activities of the Children's Defense Fund of the Washington Research Project, Inc. Cambridge, Mass.: Children's Defense Fund.

EMPEY, L. T. and S. G. LUBECK (1971) The Silverlake Experiment. Chicago: Aldine.

EMPEY, L. T. and M. T. ERICKSON (1972) The Provo Experiment: Evaluating Community Control of Delinquency. Lexington, Mass.: D. C. Heath.

FERSTER, E. Z. and T. F. COURTLESS (1972) "Post-disposition treatment and recidivism in the juvenile court: towards justice for all." Journal of Family Law 11: 683-710.

FOX, S. (1970) "Juvenile justice reform: an historical perspective." Stanford Law Review 22 (June): 1187-1239.

FREED, R. C. (1973) "Comparative urban performance," European Urban Research Paper No. 1. Los Angeles: University of California.

GIBBS, J. (1966) "Conceptions of deviant behavior: the old and the new." Pacific Sociological Review 9: 9-14.

GLASER, D. (1974) Handbook of Criminology. Chicago: Rand McNally.

GOLD, M. and D. J. REIMER (1974) "Changing patterns of delinquent behavior among Americans 13 through 16 years old: 1967-1972," National Survey of Youth Report No. 1. Ann Arbor, Mich.: Institute for Social Research.

GROSSER, C. F., W. E. HENRY, and J. G. KELLY [eds.] (1969) Nonprofessionals in the Human Services. San Francisco: Jossey-Bass.

HEALEY, E. V. (1975) "Senate testimony on Juvenile Justice Act." Juvenile Justice 26 (May): 59-61.

HOFFERBERT, R. I. (1972) "State and community policy studies," pp. 1-72 in J. A. Robinson (ed.) Political Science Annual 3.

Joint Commission on Correctional Manpower and Training (1969) A Time to Act. College Park, Md.: American Correctional Association.

KADISH, S. (1967) "The crisis of overcriminalization." Annals of the American Academy of Political and Social Science 374 (November): 157-170.

KEITER, R. B. (1973) "Criminal or delinquent? A study of juvenile cases transferred to the criminal court." Crime and Delinquency 19 (October): 528-539.

KELLER, O. J. and B. ALPER (1970) Halfway Houses: Community-Centered Correction and Treatment. Lexington, Mass.: D. C. Heath.

KILPATRICK, D. M., D. M. PAPPENFORT, and A. M. KUBY (1970) Institutions for Dependent and Neglected Children. Vol. 2 of Pappenfort and Kilpatrick (comps.) A Census of Children's Residential Institutions in the United States, Puerto Rico, and the Virgin Islands: 1966. Chicago: University of Chicago School of Social Service Administration.

KLEIN, M. W. (1972) "On the front end of the juvenile justice system," appendix I in Juvenile System Rates: Diversion. Los Angeles: Los Angeles Regional Criminal Justice Planning Board.

LEMERT, E. M. (1967) Human Deviance, Social Problems and Social Control. Englewood Cliffs, N.J.: Prentice-Hall.

LERMAN, P. (1968) "Evaluating the outcomes of institutions for delinquents." Social Work 13 (July): 55-64.

LEVIN, M. M. and R. C. SARRI (1974) Juvenile Delinquency: A Comparative Analysis of Legal Codes in the United States. Ann Arbor, Mich.: National Assessment of Juvenile Corrections.

LUGER, M. (1973) "Tomorrow's training schools—problems, progress, and challenges." Crime and Delinquency 19 (October): 545-550.

MAHONEY, A. R. (1974) "The effect of labeling upon youth in the juvenile justice system: a review of the evidence." Law and Society Review 8 (December): 597-608.

MATTICK, H. W. (1974) "The contemporary jails of the United States: an unknown and neglected area of justice," pp. 777-848 in D. Glaser (ed.) Handbood of Criminology. Chicago: Rand McNally.

MATZA, D. (1969) Becoming Deviant. Englewood Cliffs, N.J.: Prentice-Hall.

MOOS, R. (1974) Evaluating Treatment Environments: A Social Ecological Approach. New York: John Wiley.

MORRIS, N. (1974) The Future of Imprisonment. Chicago: University of Chicago Press.

National Advisory Commission on Criminal Justice Standards and Goals (1973) Corrections. Washington, D.C.: Government Printing Office.

National Conference of Superintendents of Training Schools and Reformatories (1962) Institutional Rehabilitation of Delinquent Youth: Manual for Training School Personnel. Albany: Delmar.

National Institute of Mental Health (1974) Residential Psychiatric Facilities for Children and Adolescents: United States, 1971-72. Washington, D.C.: DHEW Publication No. (ADM) 74-78.

NUTT, N. (1975) Care or Custody: Community Homes and the Treatment of Delinquency. New York: Agathon.

ORLANDO, F. A. (1975) "Status offenses: the court's role." Resolution of Correctional Problems and Issues 1 (Winter): 24-28.

PAPPENFORT, D. M., D. M. KILPATRICK, and A. M. KUBY (1970) Institutions for Predelinquent or Delinquent Children. Vol. 3 of Pappenfort and Kilpatrick (comps.) A Census of Children's Residential Institutions in the United States, Puerto Rico, and the Virgin Islands: 1966. Chicago: University of Chicago School of Social Service Administration.

PAPPENFORT, D. M., D. M. KILPATRICK, and R. W. ROBERTS [eds.] (1973) Child Caring: Social Policy and the Institution. Chicago: Aldine.

PLATT, A. M. (1969) The Child Savers: The Invention of Delinquency. Chicago: University of Chicago Press.

POLIER, J. W. (1975) "Future of the juvenile court." Juvenile Justice 26 (May): 3-10.

President's Commission on Law Enforcement and the Administration of Justice (1967a) The Challenge of Crime in a Free Society. Washington, D.C.: Government Printing Office.

——— (1967b) Task Force Report: Juvenile Delinquency and Youth Crime. Washington, D.C.: Government Printing Office.

QUINNEY, R. (1970) The Social Reality of Crime. Boston: Little, Brown.

RENN, D. E. (1973) "The right to treatment and the juvenile." Crime and Delinquency 19 (October): 477-485.

RIECKEN, H. W. and R. F. BORUCH [eds.] (1974) Social Experimentation: A Method for Planning and Evaluating Social Intervention. New York: Academic Press.

ROSSI, P. H. and W. WILLIAMS [eds.] (1972) Evaluating Social Programs: Theory, Practice, and Politics. New York: Seminar Press.

ROSSI, P. H., E. WAITE, C. E. BOSE, and R. E. BERK (1974) "The seriousness of crimes: Normative structures and individual differences." American Sociological Review 39 (April): 224-237.

ROTHMAN, D. J. (1971) "The well-ordered asylum," pp. 206-236 in The Discovery of the Asylum: Social Order and Disorder in the New Republic. Boston: Little, Brown.

SARRI, R. C. (1974) Under Lock and Key: Juveniles in Jail and Detention. Ann Arbor, Mich.: National Assessment of Juvenile Corrections.

─── and E. SELO (1974) "Evaluation process and outcome in juvenile corrections: musings on a grim tale," pp. 253-302 in P. O. Davidson, F. W. Clark, and L. A. Hamerlynck (eds.) Evaluation of Behavioral Programs in Community, Residential and School Settings. Champaign, Ill.: Research Press.

SCHULTZ, J. L. (1973) "The cycle of juvenile court history." Crime and Delinquency 19 (October): 457-476.

SCHUR, E. M. (1973) Radical Non-Intervention: Rethinking the Delinquency Problem. Englewood Cliffs, N.J.: Prentice-Hall.

SHARKANSKY, I. (1970) "Environment, policy, output and input: problems of theory and method in the analysis of public policy," in Policy Analysis in Political Science. Chicago: Markham.

SMITH, R. L. (1971) The Silent Revolution: Probation Subsidy. U.S. DHEW. Washington, D.C.: Government Printing Office (No. 1766-0007).

STREET, D., R. D. VINTER, and C. PERROW (1966) Organization for Treatment. New York: Free Press.

SUCHMAN, E. (1967) Evaluation Research. New York: Russell Sage.

THORSELL, B. A. and L. W. KLEMKE (1972) "The labeling process: reinforcement and deterrent?" Law and Society 6 (February): 393-402.

U.S. Department of Health, Education, and Welfare, Office of Youth Development (1974) Juvenile Court Statistics–1972. Washington, D.C.

U.S. Law Enforcement Assistance Administration, National Criminal Justice Information and Statistics Service (1971) National Jail Census, 1970: A Report on the Nation's Local Jails and Type of Inmates. Stat Center Publication SC-No. 1. Washington, D.C.: Government Printing Office.

─── (1974) Children in Custody: A Report on the Juvenile Detention and Correctional Facility Census of 1971. Washington, D.C.: National Criminal Justice Reference Service (No. 13403).

VINTER, R. D., G. DOWNS, and J. HALL (1975) Juvenile Corrections in the States: Residential Programs and Deinstitutionalization. Ann Arbor, Mich.: National Assessment of Juvenile Corrections.

WALD, P. M. and L. H. SCHWARTZ (1974) "Trying a juvenile right to treatment suit: pointers and pitfalls for plaintiffs." American Criminal Law Review 12 (Summer): 125-164.

WALKER, J. L. (1969) "The diffusion of innovation among the American states." American Political Science Review 63: 880-899.

WEISS, C. H. (1972) Evaluating Action Programs. Boston: Allyn and Bacon.

WILLIAMS, J. R. and M. GOLD (1972) "From delinquent behavior to official delinquency." Social Problems 20 (Fall): 209-229.

Wisconsin Department of Health and Social Services (1973) Executive Budget Policy Papers. Madison.

WOLFGANG, M. E., R. M. FIGLIO, and T. SELLIN (1972) Delinquency in a Birth Cohort. Chicago: University of Chicago Press.

Chapter 8

PREVALENCE: THE RARE DATUM IN DELINQUENCY MEASUREMENT AND ITS IMPLICATIONS FOR THE THEORY OF DELINQUENCY

ROBERT A. GORDON

INTRODUCTION

One of the most thoroughly documented known relationships concerning official crime and delinquency rates is that with socioeconomic status or SES.[1] This relationship, like most in sociology, has not been immune to challenge. One of the main challengers was Lander (1954), who claimed that his analyses showed that official rates of juvenile delinquency in Baltimore were related to "anomic" conditions, but not to SES. Lander's widely cited conclusions have since been demonstrated to be erroneous, and the result of mistaken interpretations of complex multivariate analyses (Gordon, 1967, 1968). However, there remains a body of research in which the relationship between SES and criminality is still contested on other grounds. This is the so-called "self-report" literature on delinquency and adult crime, much of which purports to show that, when persons volunteer information concerning their own criminality, no association of criminal behavior with social class is found (e.g., Short and Nye, 1958; Chambliss and Nagasawa, 1969; Williams and Gold, 1972).

Taken at face value, these findings undercut any theoretical effort which attempts to build on the association of official crime rates with SES—with one exception. That exception is the labeling theoretical approach, which would account for the manifest discrepancy between official and self-report data by treating the socioeconomic differentials in official data as though they were mainly artifacts of discrimination on the part of representatives of official agencies (e.g., Chiricos et al., 1972; Marshall and Purdy, 1972). Thus rationalized theoretically, the differentials have been more subject than ever to rejection or dismissal as "invalid." Once accepted as invalid, it requires but a short step to contend that the official data embodying such differentials should be suppressed altogether on the grounds that they constitute both a libel against those segments of society unfairly portrayed as having differentially high crime rates and a stimulus for supposed "self-fulfilling prophecy" effects (e.g., Geis, 1965).

Although the strengths and weaknesses of official crime statistics have been debated for more than a century (for reviews, see Sellin and Wolfgang, 1964: chaps. 2-5; Biderman and Reiss, 1967), the self-report and labeling approaches have stimulated an especially high level of antagonism toward such statistics in recent years. Ironically, this hostility developed rapidly during a period when the spread of computer technology and statistical expertise, as judged by their effect in other areas, could have been expected to upgrade the quality of crime statistics generally. There has been a tendency, consequently, to discourage, rather than to welcome, efforts to refine, improve, compile, and otherwise cultivate the orderly development of official crime data.[2]

Unfortunately, as I hope to show in future publication, there are certain facts that exist only in the form of official statistics that are essential for the proper evaluation of the self-report methodology, which has been the main empirical source of severe doubt concerning the value of official statistics. (Whatever other criticisms one might raise against official data appear as mere quibbles alongside the supposed discovery via self-report methods that official data cannot be trusted to hint at the correct answers to even the most elementary questions.) Consequently, we have the unusual, but probably not unprecedented, situation in science where discussion has been prematurely foreclosed by the initial success of a new method, thus interfering with the process of evaluating the new method itself.

Even before the labeling theory vogue began in the sixties, the black civil rights movement had begun to oppose racial distinctions in record-keeping of any sort. Monahan's race-specific series of delinquency rates for Philadelphia had to be terminated at 1953 because of pressure on the Philadelphia Board of Education (Monahan, 1960: 69), the Los Angeles Police Department discontinued racial breakdowns in its annual statistical reports in 1962 (Geis, 1965: 144), and the last year for which racial proportions among training school inmates were reported by the federal government was 1956 (Lunden, 1964:

Table 130). This suppression of racial distinctions in source statistics has seriously impaired the utility of existing official data by depriving whites of important information about themselves, quite aside from whether or not they have any legitimate interest in rates for blacks specifically. Since race-specific rates yield ratios of about three blacks for each white in official delinquency statistics (Gordon, 1973; Gordon and Gleser, 1974), and since the proportion black of the base population is subject to considerable variation from place to place and from one time to another, it is impossible to use racially nonspecific data in the evaluation of the self-report methodology, which is based mainly on whites. That is, since composite rates are simply a linear combination of the underlying race-specific rates, and since rates for blacks are so different from rates for whites (see also Savitz, 1973), the black rates constitute a potent source of "noise" for anyone trying to assemble a comprehensive picture of white official delinquency statistics. As Gordon and Gleser (1974: 289) point out in their discussion of statistics for Philadelphia, given the race-specific rates as intrinsic, the proportion of males appearing in juvenile court by age 18.0 could vary from 17.9% to 50.9%, as racial composition varied from all white to all black.

Attitudes toward the generation of race-specific data thus form still another impediment to scientific progress in this area. However, it is the confluence of mutually reinforcing empirical, theoretical, and political factors that is most responsible for the existing impasse, for these factors are interlocked in a manner which demands that one deal with all issues simultaneously in order to deal with any issue at all. This, of course, is not the way in which science normally progresses.

Present Purposes and Measurements

It is certainly not the intent of this paper to deal with all issues at once. Rather, its purpose is to proceed further with the exploration of official data in the form of "prevalence" rates (to be defined shortly), a task begun in two earlier papers (Gordon, 1973; Gordon and Gleser, 1974), by assembling all existing prevalence data in one place for ease of inspection, and by using the resulting network of implications as a source of information concerning basic consistencies in the data. In some cases, these consistencies will be employed to provide approximate adjustments to one or another datum in order to enhance its formal comparability to the remaining data. Essentially, these adjustments enable us to address the following kind of question: is a particular rate compatible with the assumption that it would have resembled rates in other communities more closely if it had been expressed in a more appropriate form? That is, is it compatible with the assumption that it was generated by the same basic processes as were responsible for the production of other rates, subject perhaps to certain broad influences such as might be associated, for example, with the urban-rural continuum?

When such questions can be answered in the affirmative, the consistency of the total assemblage of data is enhanced, and hence so is the possibility of eliciting new theoretical insights. Clearly, there are important advantages potentially available from considering many data points simultaneously, and from being able to employ regular features of several such points as an aid in the interpretation of new points that may appear irregular only because a basis was lacking for translating them into common terms. Irregularities that cannot be reduced by such efforts would represent genuine examples of what Monahan (1961: 160) has called "singular vagaries." Critical attention could then be concentrated upon such cases—few in number, it is hoped—to see whether there is any special explanation of why they "differ from the prevailing pattern." By proceeding in this gradual manner, and thus laying the basis for a truly comparative study, it is my hope that the empirical-theoretical-political logjam that now impedes the fruitful utilization of official crime data can eventually be picked apart.

The statistic to be employed in this discussion is one that for ease of verbal reference will be called "prevalence" (following Ball et al., 1964). Mathematically, it is described exactly as *the proportion P of an age-specific cohort that have become delinquent by a given age.* Since it relates directly to persons as the unit of measurement, this is clearly one of the most fundamental of all crime statistics, and until recently one of the most neglected. Consequently, almost all of the discussion concerning the adequacy of official information about crime has centered around *offense* rates and *victimization* rates (see, for example, the review by Biderman and Reiss, 1967). In contrast, prevalence is an *offender* rate. This rate is much more meaningful to both the layman and the criminologist than those statistics, sometimes called "incidence rates," which express the number, say, of juvenile delinquents recorded in a given year (regardless of whether they have ever been recorded before) as a fraction of all juveniles between the ages of 10 to 17, or 7 to 18. Such "incidence" rates usually yield much smaller numerical values than prevalence rates, because they include low rate ages such as 10, 11, 12, etc., in the denominator, and because they apply to only one year in the life of each individual at risk. These (absolutely low) rates cannot be translated readily into a subjective sense of the delinquency phenomenon by anyone, because a denominator such as "all juveniles 10 to 17" is not a simple phenomenological entity in the daily life of anyone.[3] An age-cohort, on the other hand, is a phenomenon that can be comprehended easily in terms of familiar experience, and offender rates based on the cohort as a base convey information that is intuitively appreciated with no difficulty. From a demographic standpoint, the traditional "incidence" rates just described do not even have the same meaning from year to year unless the population is stable (so that it has a constant proportional age distribution; e.g., see Bogue, 1969: 875); one year's denominator, for example, might reflect a greater proportion of 16-year-olds (one of the peak ages for delinquency) than another year's simply due to those fluctuations in cohort size that are usual in any natural population.

Offender rates also have another potential advantage. Much of the classic foreboding about the so-called "dark figure" of undetected or unreported crime dwells upon offenses and the known fact that not all "criminal acts" are reflected in any known recording process (Sellin and Wolfgang, 1964: 7-70; Biderman and Reiss, 1967; Biderman, 1967; Wolfgang et al., 1972: 15-17). But the concept of prevalence of offenders at, say, age 18.0 builds on the cumulative exposure to being recorded at least once that results from committing more than one offense. Although we have yet to study and determine in detail the statistical relation between offenses and offenders, it is quite clear that even a relatively low probability of recording repeated offenses by individuals could sustain a relatively high probability of recording individual offenders at least once each over a sufficiently long time interval.

As offender rates, prevalence rates are the true counterpart for official crime statistics of the measurement typically yielded by self-report techniques, wherein individuals at a particular point in the life-cycle identify themselves as offenders at some time in their past lives. For this reason alone, official prevalence rates are especially necessary for the complete evaluation of self-report methods. But other aspects of measurement having to do with delinquency and crime have received much more attention in recent years than the problem of prevalence. Most of the progress, consequently, has been confined to these other areas.

Specifically, work by Gordon and associates (1963), Sellin and Wolfgang (1964), and Rossi et al. (1974) indicates strong consensus among a wide range of population subgroups concerning the relative goodness or badness, severity, or seriousness of acts ranging from the conventional to the extremely criminal. Measurement of severity of offenses, therefore, does not appear to pose any special difficulties. Indeed, given its obvious close relationship to the most dominant factor ("evaluation") within the extensive domain investigated by means of the semantic differential (Osgood et al., 1957; Gordon et al., 1963), it would appear that the scaling of severity may actually provide more reliable measurement than the scaling of many other dimensions more familiar to social scientists.

One of the broader implications of the consensus demonstrated for severity is that the ad hoc groupings of offenders into (usually four) categories of seriousness by some investigators (e.g., Havighurst et al., 1962: 69-70; Hathaway and Monachesi, 1963: 22-23); the more sophisticated scaling procedures devised by Sellin and Wolfgang (1964) and employed by Wolfgang et al. (1972); and the juvenile justice system itself are almost certainly all in good agreement with each other concerning the ordering of offenders on this dimension. What is presently lacking is a mapping of these orderings onto each other, so that a particular point on one can be translated into a typical location on the other. Although the scale values employed by Wolfgang and associates (1972) may offer certain advantages for statistical analysis, it must be remembered that they tell us nothing about the institutional structure of the justice system, which is of great interest, unless they are explicitly related to that structure. It is to be hoped that fascination with the new method will not lead to the neglect of questions posed in terms of society's own method for scaling severity. It would make both systems more meaningful, for example, if we know that, on the Sellin and Wolfgang seriousness scale, boys taken into police custody had a certain average value, boys appearing in juvenile court had another value, and boys incarcerated had yet a third value. Values turned up in future applications of the scale could then be interpreted in light of these marker points, and institutional practices in one jurisdiction could then be compared and calibrated with nominally similar practices in another jurisdiction.

At the time of this writing, surveys of victimization appear to be evolving into an institutionalized mechanism for the regular monitoring of another important aspect of the total crime picture (Biderman, 1967; Law Enforcement Assistance Administration, 1974; Burnham, 1974). It is to be expected that once familiarity is established with the most basic facts of victimization rates, interest will turn to addressing ever more subtle questions through the use of this flexible technique.

But beyond this natural development of particular techniques lies the task of examining the relationships among all of them, so that their findings can be integrated into a total nomological network. Wolfgang and associates (1972) have already begun to do this, for example, by linking the scaled severity of offenses to prevalence (as determined by their "cohort study" method) within a single piece of research. Nevertheless, adequate prevalence data represent important pieces of the total jigsaw puzzle that are going to be in short supply when the time for integration arrives. The adequate measurement of official prevalence, especially at levels of severity corresponding to the classic stages in the juvenile justice system (i.e., police, court, incarceration), is presently the most neglected topic in delinquency research, despite signs of reviving interest.

Unnamed rates equivalent to what is here called a "prevalence" rate have been described and termed the best and most accurate measure of "real" delinquency by Savitz (1960: 205). The importance of such rates has also been stressed independently by Wolfgang et al. (1972: chap. 1), who gave reasons that were of a more general nature, however, than those stressed here. Some of these pertained to the advantages of longitudinal studies per se, rather than to the special rate which longitudinal studies are capable of yielding. In any case, Wolfgang and associates also did not actually name the rate in question. Instead, they referred to one of the methods by which such a rate might be generated, and discussed the entire subject under the rubric for that method, which they called a "cohort study." In this method, members of a cohort born in a given year are followed or traced retrospectively to see what percentage become delinquent by a given age. Gordon and Gleser (1974) point out that there are simple actuarial methods for determining analogous rates from age-specific (first-offense) rates that do not require waiting for a cohort to pass through the entire period during which they are defined to be at risk. Gordon and Gleser provide or distinguish two equally satisfactory computational methods for calculating prevalence rates, and they indicate that these methods should yield results comparable to a "cohort study" whenever the age-specific (first-offense) rates remain fairly stable over time.[4] Both Gordon (1973) and Gordon and Gleser (1974) call attention to the ease with which the keeping of age-specific (first-offense) rates could be institutionalized within any system that processes juvenile delinquents, thus making possible the yearly calculation of a variety of prevalence rates (which consist of nothing more than the cumulative sum of the appropriate age-specific rates up to the age of interest). Flexibility of the method is virtually complete, and prevalence rates could just as easily be computed for a variety of criteria ranging in severity from mere police contact to incarceration or from having at least one offense to at least two, and so on. It would be unfortunate, therefore, if the impression gained currency that the costly, ad hoc, and somewhat cumbersome cohort study was the only method for generating such important data. This is not to say that all of the information generated by a special longitudinal study such as that of Wolfgang and associates would normally be available simply as the result of institutionalizing actuarial procedures. But a variety of important prevalence rates certainly could be available.

Inexplicably, Wolfgang et al. (1972) ignore the connections between these various methods of generating prevalence rates, for in their otherwise extensive bibliographic references to cohort studies they make no mention of the two studies that pioneered the actuarial method for studying delinquency in this country, by Monahan (1960; noted by Sellin and Wolfgang in 1964: 68, n. 16) and by Ball et al. (1964). It should be mentioned that Monahan unfortunately employed an inappropriate computational paradigm, and so his calculations should not be taken as a model, although he clearly deserves full credit for first perceiving the importance of the rates he was attempting to create. His results have since been corrected by Gordon and Gleser (1974), who also provide correct models for such calculations. Ball et al.'s study is technically correct, and quite valuable (as I shall show later). Unfortunately, it stopped short of providing explicit race-specific data and so it too leaves something to be desired as a model.

Reasons for Choosing the Term "Prevalence"

For discussing the deceptively simple idea of the proportion of delinquents in a given population, two terms from the public health literature come immediately to mind:

PREVALENCE of a disease characterizes a group at a particular INSTANT of time, and is defined as the proportion of group members CURRENTLY suffering from the disease.

INCIDENCE of a disease characterizes the experience of a group during an INTERVAL of time, and is defined as the ratio of the number of CONTRACTIONS of the disease by group members during the interval, to the number of group MEMBERS—including in the numerator those contractions beyond the first for persons who contract it more than once.

The mathematical concept that can be verbalized as "the proportion of an age-cohort that have (do, or will) become delinquent according to a specified criterion by a given age" could easily be subsumed under either of these definitions, with the help of suitable changes in phrasing.

Construed as a prevalence rate, this mathematical concept would read: "the proportion of the cohort currently 'suffering' from having been a delinquent by a given age," where "suffering" is understood in a metaphorical sense. Construed as an incidence rate, the same mathematical concept would read: "the incidence of first-time delinquency during the interval from birth to the given age." Here we would have to specify "first-time" delinquency because the public health definition of incidence permits the counting of "contractions" (i.e., delinquencies) beyond the first.

As I have indicated, many of the customary delinquency rates are in fact incidence rates for which the specified interval is a calendar year rather than a segment of the life-cycle of individuals, for which successive "contractions" may or may not be counted, and for which the population at risk consists of a mixture of age levels (e.g., 10 to 17). Using the term "incidence" for the rates of interest in this paper would tend to confuse those rates with the under-informative traditional rates. The formal definition of incidence also encourages the impression that one is dealing with an essentially ephemeral event ("contractions") and that the count may embody repetitions of this event instead of being based on persons. Clearly, for present purposes, a term is needed that accords greater prominence to "persons" as the critical entity being counted, thus keeping salient the distinction between "offense" and "offender" rates.

The formal definition of prevalence offers the advantage of clearly emphasizing that it is *persons* who are being counted. This definition also allows to a greater extent for the fact that delinquency is often a persisting phenomenon, more like a chronic disease than an acute one, without necessarily committing itself to any position concerning exact duration. It might be pointed out that the abstract model underlying the concept of "prevalence" need not entail any connotation of "disease" at all, and so the surplus meaning attached to such words as "suffering" and "disease" need not be considered intrinsic to its use, the prior public health tradition notwithstanding. For example, the question, "What *is* the proportion of boys who have *ever been* to juvenile court among boys who are now 18.0?" is a straightforward request for a prevalence rate—the *current* proportion of group members who possess the experience of having been to juvenile court. Note that the issue of whether delinquency is ephemeral or persisting is left completely open. Reworded somewhat, the question would appear as a straightforward request for an incidence rate. The information produced, in either case, would be the same. With equal facility, either prevalence or incidence can refer to a time in the historic past. The concepts in question are clearly quite general and quite flexible, therefore, and it would be unnecessarily restrictive to take as their sole models the particular forms and wording that they have assumed in public health connections.

In view of these considerations, it is not surprising that there should be some divergence in terminology within the delinquency literature. Monahan (1960) has employed the word "incidence" to refer to two different kinds of rate within the same paper. One of these corresponds to the proportion under discussion here. Ball and associates (1964) distinguished between the same two rates, calling one "incidence" and the other "prevalence." Savitz (1960) and Wolfgang and associates (1972) empirically determined rates that correspond to Ball and associates' "prevalence" without giving them any label. No rationale was given in any of these publications for the terminological decisions taken. Clearly, choosing a verbal label for the kind of rate that is of main interest here is a matter of discretion. "Prevalence" has much to recommend it, and therefore this paper will follow the practice of Ball and associates (1964), of Gordon (1973), and of Gordon and Gleser (1974). The rate itself, it must be remembered, is mathematically defined, and therefore unambiguous whatever one's attitude toward the terminology chosen for discussing it.

A DETAILED REVIEW OF EXISTING PREVALENCE STATISTICS

Background and Overview

The prevailing picture with respect to *acts* of crime, as recently summarized by well-informed sources, reveals much consensus on certain points. Dinitz (1969: 7) states, "Delinquency, even more so than crime in general, *is a phenomenon of the urban community. The rural delinquent is quite rare,* and his offenses and motivation are not the same as those of the urban slum boy" (emphasis added). Sellin and Wolfgang (1964: 5) declare, "First, juvenile delinquency is chiefly an urban problem; it is in the largest cities that it exhibits the greatest variety of forms and induces the strongest demands by citizens for preventive measures." And Perlman (1964: 26) informs us, "The rate of delinquency court cases (the number of cases per 1,000 child population aged 10 through 17) was about three times higher in predominantly urban areas than in predominantly rural areas."

Wolfgang (1969: 32) reports exactly the same trend for crime in general, 65% of which is attributed to those *under* 21 years of age (thus indicating the importance of juvenile delinquency to the total crime picture). According to Wolfgang (1969: 26-27), the crime rate in large metropolitan areas, based on the seven most serious offenses, "is nearly *two times* higher than the rate in cities smaller than large metropolitan areas, and *three times* higher than crime in the rural area" (emphasis added). He continues:

> In general, the larger the city category, the higher the crime rate for all serious crimes combined, as well as for most specific offenses. For example, the 56 cities with over 250,000 inhabitants have rates that exceed the 2,000 cities with under 10,000 inhabitants in the following respects: over *twice* as high in murder and manslaughter, *four* times as high in robbery, over *three* times higher in aggravated assault, *twice* as high in burglary and larceny, *five* times higher in auto theft. . . . In general, the rate of robberies per 100,000 recorded by police ranges from about 12 in cities of less than 10,000 population to about 180 in cities over 250,000. [Emphasis added.]

The robbery rates here, it might be underscored, are higher in large cities by a factor of 15. Either there are many more criminals per capita in highly urban settings or the ones that are present commit many more crimes—or both. Certainly, there is a basis here for the presumption of much greater prevalence of delinquents and criminals in larger urban settings.

Next, let us examine briefly some genuine prevalence data for large cities, based on official statistics of one kind or another.[5] Savitz (1960) found that in a neighborhood with one of the four highest delinquency *incidence* rates in Philadelphia, 59% of all Negro boys who lived there from age 7 on became delinquent by age 18. Girls were not mentioned. Delinquency was defined here as possession of a juvenile court record, on the grounds that experience showed that delinquent behavior was usually involved regardless of the disposition of the case. The analysis by Wolfgang et al. (1972: 18-22) of the even more inclusive criterion "being taken into police custody" bore out this assumption concerning actual delinquent involvement even for that criterion, so it would certainly seem to be a safe one to apply to later stages of the juvenile justice process, in which additional screening occurs at each stage.

Wolfgang (1969: 33) reports, "In many areas in large cities 70 percent or more of all juveniles under 18 at one time or another may have been delinquent." This statement occurs in the context of a discussion using official rates, but it is not absolutely clear here what the criterion is, whether race is a consideration, or whether girls are really to be included. Given Savitz's 59%, however, it is not unlikely that 70% could be reached for Negro boys in some appropriately delineated area, such as a housing project with many mothers on ADC (e.g., New York Times, 1971; Schumach, 1971). Eisner (1969: Table 4) found two census areas in San Francisco in which 71.1 and 74.4% of the 17-year-old Negro males had acquired either police or juvenile court records *within the past year,* which was 1960.

The possibility of such high rates is clearly upheld by the results of Wolfgang and associates' study of a single birth cohort, consisting of all males (numbering 9,945) born in 1945 who resided continuously in Philadelphia at least from their tenth until their eighteenth birthday. They found the sex- and race-specific prevalence of at least one recorded police "contact" between age 7.0 and 18.0—that is, of being taken into custody by police regardless of later disposition—for this particular cohort to be 28.64% for white males and 50.24% for nonwhite males (1972: 22, 54, 218-220). (Although Wolfgang et al. usually employ the term "police contact," I am going to substitute "police custody" when speaking of their criterion, in order to emphasize that the criterion here means that an offense report is written and entered in police files. "Official arrest" constitutes only a subset of the dispositions available for the juveniles in custody. As distinct from self-report data, all of these dispositions generate "official" data in the special sense of interest in this paper.) The Philadelphia cohort was 29.18% nonwhite, and so a linear combination of the race-specific rates yields a city-wide rate of 34.94% for this criterion, which included only a few traffic or narcotics offenses (1972: Table 5.3). In 1960, 98.9% of the

Philadelphia nonwhites were Negro, so that one may read "Negro" where these authors have "nonwhite" without hesitation (U.S. Bureau of the Census, 1963: Part 40, Table 21). Dinitz (1969: 7) has given a figure similar to 34.94%, saying, " . . . there are plenty of neighborhoods in the cores of our cities in which as many as 250 to 350 of every 1,000 boys reaching 18 have experienced police and/or juvenile court contact."

For the nation as a whole, Dinitz (1969: 8) reports, it is estimated that by 1975 approximately 25.1% of the boys reaching 18 will have been *arrested* for a *nontraffic* offense. This clearly includes all races. Dinitz continues, "Comparably, 6.5 percent of the girls reaching 18 will probably have experienced an arrest," thus revealing a strong sex differential of approximately four to one. "Finally, one boy in 6 [the text reads "in 16," but this is a misprint] [6] and one girl in 23 will have come before the juvenile court by the time he or she reaches 18 years of age," Dinitz concludes, thus indicating that for the nation as a whole, the criterion of juvenile court appearance is *more stringent,* as one would expect, than that of arrest, yielding implied rates of 16.7% for boys and 4.4% for girls. The original source for these statistics is not mentioned, but when converted to percentages they appear to be remarkably close to the white prevalences given for the same criterion in Philadelphia by Monahan (1960), before these were corrected by Gordon and Gleser (1974). Originally, Monahan's white rates were 16.5% and 3.3%, respectively, for boys and girls.

Based on his extensive experience as Chief of Juvenile Delinquency Statistics of the Children's Bureau, Perlman (1959: 6) has estimated that approximately three out of four juvenile "contacts" (undefined) are dealt with by the police alone, *without a court appearance,* thus bearing out, on the single incident level, the general picture of greater severity for the criterion of juvenile court appearance that Dinitz described on the prevalence level. Lunden (1964: 188-190) has brought together published statistics, for 1,498 cities in 1961, and for Chicago for 1958-1962, showing that about 50% of juveniles in police "custody" (undefined) are referred to court. This squares with 43.5% of those arrested implied by figures for the nation as a whole in 1962 that Perlman himself presented later on (1964: 29). The implicit difference between Lunden's 50% and Perlman's earlier 25% referred to court may be due to the greater concentration of urban cases in Lunden's statistics, and perhaps to differences between Perlman's implicit definition of police "contact" and Lunden's implicit definition of police "custody." Perlman's later figures suggest that "custody" corresponds to "arrest," whereas "contact" may include more casual encounters. Both statistics support the same conclusion, however, namely that juveniles referred to court are a highly selected group, presumably for severity of the offender.

All of this may seem rather obvious, but in preparation for the more detailed analyses to follow, it is essential to have an absolutely thorough comprehension of the hierarchical ordering of the various criteria with respect to severity, of the relative magnitudes of the rates that they generate, and of the potential influence of the urban-rural continuum on these rates. For it is only when these criteria are appreciated to the maximum that it can be shown that empirical studies for particular cities or states provide estimates for different kinds of locations that are *actually highly consistent* with each other. This consistency affords us an extremely important theoretical and methodological tool. Having already introduced the police custody rates obtained from Wolfgang and associates' (1972) birth cohort study in Philadelphia, I now turn to a close examination of other examples of these rare data for particular places.

PREVALENCE IN URBAN OR HEAVILY URBAN SETTINGS

Monahan's Study: Philadelphia (1960 Population: 2,002,512)

One of the most important sources for data of this kind is Monahan's (1960) study of Philadelphia statistics for the period 1949-1954. However, in reviewing Monahan's results it was discovered that he had employed an inappropriate computational paradigm for determining prevalence, which underestimated correct values. Fortunately, it has been possible to revise Monahan's reported findings so that they are no longer subject to this mistake (Gordon and Gleser, 1974). The corrected rates will be employed throughout this discussion, accompanied by dual references to Monahan's original paper and to the table from Gordon and Gleser containing the revisions.

Although Monahan's work is rarely cited, I suspect that many of the undocumented estimates given by others concerning the prevalence of delinquency have been influenced by his results. There is reason to believe that this tacit neglect of Monahan is because he provided race-specific data; if sociologists have been made wary of SES differentials in official rates by the self-report research, a fortiori this research has led them to mistrust racial differentials even more, in view of the concentration of Negroes in lower strata. However, even if the Negro data themselves were faulty, it would still be impossible to make sense of the white data unless they were presented in race-specific form, as the rates furnished by this present example clearly demonstrate.

Monahan derived estimates for the percentage of persons who would have juvenile court experiences by their eighteenth birthday, using age-specific first-offense rates. Concerning his criterion, Monahan (1960: 70) stated:

Court figures used in this article include cases which are dismissed or adjusted by court probation officers, following an arrest or the filing of an official complaint. Traffic offenses, per se, constitute less than one-half of one percent of all cases.

It should be noted that this is practically identical to Savitz's (1960) criterion, already described, and both of these would be more severe than that of Wolfgang and associates, since not all of their police custody delinquents (but precisely how many was not stated) experienced court contact too (1972: chap. 13).

Monahan's prevalences at age 18.0, as revised by Gordon and Gleser (1974: Table 3), for the period 1949-1954 in Philadelphia, are as follows:

White girls	Negro girls	All juveniles	White boys	Negro boys
3.3%	15.8%	15.6%	17.9%	50.9%

According to the available evidence, these rates are quite stable from year to year within Philadelphia. Gordon and Gleser showed that Monahan's original rates had very small standard deviations over an eight-year period, and it would be expected that the revised rates would behave in about the same way, the two being intimately related to each other. (The standard deviations in question are exhibited later in this paper.)

The rate here for Negro boys in the city as a whole is also quite compatible with Savitz's rate of 59% for Negro boys in an especially high rate neighborhood in the same city, employing the same criterion of delinquency, for it must be remembered that relatively few Negro neighborhoods would be middle class.

The Monahan data can also be compared with a scrap of more recent information for Negro boys in the same city, from Lalli and Savitz (1972: 6-7), which also employs the juvenile court record criterion. Lalli and Savitz's sample consisted of 400 Negro 13-year-old boys, from a pool representing a cross-section of Philadelphia blacks. They found that 9.0% of the boys in the sample had already been delinquent by this age, and 12.5% of the families in the sample contained a delinquent youth (this enlarges the sample of boys, and extends it in age). Monahan's revised data (Gordon and Gleser, 1974: Table 3), which do not depend upon the completion of survey interviews, show a prevalence for Negro boys at age 13.0 of 14.8%.[7] This is not a bad match, when one allows for sampling variation in Lalli and Savitz's much smaller sample, and for the possibility that families with delinquent boys may have been harder to trace for interviewing, since the report by Lalli and Savitz is based only on the 80% of the drawn sample that had been successfully contacted thus far. At least eight important studies have reported extremely high residential mobility in antisocial populations.[8]

We do encounter a potential inconsistency, however, in connection with one important comparison. Clearly, there is an obvious need to reconcile the race-specific court record rates for males derived from the Monahan study with the race-specific rates of being in police custody at least once by age 18.0 for males from Wolfgang and associates' (1972) birth cohort study performed in the same city, but completed approximately nine years later. In order to satisfy the rate derived from Monahan of 50.9% for Negro males, virtually *all* of Wolfgang et al.'s nonwhite males who experienced being taken into police custody (50.24%) would have to achieve a juvenile court record as well, as this criterion was defined by Monahan. (The data for white males present no such problem, since the police custody percentage of 28.64 exceeds the court record percentage of 17.9 by a comfortable margin.) This particular issue concerning blacks will be taken up again in a later section.[9] Other issues concerning race will be deferred for future publication, since the present focus is mainly upon race-specific rates for whites.

It might be noted for now, however, that Gordon and Gleser's revised rates are more consistent than Monahan's original rates with all of the other rates for Negroes, with the single exception of Wolfgang and associates' police custody rate for black males, which on first appearance, at least, would seem more compatible with a rate for court appearance lower than the revised one of 50.9% given by Gordon and Gleser. However, the mathematical reasoning of their revision of Monahan's data is sound, and if there is any difficulty here, it should be sought elsewhere. The only direct, empirical check of the rates derived by Gordon and Gleser against Monahan's original data that is available shows that the revised rates do in fact provide a much better fit than Monahan's own version of these prevalences. In one of his tables, Monahan furnished a figure that represents a true prevalence rate not affected by his erroneous method of calculation (1960: Table 4, fourth column). This was for the year 1957, and it showed that 16.297% of all Philadelphia youth (both races and both sexes) would acquire a juvenile court record by age 18.0. By applying Monahan's own sex- and race-specific prevalence rates, and Gordon and Gleser's revised rates, to the appropriate proportions of the Philadelphia population, we can test to see which set does a better job at reconstituting the general rate. Here, the relative proportions of the population are estimated from a census tabulation of those who were 15 to 19 years old in 1960, and thus 12 to 16 in 1957, which concentrates them in the age range of interest (U.S. Bureau of the Census, 1963: Part 40, Table 20). Keeping in mind that the correct target figure for all Philadelphia youth is 16.297%, Monahan's original rates yield:

$$.1236(40.8) + .1400(14.8) + .3621(16.5) + .3743(3.3) = 14.32\%,$$

and Gordon and Gleser's revised rates yield:

$$.1236(50.86) + .1400(15.82) + .3621(17.87) + .3743(3.35) = 16.23\%.$$

Clearly, the revised rates are superior estimates of the actual values.

Douglas and Associates' Study: All of Great Britain

This cohort study from another country employs a delinquency criterion that appears quite similar to Monahan's court record criterion. "A delinquent in this discussion is a [child] who, before the age of seventeen years, has been *cautioned or who has appeared before the courts and been sentenced for an offence"* (Douglas et al., 1966: 295; emphasis added). In context, the criterion is ambiguous, because other passages appear to suggest that all of these delinquents "have been before the courts" (1966: 294, 299). However, a more recent report (Wadsworth, 1975: 167) of this research reveals that "cautioning" is by police, and that approximately 10.4% of the male delinquents were cautioned only. This means that actual court cases were all "sentenced" and therefore similar to those "adjudged" delinquent in Philadelphia. Since cautioned cases reflect trivial offenses, they appear to correspond to Monahan's "dismissed or adjusted" disposition. Including them seems reasonable, therefore, for they have little effect on the final rates, and none on the general argument.

The original cohort at risk was selected from the 12,468 *legitimate* single births occurring throughout England, Wales, and Scotland during the week March 3-9, 1946, so as to give unequal weight to various segments of the population. However, the authors apply the weights to their raw data so as to reconstitute estimates applicable to the original population, and these are the only values I employ (the unadjusted rate has been cited by Wolfgang et al., 1972: 10). The raw sample size in this case consists of the 2,402 boys and 2,190 girls who were living in Great Britain in 1963. Given 1946 as the birth year, it may be assumed that virtually all members of the cohort were white.

It was found that 14.6% of the male population had met the criterion between the ages of 8.0 and 17.0. This age range is one year shorter on each end than the period of risk employed by Monahan, and the upper boundary is one year short of the standard age of 18.0 employed throughout this paper.

However, it can be shown that it is safe to ignore the discrepancy at the lower bound, and that a simple adjustment can compensate for the discrepancy at the upper bound. According to Gordon and Gleser (1974: Table 3), beginning the period of risk at 8.0 rather than 7.0 would have excluded at most only 0.145% of white males and 0.006% of white females in Monahan's study. Any individuals who appear in court at this early age and who reappear later on during the period of risk would, of course, not remain excluded. At the upper bound, the figure can be adjusted by adding on the age-specific rate of new cases from 17.0 to 18.0 from Monahan's study (Gordon and Gleser, 1974: Table 3). This yields a prevalence at 18.0 of 17.295% (or 17.3%) for white males in Great Britain, which compares closely with the Philadelphia rate for a similar criterion of 17.9%.

Douglas and associates did not adjust their raw rate for girls so as to reconstitute the population estimate, as they did for boys, because they felt the number of female delinquents was too small. However, by assuming the adjustment for girls would have been proportional to the adjustment for boys, we get 1.95%, and by again adding on the age-specific rate for Philadelphia from 17.0 to 18.0, we obtain 2.414% (or 2.4%). This last figure compares closely with the rate of 3.3% actually observed for white girls in Philadelphia at age 18.0.

It might be pointed out that the adjustments I have introduced here are roughly equivalent in meaning to comparing the British rates directly with the Philadelphia rates at age 17.0 (which is possible, since the information exists in the paper by Gordon and Gleser). Although some readers might prefer a comparison between two actual rates at age 17.0 to a comparison between one actual rate and a rate adjusted on the assumption that a similar age-specific rate obtains during the eighteenth year in both places, the method I have chosen has the advantage of bringing all of the data together on a common basis (age 18.0), thus facilitating a broader range of comparisons. Age 18.0 is also a more realistic point for assessing the potential proportion of delinquents in a given cohort, since it comes later in the juvenile age range. The comparability of the numbers at 18.0 that I do present obviously depends upon the comparability of the numbers at 17.0 that I might have presented instead, so there is no real loss in information for comparative purposes.[10]

Once again, it should be emphasized that the closeness of the rates in both Great Britain and Philadelphia is quite striking. Even with an adjustment excluding "cautioned" cases, the final British rates are 15.78% and 2.21% for boys and girls, respectively.

Ball and Associates' Study:
Lexington, Kentucky (1960 SMSA Population: 131,906)

Ball et al. (1964) have also employed the age-specific rate technique for determining prevalence with data from the Lexington, Kentucky, Standard Metropolitan Statistical Area (SMSA) for the year 1960. Within the age ranges 5-19, 14.9% of the Lexington SMSA population was then black. The authors report that within this jurisdiction common traffic offenses by juveniles were handled in traffic court, and only unusual or serious traffic offenses in juvenile court. Again, the criterion of delinquency is appearance in juvenile court before age 18. Unlike Monahan's criterion, "conference" cases were not included, but Ball and associates (1964: 93) are of the opinion that their inclusion would have affected incidence more than prevalence; one presumes that this is because many individuals involved in conference cases eventually become involved in formal court appearance cases too.

Prevalence at 18.0 for boys was 20.7%, and for girls, 5.2%. To extract race-specific information from these composite rates, it is necessary to make two mild assumptions. One is that the percentage of Negroes among all 363 offenders that year, which was 31% or approximately twice random expectation, applies as well to the subset of 236 first-offenders, which figures in the actual calculation of prevalence. The other is that the rate for Negroes (as a multiple of the white rate) applies equally to both sexes (or, almost equivalently, mainly to boys, who represent 82.9% of the delinquents here). Solving for the rates for each race separately on the basis of these assumptions gives prevalences of 43.1% for Negro boys, and 16.8% for white boys. The reconstructed prevalence rates for girls, Negro and white, respectively, are 10.8 and 4.2. Except for white girls, these rates tend to be a bit lower than the corrected Monahan rates for Philadelphia, but then, Lexington, Kentucky represents a much smaller urban setting. The sex-race differentials in the rates parallel Philadelphia's.

Ball's Study: Two Kentucky Towns (Population 10,000 to 19,000)

In another study, Ball (1962: 32) found that 11% of a sample of 108 ninth grade boys in two Kentucky towns with populations between 10,000 and 19,000 were known to the *police or courts,* either officially or unofficially, for having committed crimes. Since these boys were only 15.0 years old on the average (1962: 37), this would obviously underestimate prevalence at age 18.0. It can be shown, however, that Ball's figure of 11% is much more consistent with other data than it first appears to be.

What we require for this purpose is a method for estimating the rate at 18.0, given the rate at 15.0. Consistent regularities in the relation between these two ages observed elsewhere suggest that an estimate so obtained would not be far wrong. First, Hathaway and Monachesi's data (1963: Table 18), from a study to be considered shortly using a different criterion, show that prevalence at age 15.0 doubles almost exactly for boys by age 18.0 in Minneapolis. That is, the rate of 12.6% at 15 is 48.5% of the rate of 26.0 at age 18.[11]

Second, Monahan's age-specific rates for 1957 (1960: Table 4, fourth column) show a doubling, when cumulated, from 8.198 to 16.297 for *all* Philadelphia youth, prevalence at 15.0 to prevalence at 18.0. The earlier rate here is 50.3% of the later. These particular data from Monahan are correct as they stand, incidentally, and require no revision.

Third, Monahan's rates for white boys by age 15.0 are 52.3% of the prevalence at age 18.0, for the period 1949-1954 (Gordon and Gleser, 1974: Table 3). For Negro boys, the corresponding figure was 55.8%.

Fourth, by cumulating Ball and associates' (1964: Table 2) age-specific rates for boys (of both races), we find a doubling for the Lexington SMSA, from 10.16 to 20.71, from age 15.0 to 18.0. Here the earlier prevalence is 49.1% of the later.

Fifth, by cumulating the numbers of age-specific, first-time offenders, by race, given by Wolfgang et al. (1972: Table 8.1, row B), where having been in police custody is the minimal criterion, we find that the prevalence rate at age 15.0 is 45.1% of the rate at age 18.0 for white males, and 62.2% for nonwhite males. For all males together, it is 52.2%. The rate for the nonwhite males here represents the most extreme departure of all from around half the later rate.

The average of these percentages (48.5, 50.3, 52.3, 55.8, 49.1, and 52.2) is 51.4%. For just the five white or predominantly white samples, it is 49.1%. Thus, for boys in urban settings, and perhaps mainly for whites, since even the combined data for both races and both sexes are weighted most heavily by white males, it would seem quite reasonable to double the prevalence at age 15.0 to obtain a good estimate for the eighteenth birthday, within this general range of severity.

Ball's prevalence rate of 11% at age 15.0 for his two towns may be inflated over other rates by two factors: one is his inclusion of "unofficial" police knowledge; the other is the small number of Negroes, 14 out of the 108 (p. 37). Although Ball reported (1962: 32) that race did not affect the rates "appreciably," it must be kept in mind that in Ball's small sample, each boy would count about one percentage point. Taking these considerations into account, his 11% at "average age" 15.0 is reasonably consistent with court record rates observed elsewhere, of about 17 or 18% for white boys at 18.0, for if 11% were reduced slightly, and then doubled, it would be about the same as the other rates.

More precisely, we can adjust directly for the Negroes by applying the expected rate of 28.4% delinquent at age 15.0 for Negro boys in Philadelphia (Gordon and Gleser, 1974: Table 3) to the 14 blacks to correct Ball's numerator, and then subtracting the 14 blacks from 108 to obtain the number of whites in the denominator. The Philadelphia rate predicts four (3.98) black delinquents out of 14 at age 15.0. Subtracting four from Ball's implied 12 delinquents (11% of 108) leaves eight, which when divided by 94 (108 minus 14) yields a rate of 8.51% at 15.0 for whites. Doubling this to obtain the rate at 18.0 yields 17.02%, which may be regarded as an upper bound estimate of the court record rate, in view of the inclusion of "unofficial" police knowledge.

Havighurst and Associates' Study:
"River City" (Population circa 1950-1960: 44,000)

This cohort study was performed in an anonymous, "medium-sized mid-western community" that was "the largest center of population" within 60 miles (i.e., not a satellite of a metropolis). The cohort consists of "all of the boys and girls in the sixth grade of the . . . public schools in 1951-1952," those sixth graders "who attended a Lutheran parochial school and a small, private boarding school . . . , and those in special classes (physically handicapped, mentally retarded, sight-saving) of similar grade level" (Havighurst et al., 1962: 3, 4, 7). The mentally handicapped group were all born one year ahead (i.e., in 1939) of the regular sixth grade group, this choice being made by the investigators so as "to have as homogeneous a social group as possible" (1962: 4). The unstated proportion of such slightly older retarded children was probably small, but there is no way of estimating it. By the ninth grade the initial group was supplemented by 98 additional youth who had either moved into the community or who had transferred to public schools from Catholic parochial elementary schools or "rural elementary schools at the fringes of the city" (1962: 5, 172-173). The final cohort consisted, therefore, of 247 boys and 240 girls. "About 3 per cent" of the population was Negro, and this would presumably apply to the school population as well, since both races attended school together and the city's Negroes have been "stable in numbers for generations" (1962: 9).

By the middle of 1959, when "most" of this group were "18 or 19" years old, 38.87% of the boys and 7.50% of the girls had "come into contact with police" (1962: 69). Apparently, this meant that the police recorded some information about the event ("The police would make a note of this . . . "), but this is not absolutely clear. These percentages are quite different from the court record prevalences at 18.0 that we have seen so far for whites, but this is not surprising, since the criterion of delinquency is more inclusive, the populations are a bit older than 18.0, and the races are not distinguished.

The authors themselves state, "It is much too loose a definition of delinquency, however, to call all of these boys and girls juvenile delinquents. Of the 114 offenders more than 40 have had only one contact with the police, and these were for such minor offenses as truancy, speeding, faulty automobile brakes, breaking windows or street lights. These incidents . . . never became a matter of court record. . . . Another third of the group have had more than a single contact with the police, but the reasons . . . were definitely of minor seriousness" (1962: 69).

This dissatisfaction with their "police record" criterion as a definition of "delinquency" that was sufficiently severe to be of social interest led Havighurst and associates to construct an index of severity for each contact. "The ratings varied from 1 to 4 for seriousness of the offense, and from 1 to 4 for the disposition of the case—whether the individual was let off with a warning, was brought into court, declared delinquent, fined, put in prison, sent to the state reformatory, and so on. The total delinquency scores ranged from 2 to 35" (1962: 69).

They then classified all of the delinquents into four categories of severity. The least serious category was IV, with scores below 5. Category III consisted of scores 5 to 8; "Most of these cases consisted of two contacts with the police, for relatively slight offenses" (1962: 69). Categories II and I "were definitely more serious," with category I "serious enough to suggest that there was a real danger of a criminal career" (1962: 69). The authors thereupon decided to speak only of those in categories I, II, and III as "delinquents" while stating that even "some of them are not delinquent by the usual legal definition. Nevertheless, they have done things that, if continued as they grow older, will result in arrest and punishment" (1962: 70).

Table 1 presents the distribution of cases, by sex, across the four categories, and the cumulative percentage of "delinquents" at each level of severity. Within the table, brief descriptive phrases, inspired by the text, suggest the quality of severity within each category. Only the phrase describing category IV reflects any amount of inference on my part. Given the scoring system, the authors' conviction that juveniles at this level are not "really delinquent," and the information that "more than 40" had been involved in only one minor police contact that had not been referred to court, it is pretty certain that none of the 57 youngsters strictly in category IV, with severity scores under 5, had ever been referred to court. The difference between the "more than 40" in the text and the 57 in the table is probably comprised of individuals with more than one minor police contact rather than of those who had been referred to court. Certainly, it is quite clear that at least "more than 40" of the 57 had never been referred to court. These inferences are bolstered by the authors' decision to regard only categories I, II, and III as "delinquent," and by their statement that only some of those strictly in category III "would be included in the national delinquency reports" (1962: 70), which suggests that not even all of those in almost-as-mild category III would have had a court record.

On the basis of the reasonable assumption that none of the police contacts in category IV led to a juvenile court record, we are left with the cumulative prevalences of 20.24 and 2.92% for boys and girls, respectively, as a new basis for comparison. These rates do roughly resemble the court record rates for whites already reviewed. However, we know from the authors' own remarks that not even all those in category III would be "included in national delinquency reports," that these rates reflect a point in time slightly beyond age 18.0, and

Table 1. THE PREVALENCE OF DELINQUENTS AT AGE 18 TO 19+ IN "RIVER CITY," AT FOUR LEVELS OF SEVERITY (Approximate rates for whites alone, obtained by adjusting roughly for the expected number of black delinquents, are enclosed within parentheses.)

Category, and description, from more severe to less severe	Boys		Girls	
	Category N	Cumulative prevalence (N=247)	Category N	Cumulative prevalence (N=240)
I. "real danger of a criminal career"	16	6.48% (6.18)	1	0.42% (0.36)[a]
II. "serious"	18	13.77 (13.13)	1	0.83 (0.72)[a]
III. "mostly two contacts with police, for relatively slight offenses"	16	20.24 (19.30)	5	2.92 (2.52)
IV. "Mostly one minor contact with police;" probably never became a court record	46	38.87 (38.52)	11	7.50 (----)
Total	96		18	

SOURCE: Havighurst et al., 1962: 69-70.

a. Cell N too small to yield meaningful adjustment, but entry is regarded as more informative than if simply left blank.

that the rates also reflect the inclusion of blacks (who we know from data elsewhere have rates much higher than whites). Even a modest amount of discounting applied to the above rates in view of these considerations would indicate that the "true" rate at the court record level of severity in "River City" cannot be higher than the one in Philadelphia, and might even be lower. If it were lower, this would square with our expectations concerning the relative placements of Philadelphia and "River City" on the urban-rural continuum.

The effect of the inclusion of blacks in relation to this inference can be examined by simulating the sex-specific rates that would obtain for both races when counted together, given that 3% are black, if the process generating a juvenile court record by 18.0 in Philadelphia were also operative in "River City." If 3% are black, then the male cohort consists of 7.4 blacks and 239.6 whites, and the female cohort consists of 7.2 blacks and 232.8 whites. Application of the Philadelphia rates, as reported by Gordon and Gleser, to these relative frequencies yields the following numbers of expected delinquents for boys and girls, respectively:

$$7.4(.5086) + 239.6(.1787) = 46.58,$$

$$7.2(.1582) + 232.8(.0335) = 8.94.$$

Dividing these expected numbers of Philadelphia court record delinquents by the cohort size for each sex yields expected court record rates for both races combined, at age 18.0, of 18.86% for boys, and of 3.72% for girls. The cumulative rates actually observed for categories I to III (Table 1) are 20.24 and 2.92%, respectively. Thus, the observed rates are even closer on the average to the expected rates when race is taken into account in defining the expectations.

The closeness of the observed and expected sets of rates to each other really cannot be used as totally independent evidence that the race-specific prevalence of delinquents at the court record level of severity is about the same in both Philadelphia and "River City," because we do not have an actual court record rate for "River City" or an accurately calibrated substitute (as we more or less did for Ball's Kentucky towns). However, the closeness to each other of the numbers in hand in conjunction with indications that the level III criterion is probably more inclusive than the court record criterion, and with the fact that the age of the "River City" cohort exceeds 18.0 by a small amount (perhaps six to nine months), certainly supports the conclusion that the equivalent of court record rates in "River City" do not *exceed* those in Philadelphia. As noted before, these considerations do not exclude the possibility that the "River City" rates are lower than their equivalents in Philadelphia. This outcome, however, would be consistent with expected urban-rural orderings, and we would develop a sense of inconsistency over such a difference only if it proved to be drastic and out of line with other urban-rural data points for the same criterion. The level II rate in Table 1 would seem to set a lower bound on the prevalence of delinquents of court record severity, since the descriptions of categories I and II suggest that such cases would not escape appearing in court. The level II rate for boys is not so low as to permit wild discrepancy, while the rate for girls must be judged in terms of the closeness of the expectation to zero, and the instability of small samples for estimating percentages close to zero. Thus, we can derive some assurance that the superficially noncomparable data of Havighurst and associates are actually *not visibly inconsistent* with the court record data from other studies already reviewed. When relevant studies are so few in number, this is always a worthwhile gain.

Although the fact that the proportion of blacks in "River City" is so small means that even the raw rates apply mostly to whites, it is still more convenient for present purposes to have even roughly approximate rates that apply only to whites. I have derived such rates, therefore, and placed them within parentheses in Table 1, according to the following considerations. First, it is assumed that the ratio of black delinquency rates to white delinquency rates observed at the court record level of severity in Philadelphia holds true in "River City" across the severity range represented by categories III, II, and I (category IV is considered below). Category III, we have just seen, can be sensed to be close to the level of severity represented in Philadelphia by having a court record. The extension of this proportionality to categories II and I can be justified by Gordon's (1973: Table 3) demonstration that roughly similar racial ratios apply across the severity continuum marked by having a court record in Philadelphia at one extreme and being placed in a training school (nationwide) at the other extreme. If the first of these points is close to category III, the second surely extends beyond category I (the most severe point in the "River City" data). Second, we "correct" the one level, at category III, for which there is approximately relevant data, and then we prorate this correction, within sex, across levels II and I. This correction involves removing the expected number of blacks from the level III rate on the basis of the probably more severe court record data for Philadelphia. If the court record criterion really is more severe than level III, this would amount to an undercorrection, because more blacks (and whites) would be included under a less severe criterion than under a more severe criterion. This correction would then be applied proportionally to the rates at levels II and I.

For example, if there are 7.4 Negro males expected in the cohort (3%), and the Philadelphia court record rate (of 50.86%) predicts that 3.76 of these will be delinquent, we subtract 3.76 from 50 (the cumulative number of male delinquents at level III) to obtain an undercorrected figure of 46.24 representing only white delinquents. This, in turn, is divided by 239.6 (the male cohort size minus the expected 3% Negro), to obtain a rate for whites of 19.30% (entered in Table 1). Since 19.30 is .9536 of the racially composite rate of 20.24, we employ this constant of proportionality to yield similar adjustments at levels II and I, where we lack knowledge of their relation to any established marker of approximately equivalent severity. Corresponding adjustments have also been made for females, and entered into Table 1, although the absolute frequencies at categories II and I are far too small to permit the entries to be precise estimators at those levels. However, by entering the obtained results into the table, it serves to indicate what the values *were not* in a way that is more informative than simply leaving blank spaces.

It is also possible to devise a comparison between Havighurst and associates' "police contact" criterion and Wolfgang and associates' "police custody" criterion by substituting the race-specific police custody rates for males at age

18.0 in Philadelphia into the equation employing the relative frequencies of blacks and whites in "River City." This can be done only for males, however, since Wolfgang et al. (1972) did not include females in their study. The desired equation reads:

$$7.4(.5017) + 239.6(.2867) = 72.4.$$

Dividing the result by 247 yields a rate of 29.31%. The fact that the observed rate for males in "River City" was 38.87%, which is much larger, suggests that the police in the smaller city were inclined to note down events of greater triviality than the police in Philadelphia (for it seems unlikely that the slight difference in age employed in the two studies would fully account for the difference in rates). This evidence jibes with and reinforces the opinion given by Havighurst et al. that many of the youngsters nominally qualified as delinquent by their criterion were not actually severely enough so to be of social interest. There is no reason to suppose, as an alternative explanation of the difference, that youth in "River City" are more delinquent than youth in Philadelphia. This would run against the trend thought to be associated with the rural-urban continuum. Indeed, we have already seen that there is no real evidence of such a perverse trend for the point of severity represented by the court record criterion, for which the upper bound is more clearly established in the "River City" data than is the exact point on the severity continuum at which the police contact, or level IV criterion, lies. It would seem likely that what police choose to make a matter of record might fluctuate more from one jurisdiction to another than what the court makes a matter of record, since the former entails little additional social and economic cost per case as it becomes more inclusive, while the latter entails much greater cost in time and trouble per case for all concerned.

Despite the ambiguities associated with the comparability between category IV and Wolfgang et al.'s police custody criterion, I have calculated an estimated rate for whites alone, analogous to those described above, using the Philadelphia police custody values for black males, since it is the most applicable basis for making an adjustment. This yields the parenthetical value entered in Table 1 at level IV, for males. For reasons similar to those given before, this final rate is also thought to be undercorrected.

Hathaway and Monachesi's Study: Minnesota, Statewide and Urban

The studies by Hathaway and Monachesi (1963) in Minnesota—which they describe as being in a midrange of all states economically in the late 1950s—furnish a variety of unusually comprehensive data relevant to the examination of prevalence. The definition of delinquency they employed differs in important respects from those in most of the previous studies, however, and therefore it must be studied closely. Hathaway and Monachesi state (1963: 22):

> For all the follow-up surveys the files of the probation office, juvenile police, and juvenile courts in each community . . . were examined. Each student received a severity of delinquency rating based on the records *or on any other pertinent information. A rating indicating some degree of delinquency could be given for subjects who had no official record, but this was rarely done.* [Emphasis added.]

Four levels of what is consequently almost entirely officially recorded delinquency were distinguished (pp. 22-23), which I describe below; familiarity with these definitions is essential for following the discussion to come:

Level 1. Subjects placed in this classification "were found in police records for at least one minor difficulty such as a traffic violation like overtime parking or being picked up by the police. In the latter case, involvement was either poorly established or the individual contributed to whatever disturbance occurred in such a minor way that classification into level 2, 3, or 4 was not justified."

Level 2. "The youngsters placed in this class had committed minor offenses such as destruction of property (especially when this was connected with play activities), drinking, one or more traffic offenses (escapades involving speeding, driving without a license, and/or going at high speed through a stop light or sign), *curfew violation,* and immoral conduct of a severity or frequency that did not require a rating of 3 or 4. The misbehavior was *relatively nondelinquent* in comparison to that of the other two categories. Nevertheless, these boys and girls as a group had all behaved in clearly undesirable ways." (Emphasis added.)

Level 3. "This level of misconduct involves the commission of *one serious* offense such as auto theft, grand larceny, or gross immorality, or more than one less serious offense such as petty larceny, immoral conduct, assault, disorderly conduct, malicious destruction of property, shoplifting, flagrant curfew violations, truancy, and incorrigibility. *The youngsters placed in this class were therefore not established as severely delinquent,* but, nevertheless, their offenses were worse or more numerous than those of subjects classified in level 2." (Emphasis added.)

Level 4. "This classification is used to denote those who committed *repeated offenses* such as auto theft, burglary, grand larceny, holdup with a gun, gross immoral conduct (girls), accompanied by less serious offenses. *In this category were placed all youngsters who were considered to have demonstrated a well-established delinquent pattern."* (Emphasis added.)

In the discussion to follow, *rates* based on any of these four levels of severity always include *all levels more severe* than the one named, so that, for example, "level 3 rates" are cumulatively inclusive of level 4, and "level 2 rates" subsume levels 3 and 4. This usage is similar to that which I employed for discussing the hierarchical rates given by Havighurst et al. (Note that the present four levels, indicated by Arabic numerals, run opposite with respect to severity to the four levels, indicated by Roman numerals, from the study by Havighurst and associates. In the interest of maintaining fidelity to the original reports, I have chosen not to interfere with this potential source of confusion.)

Two samples are involved. First I shall consider the one called the "statewide" sample, which *excluded* Minneapolis and St. Paul, but which included Duluth and other urban communities such that the total was composed approximately equally of rural and urban children. Twenty-eight percent of this sample resided on farms, and another 8% in towns of less than 1,000; but 44% came from urban areas and towns with populations over 10,000, and it is therefore important not to be misled by a rustic vision of Minnesota into mistaking this for a strictly rural sample (see Hathaway and Monachesi, 1963: Table 2). The sample size, divided about equally between sexes, was 11,329. Nonwhites were present in negligible numbers only (p. 16).

The second Minnesota sample is entirely from Minneapolis (1960 population: 482,872), with a total sample size of 3,971, divided between the sexes. Only the cumulative rate for level 2 is available for this sample. Here, interpolations described earlier, between what the authors call "modal" ages 17 and 19, have been used for age 18 (see n. 11, above).

Table 2 displays the cumulative percentages (prevalences) of boys and girls at each of the four delinquency levels at "modal" age 18 for the statewide sample (from Hathaway and Monachesi, 1963: Table 19), the level 2 rates for Minneapolis at "modal" age 18 (from Hathaway and Monachesi, 1963: Table 18), and, for comparison, the court record rates from Philadelphia for white boys and girls for 1949-1954 (Gordon and Gleser, 1974: Table 3), from Great Britain (Douglas et al., 1966), from the Lexington SMSA for 1960 (Ball et al., 1964), and from the two Kentucky towns (Ball, 1962), as these rates have been reconstructed or approximated. The table also includes a court record rate for Nashville that I have yet to discuss, the police custody rate for white males from Philadelphia (Wolfgang et al., 1972), rates that I derived for "River City" (Havighurst et al., 1962), and some others still to be introduced. For heuristic reasons, to be developed shortly, the out-of-Minnesota court record rates are placed in Table 2 *between* levels 2 and 3, and the police custody and contact rates ("police record") are placed adjacent to level 2. For the moment, let us disregard the placement in the table of the four categories (I to IV) from the study by Havighurst and associates.

Clearly, depending on how one chose to define delinquency (or a delinquent),

Table 2. ALL KNOWN EXISTING ESTIMATES OF THE PREVALENCE OF DELINQUENCY (in %) FOR WHITES AT ABOUT AGE 18.0, ACCORDING TO VARIOUS INTERPRETABLE CRITERIA ARRANGED IN ORDER OF THEIR SEVERITY AS JUDGED FROM AVAILABLE INFORMATION (see text for essential details)

Delinquency criterion, from more severe to less	Minnesota "statewide"		Minneapolis		"River City"		Philadelphia (two studies)		Great Britain		Lexington SMSA		Kentucky, two towns		Nashville SMSA		United States		Marion County	
	Boys	Girls	Boys	Girls	Boys	Girls	Boys	Girls	Boys	Girls	Boys	Girls	Boys	Girls	Boys	Girls	Boys	Girls	Boys	Girls
Training school																	1.02	0.23	0.90	---
Level 4	2.4	0.7																		
Category I (age 18 to 19+)					6.2	<0.5[b]														
Level 3	8.7	2.0																		
Felony charge																			13.9	---
Category II (age 18 to 19+)					13.1	<1.0[b]														
"Court record"							17.9	3.3	17.3	2.4	16.8	4.2	17.0[d]	---	16.3[d]	---				
Category III (age 18 to 19+)					19.3	2.5														
Level 2[a]	24.0	6.2	26.0	8.6																
Police record[a]							28.6	---											24.7	---
Category IV (age 18 to 19+)					38.5	<7.5[c]														
Level 1	34.6	10.4																		

a. The ordering of these two rows with respect to each other is indeterminant.
b. Original sample too small to yield a precise estimate of such a low rate.
c. No correction for small proportion of blacks (about 3%) was possible.
d. See text for assumptions underlying the derivation of this rate.

quite different rates could be had for the statewide sample from the data in Table 2. Levels 3 and 4 are unambiguously delinquent by anybody's standard and would typically involve a juvenile court appearance (see their descriptions, above). Level 1 is delinquent only in the most trivial sense; it apparently includes those numerous cases that would have been disposed of in traffic court rather than juvenile court in Philadelphia and other jurisdictions. This leaves level 2.

According to its description, level 2 seems to straddle the point of severity defined in Philadelphia by having had an appearance in juvenile court. Some of its offenses would have been handled there, but others not. This appraisal is supported by the fact that the cumulative rates for level 2 in Table 2 *exceed* the court record rates from the studies by Monahan and by Ball et al. for both sexes, despite the heavily rural component in the Minnesota statewide sample. There is no good reason to expect the statewide sample of almost entirely white Minnesota youth to be *more* delinquent than whites in Philadelphia or in the Lexington SMSA. Quite the contrary, based on what is known of rural-urban differences, as revealed in the observations by Dinitz, Wolfgang, and Savitz that I introduced earlier, the statewide sample should be *less* delinquent. This is borne out also by the fact that the level 2 rates also exceed the court rates in Great Britain, which do include rural as well as urban youth.

One would also expect the city of Minneapolis to have a prevalence rate comparable to those in other urban areas, such as Philadelphia and the Lexington SMSA, if the same criterion were employed in both places, and not a rate that was 50% higher for white boys and more than 100% higher for white girls, as would occur if the level 2 rates in Table 2 were to be equated with the court record rates in other cities. *It appears, therefore, that the level 2 criterion is much more inclusive of various types of offense than the criterion of having had an appearance in juvenile court.* Its cumulative rate, especially for Minneapolis, is quite close to the recorded police custody rate for Philadelphia (and for Marion County, to be discussed later), and we know that only 23.4% of the total number of Philadelphia police contacts with white males (that is, offenses, not to be confused with the percentage of persons contacted) were processed further in the juvenile justice system, i.e., toward court (Wolfgang et al., 1972: Table 13.1). Use of the files of the juvenile police by the Minnesota researchers undoubtedly introduced a flood of lesser offenses into the statistics—such as curfew violation (see the description)—that would *not* ordinarily have gone before a juvenile court or produced a juvenile court record. This interpretation of the relative standing of the various rates makes good sense in view of the sense of their relative severity conveyed by their descriptions.

Although there is no way of knowing from these data precisely what rates the Philadelphia and Lexington court record criteria would actually have generated if applied to whites in Minnesota, it can be seen from Table 2 and the preceding considerations that they *are not likely to be far different from those observed elsewhere,* especially in Minneapolis, since the Philadelphia court record rate is bracketed here by rates based on criteria (levels 2 and 3) that can be clearly sensed to bracket the Philadelphia criterion in their severity.

We can also see that even these highly inclusive level 2 rates, both in Minneapolis and "statewide," are *much lower* than rates based on more severe criteria for urban blacks, and that the ratio of males to females in both Minnesota samples, at every level of cumulation, stands at 3 or 4 to 1, which is the same as the ratios for whites in Philadelphia and Lexington.

If we consider only level 3 and 4 offenders together, which produce rates much lower than those at level 2, we can also gain a sense that the rate of very *severe* delinquency, as represented by the descriptions of these two levels, seems to be *quite a bit lower than the rate of delinquency defined by possession of a juvenile court record.* Even at levels 3 and 4, a further distinction can be made, since Hathaway and Monachesi regarded level 3 offenders as "not ... severely delinquent," and only the level 4 offender as having demonstrated a "well-established delinquent pattern." Judging from what we can tell of categories II and I (which included offenders regarded by Havighurst et al. as "definitely more serious" in contradistinction to their category III, which I have argued represents a criterion less severe than juvenile court), the rates of these categories too indicate by their relative standing in Table 2 that delinquency sensed to be "serious" is less prevalent than is possession of a juvenile court record.

It is a pity that Hathaway and Monachesi did not provide the rates for all of the levels for Minneapolis, for the prospect is good that they would not have been much different there, judging from the similarity in level 2 rates, and therefore they would have indicated just how prevalent mainly white official delinquents are at points of severity that correspond to the phenomenologically rich descriptions of the levels, as opposed to the operationally important but phenomenologically barren criterion afforded by the court record. This descriptive fullness, of course, is an unusually valuable property of the Hathaway and Monachesi rates, compared to which the rates of Havighurst et al. are poorly described indeed.

A certain amount of ambiguity notwithstanding, I have assigned positions in Table 2 to the rates ("categories I-IV") from the study by Havighurst and associates. Their positions in the table have been ordered with respect to the positions of other criteria so as to reflect my judgment of their relative severity in light of the information available. It should be obvious even to impatient readers that the ambiguity concerning the propriety of most of these placements is far from total. For example, "category I" is plainly more severe than "level

1." It is the subset of heterogeneous criteria that are sensed to be relatively close to each other whose relative ordering in the table is most ambiguous. Once the relative placement of adjacent criteria from different studies is settled, however, as will be seen in the case of category III and level 3, for example, the relative placement of many of the remaining criteria within each of the ordered sets with respect to members of the other set is also determined. Consequently, it is necessary to rationalize or justify only the critical subset of fairly ambiguous adjacent placements.

In the list presented as Table 3, I have furnished the rationales for the critical pairings between criteria from the two four-category systems, of Havighurst and associates and of Hathaway and Monachesi. Orderings between each of these systems and the remaining official criteria in Table 2 from conventional justice systems for juveniles have been or will be considered at other points.

Of the seven critical decisions presented in Table 3, I consider numbers 5 and 7 the most difficult to resolve. Although all of the decisions have obviously been informed by the relative magnitudes of the rates in Table 2 (a less severe criterion should produce a higher rate than a more severe criterion), I have tried

Table 3. RATIONALES FOR ORDERING TWO SETS OF CRITERIA IN TABLE 2

Less Severe	< More Severe	Reason for Opinion
1. level 1	< category IV	Because level 1 includes overtime parking.
2. category IV	< level 2	Because level 2 includes "drinking" offenses, and IV is the most inclusive in its study, whereas level 2 has been denied the level 1 offenses.
3. level 2	< category III	Because III is based usually on more than one offense, whereas level 2 can be just one offense, and both criteria apply to mild offenses.
4. category III	< level 3	Because most cases in category III are for "relatively slight offenses," implied not to be serious enough to warrant a court record, whereas level 3 is definitely serious, and would appear to warrant a court record.
5. category II	< level 3	Although category II is described as "serious," level 3 includes car theft and grand larceny, which are explicitly highly serious.
6. level 3	< category I	Because individuals in level 3 are described as "not established as severely delinquent," whereas those in category I are in "real danger of a criminal career."
7. category I	< level 4	Although category I is described as "serious enough to suggest . . . a real danger of a criminal career," level 4 is actually equated to a "well-established delinquent pattern" which requires repeated felonies such as car theft or armed robbery.

to rationalize the placements as independently of the rates as possible, with the exception of numbers 5 and 7. In their case, the relative rates have carried more influence than for the remaining decisions in resolving ambiguity. However, even here, the ordering of the rates is not contravened by any of the descriptive material available in the original studies, and in this important sense the placements are not "forced."

Gordon's Study: The Nationwide Prevalence of Commitment to a Training School—An Extremely Severe Criterion

Gordon (1973: Table 2) has derived an estimate for the nationwide prevalence at age 18.0 of commitment to a training school, by race and by sex, based upon age-specific first-confinement rates, for the period around 1964. These rates are as follows:

White girls	Negro girls	White boys	Negro boys
0.23%	0.80%	1.02%	3.90%

The fact that the rates for white boys and girls here are so much lower than the severe level 4 rates (Table 2) for the Minnesota statewide sample, which excluded Minneapolis and St. Paul, suggests that this criterion is more severe than level 4. One would probably not be able to infer this from the description of the level 4 criterion, however, which strikes one as severe enough to warrant incarceration. The same may hold true for category I in "River City" (where the only good estimator at this level is for boys).

Obviously, it is not likely that this difference in rates is due to a lower rate of severe delinquency nationwide than in the state of Minnesota minus its two largest cities. Apparently, *even severely delinquent youth are seldom confined,* and the difference between the rates testifies to the extreme severity of the confinement criterion, rather than to the "mildness" of the level 4 or category I criteria.

This assessment of the severity of the confinement criterion is also supported inferentially by data from Wolfgang and associates' birth cohort study (1972: Table 6.3). For their exclusively urban cohort, they reported the following *prevalences* at each of three levels of severity, where severity is defined by the cumulative number of times one has been in police custody by age 18.0. The abstract numbers in parentheses are these authors' mean seriousness scores for the average offense in each category (1972: 95). It can be seen in Table 4 that the seriousness of the average offense also increases with the frequency of

Table 4. PREVALENCE AT THREE LEVELS OF SEVERITY AT AGE 18.0 IN
PHILADELPHIA (mean seriousness scores of offenses in parentheses)

	In police custody at least once	More than once (recidivists)	More than four times (chronic recidivists)
Nonwhite males:	50.24% (121.2)	32.84% (130.6)	14.37% (135.5)
White males:	28.64% (83.8)	12.91% (100.3)	2.98% (107.0)

SOURCE: Wolfgang et al., 1972: Table 6.3.

offending. In this particular birth cohort, 2.5% of the boys experienced incarceration (1972: 57). Unfortunately, the information provided by the authors fails to be race-specific at this vital point. However, we can generate linear combinations for two sets of our other rates, and compare the results with the composite rate actually reported in order to get an idea of the relative severity of various criteria. Since 29.18% of the birth cohort was nonwhite, we find that the nationwide rates (from Gordon, 1973) applied to the Philadelphia cohort males would lead us to expect a composite incarceration rate of 1.86% in Philadelphia. Thus:

$$.2918(3.90) + .7082(1.02) = 1.86\%.$$

If it were assumed that all delinquents in the cohort who were in police custody more than four times ("chronic recidivists") were eventually incarcerated by age 18.0, and no one else, then the rate would be:

$$.2918(14.37) + .7082(2.98) = 6.30\%.$$

The racially nonspecific rate actually observed, 2.5%, falls *between* both of these models and is much closer to the first. This indicates, as we would expect, that the specific incarceration rates in a city like Philadelphia are higher than the national rates, which include rural settings, but by a quite reasonable amount, and that even in a large city a delinquent boy must display on the average a severity greater than that associated with merely having been in police custody four times in order to receive confinement. This squares with our appreciation of the confinement criterion as also being more severe than the level 4 criterion, since the level 4 rate of 2.4% for white males in Minnesota (Table 2) and the rate of "more than four" recorded police custodies of 2.98% for white males in Philadelphia are both quite close to each other, and we have just seen that the "more than four" custodies criterion produces much too high an incarceration rate for the birth cohort when it is imposed on the relevant fractions of the population.

This sense of the severity of delinquency implied by the incarceration criterion vis-à-vis its neighboring criteria is supported by two useful scraps of additional information. First, we know from a study in Flint, Michigan, by Gold (1963: Table 7) that only 12% of a group of 93 white boys having records of committing at least two fairly serious crimes within the previous three years were institutionalized. None of the boys who had committed but one serious crime had been sent away. This indicates that incarceration marks a more severe point than level 3, which involved only *one* serious offense. It would also appear more severe than level 4, since only 12% with "at least two" serious offenses (which qualifies for level 4) had been sent to training school. Since it has been argued that level 4 is more severe than category I, this also locates incarceration with respect to category I. Second, Conger and Miller (1966: 17) have remarked that "of the youths carried on the records of the Juvenile Court . . . only about one in eight" are sentenced to an institution. This "statistic" applies to Denver, which had a minority population of about 10% around the time of the study (circa 1960).[12] Dividing the sex- and race-specific Philadelphia court record rates from Gordon and Gleser by eight (after Denver), and comparing them with the nationwide incarceration rates from Gordon (given above), shows that the two sets of numbers are within the same ballpark, and thus continues to indicate that incarcerated delinquents are quite rare. The constructed percentages (with Gordon's in parentheses) are: white girls, 0.42 (0.23); Negro girls, 1.98 (0.80); white boys, 2.23 (1.02); and Negro boys, 6.36 (3.90). The fact that Gordon's nationwide rates tend to be a bit lower than the approximation is consistent with the rural component in the nationwide rates.

Reiss and Rhodes' Study:
Nashville, Tennessee (1960 SMSA Population: 399,743)

Our final urban prevalence datum comes from the Nashville, Tennessee, Standard Metropolitan Area (the predecessor of the SMSA), reported by Reiss and Rhodes (1961). The criterion in this 1958 study was having been referred to juvenile court and *adjudged a delinquent* either by court referees or by the presiding judge *after one's twelfth birthday.* This is more stringent than the juvenile court record standards already considered in two respects.

The most important one is that an offender has to have been *adjudged* a delinquent here, which means that the court must find that the facts alleged in a petition are substantiated (Lunden, 1964: 206), whereas in Monahan's study merely having had an appearance before the juvenile court, or appearing on court records, regardless of disposition (whether or not the case was dismissed or informally adjusted without "official" court appearance), was sufficient to classify one as a delinquent, and Ball and associates felt that their standard was tantamount to this.

Second, whatever small percentage there might be of children who appear before the court for the first time between the ages of 6 or 7 and 12, and who never reappear after 12, is lost from the Nashville rate, although these children would have contributed to the rates in Philadelphia and Lexington, and presumably also in Minnesota, and elsewhere. However, since only 3.2% of white boys acquire a court record before age 12.0 in Philadelphia (Gordon and Gleser, 1974: Table 3), and many of these undoubtedly appear again after age 12.0, this is probably not a major source of bias.

According to statistics reviewed by Lunden (1964: Table 112), 66% of delinquency *cases* in 1957, and 67% in 1961, from selected courts were placed on probation or committed, and therefore, presumably, "adjudged delinquent." Judging from other tables in Lunden's review (1964: Tables 113-116), girls and boys are treated about the same in this respect, and so we can apply these 1957 and 1961 percentages that apply to both sexes to boys alone with reasonable security to estimate full court appearance rates, regardless of disposition, for Nashville. Obviously, the general statistics are most heavily weighted by boys in any case, by a factor of about 3 or 4 to 1.

Reiss and Rhodes reported that for white boys *still in school,* and 16 or over, 8% met their definition of a delinquent. A crude, but nevertheless instructive, approximation of the more familiar court record prevalence rates at 18.0 can be obtained for these boys as follows. On the basis of the general statistics noted above, it is reasonable to assume that at least two-thirds of the boys who appear in court are adjudged delinquent. Note that while a "case" appears but once, a boy can appear repeatedly in court, and so reasoning as I am about to do from "cases" to boys can lead to an overcorrection, since repeated court exposure can eventually transform boys involved in nondelinquent "cases" into "boys" involved in cases adjudged delinquent. However, let us see where this leads. Taking into account this potentially missing third, the court *appearance* rate (adjudged delinquent or not) for Nashville becomes 12%.

Next, let us make the reasonable assumption that the age distribution of these in-school, 16 or over boys extends from 16 to 18, and that it is approximately rectangular (actually, it probably slopes downward, as a function of school leaving, and of population growth). Slight violations of these assumptions would have little influence on the outcome. Half of this distribution then falls before 17, and half after. The mean age of the lower half is 16.5, and of the upper half, 17.5. This implies that each cohort has still to acquire approximately half of the new cases that would normally occur during its age-year interval, and in addition, the younger cohort still stands to acquire all of the cases that normally are recorded in the year interval from 17 to 18. Using the increments in case numbers that would be obtained by imposing the age-specific first-offense rates for Philadelphia white boys, 1949-1954, as corrected for Monahan's data by Gordon and Gleser (1974: derived from Table 3 by subtraction), on this hypothetical Nashville distribution, or, in other words, proratedly adding half the rate for the seventeenth year for the younger half, half the rate for the eighteenth year for the older half, and the full rate for the eighteenth year for the younger half, to 12%, yields an estimated prevalence, defined approximately according to Monahan's criterion, of 14.7%. Finally, some part of the 3.2% who would have appeared before age 12.0 should be added. The amount depends on our estimate of the share who are already included because they reappeared after 12.0. If we add the full 3.2%, implicitly assuming no recidivism, we obtain 17.9; if we add half or 1.6%, we get 16.3. Clearly, any reasonable choice has little bearing on the implications of the final figure, and so I have chosen 16.3 somewhat arbitrarily as the final estimate. This estimate has been entered into Table 2, where it proves to be quite close to the rates of 17.9, 17.3, 16.8, and 17.0 for Philadelphia, Great Britain, Lexington, and the two Kentucky towns, especially if we make allowance for a presumably high delinquency rate among the school dropouts, who were not included in the Nashville data.

If the rate for the smaller urban setting of Nashville were actually to prove somewhat lower than the rate for Philadelphia this would be in keeping with long-standing expectations concerning the relative locations of these cities on the rural-urban continuum. The estimate obtained, however, even if subject to this possibility, gives us a fair sense that the statistic reported by Reiss and Rhodes is not inconsistent with those obtained elsewhere, and that all of these statistics may well refer roughly to the same phenomenon.

AN OVERALL ASSESSMENT OF PREVALENCE DATA
FOR URBAN AND HEAVILY URBAN SETTINGS

In view of the importance of prevalence data, it is amazing that there is so little to be found. Even then, much effort is required to render the various statistics reasonably comparable. The best American data appear to be those from Philadelphia, via Monahan, where the statistical procedures of the juvenile court have long been regarded as a model (1961: 162). Each of Monahan's yearly rates for a single sex has the advantage of being based on eleven age-strata samples, each one of which is about one-third larger than Wolfgang and associates' single male birth cohort, and since Gordon and Gleser's corrected rates were based on data for the six-year composite 1949-1954, the final rates derived from Monahan are in effect based on samples many times larger than the single birth cohort. Furthermore, the availability of multiple yearly observations for Monahan's sex- and race-specific rates enables us to see that they show a high degree of stability for individual years over an eight-year period, as reflected in very small standard deviations,[13] in percentage points, as follows (Gordon and Gleser, 1974: 290):

White girls	Negro girls	All juveniles	White boys	Negro boys
0.32	2.25	1.91	1.52	1.88

Most important of all, Monahan's rates have the advantage of not excluding boys who failed to meet Wolfgang and associates' rather stringent residence requirement (which was understandably imposed by the needs of the birth cohort method; see n. 4, above). The residence requirement was met by only 9,945 boys out of their initial Philadelphia birth cohort of 14,313 (1972: 38, 54). This represents a substantial loss in view of the fact that we know nothing about the delinquency characteristics of the missing 30.5%, whose crimes residents of Philadelphia were also exposed to at that time. Adjacent cohorts would also have contained boys equivalent to this missing proportion.

Monahan's cohorts include this missing fraction. For example, his cohorts of males that were age 12 in 1957, 9 in 1954, 8 in 1953, and 7 in 1952, and thus who were born in or around 1945 (Wolfgang et al.'s starting date), contain an average of 14,729 members (The Board of Public Education, 1952: Table 9; 1953: Table 9; 1954: Table 8; 1957: Table 9). This number is much closer to Wolfgang et al.'s initial 14,313 than to the 9,945 finally meeting their residence requirements.

Within race, the final numbers of nonwhite and white males meeting Wolfgang and associates' birth and residence requirements were 2,902 and 7,043, respectively. In contrast, the available race-specific data show that on the average Monahan's cohorts that were 8 in 1953 and 7 in 1952 contained 3,521 and 11,599.5 members in these categories, respectively, for a total of 15,120.5. We see, therefore, that Wolfgang et al.'s figures represent only 82.4% of the blacks and 60.7% of the whites, approximately, in the 1945 birth cohort studied by Monahan. This year's cohort should be more or less typical of the other cohorts in Monahan's data series.

It is conceivable that the kinds of persons who make up these sizable differences between the two studies by failing to qualify for one were neither typical of those who did qualify nor alike in both races. The nonqualifying blacks were probably mostly migrants from the South who came to Philadelphia sometime after age 10, and therefore after 1955. Social scientists have learned to anticipate high official delinquency rates from such children, although their rates may not be higher than those of blacks in general.[14] The nonqualifying whites, on the other hand, were very likely Jewish and middle-class Christian children whose families had moved to the suburbs by 1963, thereby terminating their eligibility for inclusion in the study. These populations generate extremely low official delinquency rates relative to whites in general.

It is intriguing to note that when the 2,017 white delinquents in Wolfgang et al.'s final cohort are divided by the total number of whites in each of the male cohorts that were 6 in 1951, 7 in 1952, and 8 in 1953 according to Monahan's sources, instead of by Wolfgang and associates' 7,043 whites, the delinquency rate becomes 17.8, 17.2, or 17.6 instead of 28.6%. These new numbers are as close to the Philadelphia court record rate for white males (17.9) as the police record rate for black males (50.2) was to the court record rate for black males (50.9). It will be recalled that the failure of the police record rate to exceed the court record rate in the case of black males was viewed as somewhat anomalous, earlier. Let us see what all of this new information suggests concerning this anomaly.

Information is lacking concerning both the exact procedural relation and the probabilistic connection between having a police record and having a court record in Philadelphia, especially by age 18.0. If the two eventually correspond, by age 18.0, despite having differed along the way, it would mean that the rates derived from Monahan and the rates reported by Wolfgang et al. are compatible for both races after all, under two assumptions. One is that the in-migrating and other excluded blacks are typically as delinquent as those who qualified for the birth cohort study (see n. 14, above), and the other is that the out-migrating whites are practically not delinquent at all (officially). This would leave us with rates that were actually similar, within race, for both the police record and the court record criteria, as just demonstrated above when the missing whites were restored to the denominator of the police record rate for whites. Since the missing blacks are assumed to resemble the included blacks in rate of delinquency, they would be restored to both the numerator and denominator, leaving the police record rate for blacks unchanged. With the reduction or elimination of the race-by-criterion interaction in rates, there would no longer be an anomaly. However, these assumptions have the severe disadvantage of implying no distinction at all between the police record and the court record as criteria of severity at age 18.0. The working assumption of a distinction here is one that I prefer not to relinquish until forced to do so by better data.

The distinction between the two criteria can be maintained, however, by replacing the above two assumptions with another pair. First, it is assumed that the excluded blacks are disproportionately lower class and therefore somewhat more delinquent than the blacks who are qualified for inclusion, some of whom would be middle class and therefore less delinquent than average. Lee's (1951) study showing that migrant black children had lower IQs than Philadelphia-born black children would support this assumption at its period in history. Unfortunately, what information we have on nonwhite migration to Philadelphia after 1955 indicates that the migrants were slightly higher in educational and occupational status than nonmigrant nonwhites (Taeuber and Taeuber, 1965: Tables 5 and 6), although this information does not preclude an increase in the variance of migrants on these dimensions and therefore a greater concentration of migrants in the lower tail of the distribution. Second, it is assumed that the excluded whites have a delinquency rate that departs from zero, but which is not as high as the rate of the whites included in Wolfgang et al.'s final cohort. This is clearly a more reasonable assumption than its earlier counterpart. The pair of new assumptions implies that the true police record rate for blacks would be somewhat higher, and the true police record rate for whites would be somewhat lower, than the corresponding rates reported by Wolfgang and associates, where "true" means with reference to the more inclusive populations studied by Monahan. It is easy to see that the probable magnitude of such changes would result in police record (or "custody") rates for both races that would be higher than their respective court record rates as defined for Monahan's populations, and thus consistent in both cases with our sense of the relative severity of the two criteria. The only trouble with these new assumptions is that the one requiring somewhat greater delinquency among the excluded blacks lacks supporting evidence.

It could be, however, that our demand that the black police record rate exceed the black juvenile court rate is totally misconceived. It will be recalled from the data in Table 4 from Wolfgang et al. (1972: 95) presented above that the average seriousness score of offenses committed by black delinquents who had been in police custody "at least once" greatly exceeds the average seriousness score even of white chronic recidivists who had been in police custody "more than four times" (121.2 vs. 107.0). Now it should be added that the average seriousness of offenses committed by blacks who had been in police custody "only once" almost equalled that of the white chronic recidivists (103.3 vs. 107.0), and far exceeded that of whites who had been in police custody "only once" (103.3 vs. 70.3). Thus, it is quite possible that the severity of black offenders is sufficient to produce juvenile court records eventually for all of those with police records, but that this does not apply within the white population. Other data from Wolfgang et al. (1972: Table 13.1) are consistent with this conjecture, since they show that 43.3% of offenses by blacks were processed toward court, but only 23.4% of the offenses by whites. Possibilities remain open, therefore, that the rates for blacks from the two Philadelphia studies may be reconcilable after all, perhaps through some combination of these various assumptions and considerations.[15]

For the purpose of estimating parameters, the Monahan study is equalled in quality only by the British study of Douglas and associates. Because it was done on a national scale, their study is practically free of the problems concerning representativeness that arise in connection with Wolfgang et al.'s cohort study. The close agreement between the British rates and the rates for whites derived from Monahan's work by Gordon and Gleser is remarkable. As nearly as one can tell from a distance, the criterion of delinquency in this study was quite similar to Monahan's, whether cautioned cases are included or not.

The Lexington SMSA data also revealed rates in good agreement with Monahan's data for whites, once a reasonable control for race was introduced. The reconstructed prevalences for blacks were not as high as those for Philadelphia blacks, although they were definitely of the same order of magnitude and thus quite different from the white rates. Perhaps city size or sample size was a factor in estimating the smaller proportion of Negro delinquents. Ball and associates' cohort sizes were only about one-fourteenth as large as Monahan's, and the Lexington data were only for a single year.

Rates for Ball's two Kentucky towns and for Nashville are the most heavily reconstructed of all, and therefore the least dependable of these various estimates. Nevertheless, they do seem consistent with court record rates for white boys observed elsewhere. When data are as rare as these, the additional corroboration contributed by such explicit reconstructions can be more valuable than one would expect.

It will be recalled that the studies by Havighurst et al. and by Hathaway and Monachesi furnished rates for various ad hoc categories and levels of seriousness. When the described severity of these rates is scrutinized closely, it appears that the court record criterion would fall between Havighurst and associates' categories II and III, or at least above III and not above II in severity. Similarly, and even more clearly, it is plausible that the court record criterion, if applied in Minnesota, would yield rates falling between Hathaway and Monachesi's level 2 and level 3 rates. These last two criteria, it has also been separately argued, fall outside of categories III and II (see Table 2), so that all of these inferred placements with respect to the court record criterion are internally consistent. The ordering of the rates attached to the level 3, category II, court record, category III, and level 2 criteria, especially for males (female delinquent samples are sometimes small) are all consistent, in turn, with the ordering of the criteria according to severity, and the rates for females are never seriously out of line.

The overall orderliness of the data in Table 2, and especially the bracketing of the court record rates by rates for other criteria observed elsewhere that also bracket that criterion in their severity, adds to our sense of the stability and generality of the rate attached to the court record, as defined by Monahan. The most important product of this analytic review, therefore, is the conclusion that when the basis for each of the various rates is understood as clearly as possible, fairly uniform rates for the several statuses appear to be in effect within urban settings and settings with a heavily urban component, *with greater differences between statuses for the same location than between locations for the same status.* Despite the heterogeneity of data sources and criteria, the sex and race differentials remain consistent and conspicuous.

It appears likely, therefore, that if the Philadelphia court record criterion were universal (and applied as in Philadelphia), the corresponding white rates for all of the heavily urban places in Table 2 would converge on Philadelphia's. The orderliness of the data and the invariance of the court record rate provide a fairly firm basis for gauging the allowances that must be made in Hathaway and Monachesi's rates in order to transform them into court record rates. With the basis for such a connection established, I turn now to Hathaway and Monachesi's rates for rural settings, for the main value of the connection is that it enables us to gain an impression from their data of the approximate magnitude of court record rates in rural settings (see Table 5, below). Finally, I will review the Marion County study, by Polk and Richmond, listed in Table 2, but not as yet integrated into the general findings.

PREVALENCE IN LESS URBAN AND RURAL SETTINGS

Hathaway and Monachesi's Study:
Rural Rates in the Minnesota Statewide Sample

Table 5 presents prevalence rates for level 2 (which is all that is available) for the Minnesota statewide sample for categories of communities ranged along the urban-rural continuum (Hathaway and Monachesi, 1963: Tables 86 and 87). Although I have already indicated that I regard the level 2 rates as much too inclusive of mild offenses in comparison to court record rates, these data are extremely informative. They possess the unusual virtues of sharing a common criterion of official delinquency (although we have no way of knowing whether legal authorities behaved *exactly* the same in all jurisdictions, we know that Hathaway and Monachesi's criteria do not depend *entirely* on the behavior of authorities), a common period in history, and common reference to a single race, despite having their origins in many different legal jurisdictions (see Hathaway and Monachesi, 1963: 76). Like our other data, they show a strong sex differential of about 3 or 4 to 1 at all points along the urban-rural continuum, and in addition, a sharp decline across the continuum to about half urban rates

Table 5. Prevalence of Level 2 Delinquency, by Community Size (Minnesota Statewide
          Sample), and Rule-of-Thumb Estimates of Prevalence of Court Record
          Delinquency Among Whites for the Same Locations

Community Size	Boys	Girls
Level 2:		
City (Duluth; 1950 pop.: 104,511)	32.28 ⎫ 32.46	8.09 ⎫ 7.39
Suburbs (of Minneapolis and St. Paul)	32.65 ⎭	6.69 ⎭
Towns over 5,000 (to 100,000)	26.80	7.58
Towns under 5,000	20.02	6.24
Farm	14.40	3.80
Rule-of-thumb conversion factor:	.5345	.5074
Court record:		
City and suburbs (generalized from other urban data)	17.35	3.75
Towns over 5,000 (estimated)	14.32	3.85
Towns under 5,000 (estimated)	10.70	3.17
Farm (estimated)	7.70	1.93

SOURCE: Hathaway and Monachesi, 1963: Tables 86-87.

for farming communities. These prevalence trends are consistent with the urban-rural contrasts described earlier by Wolfgang, Dinitz, and Perlman.

In one respect, however, the urban data in Table 5 are anomalous; the rates for boys are six points higher than the Table 2 rate for boys in Minneapolis, although all of the rates in question are for the level 2 criterion. There is no sign of any difference for girls. Except for a five-year difference in time of gathering data for the two Minnesota samples, there is no immediate explanation for this. It can be conjectured, however, that a slight social class difference between urban and suburban places in the statewide sample and Minneapolis may account for the difference in delinquency rates for males. In the statewide sample, "urban" refers to Duluth and "suburban" refers to the suburbs of Minneapolis and St. Paul. Duluth is more of a working class city than Minneapolis,[16] and the authors themselves point out that their "suburban" category "does not necessarily represent typical middle-class suburbia since it includes some rooming house and manufacturing areas" (Hathaway and Monachesi, 1963: 18-19, and Table 2). Why the rates for females are not similarly affected is still a mystery though, because their rates are more sensitive to socioeconomic status than rates for males (compare the authors' Tables 88 and 89). It is a pity that Hathaway and Monachesi did not comment upon this "vagary" in their data; apparently, they never noticed it, because they did not explicitly calculate the rates for points along the urban-rural continuum, which I have obtained from their raw frequencies, and which are presented as far as I know for the first time in Table 5.

It can be noted that the urban and suburban level 2 rates in Table 5 are approximately *double* the more severe court record rates for whites typically observed in other places (see Table 2). I would like to suggest, therefore, that halving all of the level 2 rates in Table 5 would constitute a tenable rule-of-thumb for converting these level 2 rates into estimated court record rates for all of the points along the urban-rural continuum within Table 5. This is the "connection" I alluded to in the previous section.

More exactly, the averages of the Philadelphia and Lexington SMSA court record rates for whites represent .5345 and .5074 of the averages of city and suburban rates in Table 5 for white boys and girls, respectively. Here, Philadelphia and Lexington are chosen as the standard because their court record rates were least problematic of all the places in the United States listed in Table 2. Multiplying all of the remaining level 2 rates in the top half of Table 5 by these proportions, according to sex, yields the rule-of-thumb estimates for the court record criterion in the lower half of the table. In effect, this equates urban and suburban places in the Minnesota statewide sample with the averages for Philadelphia and the Lexington SMSA, and then scales the remaining, more rural, locations with respect to these so as to maintain the proportional relations in the top half of Table 5.[17] These estimates may prove of interest for calibrational purposes when genuine court record data become available for points further along the urban-rural continuum. Meanwhile, they have heuristic value for anyone concerned with delinquency at levels of severity greater than that represented by the mild level 2 criterion, for they exploit the only major source of data for various points along the continuum that employs a uniform criterion of delinquency.

Table 5, together with Table 2, suggests that rates for boys begin to decline only when (small) "towns over 5,000" are reached on the urban-rural continuum, and then they do so steadily. Rates for girls decline, if at all, much more gradually, and the change becomes marked only when the category "farm" is reached.

The decline in rates for boys is in no way inconsistent with the apparent constancy of rates in places of various sizes observed in Table 2, for none of those places was as far along the continuum as the lower bound of the category "towns over 5,000." "River City" had 44,000 inhabitants, and Ball's two Kentucky towns ranged from 10,000 to 19,000, whereas half of the probands in the category "towns over 5,000" were from towns under 10,000 (see Hathaway and Monachesi, 1963: Table 2). Moreover, in both "River City" and the two Kentucky towns, the upper bound for the court record rate was more securely identified than the lower bound, so that even the rates for these smaller communities may be somewhat lower than they now appear. At present, however, there is no need to entertain the possibility that the rates in Table 2 shade into those for smaller places in Table 5, for it will be recalled that the cutting point explicitly employed by informed sources when contrasting city with nonurban delinquency rates (in the "overview" section, above) was "rural," and towns "under 10,000" were also mentioned in connection with crime contrasts in general. The delinquency data in Tables 2 and 5 are quite consistent as they stand with this emphasis, which locates an inflection point in crime rates at the *extreme end* of the urban-rural continuum, that is, somewhere around and beyond towns of size 10,000, and therefore outside the lower size range of places in Table 2.

The gradualness of the change in rates for girls, until the category "farm," suggests that the constancy of rates extends even further along the urban-rural continuum for girls than for boys. If it should indeed prove to be true that prevalence rates for white males remain fairly constant throughout most of the range of the urban-rural continuum, and begin to decline only when communities become extremely small, it may hold important theoretical implications for the roles of population density and anonymity in removing restraints on juvenile misbehavior. The fact that the rates for girls seem to hold constant over a greater portion of the range does not impair this derivation, for it only suggests that the kinds of offenses committed by boys are more sensitive to local population density and anonymity than the kinds of offenses (sex?) that bring girls into trouble. Hathaway and Monachesi (1963: 80) themselves suggest that community size may be better thought of as population density.

The data seem to call for more intensive study of prevalence (using a uniform, fairly severe criterion) in places in the population size range from, say, 500 to 20,000, and of the nature of any differences in type of offense according to sex of the offender. Should an inflection point first appear somewhere within this range, it would be a simple matter to attempt to relate it to the first appearance of a point in community size at which large numbers of individuals (or children) are not easily identifiable by others in the community. Clearly, the actuarial method, rather than the birth cohort method, would offer the most efficient means for conducting such an investigation on a scale large enough to gain reasonable precision in the estimation of parameters.

Marion County, Oregon: A Study of "Nonmetropolitan" Delinquency

The amount of information available concerning this recent study is still quite modest. Sources are Research Report 5 of the Center for Studies of Crime and Delinquency (CSCD, 1974), a dittoed report (Polk?, 1974) which was the basis for Research Report 5, and helpful telephone conversations with Dr. F. Lynn Richmond, who is study director (personal communication). Kenneth Polk is the principal investigator.

The population cohort at risk was defined as "all boys who were sophomores in 1964 in [all] 14 high schools" of Marion County, Oregon (CSCD, 1974: 1). This cohort included 1,227 boys (personal communication). There was no birth or residence requirement, apparently, beyond that implied by being a sophomore in one of the county high schools, public or parochial. As defined, the cohort had a median age of about 15 in the fall of 1964, and would have completed its exposure to risk by 18.0 in about 1967, just prior to the major drug epidemic of the late sixties, and its associated upsurge of drug-related offenses.

The criterion of delinquency was having "an official record with the county juvenile department . . . with minor traffic offenses excluded" (CSCD, 1974: 2), by age 18.0. Judging from reported analyses which single out boys who committed their offenses during the period "0-15" years of age, and which also draw explicit comparisons with the results of the Wolfgang et al. (1972) birth cohort study, the period at risk in this study extends back in principle over the entire juvenile period. I mention this only because the lower age bound is not explicitly reported, and therefore it must be assumed to have been comparable to the age range employed in Philadelphia (but without the residence requirement).

I have placed the Marion County study last, and among the "rural" studies, because of the emphasis given by the investigators to the failure of their data to yield anticipated contrasts with *urban* rates of delinquency, especially as manifested in the Philadelphia study of Wolfgang et al. (1972), which employed a criterion of delinquency that was apparently similar to that used here. This emphasis appears in the title of Research Report 5, "Teenage Delinquency in small town America," in the title of the dittoed report mentioned above (Polk?, 1974), "Rural Delinquency and Maturational Reform," and in related expressions of surprise over how much delinquency was found in a "nonmetropolitan" area (Polk?, 1974: 1; CSCD, 1974: 1-2). Given the study's emphasis on the lack of expected contrast with urban rates, many persons are apt to read the term "nonmetropolitan" to mean "rural," despite the fact that "small city" populations are mentioned as being included with rural ones. The anonymity of the actual study site in published reports makes it unlikely that these impressions will be challenged. Before trying to fit this study's results into the pattern of findings in Tables 2 and 5, therefore, it is necessary to know more about the actual setting to which these results apply.

According to 1960 census data, Marion County had a population of 120,888, 63.5% of which was classified as "urban." Salem, the largest city, had a population of 49,142, which makes it slightly larger than "River City" (pop.: 44,000), but smaller than Duluth (1950 pop.: 104,511). Thus, the city of Salem itself contained 40.7% of the county population at a point in time corresponding roughly to the beginning of adolescence (age 11) for the cohort at risk. After Salem, the next largest place (town) in the county had a population of only 10,948, and thereafter the remaining towns ranged in size from 3,000 to 6,000 (U.S. Bureau of the Census, 1963: Part 39, Tables 5-7). About half of the cohort (more than those living in Salem proper) actually come from Salem schools, because the Salem school district extends into the surrounding countryside (personal communication). This suggests that a fraction over and above those residing in Salem would also have been able to reach the city on weekends and other occasions, where they would have been exposed to opportunities for getting into trouble that are essentially urban in many important respects.

By 1970, three years beyond the end of the period at risk, Marion County contained 151,309 persons, 68,296 of whom lived in Salem. Thus, Salem now included 45.1% of the county population, up from 40.7% in 1960. The Salem Urbanized Area, some small portion of which lies in adjacent Polk County, contained 93,041 persons. As of 1970, both Marion and adjacent Polk County had been designated the Salem Standard Metropolitan Statistical Area, with a population of 186,658, which is larger than the Lexington, Kentucky, SMSA was in 1960 (pop.: 131,906). This fact alone raises questions concerning the aptness of the description "nonmetropolitan" for delinquency rates obtained just a few years earlier within this same jurisdiction (U.S. Bureau of the Census, 1973: Tables 7, 10, 11, and 13).

It will be recalled that 44% of the Minnesota statewide sample came from urban areas and towns with populations over 10,000. Even in 1960, 49.7% of the persons in Marion County lived in urban places and towns with populations over 10,000 (Salem plus the next largest town). Perhaps another 10% could legitimately be added to this percentage to take into account boys from the surrounding countryside who attended school in Salem. In the years between 1960 and 1970, the total of these percentages would have grown larger still.

Thus, the Marion County sample is actually slightly more urban than the Minnesota statewide sample. Although the Marion County study does contain a strong rural component, it is important that the composition of its sample be thoroughly understood in order to assess this study's exact contribution to our total assemblage of data, especially in view of the investigators' emphasis upon the surprising failure of the rates they observed to contrast with urban rates for a similar criterion.

Before examining the prevalence rates actually obtained, it should be explained that although race was not controlled, the percentage of blacks in the area is small. In 1960, only 0.7% of the county's 11-year-old cohort (which would have been 15 in 1964) was nonwhite. Only 1.0% of the population in Salem proper was Negro. By 1970, the percentages of blacks in the county and in Salem had grown to only 1.6 and 1.8%, respectively, and most of this growth would have occurred after the definition of the cohort (U.S. Bureau of the Census, 1963: Tables 13 and 27; 1973: Table 16).

Given the small proportion of blacks, any attempted correction for their inclusion would alter this study's prevalence rates by no more than half a percentage point. No such effort has been made, therefore. It might be noted, however, as a critical comment that the study's indifference to the value of controlling for race reflects more than the conviction that doing so would have produced little change in its own data. This conclusion is based on comparisons that the investigators draw between their own rates and rates reported by Wolfgang et al. (1972), where these comparisons do not consistently employ the rates for whites alone that are provided in the latter study despite the recognition that doing so reduces differences between the two studies, and thus strengthens the investigators' own interpretations concerning the failure of their rates to differ from metropolitan ones (Polk?, 1974: 2), as will be apparent below. Plainly, there is much uncertainty or ambivalence about controlling for race.

Comparing prevalence rates for males in the virtually all white Marion County sample with the white sample from Philadelphia at each of three levels of severity defined by Wolfgang et al. (1972: 89-90), we obtain the figures given in Table 6. Here, the two smaller prevalence rates for Marion County have been derived from reported comparisons which employ the total number of delinquents (as defined by the larger rate) as the base, instead of the entire cohort. This switch in bases suggests that the value of prevalence rates based on the cohort is not yet fully appreciated by sociologists.

It should be added that the Oregon study reports a fourth criterion, "charged with committing a felony," which had no counterpart in the Philadelphia results. This fourth criterion produced a prevalence of 13.9%. The investigators

Table 6. PREVALENCE FOR MALES AT AGE 18.0 IN TWO STUDIES,
AT THREE LEVELS OF SEVERITY

	In police custody at least once	More than once (recidivists)	More than four times (chronic recidivists)
Marion County:	24.69%	11.11%	2.72%
Philadelphia:	28.64%	12.91%	2.98%
Ratio, M.C./Phil.:	.86	.86	.91

characterize offenses in this category as "serious," and it seems certain that this criterion would constitute a lower bound for the court record rate (since felonies would usually be referred to court), which elsewhere hovers around 17% for white males. This felon rate from Marion County is quite close to the category II rate of 13.1% for "River City," a criterion which also has been characterized as "serious," by Havighurst and associates (see Table 1, above). It will be recalled that I have already argued, in connection with Table 2, that category II represents a criterion more severe than the court record criterion, and hence that it constitutes a lower bound for that unobserved rate in "River City." Thus, both the felony criterion and category II indicate a lower limit for court record rates in their locales that are only a few percentage points lower than the five court record rates already displayed in Table 2, and both are close to each other in value and not distinguishably different from each other in severity. These fresh comparisons add to the consistency of the prevalence picture.

Aside from the higher rate of the felony criterion, and the plausibility of its being equivalent to category II in severity, I see no way to determine from content alone that the felony criterion is less severe than level 3 (with a rate of 8.7%); conceivably, it could be *as* severe (see the complex level 3 description, above, which includes some felonies), thereby producing a disparity in rates. There is no reason to think the felony criterion is more severe than level 3, however, so category II and level 3 may be regarded as bounding its severity. Accordingly, I have placed the felon rate between level 3 and category II in Table 2. Obviously, in view of the similarity in their rates, the closer to category II the felon rate actually belongs, the prettier the picture.

The Marion County investigators also report an "institutionalization" rate of 0.90% for their cohort (personal communication).[18] This refers to incarceration in the state training school, and not just "overnights" in jail. Their rate is extremely close to Gordon's (1973) nationwide rate (1.02%) for white males for the same criterion, obtained by the actuarial method. The comparability here is of special interest because both estimates apply to populations that are roughly equal in their rural component.[19] Again, the incarceration rate is substantially lower than the local rate of having been in police custody "more than four times" (2.72%), just as was the case in Philadelphia. For Marion County, however, the relation between these two criteria is established entirely by direct observation, whereas for Philadelphia this required the help of a linear model.

It will be noted that the two prevalence criteria based strictly on frequency of police custody ("more than once" and "more than four times") from both Marion County and Philadelphia have not been placed in Table 2. This is because it is difficult to determine their severity relative to that of the criteria already in the table that are founded either on longstanding institutional procedure or on more or less detailed descriptions. Entering the two recidivist criteria would have required depending entirely on the sizes of their rates relative to the rates associated with other criteria, thus begging the question of whether or not they contribute to the consistency of the overall picture.[20] This uncertainty does not, of course, afflict comparisons made within the subset of frequency-based criteria themselves, since their levels of severity relative to each other are unambiguously defined. These comparisons, which I discuss next, clearly do lend support to the general picture (see Table 6, above).

Thus, when we examine the exhibited comparisons at three levels of severity between Marion County and Philadelphia, great similarity in rates between the two locales at all three levels can be observed. This similarity is a further indication that the rate structure for white populations remains practically invariant over a wide range of the urban-rural continuum—and consequently over a wide range of types of places. The close agreement between heavily urban Marion County (24.7%) and Philadelphia (28.6%) in their basic police record rates extends as well to the level 2 rates in the Minnesota statewide (24.0%) and Minneapolis (26.0%) samples in Table 2. In both comparisons, partly urban samples (Marion County and Minnesota) produce rates that are quite close to rates for fully urban samples (Philadelphia and Minneapolis). Level 2, it will be recalled, is quite similar to the police record criterion in its severity and import, since it excludes overtime parking and being picked up by police where involvement was poorly established or the individual contributed to a disturbance in only a minor way, which qualify for level 1 (Hathaway and Monachesi, 1963: 22).

The rates from Oregon need not occasion much surprise, therefore, in view of the prior existence of comparable rates in the two Minnesota samples, one of which was demographically similar in composition to the Marion County sample, that is, partly rural. It is of interest to note, however, that Hathaway and Monachesi (1963: 77) reported that the magnitude of their Minnesota rates occasioned "shock" among some persons. These authors accounted for their rates by the fact that they tried to include "all cases, including those who usually escape mention in reports on delinquency." From this, some persons concluded "that statistics on juvenile delinquency are not readily comparable from city to city, from county to county, or from state to state" (United Community Fund of San Francisco, 1961: 29)—which is exactly the wrong conclusion, although typical apparently. The high rates in all four samples are accounted for by the fact that they all employ a criterion that is less severe than that usually reported by official agencies, such as juvenile courts. Once the severity of the criterion is taken into account, along with race and sex, the rates from place to place along most of the urban-rural continuum prove quite comparable, as I have shown in Table 2, above.

As presently analyzed, the Marion County sample really does not inform us about delinquency rates at points further along the urban-rural continuum than the range in which such rates have already been shown to be relatively invariant. The little we know about the rural extreme comes from Hathaway and Monachesi's research, which indicates that a decline in rates actually does appear when we pass below towns of about 10,000 inhabitants (see Table 5, above). It is important that the "surprise" aspect of the Marion County study be placed in perspective, therefore, so that it does not cloud our knowledge of this portion of the continuum obtained from the one study that actually investigated it, and with extremely large samples at that. Hathaway and Monachesi (1963: Table 2) had 1,593 boys from farm settings alone, and 307 from towns under 500 in size, to give some idea of the strength of their design. The Marion County study has only 1,227 boys in its entire cohort. Despite this more modest size, it would increase the value of their already important study if the Marion County investigators provided a detailed analysis of rates in the extremely rural settings of their county. Hathaway and Monachesi's invaluable data are also capable of being analyzed in much finer detail, concerning the effect of the size of small communities, than has so far been done (see, for example, the stub of their Table 2).

In a third line of entries, below the exhibited rates at three levels of severity for Marion County and Philadelphia, I have presented the ratios of the rate in one study to the rate at the same level of severity in the other study (Table 6). All of these ratios, if rounded-off, would equal 0.9. This relatively constant proportionality, at each of three widely separated levels of severity (judging from the rates), between prevalence rates in Philadelphia and prevalence rates in Marion County with its strong rural component, indicates that we could have predicted the rates at the two more severe criteria in Marion County accurately if given all three rates for Philadelphia and just the general police record rate for

Marion County. In such a case, the proportional predictions for Marion County at the two more severe criteria would have been 11.13 and 2.57%, whereas the actual rates are 11.11 and 2.72%, respectively. This prediction task is closely analogous to the one performed in the bottom half of Table 5, where more severe court record rates were derived from less severe level 2 rates at various points along the urban-rural continuum on the basis of the known proportional relation between these two rates in large cities. The obvious success of the predictions in the present instance is an indication that the estimation procedure used in connection with Table 5 was reasonable.

Since there are only two studies dealing with delinquency in less urban settings, and since I have discussed their relation to each other in presenting them, there is no need for a special section in which to evaluate them. It is quite clear that they are in good agreement with each other at all points of visible comparability, especially when the interpretations of the Marion County study concerning the lack of contrast between metropolitan and "nonmetropolitan" rates are placed in proper perspective. Once this is done, both studies yield results which are consistent with other evidence (in Table 2) that race-specific delinquency rates are relatively invariant over an enormous span of the urban-rural continuum, but which also allow for a decline in rates for settings that are extremely rural.

CONCLUSION: THEORETICAL AND PRACTICAL IMPLICATIONS

To a degree never before attempted, this paper has assembled data specifying the proportions of juvenile delinquents present in representative or nearly representative age-cohorts. The criteria of delinquency have all been official ones. For whites, a total of 42 data points have been marshalled (Tables 2 and 5 contain 38 relevant points, and four more based on recidivism occur in Table 6). In view of their small standard deviations over an eight-year period, it would be justified to regard the court record rates derived from Monahan's work as being equivalent to eight data points apiece, thus adding 14 more to the total, now 56. All of these data points are in good agreement with each other concerning the apparent invariance of race- and sex-specific prevalence rates within urban places that exceed in size a point lying somewhere in the range between 10,000 and 44,000. Between a few of the data points the ordinal relations are not as sharply defined as is the case for most of them. Even in the case of the doubtful few, however, existing information provides no evidence of inconsistency, that is, of improper order coupled with a difference of substantial magnitude. The overall structure of the argument is far stronger, consequently, than its weaker links, and it merits serious attention, at least until proved wrong by future studies.

In order to incorporate data from as many sources as possible, it has often been necessary to apply one or more adjustments—based on observations elsewhere—assuming uniformity in prevalence rates for blacks. Such assumptions concerning external parameters in no way bias the affected estimates for whites toward uniformity, since the latter remain free to attain any value. Other adjustments have encroached slightly on the independence between studies, but these have been employed mainly in a formal role in order to impose a common age standard on all of the studies, insofar as possible. To emerge after such an age adjustment, uniformity had to be present initially with regard to some age, at least, in the unadjusted data. The only question begged in such cases, therefore, by the lack of total independence is whether the uniformity observed at an earlier age persists until the later age. Regularities observed in the association of rates with ages seem to make this assumption of persistence a safe one. When the span of years involved in an age adjustment is small, the slight riskiness in this assumption is reduced even further. As for other residual uncertainties stemming from ambiguities in original sources—or from sometimes audacious adjustments—it should be remembered that uniformity is seldom improved by heterogeneous influences.

By demonstrating the importance of prevalence data, and of how troublesome inadequacies can be, it is hoped that this report will stimulate a higher standard of reporting and design in future studies. More attention must be paid to the practical meanings and exact definitions of criteria of delinquency, to issues surrounding representativeness of cohorts, to age boundaries, to local peculiarities underlying nominally similar concepts, to the selection of settings along the rural-urban continuum, and to the value of reporting all of one's data for both sexes at all of the criterion points potentially available, even when the rates in question approach zero. Since it has been shown that rates in other studies confirm that rates for whites within the studies that do provide race-specific data for blacks and whites are typical, the failure to maintain race-specificity should no longer be excusable. Especially for rates under 10%, the number of decimal places employed should always be generous.

On their face, the scattering of existing prevalence statistics has appeared to be a hopelessly disparate collection of idiographic facts, presumably reflecting differences in time and place, social practice, and perhaps true rate, to unknown degrees. Analysis shows, however, that the major differences in rates, once racial and sexual status are held constant, can be understood primarily in terms of nomothetic principles governing differences in severity of the offenders and offenses subsumed by definitional criteria, and governing differences in the ages to which the data pertain; and secondarily, in terms of principles which may involve the population density of strangers.

In this context, density is understood not as an "irritant," but rather as a measurement indicative of the amount of anonymity in daily encounters and of the extent to which bonds of immediate personal interdependence are absent. These conditions in turn are thought to act as releasers of noxious behaviors (e.g., stealing, aggression), especially on the part of males, that might otherwise be held in check when the potential victim is an acquaintance, an associate of acquaintances (a relative being viewed as a special case of acquaintance), or a member of a kinship network with longstanding friendly relations with one's own kinship network, and membership status is visible even when individual identity is not. The threat of vengeance—and hence of punishment by one's own kin to avert group retaliation—would be the key concomitant of this last condition.[21]

The checks described would hold within human communities throughout most of the history of the species, and perhaps even in large preindustrial cities wherein artisans and skilled craftsmen, often linked by ethnicity, were apt to constitute a very high proportion of the population (e.g., Moseley, 1975: 224), and to establish themselves in special quarters or streets (Sjoberg, 1965: 58) thus creating the moral equivalent of contiguous villages. Within such settings there would still be delinquency, of course, but at reduced rates (e.g., Table 5). In highly mobile, industrial society, however, the checks inevitably cease to be operative once certain critical densities are achieved, and this apparently occurs relatively early in the ranking of communities in order of increasing size. Consequently, there is remarkably little variation in specific prevalence rates within all but the rural extreme of the rural-urban continuum. Surveys of village life among Eskimos, Mexicans, and in India, in contrast to urban life, are consistent with this general picture (see Cavan and Cavan, 1968).

Given this apparent lack of variation in the prevalence of white delinquency over the greater portion of the rural-urban continuum, two major theoretical questions arise. First, how can we account for the strong, widespread impression that something called "urbanization" contributes to delinquency in recent times? Second, what accounts for the surprising constancy in rates? It will become evident as I attempt to answer them that these two questions are closely intertwined.

Reconsidering the Contribution of "Urbanism" to Juvenile Delinquency

Some time ago, Angell (1951: 15-16) noted that once population size passed 100,000, city size ceased to be related to the crime rate. Angell's measure of crime was offenses known to the police, but this appears to be a direct function of the number of offenders, so let us disregard the distinction in order to pursue the main point. Below 100,000, there was a fairly consistent relation with size (except for homicide). Angell's data were for 1940 and 1947. The correlation between population size and "crime" in the 43 relatively independent cities *over* 100,000 used in his major 1940 study was only —.06 (the sign may be ambiguous in view of the reverse scoring of his crime index, which was used as a measure of "moral integration").[22] Angell's various observations conform to those reported here, except that here the data indicate that this fundamental lack of variability may extend even further down in the range of community size, perhaps to 44,000 or even 10,000. On the other hand, more recent data for 1965 show that offense rates continue to increase even in the upper range of city size, so that the concept "urbanization" has again been brought into the discussion (President's Commission . . . , 1967: 28-29).

As an initial step toward clarification of the picture, let us recognize that much of the classic association in the public's mind between urban life and crime is probably a carryover from times when most of the population was rural, and the rural-urban differential in Table 5 (above) was consequently more conspicuous. Kingsley Davis (1973: 5) comments, "As long as there were few cities in the world, complaints against them had the character of complaints about an abnormality." He also notes that moral condemnation has long been a prominent theme in the social criticism of cities. The spatial organization of large populations according to socioeconomic status within industrialized cities, moreover, has always led to the creation of districts in which delinquents are especially concentrated, and hence especially visible. Although crime rates within such districts would impress observers as far exceeding anything ever seen in the countryside or in small towns, only sophisticated statistics would be capable of revealing that the prevalence rate of delinquency for the local white population *as a whole* did not in fact differ much from rates in smaller towns. Finally, the inflection point in city size may be pushed upward in Angell's statistics (to 100,000) by the inclusion of adult offenses. Conceivably, many adult offenders are drawn from rural places to the nearest large city, to concentrate there, by the opportunities afforded to those pursuing deviant life-styles.[23] Juveniles, on the other hand, are less mobile, and migration in their case would reflect the motives of their parents rather than of the juveniles themselves. Delinquency data, therefore, ought to present a truer picture of the effect of "urbanism" on indigenous crime, and cohorts of juveniles ought to remain more representative of communities in general, thus permitting juvenile offender rates to remain invariant over a greater range of city size than Angell's statistics would lead us to expect.

Next, let us also recognize that contemporary impressions of urban delinquency do not distinguish rates according to race very precisely, say, as compared to Tables 2 and 5. In view of the higher delinquency rates of blacks, racially composite rates for cities containing sizable proportions of blacks would exceed rates in mainly white rural communities by noticeable amounts. Such high overall rates would, of course, feed into the classic stereotype of urban-rural differences regardless of whether or not there was also an impression that real differences in rates between races did in fact exist. The paucity of race-specific prevalence data would do nothing to disturb the urban stereotype that is thus reinforced. Let us pursue this plausible connection between race and the persistence of impressions that link "urbanism" to criminality in greater detail.

Although size among cities over 100,000 was uncorrelated with crime in the 1940s, the fact that there seems to be a correlation in 1965 is corroborated by Angell's recent attempt to replicate his earlier study of "moral integration." Using 1970 data for 112 SMSAs, he found that the correlation between population size and his crime index (with scoring reversed) was now $-.42$ (1974: Table 8). This was larger than the correlation with crime of any other independent variable that Angell employed. However, this change in the magnitude of the correlation over time, from $-.06$ in 1940, straddles the massive migration of blacks from the South to the urban North between 1940 and 1970. There is a good possibility, therefore, that city (or SMSA) size is confounded with the proportion black to a greater degree in the later period (e.g., Grodzins, 1958; Rosenthal, 1971).

Appropriate analysis shows that racial composition is related to crime rates of cities at both periods to a much greater extent than has generally been realized. Let us examine Angell's crime index data, for both 1940 and 1970, for 40 of the 43 cities in his original 1940 study (1974: Table 9). In this analysis, I correlate his crime index (which he presents in the form of standard scores) at each time with the proportion of males who are black in the 10 to 24 age-cohort. For 1940, the correlation between the proportion black and the crime index is $-.676$; for 1970, when as the result of migration the distribution of proportions black over the 40 cities is less skewed so that blacks are more evenly distributed, it is $-.478$. Both of these correlations are larger than any of those in Angell's own analyses for the same year, using independent variables that he considered to be causally related to "moral integration" (1951: 125; 1974: Tables 1, 2, 4, 6, and 8).

Next, let us apply these ideas to changes over time. When the proportions black at the two times are converted to standard scores (so as to be on the same scale with Angell's crime index), we find that the change from 1940 to 1970 in the proportion black correlates $-.474$ with the change in the crime index. This means that as a city increased its relative standing with respect to the proportion black, it declined in its relative standing with respect to its freedom from criminality. The correlation here and the two in the preceding paragraph are larger than the one of .41 that Angell found between the crime index rank of a city in 1940 and its rank in 1970 (1974: 626).[24] Thus, both static and dynamic aspects of racial composition predict the crime index values of these cities better than their own past history of criminality. It should also be pointed out that all of the correlations involving the proportion black are larger than the correlations with population size that have been noted.

Quite clearly, the regularity of the rates for whites together with the large differences between blacks and whites in race-specific prevalence rates discussed earlier (Gordon, 1973; Gordon and Gleser, 1974; Wolfgang et al., 1972) imply that if such racial differences are general, variation in the proportion black should be strongly correlated with variation in the total volume of crime within homogeneous segments of the urban-rural continuum. My analyses of Angell's urban data for two different times show that this expectation has been met (see also McKeown, 1948: Table IV; Schuessler, 1962: Table 3). This establishes the main point of this section, namely, that the high prevalence rate of delinquency among blacks is deeply implicated in the contemporary phenomenology of "urbanism" and crime.

This is not to say that blacks are the only group that contributes to this impression. They are merely the largest such group. Angell, for example, explicitly noted that the crime index for Denver in 1970 was heavily influenced by an influx of Mexican-Americans (1974: 628). This ethnic group had a delinquency incidence rate for both sexes in Los Angeles County in 1956 that was 3.1 times the rate for "Anglos" (Eaton and Polk, 1961: 25); this is close to the analogous ratios of 3.6 and 3.8 in the prevalence data for blacks and whites (Gordon, 1973: Table 3). Had I taken account of Mexican-Americans and some other minority groups in establishing the variable of population composition, it probably would have raised the correlations in my analyses of Angell's data. In view of these considerations, the uniformity in prevalence rates for *whites* over a vast portion of the urban-rural continuum reported in this paper does not stand in opposition to current impressions concerning the relation of crime to cities after all.

IQ Distributions as the Source of the Regularities and Consistent Irregularities?

The regularities in delinquency rates for white populations over a wide range of urban settings suggest that the substrate of this behavior lies in some equally regular feature common to all of these populations. The IQ distribution is such a feature. Although some might argue that the regularity inheres in the urban settings themselves, sociologists have not heretofore regarded cities as being as similar to each other in the dimensions that such a traditional argument would invoke as an adequate explanation would seem to require. Judging from the data in Table 2 and especially in Table 5, it is only when truly drastic changes are introduced in the lower range of the relatively crude and essentially physical variable of community size that we begin to detect some concomitant variation in the prevalence rate for whites.

This suggests that the key source of variation in the community setting is some property associated closely with population size, a property, moreover, that does not itself change very much once a critical size threshold is reached, such as a minimal density of strangers. As it has been conceived here, this is a relatively passive variable which does not provoke noxious behavior, rather, it releases it. This release is thought to result from the absence of certain obvious checks in the interpersonal network that would be present within all human communities throughout all but the most recent history of the species. It is the passivity of the density variable and the reactive rather than proactive nature of the checks that restrict the active source of delinquent behavior to within the population itself, even with respect to that part of the variation that is associated with population size (in the lower range). Thus, both the constancy of the rates in settings over a critical size and the variation that does occur between settings above and below the critical size are consistent with viewing the population as the proper locus of causality.

A number of facts, considered together, point to the IQ distribution as the relevant population feature.[25] Here, they can only be indicated briefly.

First and foremost, the IQ distribution has the requisite constancy from one place to another, and from one cohort to another. Although it is likely that this distribution does exhibit an extremely modest amount of variation from place to place (e.g., Johnson, 1948; Nichols, 1969), the available data for entire white communities are insufficiently sensitive to justify concern with such a minor effect within the context of the present discussion.

Second, IQ is associated with delinquency within the white population. I am well aware that this last statement flies in the face of literature which contends or seems to show that IQ is not related to delinquency. At some future time I will treat that literature. This association between IQ and delinquency within populations would account for the classic association between socioeconomic status and delinquency within populations that was noted in the opening paragraph of this paper. The heavily biological basis for IQ that has been established among whites (Jensen, 1969a) would account for the reproduction of similar distributions of delinquents from generation to generation, and hence from cohort to cohort. It should be noted that biological sources of variation in IQ are not restricted simply to the genetic component, but include also sources in the environment (e.g., the uterus) over which there is relatively little social control (Jensen, 1969a: 51, 65-74; 1970: 144-146).

A strong biological foundation for stability in the population would also account for remarkable regularities that occur from year to year when certain crime statistics are based on large populations. Blumstein (1974: Table 5), for example, showed that the seven index crimes reported by the FBI correlate .98 with each other on the average over a 13-year period. The lowest correlation was .958. Why should the number of burglaries be such a regular multiple, say, of the number of homicides? A similar stability in the percentage distribution of juvenile offenses over seven crime categories for three years can be observed in rare data from the Archangel *oblast'* (administrative district) in the Soviet Union, presented by Connor, who also notes that the "working-class milieu seems to be the major source of Soviet delinquents" (1970: Table 1, and p. 295). Percentage distributions of juvenile offenses over 13 crime categories for a 15-year interval also turn out to be strikingly stable in Philadelphia, especially when changes in racial composition during the period (1940-1954) are taken into account (Municipal Court of Philadelphia, 1954: Table 9), for blacks and whites are not distributed the same over crime categories, and between 1940 and 1960 the percentage nonwhite in Philadelphia went from 13.1 to 26.7 (U.S. Bureau of the Census, 1946: Table 21; 1963: Part 40, Table 13).

Third, IQ could account for the scattering of studies showing greater concordance rates for criminality among monozygotic than among dizygotic twins, using various criteria of zygosity, as reviewed by Rosenthal (1970: 222-239; see also Crowe, 1972: 600). The average IQ difference of 11 points between dizygotic twins is about the same as that of siblings reared together, which is 12 points, whereas the average IQ difference between monozygotic twins reared together is only about 5 points (Jensen, 1970: 141, Table 4; Reed and Reed, 1965: Table 45). It might be noted that Rosenthal's conclusion that rising crime rates in the United States "provide additional testimony to the overriding importance of environmental factors in crime" (1970: 239) fails to take account of the large differentials in crime rates between racial groups mentioned earlier and of changes over time in their relative proportions of the nation's population, especially in cities. Since these groups obviously represent different gene pools at least with respect to visible characteristics like physical appearance, such recent changes in national crime rates cannot be used to throw doubt on genetic contributions to crime.

Fourth, the high heritability of IQ would account for the results of Crowe (1972), who found that among the 52 adopted offspring of white women criminal offenders there were significantly more criminal records, convictions, and incarcerations than among a matched group of adopted children of unknown parentage. In this Iowa study, two of the 25 female offspring (but none of the 27 males, and no controls) had been confined in the state training school, for a rate of 8.0% for females. Although the sample is small, it is worth noting that this rate is 34.78 times as large as the rate of 0.23% for white girls, nationwide, in Table 2. One explanation for the fact that the offspring of offenders were considerably less criminal than their mothers would involve the well-established phenomenon of regression toward the mean (in this case, upwards) for polygenic characteristics such as IQ (for a numerical example, see Burt, 1961: Tables I and II).[26]

In examples such as the preceding one, where there does appear to be evidence of genetic transmission, IQ is not necessarily the sole causal factor determined by genetics. Quite possibly, genes for other desirable human traits have come to be correlated with genes for IQ, most likely through mechanisms such as assortative mating decisions and natural selection for coadaptive gene complexes rather than for individual genes (Caspari, 1967). Galton (1869: 279), who observed that men of above average intellect tended also to be above average in physical constitution, was the first to comment upon the tendency toward positive correlation among desirable traits. As another example, modest positive correlations are usually reported between physical attractiveness and intelligence (Mohr and Lund, 1933). In the present context, genes for undesirable temperamental or personality traits that were conducive toward criminality could be associated with genes for low IQ, and the two types of variable could combine additively or interactively to favor behavior so noxious to others that it is made criminal. In this situation, the more visible IQ variable would serve as an index of the presence or absence of the unknown other variables (perhaps, for example, psychopathy or hysteria; see Trasler, 1962; Eysenck, 1964; Robins, 1966).

Fifth, substantial IQ differences between groups are associated with substantial differences in the prevalence of juvenile delinquency and criminality in general. For a long time, however, widespread conviction about supposed "cultural bias" in IQ tests (e.g., Mercer, 1973) has deprived this observation of its proper scientific value. The cultural bias hypothesis has now been subjected to rigorous research for both blacks and Mexican-Americans. Elsewhere I have reviewed this research and cited other concurring reviews (Gordon, 1975: 91-102). The evidence shows conclusively that IQ scores have the same meaning for both blacks and whites. Evidence for Mexican-Americans is less extensive, but I was able to add to existing material the fact that ability tests for whites, blacks, and Mexican-Americans in the Coleman Report (Coleman et al., 1966) are clearly not biased against members of the two minority groups. Taken together, all of this evidence leaves no doubt that there are substantial real differences between these two minority populations and whites in average IQ, on the order of at least 10 IQ points for Mexican-Americans, and about one white standard deviation for blacks (16 points). Given these facts, it follows a fortiori that socioeconomic bias in the meaning of IQ scores within the white population itself poses no problem of any consequence.

For present purposes, it is particularly fortunate that these two minority populations have figured in IQ test research, for these are also the two minorities for which I have been able to present either prevalence or incidence rates of delinquency. These rates showed the minorities to exceed "Anglos" by factors of more than three to one (counting the sexes together). Elsewhere, in a work on mental retardation, I show that minority/"Anglo" ratios of at least three to one are generated simply by establishing cutting points in the lower range of the IQ distribution wherever it would be reasonable to do so for the purpose of defining presumptive retardation (Gordon, 1975: Table 4.4). These large ratios follow from the properties of unimodal (and roughly normal) distributions that have different means, and perhaps different variances. One might call them "distribution effects," since they create dramatic disproportionalities between two populations in the percentages falling above or below a given point. The further out in the tail such a point is located, the greater the disproportion. Distribution effects have been known for a long time, but they are still unfamiliar to many social scientists.

Let us focus for the moment on black-white comparisons alone, since these are the only populations for which we have genuine prevalence rates, and such rates are far more appropriate than incidence rates for the study of individual differences in conjunction with another individual differences dimension such as IQ. In Table 7, I have created a model of the relation between prevalence rates and IQ parameters that is intended solely for the purpose of revealing any potential correspondence between them. The model converts observed prevalence rates to IQs consistent with the means and standard deviations (from other research) of the IQ distributions in question. It does this, with the help of tables of the unit normal distribution, by assuming that the prevalence rate is generated by a fictitious process that causes everyone under a certain IQ, and no one over it, to become delinquent according to a specific criterion. We simply look up the z-score associated with the prevalence rate (as a percentage of the area under the normal curve), and then calculate the IQ associated with that z-score (in units of the IQ standard deviation), as a deviation from the IQ mean of the population of interest.

Obviously, no one is suggesting that this step-function model represents the exact relation between IQ and delinquency. The point is, when various rates from the two most representative studies available are employed, the model always yields as the critical IQ a value that is almost identical for blacks and whites. These "coincidences" virtually necessitate that there be some more

Table 7. IQs IMPLIED BY VARIOUS PREVALENCE RATES UNDER THE SIMPLIFIED
ASSUMPTION THAT EVERYONE UNDER A CERTAIN IQ BECOMES
DELINQUENT ACCORDING TO THE CRITERION IN QUESTION

	Blacks	Whites	Difference
Philadelphia parameters:			
Assumed IQ mean	86.0^a	101.8^c	-15.8
Assumed standard deviation	12.4^b	16.4^c	---
Philadelphia, court record:^{d}			
Boys (implied critical IQ)	86.3	86.7	-0.4
Girls (implied critical IQ)	73.6	71.7	1.9
United States parameters:			
Assumed IQ mean	83.4^e	101.8^c	-18.4
Assumed standard deviation	12.9^e	16.4^c	---
Nationwide, training school:^{f}			
Boys (implied critical IQ)	60.7	63.8	-3.1
Girls (implied critical IQ)	52.3	55.3	-3.0

a. Based on Negro mean of 95.9 for Philadelphia blacks (Wolfgang et al., 1972: Table 4.5)
and knowledge that the Philadelphia Verbal Ability Test yields IQs 10 points too high.
b. Based on sample of Kennedy, Van De Riet, and White (1963: Table 38) and assumption
of homoscedasticity in North and South.
c. Based on 1937 Stanford-Binet normative sample (Terman and Merrill, 1960: Fig. 4).
d. Based on prevalence rates of Gordon and Gleser (1974: Table 3).
e. Mean based on weighted combination of Shuey's (1966: 205) North (87.6) and South
(80.5) means for blacks, using weights for 1960 census distribution of blacks 5-19, namely
.4026 (North) and .5974 (South). Standard deviation based on substituting these weights
and means and 12.4 into McNemar's (1955: 26) formula for standard deviation of combined distributions. For post-1945 testings, Shuey's (1966: 503) U.S. means are 83.0
and 83.6.
f. Based on prevalence rates of Gordon (1973: Table 2).

reasonable functional relationship within sex between IQ and delinquency that is
common or nearly common to both races. Rather than a step-function, some
more gradual monotone function over most of the range of interest seems
plausible. For example, Hirschi (1969: Table 17) reports official police "record"
rates for a sample of Negro and white male high school students (see n. 9,
above), within various Verbal Reasoning score ranges of the Differential
Aptitude Test, as shown in Table 8. Note that there is a consistent monotone

Table 8. POLICE RECORD DELINQUENCY RATES FOR MALES WITHIN
         VARIOUS DAT VERBAL SCORE RANGES

	0-9	10-19	20-29	30 and above
Negro:	47%	34%	23%	0% (N=9)
White:	43%	26%	20%	6%

SOURCE: Hirschi, 1969: Table 17.

function for each race: the percentages decrease from left to right. However, when we take into account that individuals in the lowermost IQ range may be too incapacitated to function even as a delinquent, we see that the function may have to be one of the second degree (inverted U-shape). Ferguson (1952: Table 55) has provided data for Glasgow which show that no retarded boy under IQ 50 was *convicted* by age 18; the percentage jumps to 20.6 for the IQ range 50 to 59, and then rises more gradually to 25.4 and 27.1 in the ranges 60 to 69 and 70 to 89. Presumably, somewhere after IQ 89 the percentage becoming delinquent would begin to decline again. Hirschi's lowest DAT score category has IQ 86-90 (approximately) as its upper bound, and so it includes all or most of Ferguson's categories, thus accounting for the discrepancy between their results and confirming the second degree function, which is revealed only when the full IQ range is adequately sampled and explicitly examined.

The two sets of delinquency data in Table 7 are based on hundreds of thousands or millions of cases in the base populations. The best set, for Philadelphia, exhibits the best fit. Conceivably, the IQ average for blacks ought to be a point higher than given, but this would not disturb the fit appreciably. The median IQ at sixth grade in 20 Harlem public schools that were virtually all black has been reported as 86.3 (Harlem Youth Opportunities Unlimited, Inc., 1964: Table 38), which is quite close to 86.0, the value employed here. For the nation as a whole, I have used a black IQ average that is more than one white standard deviation below the white mean, and hence lower than the value that is usually cited by about two points (e.g., Jensen, 1969a: 81, 87). Changing to the conventional value here would improve the fit. However, I have chosen to remain with the figure produced by an objective estimate rather than juggle numbers to suit the model. This figure, of 83.4, is quite close to Shuey's grand values of 83.0 and 83.6 for testings of Negro school children since 1945 (1966: 503). The training school data may also be the "noisier" of the two sets as the result of being subject to some interjurisdictional variation in applying the criterion of delinquency. The absence of this source is another advantage of the Philadelphia rates. Finally, the necessity of using 1956 data to estimate the racial split amongst training school inmates in 1964 may have led to a slight underestimation of prevalence among blacks and a slight overestimation of prevalence among whites, since the relative proportion of blacks in the U.S. population had increased during the interim (see Gordon, 1973: 549). This would contribute to the slight discrepancy in Table 7. When prevalence rates for a criterion are extremely low, as in the case of the training school data, it should be realized that the model is exquisitely sensitive to small errors in the low percentages that constitute the prevalence rates. For this criterion, a decrease of only 0.1 percentage points for whites and an increase of only 0.1 percentage points for blacks changes the racial difference in IQ between boys 0.8 points, and the racial difference in IQ between girls by 3.5 points! Corresponding changes in the court record rates, in contrast, produce changes in the racial difference of only 0.1 and 0.3 IQ points, respectively.

The close fit between blacks and whites which results from taking account of differences between them in the two main parameters for IQ (mean and standard deviation) is important evidence for the relevance of IQ to delinquency. Although some reduction of the IQ difference between races could have been anticipated simply as the result of the known relationship of both IQ and delinquency to social class, it is unlikely that many persons would have anticipated that practically all of the IQ difference would be accounted for by the model. The success of the model suggests that there is a unimodal subdistribution of delinquents for each of the official criteria of delinquency nestled mainly under the lower half of the white IQ distribution, and that displacements of the parent distribution up or down the IQ continuum consequently affect the size of the proportion that does become delinquent out of the total population. This would account for Hirschi's ability to reduce the race difference in delinquency to about one-fourth its zero-order value (16%) by controlling for DAT Verbal score, as demonstrated above. The DAT Verbal Reasoning test is a good measure of general intelligence (Carroll, 1959: 671; Frederiksen, 1959: 676).

At present, I know of no other data as good as those in Table 7 for capitalizing on intergroup IQ differences as natural experiments in the study of delinquency. However, general impressions indicate that blacks and whites are no special case, and that the delinquency and crime rates of other groups display orderings consistent with the orderings of their IQ means. Gold (1963: 186), for example, has stated that "The Japanese, Chinese and Jews have maintained low delinquency rates despite their minority group status and despite periods in their history in America when they were for the most part in lower socioeconomic strata."[27] Jensen (1969b: 480) hypothesizes, on the basis of evidence familiar to him (e.g., Jensen, 1973: 252-253), that Orientals average somewhat higher than Caucasians in general intelligence. Within a national cross-section of tenth-grade boys, I have calculated that the Jewish subsample has an average intelligence test score commensurate with a mean Stanford-Binet IQ of 111 (Bachman, 1970: Tables E-4-5 and E-4-8), as compared to about 100 for whites in general. Evidence that I have reviewed shows that Jews do indeed have lower crime and delinquency rates than whites in general. In Israel, however, the non-European or "oriental" Jews have a much lower average IQ (personal communication from an Israeli social scientist), and they are reported to have high crime and delinquency rates (Smooha, 1972; Iris and Shama, 1972). In Australia, aborigine women have been reported to comprise 60% of the female prison population in areas where they represent only 2.5% of the general population (of women or of men and women is unclear; Newsweek, 25 December 1972: 38). A majority of true aborigines examined on Piagetian conservation tests (which load on the general intelligence factor) do not show conservation by adolescence, although most European children do so by age seven (De Lemos, 1966, after Jensen, 1969b: 450-451). The Australian aborigines also lag far behind in educational attainment, but not all of this lag seems attributable to simple opportunity, for one source informs us that of the 65% who had completed primary education in one state, only 2% "had qualified to pass into the higher forms of secondary education" (Roper, 1970: 54). I also noted earlier that the delinquency incidence rate and average IQ of the Mexican-American population were at least roughly commensurate with each other. Casual observations concerning deviance rates of other groups in contemporary American society show no sign of an exception to this general picture.

I am quite aware that the model in Table 7 depends on the validity of intergroup differences in crime and delinquency rates, just as it depended on the validity of intergroup differences in IQ (now established for blacks, whites, and Mexican-Americans), and that the validity of such differences in crime rates is often questioned or denied. Much of this questioning arises from self-report and other methodologies. As I pointed out before, the present paper is a crucial stepping-stone toward the eventual review of this body of research. For now, it can be noted that the commensurability between the differences in rates and the differences in IQ parameters established in Table 7 constitutes important external evidence of the validity of the differences in prevalence rates. Simple discrimination models do not differentiate between varying degrees of excess criminality, and therefore they can be invoked quite casually to account for any size difference whatever between groups. In contrast, the IQ model comes extremely close to predicting the exact magnitude of the difference in delinquency. Moreover, the essence of discrimination models is that all members of the oppressed group are arbitrarily treated alike, without regard to their individual differences. The IQ model, however, works as well as it does precisely because it takes full account of individual differences along the IQ dimension. Ingenious ad hoc assumptions would have to be introduced into the discrimination model to account for the fact that an unfair discriminatory process is as sensitive to IQ as Table 7 requires. As it stands, therefore, the relation between IQ and delinquency rates for entire populations contributes predictive validity to the meaning of both IQ scores and official delinquency rates for those populations. If both the IQ and delinquency measurements were to be taken from the exact same large population of individuals, the model might perform even better.

The sixth, and final, fact which implicates the IQ distribution is the comparatively high rate of delinquency in black neighborhoods that fall within the middle class range, a phenomenon that is occasionally remarked upon by interested observers (e.g., Hardin, 1972). It is sometimes said, as a neutral reaction, that the blacks who move into new neighborhoods are "followed by" the problems of the ghetto. Regression toward the mean in the IQs of the children would account for this surprising amount of delinquency, however. It is well-established that middle class black children regress further on the average than middle class white children in IQ, and hence also in correlates of IQ. This is because even when the IQs of fathers are matched across race, the black children are regressing halfway back to a mean (of about 80 to 87) that is more distant than the mean for whites (of about 100). Examples or discussions of this effect can be found in Duncan, Featherman, and Duncan (1968: 69), Heber, Dever, and Conry (1968: 12), Scarr-Salapatek (1971: Table 3), and Jensen (1973: 118-119, 185-186, 239-240; 1974: 713). The example in Scarr-Salapatek's work is of special interest, because it shows that the regression effects are strong enough to produce slightly lower general intelligence means for upper SES black children than for lower SES white children: the two classifications regress in opposite directions and cross. Since both classifications have similar standard deviations, the data suggest that, if it is the IQ of the children rather than the IQ of the parents that is critical, the upper SES black neighborhoods (as defined there) should have delinquency rates comparable to those of lower SES white neighborhoods. This would certainly be sufficient to impress observers as worthy of comment.[28]

As far as I know, there have been only two other recent attempts to examine the crime difference between blacks and whites with an eye to relating it to the IQ difference. The other two came to my attention after my own data, developed for other reasons, suggested the possibility, and it appears that all three efforts have been independent of each other. Plainly, there is a phenomenon here that leads to convergent hypotheses.

The first person to undertake such an analysis was the physicist William Shockley (who included Orientals), in an address to the National Academy of Sciences (1967: 1773, Items 9-12). Shockley worked with incidence data rather than prevalence data out of necessity, and employed an analytic approach similar in some respects to mine, except that he used an empirical IQ distribution obtained from Burt's work rather than the normal distribution. Shockley also made the simplifying assumption, which I have been able to avoid (but at the cost of having to specify a somewhat artificial model), that the black and white IQ distributions shared the same standard deviation. Because this assumption is not strictly true, Shockley's z-score differences between the two races are not readily convertible into genuine IQ differences, although it must be recognized that his average z-score difference, over "a very diverse assemblage of behaviors," of 1.2 standard deviations (1967: 1769) was certainly close to the 1.1 white standard deviation difference that I have employed in Table 7 on the basis of data from Shuey (see note e) and from Terman and Merrill (see note c). Shockley's average z-score difference for four deviant behaviors alone was 1.0, and the four values themselves ranged from 0.8 to 1.2.

Shockley also attempted to take into account possible differences between black and white IQ standard deviations, but this led to a varying z-score difference which ranged from about 1.2 to 1.7 for the deviant behaviors, and which was far below 1.0 for outstanding educational and professional attainment. The exact interpretation of such results is unclear. Shockley himself gave none, although they are conceivably compatible with an interactive model in which low IQ blacks experience a harsher fate than a white of similar IQ, and high IQ blacks experience a better fate than a white of similar IQ. It is not hard to fantasize mechanisms that would produce such effects. There is considerable scatter among Shockley's results, no doubt due in part to the make-do nature of the data he had to employ. Although his results certainly have implications for the global difference between blacks and whites, more precise data are needed for the development of appropriate theory in any given behavioral area, particularly those areas that do not reflect educational attainment—and hence the more obvious aspects of IQ—in strong measure.

Hirschi (1969: 80) was the second person to examine the race-crime-IQ difference empirically, in the analysis summarized earlier. However, Hirschi's deliberate decision to use the term "academic competence" rather than "intelligence" (1969: 111, n. 3) in discussing this analysis leads one away from the rich heuristic implications of general intelligence as a pervasive influence on personality formation and dyadic relations, and favors instead a narrower focus upon school success and, ultimately, occupational prospects. Because the school is the first extrafamilial institution in the life cycle that is intensively studied, and because intellectual and behavioral difficulties are likely to appear there first simply because of timing, some persons may be overly hasty in assigning educational difficulties a primary role in the causation of delinquency. There is no reason to believe that delinquency would not occur just as often even if school did not exist (e.g., Ferguson, 1952: 146-147).

Hirschi's success in reducing differences between races in delinquency by controlling for intelligence was due in part to eliminating whites from virtually "all-white" schools from the analysis (1969: 77, and Táble 29B). When this large contingent is restored to the analysis, controlling for general intelligence reduces the average racial difference to only about 43% of its zero-order value (24%). The excluded whites from "all-white" schools had lower delinquency rates and higher intelligence, and hence were presumably from higher socioeconomic strata than the included whites. While residual variation in intelligence scores within the categories of the analysis could account for the failure of delinquency rate differences to "vanish," there is another possibility that brings home the potential importance of the IQ dyad, concerning which there is no real social psychological theory at the present time.

This possibility takes account of the IQ linkage between parent and child. The parents of white children as compared to black children, and of higher SES white children as compared to lower SES white children, will have higher IQs, even though the children in these categories are all matched exactly for IQ.[29] To put it simply, a black child of IQ 90 will on the average have parents whose midparent IQ is *lower* than his, and a white child of IQ 90 will on the average have parents whose midparent IQ is *higher* than his. This follows from the law of filial regression to the mean, which works in both directions, from parent to child and from child to parent. Note that the genetic and environmental contributions of the parents to the IQs of the children are already discounted by having stipulated the IQ of the children. The potential effect of interest derives from the environmental contribution of the parents, given their IQs, to the delinquency proneness of the children, over and above the genetic and environmental contributions of the parents to IQ itself. As a dramatically exaggerated example whose values have nothing to do with the average amounts of regression it would be reasonable to expect, consider that 120 IQ parents might be more effective in socializing a 100 IQ child than, say, 80 IQ parents. In actuality, based on estimates of key parameters in the white population, we would expect the black midparent IQ to be only about 5.3 IQ points below the white midparent IQ nationwide when their children are matched for IQ.[30] This average difference may be too small to produce much of an effect (hence the "dramatic" preceding example). However, if such an effect were potent it would constitute a regular causal distinction between two populations that

regularly differed in IQ. A five-point difference in parental IQ is roughly
equivalent to at least half of a social class when occupations are stratified in
accordance with the usual six-category system (Burt, 1961: Table I; Johnson,
1948: 223-224).

If the IQ of parents is related to the delinquency proneness of their children
over and above the effect of the IQ of the children, the probability of becoming
a delinquent for a child of given IQ would vary across the races, and blacks and
whites would have separate probability functions of delinquency over the range
of IQ. For roughly similar reasons, the IQs of peer-group contexts could also give
rise to such a race difference in the probability of delinquency for a child of
given IQ. These effects would result in a residual difference in delinquency rates
between races that could not be eliminated, as in Hirschi's data, even by
controlling for individual IQ exactly (see n. 29, above), which Hirschi did not
attempt. Whether or not taking the IQs of the full parent-child unit into account
improves the prediction of delinquency remains to be seen, however. The data in
Table 7 do not indicate the need to take into account the IQ of more than one
individual: on the average, there is no unexplained surplus of black delinquency.
Perhaps the regression effect difference between the races is so small that the IQ
of the child already contains all of the extractable information.

IQ-specific delinquency prevalence rates (within race and sex) at age 18.0
represent the most powerful measurements I can imagine for testing the relation
between IQ and delinquency. To establish such a relation, the rates would have
to vary over the IQ range, the higher rates would have to cluster together in
some meaningful distribution (unimodal, for example), and this distribution
would have to reappear in successive cohorts. A still more critical test involves
comparisons across race, using well-chosen criteria of delinquency, with all
populations located within the same or similar jurisdictions. If the rates describe
the same or nearly the same function in each race, despite all of the social
differences known to obtain between races in other respects, the simplest model
would be upheld. If the functions differ, such that there is a surplus of black
delinquents at any given IQ level, it may prove appropriate to replace the simple
one-generational model with a two-generational one which also takes explicit
account of the IQ of parents and of the differential regression effect on
midparent (or even single parent) IQ that I described above. For this purpose,
data on Jewish populations would be especially precious because the extremely
high average IQ of Jews would magnify any potential differential regression
effect involving parents in comparison with blacks. Other discrepancies or
patterns brought to light by the first examination of data such as these might
suggest other refinements rather than abandonment of the general model.

Within this general model, IQ is treated as an "actuarial" variable, much like age. Just as there are many possible causal connections between age and mortality, there would be many possible causal connections mediating between IQ and delinquency. In theory, for example, the low IQ child-low IQ parent dyad is fraught with potential for poor socialization outcomes, and the inappropriate or erratic child-rearing practices often found within the families of delinquents are plainly suggestive of inadequate cognitive analyses of the interpersonal child-rearing task. If spelled out in detail so as to take account of other information, both the simple and the regression effect models carry the implication that a low IQ child is usually reared by low IQ parents, which is empirically true. Neither special model actually distinguishes between the IQ of the filial generation and the IQ of the parent generation, since both carry the same distribution, and the models really address the distribution. The close connection between generations in IQ, however, means that information about a member of one carries information about his kin in the other: the correlation between midparent and offspring at age 18 is about .70 (Jensen, 1969b: 461). In this sense, both models reflect the realities of the parent-child IQ connection. If both generations contribute to delinquency, the fact that the midparent-child IQ correlation is less than 1.0 would produce greater dispersion in the distribution of delinquency rates as a function of IQ than if only one generation contributed, because at least some of the time a low IQ in one generation will be paired with an offsetting high IQ in the other generation, and vice versa. This would also tend to reduce the IQ-delinquency correlation among individuals, thus bringing out one important difference between thinking at the population as opposed to the individual level.

As I have noted elsewhere (Gordon, 1975), once it is established that IQ scores have the same functional meaning, or very close to the same meaning, in all of the racial-ethnic populations considered here, virtually all of the unfavorable practical consequences that are commonly and mistakenly identified only with the controversial issue of genetic differences are already upon us. If the differences are valid, and if they prove extremely resistant to remedial measures by environmental means—as they have proven for blacks—then for all usual intents and purposes it makes little difference whether they are genetic or not. Nothing that I have said thus far entails a genetic explanation of race differences in IQ. However, as I noted elsewhere (Gordon, 1975), once a genetic explanation is introduced to account for some behavior among whites for which there also exists a strong differential between races, psychological tension is created concerning the applicability of the same genetic explanation to the even larger proportion of blacks who exhibit the same behavior. For once the genetic explanation is accepted for the affected blacks, it tends to drag the rest of the black population with it for explanatory purposes, and the issue of genetic differences between entire breeding populations is raised in full. Thus, it is difficult to evade the issue.

As a recent reviewer of Jensen's work has said, "the genetic hypothesis is a viable one and ... it must be considered seriously" (Denniston, 1975: 162). Hopefully, greater recognition of the extent to which all groups suffer from the crime among us, including criminals themselves, will encourage us to adopt a more constructive attitude toward the genetic issue when it eventually has to be faced. A willingness to cooperate by sharing the information that is contained within our relatively separate ethnic-breeding populations—as natural experiments—could lead to solutions for problems that now seriously threaten us all.

What Criterion Should We Focus Upon?

It is my conviction that the court record criterion represents a lower bound for the degree of severity that defines "delinquent" in a manner with which it is profitable for society (and hence social science) to concern itself. Lesser degrees of misconduct are quite possibly of interest in their own right, especially for studying the full juvenile justice system. However, I feel that any investigation focusing principally on such lesser degrees of the dependent variable should clearly identify itself as dealing with a phenomenon that regularly ranges an order of magnitude lower in severity than court record delinquency. This viewpoint is in accord with one of Sellin and Wolfgang's (1964: 115) basic assumptions concerning the measurement of delinquency: "That the community is interested, for measuring purposes, in serious delinquent events rather than symptomatic or predelinquent behavior."

Even at the court record level of severity, and especially at the still more inclusive level 2 and police record criteria, many acts are considered delinquent mainly because they are performed by juveniles, and not because they are socially noxious per se (e.g., drinking, sex, underage driving, truancy, etc.). This is not to say that such behaviors do not often have serious antisocial impact. The point is that they are not criminal per se when performed by adults; and although technically illegal for juveniles, it is possible for some of them to be performed by some juveniles in a relatively responsible manner. If this inclusiveness holds at the court record level, what of less severe criteria?

Hathaway and Monachesi, judging from their remarks concerning the four levels, had reservations about level 2 themselves. Recall that they considered level 3 "not ... severely delinquent." Since they were sometimes forced to include even level 1 in the definition of delinquency for girls, in order to have enough cases for analysis (1963: 78), we can legitimately wonder whether the placement of their cutting point at level 2 was not a similar concession which they would have avoided had levels 3 and 4 yielded higher rates. This surmise is supported by their statement, "The problem of sample size is especially vexing in the case of girls, for whom the delinquency rate is only about one-third that for boys" (1963: 78). Since the level 3 rate for boys was also about one-third their level 2 rate (see Table 2, above), it presumably would have been as vexing to use level 3 for boys as it proved to use level 2 for girls. Evidently there are pressures stemming from sample size considerations that lead investigators to define delinquency more inclusively than they would on the basis of severity alone.

Havighurst and associates (1962: 69) expressed strong dissatisfaction with their police record criterion as a definition of important delinquency, and finally settled for category III, which I have argued is close to court record severity. Conger and Miller (1966: 17) were convinced that use of the police record criterion "would have diluted the meaning of the term delinquency to the point of absurdity." Accordingly, they chose the juvenile court record, on the grounds that it "had the greatest promise for scientific investigation, and was also in closest accord with common usage."

I call attention to these opinions because Wolfgang et al. (1972: 15) have stated that "it is generally admitted today that to limit oneself to court-determined delinquency would result in a highly biased view of the problem." For the purpose of establishing rates at meaningful levels of severity, however, a "bias" in severity is entirely appropriate. Common sense would suggest that a classic institution for dealing with delinquency would focus on delinquents at or somewhat beyond a point in the range of severity where the cost of not dealing with them begins to exceed the considerable cost of dealing with them. Since the court is an expensive institution, the average social utility of bringing a juvenile to court would have to be fairly high, but the errors would probably be pitched in the direction of over-inclusiveness rather than under-inclusiveness.

The balancing-off of costs in either direction would account for the apparent siting of courts for dealing with juveniles at a relatively constant position along the severity continuum. Without such stability, we would not find the invariance in rates for the court record criterion proper that appears in Table 2, even if the populations themselves produced a constant proportion of delinquents at that level of severity. Detection of a regular measurement obviously requires a reasonably stable measuring device. Thus, it is not entirely fortuitous that the delinquency criterion of greatest interest happens to be associated with an institution that is strategically located for recording it and collecting other data. The absence of comparable constraining costs at the police record level (where processing of a case is relatively inexpensive) undoubtedly accounts for much of the raggedness among rates along the lower border of Table 2. For these mild criteria (police record, category IV, level 1, and level 2) there is little natural constraint on accepting cases of ever decreasing severity. The lesson to be drawn is that tests of the models described in the preceding section ought to be based on the more stable criteria of delinquency, such as the court record, rather than on the police record.

If the court record is accepted as the most inclusive criterion of reasonably severe delinquency, the court record and other data reviewed here put us in position to pose a key question concerning self-report studies, which sometimes employ cutting points as high as 42% for defining delinquency in the white population. With an official prevalence rate for white males in cities of about 17%, and an estimated prevalence rate in "Towns over 5,000" of 14% (Table 5), are self-report studies capable of detecting a relation between social class and reasonably severe delinquency if indeed one existed, and the official rates were accurate?

The robustness of the race- and sex-specific prevalence rates exhibited for whites in this review, the apparent ability of the processing agencies to adjust their capacity so as to accommodate a larger volume of delinquency from blacks, and the commensurability maintained between rates for each race (within sex) and their IQ difference, vindicate those few individuals (e.g., Lejins, 1960, 1966) who have defended official statistics in the face of severe, but often nonempirical criticism, frequently emanating from official agencies themselves: "No evaluation, however, appears necessary. Juvenile court statistics, the [U.S. Children's] Bureau observes in its introduction, not only fail to measure the full extent of delinquency but also can be particularly misleading when used to compare one community with another" (Center for Studies of Crime and Delinquency, no date). The robustness and invariance over most of the urban-rural continuum which the reviewed data exhibit is quite consistent with the finding that even conventional delinquency prevention programs have little impact on the phenomenon of delinquency (Robins, 1973). If deliberate interventions have little effect on delinquency rates, it is reasonable to suppose that the rates are similarly unresponsive to many other variables. Indeed, the unsuspected regularity in the capacity of human populations for emitting and responding to noxious behaviors that has been revealed may be the most significant finding of all. Since "labeling" approaches to delinquency attribute the main source of variance in rates to audiences, this finding, if sustained, will impose new limits on the potential applicability of those approaches.

NOTES

1. See Blum and Rossi, 1969: 363-366; Chilton, 1964; Cohen, 1955: 36-44; Cressey, 1961: 41-43; Douglas et al., 1966; Ferguson, 1952: Table 6; Gold, 1963: 5-9; Gordon,

1967, 1968; Harlem Youth Opportunities Unlimited, Inc., 1964: chap. 5; Hathaway and Monachesi, 1963: Tables 84 and 85; Havighurst et al., 1962: Table 18; Hirschi, 1969: Tables 12-13; Kvaraceus, 1945: chap. 9; Lander, 1954: 30; Reiss and Rhodes, 1961; Robins et al., 1962; Robins, 1966: chaps. 5 and 8; Trasler, 1962: 75; Trenaman, 1952: Table 16; Werner and Gallistel, 1961; West, 1967: chap. 3; Wolfgang, Figlio, and Sellin, 1972: Table 4.1.

2. Contributions with which I have been associated, for example, encountered more resistance than I personally have experienced with articles in the past—until they were submitted to journals that were highly quantitative in emphasis. Some of the referees also seemed to find the effort to derive estimates of prevalence parameters tedious and uninteresting. The groundwork for establishing important scientific facts often is tedious, of course, and it is a sad commentary when this becomes a consideration in journal publication.

3. For example, Perlman (1964: 29) notes that "only about 4 percent . . . of the juveniles aged 10 through 17 were arrested by the police in 1962, only 1.8 percent were referred to juvenile courts for delinquent behavior, and only 0.2 percent were committed to institutions for delinquent children." These low numbers, of "only" 4, 1.8, and 0.2%, may be compared to sex- and race-specific prevalence rates at age 18.0 for white males at corresponding levels of severity, given elsewhere in the present paper, of about 25 to 28%, 17 to 18%, and 1.02%, respectively. I would suggest that the kind of rate employed by Perlman is far more conducive to complacency than rates in the form I am calling "prevalence," even if Perlman's rates were simply doubled to approximate their values for males alone. Unlike Perlman's rates, the prevalence statistic conveys a sense of the proportion of delinquency-prone youth that one would be surrounded by as a member of the cohort. For essentially similar observations, see Savitz (1960: 204-205).

4. Another influence that could affect the comparability between rates derived from "cohort studies" and those derived by actuarial methods is the requirement that all members of the cohort reside continuously within a given city during all or most of the period of risk, say from "their tenth until their eighteenth birthday" (e.g., Wolfgang et al., 1972: 27). Although it is understandable that cohort investigators would desire to standardize the exposure to risk by means of this requirement (1972: 31), it can have the effect of purging the population at risk of members high in intercity residential mobility. Such members would not normally be excluded by an actuarial study, since if a boy lived in the city only for one year, he would contribute to the age-specific rate (either as a delinquent or a nondelinquent) appropriate for his age level during his time of residence. Obviously, the amount and direction of bias would depend on how representative of the qualified cohort the pool of those disqualified by intercity mobility happen to be, and on the size of this pool. I am not suggesting that this consideration necessarily represents a serious source of bias, but it should be kept in mind as a potential source whenever differences between cohort and actuarial rates are being reconciled, as I shall demonstrate later. Presumably, the more inclusive the jurisdiction, the less of a problem posed by interjurisdictional mobility.

5. In this paper the term "official" shall refer to statistics created by some action of a public agency, such as arrest, whether or not they have been assembled by a public agency or by, for example, a research sociologist going through the files of a public agency. Thus, "official" is in contradistinction to self-reported statistics. I shall try to avoid the word "unofficial." Within juvenile courts, and consequently among sociologists, a distinction is often made between cases processed "officially" and "unofficially," with the understanding that in the latter situation, a case does not leave a "record." But here too, "record" is being

used in a strictly local sense, to mean "official record," for it is widely acknowledged that "unofficial" dispositions also are recorded, and therefore leave records that are equally official in the sense of this paper, as are many police "contacts" in some jurisdictions. The words "formal" and "informal," and "judicial" and "nonjudicial" are coming into use for distinguishing between different dispositions of official cases, and seem preferable to "official" and "unofficial" (Lunden, 1964: 196; Sheridan, 1966: 57). As the meanings of the various rates become better understood, it will be more important than ever to report them in precise and unambiguous terms. Police "contact" seems to be a term in wide use that is especially unhelpful, unless further defined (as in Wolfgang et al., 1972: 22, 43-44, 218-220).

6. Simon Dinitz kindly clarified this for me in a personal communication.

7. The interim report of the Lalli and Savitz (1972) study provides a useful demonstration of the utility of age-specific rates and of the cumulative prevalence that they yield at each individual year of age. Lalli and Savitz compare the 12.5% of families containing any delinquent youth by about age 13.0 (of the proband boy) with the remainder of their Philadelphia Negro cohort (not containing a youth with a court record). For some of the variables involved in these comparisons, they found little difference between the two subsamples. However, the information from Monahan and from Gordon and Gleser (1974: Table 3) concerning Negro boys in the same city, and employing the same criterion of delinquency, indicates that 50.9% of a representative cohort meets this criterion by age 18.0. This means that approximately 44% of the "nondelinquent" group in the comparisons made by Lalli and Savitz may actually consist of boys who will meet the criterion by age 18.0. Clearly, the presence of a delinquent proportion this large in the "nondelinquent" group would serve to undercut any comparisons made between the two groups, and it may account for the rarity of differences. This sobering example also illustrates the point of employing the perspective of "prevalence," which encourages the realization that there is *currently* present in the cohort a certain proportion who will all qualify as delinquent, within a very few years, and who presumably do not differ very much at any given time from those already so qualified.

8. These studies are by Kvaraceus (1945: 96-97); Glueck and Glueck (1950: 80, 156); Savitz (1960: 200); Essen-Möller (1961: 12); Ball and Pabon (1965: 405-406); Putnam and Ellinwood (1966); Robins (1966: 92-95); and Wolfgang et al. (1972: Tables 4.2 and 5.1). Since another study (Downie, 1953) reveals that mobility per se does not cause either social or cognitive maladjustment, the relation between antisocial persons and mobility must be due to the characteristics of the deviants before they moved. This interpretation is supported by Savitz's (1960) study of black migration, which found that migration per se within the life of the proband boy was not criminogenic.

9. Hirschi (1969: Table 2) has presented "police record" rates for male Negroes and male "Others" (consisting mainly of whites, with small percentages of Mexican-Americans and Orientals which I estimate at roughly 5.3 and 2.6%, respectively, from 1970 census data), in Western Contra Costa County, which is part of the San Francisco-Oakland metropolitan area, for 1964. Hirschi's rates show prevalences of 57% for Negroes and 32% for "Others." Clearly, this high "police record" rate for Negroes would accommodate a court record rate of about 50% with no difficulty. However, it is hard to believe that Hirschi's California criterion is the same as Wolfgang and associates' Philadelphia one, since Hirschi's sample consists of seventh to twelfth graders, with an average age which I estimate to be only 15.8 for the whites proper (from his Table A-1). The magnitude of these rates, long before the boys have all reached 18, compels us to assume that the criteria are not

equivalent in both studies, despite their superficial terminological resemblance. Unfortunately, as is all too common, Hirschi provides little information concerning the concrete nature of his delinquency criterion, although in other respects his research report and analyses are of the highest quality.

10. Some persons might have chosen a slightly different method for making these adjustments. For example, if the British rate at age 17.0 was 96% of the Philadelphia rate at 17.0, they would have added only 96% of the Philadelphia age-specific rate in the interval 17.0 to 18.0, instead of 100%, thus maintaining the proportional discrepancy. This line of reasoning assumes that the slight discrepancy observed between the two series at 17.0 is not a random deviation potentially compensated for in the next year of age (the longer series being more reliable), but rather an estimate of the true proportional difference between the two series. The method I employ attaches greater weight to the assumption of no true difference between the two series and maintains the observed discrepancy as a constant percentage difference rather than a constant proportional difference. It is easy to see that the method I have rejected could exaggerate extremely small percentage differences appearing in the early years of a series, when base rates are usually quite low. Perhaps the most important consideration is that the two methods differ only slightly in the results produced whenever the amount of the adjustment is but a modest proportion of the sum of the observed figure plus the adjustment.

11. I have obtained rates for age 18 here by interpolation between published rates for 17 and 19. Since the difference between the rates for 17 and 19 amounted only to 4.9 percentage points, the interpolation (a simple average) cannot be far off the mark.

12. Incidental to other research purposes, Conger and Miller found that 11.54% of a male cohort whose relation to the general white population is exceedingly ill-defined had a juvenile court record by 18.0 (1966: 16). I have not been able to improve our understanding of this datum so as to relate it to other rates in this paper. The same applies to the rate of 12.2% "convicted" by age 18.0 in a Glasgow cohort of males who left school at age 14, studied by Ferguson (1952).

13. As I indicated earlier in the text, these standard deviations are based (of necessity) on what Gordon and Gleser call Monahan's "pseudoprevalence" rates; it is quite reasonable to expect that for a given population the actual prevalence rate would show about the same variance, since the two quantities are intimately related to each other.

14. Savitz's (1960) study of delinquency among black migrants residing in a neighborhood with one of the four highest incidence rates of delinquency in Philadelphia indicates that these migrants acquired juvenile court records at rates quite close to those established by Gordon and Gleser (1974: Table 3) for black males in the city as a whole. Savitz's discussion suggests that he performed his juvenile court record search in 1958, which would establish the ages of his migrants in his Table III as 13, 14, 15, 16, 17, and 18. Comparing his delinquency prevalence rates at these ages for his small migrant samples with Gordon and Gleser's prevalence rates at corresponding ages (13.0, 14.0, etc.), we obtain:

Savitz:	17.6	28.6	17.9	31.1	42.5	50.0
G. and G.:	14.8	21.0	28.4	36.6	44.5	50.9

Savitz's cumulative rates are higher at two out of six ages, and lower at four out of six. However, the nonmonotonicity produced by his rate (of 17.9) at age 15 is a clear indication of a sampling fluctuation. Interpolation suggests this rate is actually higher than Gordon and Gleser's at age 15.0, which would lead to a tie at three apiece for which series displays the higher rate. These considerations and the close agreement in actual rates, on the average, indicate that if the migrants in this one neighborhood are typical of migrants in the city as a whole, there is little difference between migrants and nonmigrants in delinquency rates. If black migrants tend to be lower class, it is quite conceivable that Savitz's migrants were more typical of migrants throughout Philadelphia than the Philadelphia-born blacks in the same high-delinquency neighborhood were of native-born blacks throughout the rest of the city. Those familiar with Savitz's study will recall that native-born blacks in this neighborhood had delinquency rates that were usually higher than those of the migrants, although the differences were not significant. The import of Savitz's data for present purposes hinges on how representative his migrants in this one neighborhood were of migrants in general, and this cannot be determined.

15. Another potentially reconciling influence can be found in the following statement of Monahan's (1961: 164): "Court data include more than police arrest cases. Parents, relatives, private police, agencies, schools, and individuals may file petitions against children for delinquent acts." Until forced by appropriate data, I would certainly not interpret this to mean that Wolfgang and associates' police custody criterion is not more inclusive overall, and therefore less severe, than the court record criterion. This is because I doubt that such petition cases, initiated by other than the police, would outweigh the inclusiveness of police custody. However, if the proportion of petition cases were to be correlated with being black, this would contribute to reducing the anomaly concerning rates for blacks in the two Philadelphia studies.

16. The 1950 census shows that among employed males, the percentage of "Professional, technical, and kindred workers" was 10.8 in Minneapolis, but only 8.0 in Duluth, and the percentage of "laborers, except farm and mine" was only 6.3 in Minneapolis, but 10.8 in Duluth. The median number of school years completed by persons 25 years old or older was 11.5 in Minneapolis, but only 10.2 in Duluth. The percentage unemployed was 5.5 in Duluth, but 4.2 in Minneapolis (U.S. Bureau of the Census, 1952: Part 23, Tables 10 and 35). The statistic for laborers is especially meaningful, because elsewhere it has been shown that variation in the proportion in the bottom-most stratum of the socioeconomic distribution is most relevant to variation in official delinquency rates (Gordon, 1967: 944).

17. In view of the six-point difference between Minneapolis and Duluth in level 2 rates, it might occur to some persons that an average of level 2 rates in Minneapolis, Duluth, and the suburbs would provide a better measure of this rate in urban locales than just the one for Duluth alone, especially for the purpose of deriving the proportional estimates of court record rates in the lower half of Table 5. However, using such an average would change the final estimates by only one percentage point or less.

18. The published report (CSCD, 1974: 2) states that "only 4 percent of the group were institutionalized." Here, apparently, the total number of 303 police record delinquents was taken as the base. Dr. Richmond clarified this point, and the rate I employ is consistent with the published figure of 11 boys incarcerated out of the entire cohort of 1,227.

19. In 1960, 49.7% of Marion County and 54.3% of the nation as a whole lived in communities of 10,000 or more (U.S. Bureau of the Census, 1963: Tables 5-7; 1971: Table 16).

20. Although suggestive, the average seriousness scores (given earlier) for the offenses committed by offenders in the two recidivist categories cannot be used to place them in Table 2 because it tells us nothing about their most serious offenses, upon which their proper location depends. For seriousness scores, see Table 4.

21. Those familiar with Hirschi's (1969: chap. 2) useful classification of deviance theories will recognize this explanation as an example of what he calls a "control theory."

Hirschi's own research tends to favor "control theory" explanations of delinquency, which are based on the absence of controls. For another compatible view, see Reiss (1951).

22. Angell's (1951: 123-124; 1974: 611) crime index was based on a weighting of FBI Uniform Crime Report statistics for homicide, robbery, and burglary. For a demonstration that all indices based on crimes known to the police in these three categories would correlate almost perfectly with each other or with an index based on the Sellin-Wolfgang seriousness scores, see Blumstein (1974). There is reason to believe, however, that the inclusion of aggravated assault would have increased the correlations with race that I present below (see McKeown, 1948; Schuessler, 1962).

23. On the greater criminality among adult migrants, see Spirer (1940: 41-44), Amarista (1959), Kinman and Lee (1966), and Green (1970: Tables 3-5). All four studies show this effect for whites, and the first and fourth show it for blacks at the particular times and places concerned. Studies which fail to show this effect for blacks (Kinman and Lee, 1966; Crain and Weisman, 1972: Table 2.2) may only demonstrate that the recruitment effect which draws antisocial adults to cities may be overridden by other trends during periods of mass migration. Kinman and Lee's (1966: 8) observation that "rates of migration are highest among young males" is, of course, extremely relevant to the connection between migration and criminality.

24. The product-moment correlation is .403.

25. By IQ I mean the variable measured by IQ tests and other standard tests of intelligence (whether their scores are expressed in IQ form or not) which load on the general factor common to such tests. As Jensen (1969a: 19) points out, "Any one verbal definition of this factor is really inadequate, but, if we must define it in so many words, it is probably best thought of as a capacity for abstract reasoning and problem solving." For a good, nontechnical discussion of the issues surrounding the general factor interpretation, see Herrnstein (1973: chap. 2).

26. Rosenthal (1970: 238) cites an early German adoption study by Zur Nieden (1951) as indicating "that criminals' children reared in good homes behave well." However, there is actually no evidence for this conclusion. Although Zur Nieden dismisses what she regards as "little criminality" among her total group of adoptees, it is impossible to tell whether the observed criminality rates are low or high, since she fails to draw explicit comparisons between rates among adopted offspring of known criminals and rates among control offspring. Among her 138 adoptees, only 21 cases at most, and perhaps as few as 15, were of criminal extraction. Moreover, 74% of the adoptees were girls, and 46% were adopted after the age of six (unlike Crowe's study, where none was adopted later than age four). These additional facts also mitigate against high criminality rates in the sample because rates for females are low in general, and because late adoption permits more opportunity for screening out troublesome youngsters. It may be revealing, however, that two of the 102 girls had to be "institutionalized on account of waywardness and unwillingness to work" (Zur Nieden, 1951: 94). If these two incarcerations are equated to commitment to a training school by age 18.0, the rate for this mixed group of white girls would be 1.96%. This is 8.52 times higher than the recent rate of 0.23% for white girls in the United States reported by Gordon (1973: Table 2), and almost twice Gordon's rate for white boys.

27. In their study of probation department referrals in Los Angeles County in 1956, Eaton and Polk (1961: 25) found that Japanese-Americans had a delinquency rate that was 0.500 times (half) the "Anglo" rate (both sexes counted together). In New York's "Chinatown," a minor outbreak of teen-age violence prompted a shocked newspaper reaction, although yearly arrests for serious crimes in the community of 45,000 still ran at

the rate of only 0.67 per 1,000 (Arnold, 1970). Crime rates are also reported to be low in Tokyo, in China (Evening Sun, 1974; 1975), and in Hong Kong (Michelson, 1970: 154-155), despite extremely high population densities and a variety of political systems. See also Kitano (1967) and Eisner (1969: Table 1).

28. Some readers who follow newspaper descriptions of crimes closely and who have had first-hand exposure to criminals and delinquents may also find convincing the impulsive, irrational quality of many offenses, in which the self-interested motivation of the offender seems inadequate to account for his actions in, say, killing a friend or relative over slight provocation with little hope of avoiding detection. The low IQ, high associative learning profile which Jensen has identified as more prevalent among low SES populations (1972: 204-293) would certainly be capable of supporting such crimes, as well as more opportunistic ones (such as drug abuse) where the disadvantageous consequences are apparent mainly over the long range. Quite possibly, the cognitive models discussed in connection with Table 7, above, would benefit from taking explicit account of associative learning ability as a second cognitive dimension. For additional discussion of this second dimension, and its role in the community, see Gordon (1975).

29. Jensen (1973: 120, n. 7) points out that in this and comparable designs mentioned below it is necessary that the matched individuals be matched on "regressed true scores" rather than raw IQs, "that is, the IQ scores they would be expected to obtain if errors of measurement were eliminated." This would involve taking account of the mean IQ and the reliability of the test for each population.

30. The midparent IQ, P, can be calculated from the formula $P = h^2 (O-M) + M$, where h^2 equals heritability in the narrow sense, O equals the IQ of the child, and M equals the mean IQ of the population in question. The best estimate of h^2 in the white population is .71 (Jinks and Fulker, 1970).

REFERENCES

AMARISTA, F. J. (1959) "Experiencia en la Prueba de Raven." Psychological Abstracts 33 (October): 1034.

ANGELL, R. C. (1974) "The moral integration of American cities. II." American Journal of Sociology 80 (November): 607-629.

――― (1951) "The moral integration of American cities." American Journal of Sociology 57, no. 1, part 2 (July): 1-140.

ARNOLD, M. (1970) "Teen-age gangs plague merchants in Chinatown." New York Times (August 5): C23.

BACHMAN, J. G. (1970) Youth in Transition, Volume II: The Impact of Family Background and Intelligence on Tenth-Grade Boys. Ann Arbor, Michigan: Institute for Social Research, University of Michigan.

BALL, J. C. (1962) Social Deviancy and Adolescent Personality. Lexington: University of Kentucky Press.

――― and D. O. PABON (1965) "Locating and interviewing narcotic addicts in Puerto Rico." Sociology and Social Research 49 (July): 401-411.

BALL, J. C., A. ROSS, and A. SIMPSON (1964) "Incidence and estimated prevalence of recorded delinquency in a metropolitan area." American Sociological Review 29 (February): 90-93.

BIDERMAN, A. D. (1967) "Surveys of population samples for estimating crime incidence." Annals of the American Academy of Political and Social Science 374 (November): 16-33.

——— and A. J. REISS, Jr. (1967) "On exploring the 'dark figure' of crime." Annals of the American Academy of Political and Social Science 374 (November): 1-15.

BLUM, Z. D. and P. H. ROSSI (1969) "Social class research and images of the poor: a bibliographic review," pp. 348-397 in D. P. Moynihan (ed.) On Understanding Poverty. New York: Basic Books.

BLUMSTEIN, A. (1974) "Seriousness weights in an index of crime." American Sociological Review 39 (December): 854-864.

Board of Public Education (1957) One-hundred Thirty-ninth Annual Report of the Board of Public Education, School District of Philadelphia.

——— (1954) One-hundred Thirty-sixth Annual Report of the Board of Public Education, School District of Philadelphia.

——— (1953) One-hundred Thirty-fifth Annual Report of the Board of Public Education, School District of Philadelphia.

——— (1952) One-hundred Thirty-fourth Annual Report of the Board of Public Education, School District of Philadelphia.

BOGUE, D. J. (1969) Principles of Demography. New York: John Wiley.

BURNHAM, D. (1974) "Poor main target of violent crime." New York Times (November 28): 21.

BURT, C. (1961) "Intelligence and social mobility." British Journal of Statistical Psychology 14, part 1 (May): 3-24.

CARROLL, J. B. (1959) "Differential aptitude tests," pp. 670-673 in O. K. Buros (ed.) The Fifth Mental Measurements Yearbook. Highland Park, N.J.: Gryphon Press.

CASPARI, E. (1967) "Introduction to Part 1 and remarks on evolutionary aspects of behavior," pp. 3-9 in J. Hirsch (ed.) Behavior-Genetic Analysis. New York: McGraw-Hill.

CAVAN, R. S. and J. T. CAVAN (1968) Delinquency and Crime: Cross-Cultural Perspectives. Philadelphia: Lippincott.

Center for Studies of Crime and Delinquency (1974) Teenage Delinquency in Small Town America, Research Report 5, Publication No. (ADM) 75-138. Washington, D.C.: Government Printing Office.

——— (n.d.) Criminal Statistics, Publication No. (HSM) 72-9094. Washington, D.C.: Government Printing Office.

CHAMBLISS, W. J. and R. H. NAGASAWA (1969) "On the validity of official statistics: a comparative study of white, black, and Japanese high-school boys." Journal of Research in Crime and Delinquency 6 (no. 1): 71-77.

CHILTON, R. J. (1964) "Continuity in delinquency area research: a comparison of studies for Baltimore, Detroit, and Indianapolis." American Sociological Review 29 (February): 71-83.

CHIRICOS, T. G., P. D. JACKSON, and G. P. WALDO (1972) "Inequality in the imposition of a criminal label." Social Problems 19 (Spring): 553-572.

COHEN, A. K. (1955) Delinquent Boys. Glencoe, Ill.: Free Press.

COLEMAN, J. S., E. Q. CAMPBELL, C. J. HOBSON, J. McPARTLAND, A. M. MOOD, F. D. WEINFELD, and R. L. YORK (1966) Equality of Educational Opportunity. Washington, D.C.: Government Printing Office.

CONGER, J. J. and W. C. MILLER (1966) Personality, Social Class, and Delinquency. New York: John Wiley.

CONNOR, W. D. (1970) "Juvenile delinquency in the U.S.S.R.: some quantitative and qualitative indicators." American Sociological Review 35 (April): 283-297.
CRAIN, R. L. and C. S. WEISMAN (1972) Discrimination, Personality, and Achievement: A Survey of Northern Blacks. New York: Seminar Press.
CRESSEY, D. R. (1961) "Crime," pp. 21-76 in R. K. Merton and R. A. Nisbet (eds.) Contemporary Social Problems. New York: Harcourt, Brace & World.
CROWE, R. R. (1972) "The adopted offspring of women criminal offenders." Archives of General Psychiatry 27 (November): 600-603.
DAVIS, K. (1973) "Introduction," pp. 1-6 in K. Davis (ed.) Cities: Their Origin, Growth, and Human Impact. San Francisco: W. H. Freeman.
DE LEMOS, M. M. (1966) "The development of the concept of conservation in Australian aboriginal children." Ph.D. dissertation. Perth: University of Western Australia.
DENNISTON, C. (1975) "Accounting for differences in mean IQ." Science 187, no. 4172 (January 17): 161-162.
DINITZ, S. (1969) "Emerging issues in delinquency," pp. 1-19 in The Threat of Crime in America; the 1967-68 E. Paul du Pont Lectures on Crime, Delinquency and Corrections. Newark: University of Delaware.
DOUGLAS, J.W.B., J. M. ROSS, W. A. HAMMOND, and D. G. MULLIGAN (1966) "Delinquency and social class." British Journal of Criminology 6 (July): 294-302.
DOWNIE, N. M. (1953) "A comparison between children who have moved from school to school with those who have been in continuous residence on various factors of adjustment." Journal of Educational Psychology 44 (January): 50-53.
DUNCAN, O. D., D. L. FEATHERMAN, and B. DUNCAN (1968) Socioeconomic Background and Occupational Achievement: Extensions of a Basic Model. Final Report, Project No. 5-0074 (EO-191), Office of Education, U.S. Department of Health, Education, and Welfare.
EATON, J. W. and K. POLK (1961) Measuring Delinquency: A Study of Probation Department Referrals. Pittsburgh: University of Pittsburgh Press.
EISNER, V. (1969) The Delinquency Label: The Epidemiology of Juvenile Delinquency. New York: Random House.
ESSEN-MOLLER, E. (1961) "A current field study in the mental disorders in Sweden," pp. 1-12 in P. H. Hoch and J. Zubin (eds.) Comparative Epidemiology of the Mental Disorders. New York: Grune & Stratton.
Evening Sun (1975) "China warns peasants against crime." (February 5): A10.
——— (1974) "Law and order are Tokyo norm." (April 22): B1.
EYSENCK, H. J. (1964) Crime and Personality. New York: Houghton Mifflin.
FERGUSON, T. (1952) The Young Delinquent in his Social Setting. London: Oxford University Press.
FREDERIKSEN, N. (1959) "Differential aptitude tests," pp. 673-676 in O. K. Buros (ed.) The Fifth Mental Measurements Yearbook. Highland Park, N.J.: Gryphon Press.
GALTON, F. (1869) Hereditary Genius. London: Macmillan.
GEIS, G. (1965) "Statistics concerning race and crime." Crime and Delinquency 11 (April): 142-150.
GLUECK, S. and E. GLUECK (1950) Unraveling Juvenile Delinquency. Cambridge: Harvard University Press.
GOLD, M. (1963) Status Forces in Delinquent Boys. Ann Arbor: Institute for Social Research, University of Michigan.
GORDON, R. A. (1975) "Examining labelling theory: the case of mental retardation," pp.

83-146 in W. R. Gove (ed.) The Labelling of Deviance: Evaluating a Perspective. The Third Vanderbilt University Sociology Conference. New York: Halsted/Sage.

——— (1973) "An explicit estimation of the prevalence of commitment to a training school, to age 18, by race and by sex." Journal of the American Statistical Association 68 (September): 547-553.

——— (1968) "On the interpretation of oblique factors." American Sociological Review 33 (August): 601-620.

——— (1967) "Issues in the ecological study of delinquency." American Sociological Review 32 (December): 927-944.

——— and L. J. GLESER (1974) "The estimation of the prevalence of delinquency: two approaches and a correction of the literature." Journal of Mathematical Sociology 3 (No. 2): 275-291.

GORDON, R. A., J. F. SHORT, Jr., D. S. CARTWRIGHT, and F. L. STRODTBECK (1963) "Values and gang delinquency: a study of street-corner groups." American Journal of Sociology 69 (September): 109-128.

GREEN, E. (1970) "Race, social status, and criminal arrest." American Sociological Review 35 (June): 476-490.

GRODZINS, M. (1958) "The metropolitan area as a racial problem," pp. 85-123 in E. Raab (ed.) American Race Relations Today. New York: Anchor Books, 1962.

HARDIN, W. (1972) "New problems replace old ones, blacks find." Baltimore Evening Sun (May 17): D1.

Harlem Youth Opportunities Unlimited, Inc. (1964) Youth in the Ghetto. New York: Harlem Youth Opportunities Unlimited, Inc.

HATHAWAY, S. R. and E. D. MONACHESI (1963) Adolescent Personality and Behavior; MMPI Patterns of Normal, Delinquent, Dropout, and Other Outcomes. Minneapolis: University of Minnesota Press.

HAVIGHURST, R. J., P. H. BOWMAN, G. P. LIDDLE, C. V. MATTHEWS, and J. V. PIERCE (1962) Growing Up in River City. New York: John Wiley.

HEBER, R., R. DEVER, and J. CONRY (1968) "The influence of environmental and genetic variables on intellectual development," pp. 1-22 in H. J. Prehm, L. A. Hamerlynck, and J. E. Crosson (eds.) Behavioral Research in Mental Retardation. Eugene: School of Education, University of Oregon.

HERRNSTEIN, R. J. (1973) I.Q. in the Meritocracy. Boston: Little, Brown.

HIRSCHI, T. (1969) Causes of Delinquency. Berkeley: University of California Press.

IRIS, M. and A. SHAMA (1972) "Black Panthers: the movement." Society 9 (May): 37-39.

JENSEN, A. R. (1974) "Educability and group differences." Nature 250, no. 5469 (August 30): 713-714.

——— (1973) Educability and Group Differences. New York: Harper & Row.

——— (1972) Genetics and Education. New York: Harper & Row.

——— (1970) "IQ's of identical twins reared apart." Behavior Genetics 1 (no. 2): 133-148.

——— (1969a) "How much can we boost IQ and scholastic achievement?" Harvard Educational Review 39 (Winter): 1-123.

——— (1969b) "Reducing the heredity-environment uncertainty: a reply." Harvard Educational Review 39 (Summer): 449-483.

JINKS, J. L. and D. W. FULKER (1970) "Comparison of the biometrical genetical, MAVA, and classical approaches to the analysis of human behavior." Psychological Bulletin 73 (May): 311-349.

JOHNSON, D. M. (1948) "Applications of the standard-score IQ to social statistics." Journal of Social Psychology 27 (May): 217-227.

KENNEDY, W. A., V. VAN DE RIET, and J. C. WHITE, Jr. (1963) "A normative sample of intelligence and achievement of Negro elementary school children in the Southeastern United States." Monographs of the Society for Research in Child Development 28 (no. 6): 1-112.

KINMAN, J. L. and E. S. LEE (1966) "Migration and crime." International Migration Digest 3 (Spring): 7-14.

KITANO, H.H.L. (1967) "Japanese-American crime and delinquency." Journal of Psychology 66 (July): 253-263.

KVARACEUS, W. C. (1945) Juvenile Delinquency and the School. Yonkers-on-Hudson, N.Y.: World.

LALLI, M. and L. SAVITZ (1972) Delinquency and City Life. Washington, D.C.: U.S. Department of Justice, Law Enforcement Assistance Administration, National Institute of Law Enforcement and Criminal Justice.

LANDER, B. (1954) Towards an Understanding of Juvenile Delinquency. New York: Columbia University Press.

Law Enforcement Assistance Administration (1974) Crime in the Nation's Five Largest Cities. Washington, D.C.: National Criminal Justice Information and Statistics Service, Law Enforcement Assistance Administration, U.S. Department of Justice.

LEE, E. S. (1951) "Negro intelligence and selective migration: a Philadelphia test of the Klineberg hypothesis." American Sociological Review 16 (April): 227-233.

LEJINS, P. P. (1966) "Uniform crime reports." Michigan Law Review 64 (April): 1011-1030.

––– (1960) "Measurement of juvenile delinquency." American Statistical Association, Proceedings of the Social Statistics Section 1960: 47-49.

LUNDEN, W. A. (1964) Statistics on Delinquents and Delinquency. Springfield, Ill.: Charles C Thomas.

MARSHALL, H. and R. PURDY (1972) "Hidden deviance and the labelling approach: the case for drinking and driving." Social Problems 19 (Spring): 541-553.

McKEOWN, J. E. (1948) "Poverty, race and crime." Journal of Criminal Law and Criminology 39 (no. 4): 480-484.

McNEMAR, Q. (1955) Psychological Statistics. 2nd ed. New York: John Wiley.

MERCER, J. R. (1973) Labeling the Mentally Retarded. Berkeley: University of California Press.

MICHELSON, W. (1970) Man and His Urban Environment: A Sociological Approach. Reading, Mass.: Addison-Wesley.

MOHR, A. and F. H. LUND (1933) "Beauty as related to intelligence and educational achievement." Journal of Social Psychology 4 (May): 235-239.

MONAHAN, T. P. (1961) "On the trend in delinquency." Social Forces 40 (December): 158-168.

––– (1960) "On the incidence of delinquency." Social Forces 39 (October): 66-72.

MOSELEY, M. E. (1975) "Chan Chan: Andean alternative of the preindustrial city." Science 187, no. 4173 (January 24): 219-225.

Municipal Court of Philadelphia (1954) Forty-first Annual Report of the Municipal Court of Philadelphia, 1954. Compiled and edited by F. S. Drown and T. P. Monahan.

Newsweek (1972) "Down Under's downtrodden." Vol. 80, no. 26 (December 25): 38-39.

New York Times (1971) "Crime engulfs Buffalo project." (July 19): 26.

NICHOLS, R. C. (1969) "Where the brains are." National Merit Scholarship Corporation Research Reports 5 (no. 5).

OSGOOD, C. E., G. J. SUCI, and P. H. TANNENBAUM (1957) The Measurement of Meaning. Urbana: University of Illinois Press.

PERLMAN, I. R. (1964) "Antisocial behavior of the minor in the United States." Federal Probation 28 (December): 23-30.

——— (1959) "Delinquency prevention: the size of the problem." Annals of the American Academy of Political and Social Science 322 (March): 1-9.

POLK?, K. (1974) "Rural delinquency and maturational reform." Eugene, Oregon: Marion County Youth Study (mimeo).

President's Commission on Law Enforcement and Administration of Justice (1967) The Challenge of Crime in a Free Society. Washington, D.C.: Government Printing Office.

PUTNAM, P. L. and E. H. ELLINWOOD, Jr. (1966) "Narcotic addiction among physicians: a ten-year follow-up." American Journal of Psychiatry 122 (January): 745-748.

REED, E. W. and S. C. REED (1965) Mental Retardation: A Family Study. Philadelphia: W. B. Saunders.

REISS, A. J., Jr. (1951) "Delinquency as the failure of personal and social controls." American Sociological Review 16 (April): 196-207.

——— and A. L. RHODES (1961) "The distribution of juvenile delinquency in the social class structure." American Sociological Review 26 (October): 720-732.

ROBINS, L. N. (1973) Review of 400 Losers, by W. M. Ahlstrom and R. J. Havighurst. American Journal of Sociology 79 (July): 236-238.

——— (1966) Deviant Children Grown Up. Baltimore: Williams & Wilkens.

——— H. GYMAN, and P. O'NEAL (1962) "The interaction of social class and deviant behavior." American Sociological Review 27 (August): 480-492.

ROPER, T. (1970) The Myth of Equality. North Melbourne, Australia: National Union of Australian University Students.

ROSENTHAL, D. (1970) Genetic Theory and Abnormal Behavior. New York: McGraw-Hill.

ROSENTHAL, J. (1971) "One-third of blacks found in 15 cities." New York Times (May 19): 20.

ROSSI, P. H., E. WAITE, C. E. BOSE, and R. E. BERK (1974) "The seriousness of crimes: normative structure and individual differences." American Sociological Review 39 (April): 224-237.

SAVITZ, L. (1973) "Black crime," pp. 467-516 in K. S. Miller and R. M. Dreger (eds.) Comparative Studies of Blacks and Whites in the United States. New York: Seminar Press.

——— (1960) "Delinquency and migration," pp. 199-205 in M. E. Wolfgang, L. Savitz, and N. Johnston (eds.) The Sociology of Crime and Delinquency. New York: John Wiley.

SCARR-SALAPATEK, S. (1971) "Race, social class, and IQ." Science 174, no. 4016 (December 24): 1285-1295.

SCHUESSLER, K. (1962) "Components of variation in city crime rates." Social Problems 9 (Spring): 314-323.

SCHUMACH, M. (1971) "Protest on Brooklyn Heights welfare hotels on rise." New York Times (August 14): 1.

SELLIN, T. and M. E. WOLFGANG (1964) The Measurement of Delinquency. New York: John Wiley.

SHERIDAN, W. H. (1966) Standards for Juvenile and Family Courts. Children's Bureau Publication Number 437-1966. Washington, D.C.: Government Printing Office.

SHOCKLEY, W. (1967) "A 'try simplest cases' approach to the heredity-poverty-crime problem." Proceedings of the National Academy of Sciences 57 (June): 1767-1774.

SHORT, J. F., Jr. and F. I. NYE (1958) "Extent of unrecorded juvenile delinquency: tentative conclusions." Journal of Criminal Law, Criminology and Police Science 49 (no. 4): 296-302.

SHUEY, A. M. (1966) The Testing of Negro Intelligence. 2nd ed. New York: Social Science Press.

SJOBERG, G. (1965) "The origin and evolution of cities." Scientific American 213 (September): 54-63.

SMOOHA, S. (1972) "Black Panthers: the ethnic dilemma." Society 9 (May): 31-36.

SPIRER, J. (1940) "Negro crime." Comparative Psychology Monographs 16 (June): 1-64.

TAEUBER, K. E. and A. F. TAEUBER (1965) "The changing character of Negro migration." American Journal of Sociology 70 (January): 429-441.

TERMAN, L. M. and M. A. MERRILL (1960) Stanford-Binet Intelligence Scale: Manual for the Third Revision Form L-M. Boston: Houghton Mifflin.

TRASLER, G. (1962) The Explanation of Criminality. New York: Humanities Press.

TRENAMAN, J. (1952) Out of Step. London: Methuen.

United Community Fund of San Francisco (1961) Juvenile Delinquency: An Analysis of Theory and Research towards a Program of Action. San Francisco: Social Planning Department, United Community Fund of San Francisco.

U.S. Bureau of the Census (1973) U.S. Census of Population: 1970. Vol. I, Characteristics of the Population. Washington, D.C.: Government Printing Office.

——— (1971) Statistical Abstract of the United States: 1971. Washington, D.C.: Government Printing Office.

——— (1963) U.S. Census of Population: 1960. Vol. I, Characteristics of the Population. Washington, D.C.: Government Printing Office.

——— (1952) U.S. Census of Population: 1950. Vol. II, Characteristics of the Population. Washington, D.C.: Government Printing Office.

——— (1946) Statistical Abstract of the United States: 1946. Washington, D.C.: Government Printing Office.

WADSWORTH, M.E.J. (1975) "Delinquency in a national sample of children." British Journal of Sociology 15 (April): 167-174.

WERNER, E. and E. GALLISTEL (1961) "Prediction of outstanding performance, delinquency, and emotional disturbance from childhood evaluations." Child Development 32 (June): 255-260.

WEST, D. J. (1967) The Young Offender. New York: International Universities Press.

WILLIAMS, J. R. and M. GOLD (1972) "From delinquent behavior to official delinquency." Social Problems 20 (Fall): 209-229.

WOLFGANG, M. E. (1969) "Crime in urban America," pp. 21-43 in The Threat of Crime in America; the 1967-68 E. Paul du Pont Lectures on Crime, Delinquency and Corrections. Newark: University of Delaware.

——— R. M. FIGLIO, and T. SELLIN (1972) Delinquency in a Birth Cohort. Chicago: University of Chicago Press.

ZUR NIEDEN, M. (1951) "The influence of constitution and environment upon the development of adopted children." Journal of Psychology 31 (January): 91-95.

ABOUT THE AUTHORS

ROBERT M. CARTER is Director of the Center for the Administration of Justice and Professor of Public Administration at the University of Southern California. In 1968 he served as Executive Director of the San Francisco Crime Commission. He has been a Correctional Officer at California State Prison, San Quentin, and a U.S. Probation and Parole Officer. From 1971 to 1974, he was Director of the Delinquency Control Institute. He has written numerous books, articles, and research reports on such subjects as probation and parole, corrections, and juvenile justice management.

LaMAR T. EMPEY, Professor of Sociology at the University of Southern California, was formerly Chairman of the Sociology Department and Director of the Youth Studies Center there. His research interests include delinquency causation and the evaluation of sociological theories of delinquency. He has been a member of research review panels at the National Institute of Mental Health, the Department of Health, Education, and Welfare, and the National Institute of Law Enforcement and Criminal Justice, and has served as consultant to the President's Commission on Law Enforcement and the Administration of Justice and to the National Commission on the Causes and Prevention of Violence.

ROBERT A. GORDON is Associate Professor of Social Relations at Johns Hopkins University. He received his Ph.D. from the University of Chicago and was Associate Director of the Youth Studies Program there. His major research interests include the social psychology of deviant behavior, values, small group interaction, the sociology of intelligence, and causes of crime and delinquency. In 1974 he shared the American Association for the Advancement of Science Socio-Psychological Prize with William E. McAuliffe for their research on opiate addiction.

MALCOLM W. KLEIN is Professor and Chairman of the Department of Sociology at the University of Southern California. His primary research interests are juvenile gangs and gang intervention programs, diversion of juvenile offenders, deinstitutionalization of status offenders, and evaluation of practical and policy-oriented delinquency programs. He is the author or editor of *Juvenile Gangs in Context* (1967), *Street Gangs and Street Workers* (1971), and, with Robert Carter, *Back on the Street: The Diversion of Juvenile Offenders* (1975).

SUSAN LABIN-ROSENSWEIG is currently a graduate student in the Department of Sociology at the University of Southern California.

SUZANNE BUGAS LINCOLN is currently a graduate student in the Department of Sociology at the University of Southern California.

WILLIAM T. PINK is Associate Professor and Chairperson of the Department of Educational Foundations at the University of Nebraska—Omaha. His major research interests are youth subcultures, alternative education models, delinquency prevention programming, and half-way house rehabilitation programming.

H. TED RUBIN served as a Colorado State Representative from 1961 until 1965 and then as Judge of the Denver Juvenile Court from 1965 until 1971. Since 1971, he has been Director for Juvenile Justice Management at the Institute for Court Management, Denver, Colorado. He is a visiting lecturer in both the School of Law and the Department of Sociology at the University of Colorado, and is the author of numerous articles on juvenile courts and juvenile justice.

ROSEMARY C. SARRI is Professor of Social Work at the University of Michigan and Co-Director, with Robert D. Vinter, of the National Assessment of Juvenile Corrections, a national field study of correctional programs for juveniles. She was a member of the Task Force on Corrections of the National Advisory Commission on Correctional Standards and Goals and a consultant to the President's Committee on Juvenile Delinquency and Youth Crime. Currently, she serves as a member of the Committee on Correctional Education of the Education Commission of the States and a member of the Advisory Committee of the National Resource Center on Women Offenders.

IRVING A. SPERGEL is Professor in the School of Social Science Administration and Chairman of the Advanced Study Committee at the University of Chicago. He is the author of books and articles on comparative community development, youth gangs and youth manpower, delinquency, and deviant behavior. From September 1970 until September 1971, he served as United Nations Advisor in Youth Work to the Hong Kong government.

JOSEPH A. STYLES is currently a graduate student in the Department of Sociology at the University of Southern California.

KATHIE S. TEILMANN is currently a graduate student in the Department of Sociology at the University of Southern California.

ROBERT D. VINTER is Professor of Social Work at the University of Michigan and Co-Director, with Rosemary C. Sarri, of the National Assessment of Juvenile Corrections. He has served as a consultant to the President's Committee on Juvenile Delinquency and Youth Crime, the President's Commission on Law Enforcement and Criminal Justice, the Office of Juvenile Delinquency in the Department of Health, Education, and Welfare, the National Institute of Mental Health, the U.S. Bureau of Prisons, and the Probation Services of the government of Jamaica. He has been a member of the Research Council of the National Council of Crime and Delinquency.

MERVIN F. WHITE is Assistant Professor of Sociology at Washington State University in Pullman and has been a Visiting Professor at California State University at Hayward. His research interests include juvenile delinquency, decision-making in premarital sexual behavior, and cohabiting relationships among college students.